Multicultural Research

Multicultural Research:
A Reflective Engagement with Race, Class, Gender and Sexual Orientation

Edited by

Carl A. Grant

FALMER PRESS
Taylor & Francis Group

UK	Falmer Press, 1 Gunpowder Square, London, EC4A 3DE
USA	Falmer Press, Taylor & Francis Inc., 325 Chestnut Street, 8th Floor, Philadelphia, PA 19106

First published in 1999

A catalogue record for this book is available from the British Library

ISBN 0 7507 0881 6 cased
ISBN 0 7507 0880 8 paper

Library of Congress Cataloging-in-Publication Data are available on request

Jacket design by Caroline Archer
Cover printed in Great Britain by Biddles Ltd.

Typeset in 9.5/11pt Times by
Graphicraft Limited, Hong Kong

Printed in Great Britain by Biddles Ltd., Guildford and King's Lynn on paper which has a specified pH value on final paper manufacture of not less than 7.5 and is therefore 'acid free'.

Every effort has been made to contact copyright holders for their permission to reprint material in this book. The publishers would be grateful to hear from any copyright holder who is not here acknowledged and will undertake to rectify any errors or omissions in future editions of this book.

Contents

Contents

Acknowledgments

Much appreciation and gratitude is extended to Kim Wieczorek for her tremendous assistance with this project. Many thanks to Nadine Goff, Joy Lei, and LeVon Williams for editorial assistance with some chapters. Also, a big thanks is extended to Christine Kruger for her help with word processing.

1 Introduction: The Idea, the Invitation, and Chapter Themes

Carl A. Grant

The Idea

We teach and learn in a time when human agency and authentic voice, diversity and multicultural education are receiving attention like no other time in the history of the United States and we can include the world. This attention is brought on by an increase in the population of people of color, and the development of a climate that encourages, although reluctantly, increased respect for group empowerment. Another factor stimulating the change is the acceptance of the importance of social cultural factors in learning and the movement toward challenging traditional assumptions and envisioning multiple possibilities for change.

Simultaneously, we teach at a time when the elementary to college aged students are not beholden to, or impressed by, academic tradition and professional mystique. Instead these students come to school with a curiosity that is somewhat cynical, and an outspokenness, wondering and/or searching to discover if the emperor has clothes — that is in this case, searching to see if their professors and teachers have a genuine legitimate understanding of teaching and learning in today's world. This outspokenness has merit, especially when considered in relationship to how schools have served to sort and select students depending on their race, class and gender; and how the cultural politics of United States education and the cultural capital highlight in schools have and still remains, at least for the most part Euro-centric.

I believe that when teachers share with students personal histories, reasons for their teaching actions, perspectives behind certain knowledge construction, along with using a teaching philosophy that embraces cultural pluralism and educational equity this will inspire student learning. Additionally, I believe that multicultural education and social justice scholars must teach and conduct research in a way that demystifies the systems of reasoning behind why we do what we do.

The Invitation

Based upon this belief I invited several scholars to share, why they do what they do. More specifically, the invitation read:

> Dear _____ ,
> I am writing to invite you to write a chapter for a book (tentatively titled), *Multicultural Research: A Reflective Engagement with Race, Class, Gender, and Sexual Orientation*, to be published by Falmer Press. You have engaged in scholarly work in which you

have included in your methods and procedures, analyses, and discussion attention to issues of race, class, gender, sexual orientation, and/or education that is multicultural. The purpose of this edited volume is to explain to the readers (e.g., graduate students, colleagues) what guides you during your research and writing in the area of equity, social justice, and power and/or the interrelationship between your life experiences and the theoretical underpinnings of your scholarship. There are at least two interrelated questions that are important to the book: (a) What are the historical influences on your life? (b) What are the personal and/or professional decisions that guide your research? For example, are the influences and/or decisions that guide your research? For example, are the influences and/or decisions; e.g., autobiographical, philsophical, ideological, a desire to question, and/or a desire to illuminate privilege and power?

How does the paradigm(s) that guides your research support your engagement in different analyses and discussion? For example, sometimes I use conflict theory to frame my analyses. This paradigm supports my examination of issues of power and equity. Also, by using this framework, I have a context through which to discuss issues of race, class, and gender and the intersection of the three. Another example is that sometimes I use 'social reconstruction' to frame my arguments. This framework probably suits me better, because as a teacher in Chicago, a graduate student at Loyola and UW-Madison and as a professor I have always been searching for ways to argue for change and/or to implement change to improve schooling, especially for those who are marginalized. Also, this framework affords me a way to discuss my personal life history, as well as United States and world history; and it has been supportive of my development of a scholarly chain of inquiry.

Another point you may want to consider in developing your chapter is, 'why' you chose your subject matter focus. For example, some scholars study school math because of the way mathematics frames social debates. Often in school, math students are taught to be consumers of mathematical knowledge, rather than critics, and producers of mathematical arguments. This volume welcomes insights into the historical accounts of your chosen subject areas, your experiences, and the role of your scholarship in illuminating equity dilemmas.

An additional point you may wish to consider is why you do the research projects you do. For example, is it out of personal interests, invitations from colleagues that you cannot refuse, you are playing your cards right for tenure, promotions, etc.

In order to provide a context for the reader, please review different sections and/or aspects of your research and/or writing and use material from it to illustrate that choices you made.

The reflective analyses in the collected chapters in this book will help our graduate students and colleagues to know why we made the choices we made, where we place our values, where our interpretations come from, and the goals we are trying to achieve.

My purpose in presenting these different examples and suggestions is not to confuse but to illuminate, to let you understand the purpose of this volume. So if confusion is going on, 'reach out and touch me'.

Most invitations were accepted, and everyone invited saw this as a thoughtful, rewarding undertaking. Some authors stated this task was: cathartic, difficult, 'most interesting of writing activities in which I ever engaged', 'the personal essay was an interesting genre to tackle, or better, to be tackled by'.

The book contains 18 chapters. The chapter authors did an outstanding job of responding to the requests in a the letter. The chapters are powerful, insightful, instructional and told me, in a modest way, that this was a good idea and would be helpful to our students and colleagues.

The Themes

After reading the chapters, numerous themes emerged and there were intersections of these themes in the work of most authors. Race, class, gender, power, struggle, theoretical/philosophical underpinning were often at the nexus of these discussions. Five themes can be suggested as advance organizers to help the readers' scaffolding process in understanding multicultural education research and more fully appreciate the chapters. These five themes are: systems of reasoning; power in relationships; ideology in response to ethnicity and issues of social justice; involvement in struggles and forming alliances; and methods and procedures. It will not be surprising if you come up with different themes as you read these chapters. That's OK; the main purpose for this book is for you to better understand why scholars do the work they do and to learn more about multicultural education.

Systems of Reasoning

In each chapter authors describe why and how they reason as they do. The reason(s) they give are not difficult to understand. They arise from personal commitment, activism, a search for understanding, and the desire to work in multiple relationships. They come from a constant questioning of values and ways of reasoning and acting. Popkewitz argument is that we need to examine these 'systems of reasons', for they may tell us more about why (urban and rural) schools are the way they are more so than studying the notions of success or failure we often study when conducting research on urban and rural schools. Popkewitz states:

> It seemed to me that the languages of helping children embodied ways of reasoning about teaching and children that itself was the problem. That language of schooling, I thought, carried norms and values that historically function to intern and enclose children. What needed to be investigated, I felt, is not who and how success or failure is achieved but the systems of reasoning embodied in the ways we talk about success and failure.

In chronicaling her experiences from graduate to the present day Elizabeth Ellsworth gives up a rare look into the personal and professional growth of a scholar. She poignantly describes how the dominant eurocentric heterosexual male discourses influenced her life and scholarship from graduate school to her early days as a professor and she provides an engaging account of how she made changes. Important to her essay is the argument that 'multicultural' is an inappropriate concept, instead she argues for the use of 'multiculture.' The differences, she writes, are more than grammatical:

> 'Multicultural' is an adjective. 'Multiculture' is a noun. But the difference isn't just grammatical. Framing my work in terms of 'multiculture' instead of 'multicultural' has changed that work and my relationship to it. 'Multiculture' makes approaches to research and teaching possible and intelligible for me that are otherwise impossible and unintelligible when I frame my work in terms of 'multicultural'. I'm going to try to explain here how and why the differences between these two terms have taken on larger theoretical, methodological, and political meanings for me as an educator.

Ellsworth goes on to describe her journey from 'multicultural' to 'multiculture', telling about her constant questioning of her own reasoning and ways of working.

Jennifer Obidah, a scholar just completing her PhD discusses her own struggles to find a balance between competing discourses learned during graduate school socialization, her prior college experiences and classroom teaching in a urban area. She describes how writing her dissertation was an 'act of synchronicity':

> I synchronized the knowledge that I was taught in university classrooms with the knowledge that I brought to graduate school and the knowledge-in-action I observed in classrooms where I taught and/or conducted research. My previous unconscious attempts to subscribe to this university norm of finding one voice, one definitive writing style, one hierarchy of knowledge, has been detrimental to my learning process. Acknowledging the training and preparation I derived from my life outside the walls of the university propels my resolute conclusion that I know what I know.

Ellsworth, Popkewitz, Obidah, as well as many of the other chapter authors invite us to discover how certain systems of reason influence the scholar that they do.

Power in Relationships

Power in relationships is a theme that is threaded through all the chapters. This discussion is approached using different concepts and tools, such as gender, race, official knowledge, and methodology. For example, Michael Apple argues that 'education has been one of the major arenas in which the conflict between property rights and person rights has been fought' (Apple, 1993, 1995, p. 12) and in making this claim he provides the readers with examples and of how power operates in a relationship where 'person' or 'property' are the 'end' result.

Interactions between males and females are often seen as power relationships. In regard to adolescents' reading, Donna Alvermann believes 'it is critical that we not dismiss students' gendered positionings of each other in their talk about texts as 'natural' or 'just the way things are'. She argues that '[m]ore is at stake than simply an essentialized view of adolescent male and female behaviors. Exercises in power relations spill over to society at large and affect how men and women deal with one another throughout their lives — in political and economic, as well as social, ways.'

To Mary Gomez power is in the relationship she develops with her students through the use of narratives that she used to inform, to heal, and to reconsider who she is and how she came to be. She states:

> For my students, for the children and adolescents whom they will teach, as well as for myself, I hope and plan for continuing opportunities to tell our stories in the service of creating a more just world for all people. In telling stories about my childhood and my adulthood as a teacher here, I have found a way to heal some wounds, to reconsider who I am and how I came to be so, and to articulate the power of our words and the words of those with whom we live and labor in shaping our ideas, our actions, and our possibilities.

From reading the various chapters in the book readers will come away with different notions of power in relationships, and how power exists and the extent of its visibility in institutions, organizations and within groups and individuals.

Ideology in Response to Ethnicity and Issues of Social Justice

One's ideology is developed and/or acquired in response to one's lived and learned experiences. Chapter authors are straightforward in explaining their ideology and advocating a way to think about issues of justice and diversity. Eugene García, Carl Grant, Joyce King, Sonia Nieto, Jennifer Obidah, Mildred Hudson, and Michael Thornton provide some rich accounts of how ethnicity and social justice issues influence their scholarship. Some educators invalidate the research of scholars of color, saying they are just studying their own problems. This seems nothing more than 'a dirty trick' or technique of control to prevent the exposure of the evils of racism, sexism and other narrow-minded thinking. For example, Eugene García speaks eloquently about how his work is a 'complexification of the issues of "culture" and its conceptual meaning in today's diverse societies.'

Joyce King explains how the power of blackness for black people enables them to participate and do things that are excellent and worthwhile society. Explicitly she states:

> Black cultural expression, which is most often collective, participatory, and life-affirming, validated our being within an existential social reality where everyone could be and do something excellent and worthwhile. This is the power of blackness that could not easily be contained, repressed, or simply erased from our collective cultural memory.

Mildred Hudson discusses how the evils of racism that she and her family suffered when she was a young child have served as a powerful drive for her work to combat racism in the US. She describes one of two important incidents in her life as follows:

> I can still remember the pain in my father's face when he vowed never again to speak to my mother's uncle, Mose Wright, for allowing the white mob to murder my 14-year-old cousin, Emmett Till, and dump his body into the Tallhatchie River.

Michael Thorton's ethnicity and ideology leads him to investigate important problems that other scholars do not consider: 'I see my work supporting the struggle to resist oppressive forces in two ways: I choose topics others typically describe as esoteric and marginal, and I use them as examples of how people of color alter their environments in meaningful ways, overcoming obstacles, making something new (at least different from what would "normally" be expected), changing their environment to better work in their own interests.'

A clearer connection between ideology, ethnicity, identity and scholarship offered by Sonia Nieto would be difficult to locate. She poignantly argues how a simple phrase about identity served as a catalyst that influenced her thinking about the tension between unity and diversity in US society: My own struggle with identity was no doubt one of the factors that led me to teaching. 'Funny, you don't look Puerto Rican', a generally innocent statement made with the best of intentions, became for me a catalyst for questioning my own identity as well as those conditions in our society that make that backhanded compliment so acceptable. The statement itself is a symbol of that most basic of tensions in a pluralistic society: the need to reconcile diversity and unity.'

For other chapter authors, ideology is shown through their alliances, political commitments, their activism, their methodology, their work with organizations and the way they question established norms. Simply put, their way of life!

Carl A. Grant

Involvement in Struggles and Forming Alliances

The history of the United States is rich with accounts of people becoming involved in struggles for social justices for others and in essence for themselves. Some of these accounts tell of those who, while struggling for themselves, learned about injustices done to others, leading to the forming of alliances and the realization that all struggles for social justice have much in common. Among others, Peter McLaren, Christine Sleeter, and Beth Blue Swadener discuss how becoming involved in struggles for social justice, and forming alliances with others has influenced their scholarship. Peter McLaren insists that solidarity is essential to the struggle to achieve equity and equality in education for all. His discussion is passionate and powerful:

> Only fists raised in solidarity with our brothers and sisters in struggle, and a commitment to make critical pedagogy a practical tool for the common good, can bring about the social and educational conditions necessary to rescue those we have lost and betrayed.

He goes on to add 'If we are not prepared to spend time in struggle with our Chicano brothers and sisters and our African-American brothers and sisters then ours is a pedagogy of hollow hope.'

With a commitment that began before her graduate school days, Christine Sleeter describes how she pledged to 'work with multiracial coalitions, in support of how people of color are framing issues.' She also considers her most useful work as an ally to help people like herself 'confront and deal with white supremacy.'

Similarly, Beth Blue Swadener recognizes the importance of developing multicultural alliances. She speaks of them being rooted in her experience of coming of age in the early 1970s and participating in the civil rights and women's rights movements. She also explains the importance of collaboration in early childhood contexts when she states:

> I continue to learn from collaborative experiences, and share a vision with many of my collaborators of far more teacher and student voice in research, the active co-construction and negotiation of meaning and shared writing of interpretive accounts which are multi-vocal and avoid essentializing descriptions of early childhood settings and contexts.

The developing of alliances is a common thread throughout the chapters. Chapter authors discuss these alliances both explicitly and implicitly. Explicitly, they discuss their travels to meet and work with others, their work with teachers and community people in schools, and working with other scholars. Implicitly, the forming of alliances is discussed as chapter authors explain how students, family members and other colleagues have influenced their work.

Methods and Procedures

Besides helping us to understand the problems we are pursuing, the methods and procedures we use often help us to gain greater insight into ourselves and this sometimes leads to personal change. In the chapters, authors address not only 'why' they do what they do, but 'how' they do what they do. In this context, they illuminate the purpose and expectations for their choice of method and procedure. The chapters by Mary Gomez, Becky Ropers-Huilman and Elizabeth Graue, Mary Lou Fuller and Reba Page are particularly informative because they illustrate the importance of methods and procedures to the research and the researcher.

Mary Gomez discusses how the use of narratives can be important to helping education students to gain insights into their professional and personal selves. She argues that teaching stories are a way for prospective and practicing teachers to reconsider their actions and the grounds on which they have been developed. She states:

> The goal for this work is that our discourses and our actions will be reflected to us in ways that simultaneously affirm our good intentions and problematize our pedagogy.

Ropers-Huilman and Graue provide another discussion that shows a connection between method and identity. They state:

> We learned that techniques in research methodology have implications for practice that go far beyond measures of correct application. While some have posed a framework by which methodology, method, and epistemology can be tentatively separated (Harding, 1987), we believe that there are values and practices linked to identities that are inherent in each stage, or layer, of research. Through multiple layers and their corresponding lenses, definitions of qualitative research became complicated, with increasingly blurred boundaries.

Ropers-Huilman and Graue elaborate on this point when they argue that the quality of knowing is linked to our cultural identities. They state:

> In teaching, learning and enacting qualitative research and knowing in a variety of settings, methods are much more than just techniques and strategies. Standards for measuring the quality of knowing are not simply measures of correct application of certain methods. Rather, our standards for our own and others' knowing are strongly influenced by positioned statuses we bring to that knowing. Our knowing processes exist in synergy with our cultural identities — each enhancing and disrupting the other.

Fuller continues to point out the connection between research and self when she states: 'The process of doing empirical research changes the researcher, and major theories of human behavior describe the changes in researchers' lives just as they do others'. She also describes how she uses the work of several psychologists as her method and procedure to achieve personal development and growth as a multicultural scholar. Speaking directly to her chapter readers, she states:

> All of this means that you, as a critical reader, can view these observations on my life as an exercise in understanding how issues such as psychological needs running across the human life span (Maslow) related to those to specific stages (Erikson) and gender (Gilligan, Levenson) and play out in the kind of thinking (Schon) that allows a person to extract insight from experience.

As part of Reba Page's discussion of her methods and procedures she analyzes her own personal use of 'reflection' and discovers how her way of thinking has roots in her early family life and growing-up. Page observes:

> In reflecting, I have run up against what seems an ongoing circling of schooling, family, and the times I grew up in. I am somewhat startled to see what could be read as a relatively steady, if slow and circuitous, march right toward field research.

Carl A. Grant

On the other hand, Page like many of the authors stresses the importance of not having the methods and procedures become the primary focus of research. She argues:

> As important and enduring as the methods I use are the questions that drive them, and me. I continue to be preoccupied with the diverse ways we humans carve up the world and how, using indeterminate symbols, we are able to bring meaningful and consequential realms into being. The domain I examine these processes in has shifted somewhat, from a suburban community to school communities.

I often tell students in my research and multicultural education class that the desire to use particular method(s) and procedure(s) should not be the major reason for pursuing a particular research topic. Sometimes they listen to me, and other times they do not. Perhaps, this is so, I am learning from the chapter authors in this book, because consciously or unconsciously their cultural identity and/personhood is directly connected to both their studying particular questions and their deciding on the methods and procedures for investigating their questions.

Conclusion

Between the covers of this book are 18 personal journeys, journeys that provide rich penetrations into academic research and scholarship. These penetrations are tools, both important and powerful for helping students to better understand what personal and professional life blood lies behind the book or article they read. These tools are also important because they give added understanding to the educational context, that is, experiencing demographic changes, an increased tolerance for group rights, and the acceptance of the importance of cultural social histories in learning. They are also powerful tools because they can lessen suspicions on the part of many students about the material they are given to learn, they contribute to, and support, our post-modern way of viewing events, and they can help to explain why education in the United States is in major need of reform in order to fully include those that have been historically marginalized.

Finally, achieving a result or outcome from an idea is no small undertaking. The process is often filled with regrets, resistance, and/or discovery that it really wasn't a good idea. In no way has this been the case with *Multicultural Research: A Reflective Engagement with Race, Class, Gender, and Sexual Orientation*. Each chapter author(s) delivered much more than I hoped for. They took seriously the charge and challenge in my letter and have produced excellent accounts of why they do the research that they do. It is because of their scholarships that researchers, scholars, and students will better comprehend the connections between conducting research, producing scholarship and understanding cultural identity.

References

APPLE, M.W. (1993) *Official Knowledge*, New York: Routledge.
APPLE, M.W. (1995) *Education and Power* (2nd. ed.) New York: Routledge.

2   Reconstituting Ethnography: Social Exclusion, Post-modern Social Theory, and the Study of Teacher Education

Thomas S. Popkewitz

In 1990, I was asked to evaluate 'Teach for America'. The program is an alternative teacher education program. It lies outside university certification programs and is designed to recruit and train people with degrees in fields other than education. The program focus was on for urban and rural schools where there are chronic shortages of teachers. The data collection for the research entailed 'traditional' procedures associated with an ethnography — during the first year of the program, I observed and interviewed the staff and the program's recruits (corps members) as they worked full time in the different schools around the country.

The study began as one of socialization: what norms, patterns of practice, and systems of ideas construct the teacher. Underlying this question was a concern with issues of power and inequity. Teach for America was to provide teachers for schools that have consistently failed their children. How were the issues of miseducation being addressed, encountered, and countered?

But an uneasiness began as I struggled to think about the study of teacher education and schooling.[1] An uneasiness related to my own thinking about the concept of socialization.

First, I realized that conventional notions of socialization of teachers did not tackle a persistent concern about how unequal education occurs. I felt that the 'hidden curriculum' studies since the 1970s forcefully directed attention to the social, political and economic effects of pedagogical practices (see, e.g., Young, 1971, as an icon of this period). Yet as I compared those studies with today's literature, the major differences between then and now seemed to lie in the public policies spoken about rather than in the substantive development of the issue of power in schooling. This chapter, is about advanced liberal societies, the New Right, conservative restorations; 'empowerment' and 'voice'. The discussions point to different policy languages and 'contexts' from those of the 1970s, but the conclusions are the same — some groups use the resources of schools to their advantage while others do not; and we still have an unequal society which we need to challenge. No matter how hard reformers work to redress the conditions of inequity in the USA schools, the concrete practices that produce inequities seem to continue uninterrupted.

As I read my first draft to tell the story of Teach for America, I felt I was reproducing the conventional 'wisdom' about power that travels within the folklore of educational reform.[2] My story would 'tell' of the difficulties already known about urban and rural schools. The story would appear within the critical genre that raises questions about issues of schooling as a social and political enterprise.

Yet, as I wrote, I did not 'see' anything in these first drafts that contributed to understanding the *concrete pedagogical practices* which qualifiy/disqualifiy children in social affairs. I knew of the structural analysis that 'told' of school practices as 'tools' of outside social forces, but felt that different questions needed to be asked. Although I wanted to maintain a sensitivity to issues of race, gender, and class, I wanted to give attention to the everyday details of teaching and learning in the practices of the teacher. My interest was in the knowledge by which teachers 'saw' and administered children; examining the concrete practices that embodied principles by which teachers organized, observed, supervised and evaluated children. As Teach for America was a program for children of color and poverty, my suspicion was that to focus on pedagogical ideas would give attention to how children were divided and differentiated in the everyday practices of the teacher. Through identifying the dividing and differentiating strategies, I could better understand the disabling and disqualifying practices of teaching.

Drawing from readings in post-modern social theories, I viewed the pedagogical ideas as 'making' (constructing) the teacher who administers the child. I looked at the ideas about childhood, learning, self-esteem, and intelligence in classroom practices. These ideas, I argued, 'made' the objects that teachers reflected and acted on. Structural issues about the 'state', economy, race, and gender, among others, were placed as an horizon, in a phenomological sense, to the study as I focused on principles that ordered the reason and the reasonable person in teaching. The investigation of Teach for America looked at the pedagogical ideas as micro-practices through which the teacher constructed the child as a child in urban and rural schools.

Second, my rethinking about the problem of power in schooling required a rethinking about the methods of ethnography. In one sense, this is an old argument: all research involves theoretical considerations as there are no data without theory. When we look at the classroom, we are involved in a process of selecting things to see and interpret. Our world is never one of *tabula rasa* but one organized through the principles of classification that are available for us to see and talk about our world. My research focus on the 'making' (constructing) of the teacher and the child shifted the analysis from previous concerns with what teachers mean when they talk about their work, I examine the rules and standards by which that meaning is constructed.

This chapter, then, is about how I began the study of Teach for America, how it changed over time, and how it formed eventually into a book entitled, *Struggling for the Soul: The Politics of Schooling and the Construction of Teachers* (1998). I can say here that even selecting the title was a struggle to find the right words, words that focused on the complexities of how schooling objectively separated and ranked the children in schools who are predominantly people of color and poor.

Teach for America: Who the Book Is About

Teach for America was constructed by a recent graduate of Princeton whose senior thesis argued that a private organization be created to find a solution to the shortage of teachers for urban and rural schools. The program would attract recent liberal arts graduates into teaching, adding to the existing pool of teachers a group whose original education was not in university educational certification programs.

In what would be an oddity to anyone outside the USA, the program solicited funds from private businesses and foundations. It was a private initiative to change the recruitment and preparation of a public enterprise — the public schools.

The program drew its first 500 recruits from the private and public universities in the nation. After an eight-week training at a private institution, The University of

Southern California, the students were placed as full time teachers in rural Georgia and North Carolina, Baton Rouge and New Orleans, Louisiana, New York City, and the metropolitan areas of Los Angeles.

Teach for America held a great fascination for the American media, business and philanthropic communities and government. Numerous articles and editorials in *The New York Times*, news reports on the network news programs, a Public Broadcasting System special about the first year, as well as reports in *Newsweek, US News* and *World Report*, and *Forbes* magazine provided a somewhat romanticized gloss to the program and the first summer institute.

The discourse concerning Teach for America claimed legitimacy within a wider American discourse about privatization and 'choice' as a practice of educational policy. The media attention concerning Teach for America came largely from the way in which its goals and justifications meshed with multiple streams of a general American social and political ideology in the 1980s. First of all, Teach for America drew on the idea that individual initiative and private enterprise can find solutions to the grave social issues of our time, represented the utilitarian spirit of American enterprise, Teach for America a 'can-do' attitude towards social problems. The program was to change how teachers were recruited, and it attacked what was seen to be the entrenched ineptness of governmental bureaucracy as personified in teacher education. This last point was a legacy of Reagan Era rhetoric about pulling government back from involvement in social affairs.

The program also epitomized an idealism of youth that the country had not witnessed since the early days of the Kennedy era and the creation of the Peace Corps. Five hundred youths who had grown up with privilege were committing themselves to spend two years working with people who were often denied any privilege. As if to evoke the image of the Peace Corps, Teach for America recruits were called 'corps members'.

Recruitment to the Summer Institute was modeled on the Peace Corps — active recruitment, a short time commitment, a selective and centralized application process, intensive training, placement, and a support mechanism. The 1990 Summer Institute was designed to immerse corps members in the career of teaching. There was an intensive 15-hours-a-day, six-days-a-week, eight-week training program to prepare the corps with teaching skills and cross-cultural understanding. It also provided them with intensive experience in Los Angeles schools as student teachers.

A different goal of the first Summer Institute was to make the teacher an agent of change. Drawing on a curriculum tradition of social reconstruction that emerged during the Depression of the 1930s, the Institute focused on contemporary issues of social inclusion/exclusion in a demographically and economically changing United States. The three over-arching themes of the Institute — professionalism, reflection, and multiculturalism — gave emphasis to the social and cultural issues of teaching.

The program was symbolized by its juxtapositions. There was the general affluent background of the corps members and of the private educational setting of the University of Southern California. Then there was the location of the university within its immediate surroundings of the poorest urban areas of Los Angeles. The intersection of the three — the affluence of America's privileged, the commitment towards those who have been denied privilege, and the need to address social and cultural diversity — publicly constructed an image for Teach for America.

In the fall, the corps members began full time teaching. They faced the difficulties and challenges that are well documented with American schools (see, e.g., Kozol, 1991 about its horrors, Sleeter and Grant, 1994 and Ladson-Billings, 1994 about its possibilities).

Thomas S. Popkewitz

As the different schools around the country were visited, the driving question in the research concerned the data — what data were worth collecting to understand the effects of the program? I was continually confronted with schools that existed within an unequal playing field. The language of schooling spoke about enabling children to participate and profit from their involvement. But the talk about inclusion also contained discussion about exclusion. The children of the school were spoken about as not 'succeeding', having low 'self-esteem', and having little motivation. School programs that were not relevant to the cultural diversities of the children who came to school.

My problem in the research was not to accept the classifications of success or failure given in pedagogical discussions and policy statements of schools. These explanations of children's success and failure were not just neutral expressions to help the child learn and succeed. Nor was the problem, as so often stated in reform literature, merely to get teachers to feel positive that they and the children could be successful and stop labeling of children. It seemed to me that the languages of helping children embodied ways of reasoning about teaching and children that itself was the problem. That language of schooling, I thought, carried norms and values that historically function to intern and enclose children. What needed to be investigated, I felt, is not who and how success or failure is achieved but the systems of reasoning embodied in the ways we talk about success and failure.

To tell this story required a lot of rethinking and rewriting (6 years to be exact) after the data were collected. My travels were also about what it meant to do educational research.

Constructing an Ethnography: What Do I Mean by Power?

As I said earlier, after several decades of state educational planning and research to identify better approaches to classroom teaching — with the multitudes of 'remediation' programs, community action projects and state funded research projects to identify 'what works' and successful teaching — the differences in an uneven playing field of schools continue almost uninterrupted, and the lives of children in schools are often worse now than when I started teaching in the 1960s. Large scale state interventions and research closely tied to state programs to 'rescue' children from the cycles of poverty and racism have not substantially changed the school. Sometimes, as I read critical educational literatures with a different rhetorical focus, I am at a similar loss. It seems almost as if the rhetorical and constant reiteration of the need to redress inequalities makes the problem confrontable and the ethical commitments reachable.[3]

My discomfort in contemporary educational debates made me think that possibly we have been asking the wrong questions. I thought about this in relation to my previous studies of schooling.[4] In The *Myth of Educational Reform* (Popkewitz et al., 1982), for example, my colleagues and I studied how an elementary reform program was realized with the cultures of schools. After visiting 17 schools around the country and intensively observing six schools, we constructed case studies to describe the different practices, school environments, and educational implications. Three different categories were created to talk about the distinctions found: illusory schooling, technical schooling, and constructivist schooling. For example, the one constructivist school emphasized children's questioning, an integrated of curriculum, the tentative qualities of knowledge, and the active questioning involvement of children. The three technical schools, in contrast, focused on the certainty of curriculum knowledge and procedural concerns in the tasks of learning. The two illusory schools were places where the symbolic facades of learning provided practices that seemed to direct attention to the teaching of reading, writing, adding, and thinking, but the actual teaching had little substantive content. The study also considered how these different cultures of schools related to professional ideologies, school district politics and social/cultural factors of the school's community.

As I now think about this and my other studies, I realized that I was thinking about power in a very particular way. Power was treated as 'something' that was owned, as a sovereign did in the days when the King ruled. But modern sovereignty was owned by bureaucracies of the schools that did not allow thoughtful teaching. In the *Myth of Education*, the accountability measures of central school administration, for example, restricted the options of teachers and limited the educational opportunities of children. Power was also owned in the interplay of religious, social-economic groups and racial differentiation. The combination of actors played into my equation about the inequities in schooling.

But this conclusion itself was based upon certain assumptions about power that I now wanted to rethink, but not totally reject. The focus on sovereign power pointed to its ownership by professionals, the wealthy, the white, and so on (the actual kings and queens in modernity no longer play a role in the construction of sovereign power it is displaced to other social actors). Modern ownership is not straightforward and unambiguous, but if properly identified, it is believed that strategies of change would be promoted. This power was to be confronted directly through identifying the practices that gave some groups power and therefore limited the access of others — community groups, parents. Access for those who were excluded from participation was to be equalized in this manner. Less directly, inclusion (access) is provided through school achievement and success for those who have previously not had success.

The reasoning of the sovereignty notion of power is, implicitly if not explicitly, like a mystery novel. If we can identify who perpetuated the inequities and how they dominate, then it is possible to change the distribution of power so that all groups can participate equally. The argument is a beguiling belief of twentieth-century social theory and policy, particularly in post-World War Two education. It underlies, as Hunter (1994) points out, the left and the right as they assume that the problem of schooling is a principled; the difficulty is how to enable all groups to be included through the processes of schooling. It does not question how those principles are constructed as the effects of power.

This sovereign assumption of power shapes discussions of the inclusion/exclusion in educational policy and research. Efforts are to identify what 'successful' teachers do in order to make their practices as universal practices for all teachers to follow. Discussions about empowerment and 'voice' in education focus on the problem of how to include those people who have been previously marginalized and excluded.

These political projects of inclusion are important in a society that categorically has excluded different groups of people. But the focus on the categorical exclusion of groups does not answer the question about the systems of reasoning that organize the practices of 'success', 'empowerment', 'voice'. That is, my attention moved to how the systems that classify reason and reasonable people in schools produce norms that inter and enclose children in a manner that disqualifies them for participation. *My* reasoning was that we needed to look at the concrete levels of pedagogical practices to understand the technologies that exclude and disable children. (I discuss this in Popkewitz, 1998, and Popkewitz and Brennan, 1998).

Knowledge As the Effects of Power: My Post-modern Sensitivity

This interest in the reasoning of schooling, however, did not come out of nowhere. I had been reading since the middle 1980s literature that is now called 'post-modern social theory'. While I use the term 'post-modern social theory', I do not think of it as anything 'post' but as a broad band of literature that gave me a historical specificity to the questions I had about schooling and inequality. The post-modern literature suggested to me that the very ways in which I have been thinking about schools, culture and power assumed more than I should in a critical stance towards schooling. The literature 'told' me that I should pay more attention to the knowledge by which we reason about our 'self' as teachers (and researchers). That is, much of our modern life is ordered through expert systems of knowledge that disciplines how we participate and act. In a commonsense way, expert knowledge shapes and fashions 'our' thinking and acting towards the calories in our diet as part of our personal health, about the pollution in our environment as affecting our lives; our body and mind as having stages of development, personality, and processes of self-realization; and towards children as having intelligence, growth and the normalities of childhood. Each of these thoughts that we assume as natural, are not natural thoughts but thought built from expert systems of knowledge. The power of such expert knowledge is that it is not only knowledge; ideas function to shape and fashion how we participate as active, responsible individuals.

We can think of this fusion of public/personal knowledge that disciplines our choices and possibilities as the effects of power. This notion of the effects of power is very different from that of sovereignty. I can say that the former concerns the productive actions for our participation, where the latter focuses on what dominates and represses our actions.

The post-modern social theory, then, is also a political theory that could be used to study teaching. It directed me to understand that the very knowledge that organizes teaching, learning, classroom management and curriculum inscribes a certain selectivity. That selectivity refers to the ways in which the teachers 'see', think, feel and talk about children and school subjects. The effects of that selectivity, I argue in the book, is to generate principles that disqualify from participation many of the children in the schools.

This insight, by itself, is not original to post-modern literature as critical research has continually alerted us to the relation of knowledge and social divisions. But what the post-modern literature enabled me to do is provide more nuanced strategies to investigate pedagogical knowledge.[5] As I stated this beginning of this essay, it enabled me to rethink the idea of socialization by focusing on what we think of as true about teaching and children. It enabled me to think about why it is that what we want to know about children in the ways that we do — why it is that we talk about what is true, for example, about teaching through psychological categories of childhood. It also enabled me to ask how teachers' reasoning about children's childhood relates to other ideas, such as classroom management, 'the wisdom of teachers' knowledge', and the schools as inner-city and rural.

The different linguistic organizations (discursive practices) about teaching and children in school, I argued in the study, are important social practices because they normalize. That is, our ways of talking about children, learning, achievement, intelligence, and classroom management, produce systems to order and classify children. Further, the ordering of the attributes of children embodies a continuum of value, about what is normal and not normal. To say, for example, that a child 'needs to work harder to get better grades' inscribes norms about the appropriate work that the child is not doing, as well as unspoken values expressed in the ordering produced by 'grades'. In the discourses of the teaching in the schools, such expressions provided principles that 'told' the teacher about the average, the normal and the not-average and not-normal. The norms of the average, normal and not-so-normal are not what we typically talk about as teachers' beliefs or their philosophy of education. Nor are the norms necessarily what is publicly spoken about as educational purposes. Rather the norms are embodied in the categories, distinctions, differentiations and divisions by which teachers come to 'see' and act towards children.

For example, when teachers talked about children's intelligence, the idea of intelligence was related to social categories of 'urban' schools, a psychology about 'low self-esteem', and a view of learning by 'doing' rather than thinking abstractly. The cumulative set of ideas differentiated the children of the urban and rural schools as different from other 'normal' children.

For me, at this point, the reasoning about children in schools was the culprit that needed to be investigated. I wanted to explore the divisions and distinctions produced in the everyday, commonsense activities and ideas about schooling. The ethnography was directed towards the different school systems of ideas (discourses) through which the teacher 'saw', observed, evaluated, and supervised the child. Ideas about childhood, learning, self-esteem, and intelligence embodied norms that separated the children who succeed from those who fail in schools. This separation was produced because the child did or did not possess the norms of reason. The reasoning of success was deeply embedded in the dispositions and sensitivities that formed the inner qualities of the child.

Pedagogical Discourses As Principles of Inclusion/Exclusion: An Example

To consider how reason selects and distributes norms of division, we can focus on the distinction of inner-city and rural schools that organized the program. The ideas of inner-city and rural were introduced to point to the special obligations and needs of American schools. But these ideas of inner-city and rural do not stand alone. They are joined with other ideas and distinctions to order the practices of teaching. Inscribed in the practices of Teach for America, for example, was a societal 'feeling' about the needs and deficiencies of urban and rural schooling. This occurred through discourses of mission within Teach for America. The social mission was not only of this program but of modern schooling which tied religious commitments of saving the soul with the problem of social engineering. Modern schooling makes the child's (and the teacher's) capabilities as the site of pedagogical intervention to rescue the child from the moral conditions of their communities and to make the child into a productive citizen.

The fact that Teach for America and its corps members carried religious connotations of a 'mission', was not unique. What is significant, however, was the operative discourse through which the 'mission' was given direction and purpose. The sense of mission did not form around abstract principles, but coalesced in pedagogical distinctions to classify school competence/incompetence, and achievement/non-achievement.

One of those operative discourses was the wisdom of teacher's practice. The wisdom of practice was not only to gain information about teaching. The 'practices' involved norms about the child that organized and evaluated teachers' actions. An inservice program for the corps members, for example, imparted practical information about 'what works' in the classroom. The 'practical information' was based on the assumption that future teachers can best learn their craft through the telling of experience. The 'practical reasoning' was storytelling about teaching.

Yet as I looked at this emphasis on 'what works', it established a particular way of reasoning about teaching, 'childhood' and children. The storytelling of the wisdom of practice placed boundaries upon what was acceptable and 'normal', and its opposite — the unacceptable and abnormal — in schooling. The distinctions about inner-city schools, for example, were related to concepts about the 'street-wise' intelligence of the children. The category was intended as a positive expression about the children of the 'inner-city' school. The child in the school was to be viewed as having the potential to be as smart as any other child. But immediately we can see that the categories of street-wise intelligence and inner-city are caught in a web of ideas that function to compare and classify the capabilities of children. There were distinctions about children's mastery of school subjects (the children 'did not learn' mathematics); distinctions about psychological capabilities (the children 'were not motivated', had 'low self-esteem', and had 'different learning styles'). The different ideas differentiated the learning of the children from other children (*these* children required greater attention to hands-on activities and 'field dependent' learning experiences). The teaching procedures constructed the 'mental' capabilities of children by abandoning any possibilities that children might want to learn anything but the most limited materials.

The different systems of ideas governed teachers' actions and participation. The patterns of distinctions make the children with the 'street-wise' intelligence of children in 'inner-city' schools as 'troubled' and somehow different from children who were not present. These *other* children, who were not present, had unspecified capabilities of 'intelligence' that the children in the 'inner-city' school lacked. The dividing occurs not in only what is cognitively understood, but in the production of norms which separate and divide children according to their available sensitivities, dispositions, and awarenesses.

The principles that governed actions, I argued, are not of a principal who says that a teacher needs to give a test every week, or of the governing of a Department of Education that mandates the teaching of local history in third grade. These are sovereign notions of power that limit action. The governing that I speak about is positive and productive through providing the reasoning for actions and reflection about teaching. The principles of reasoning discriminate, distinguish and normalize what the child is and is to become (e.g. on a lower level than non-'inner city' students).

The book, then, is about my journey to understand the politics of knowledge as the corps members learned to be a teacher. The study expressed my interest in how the different sets of ideas about children, teaching and learning that ostensibly to help children become productive citizens, actually work in ironic ways to 'make' (construct) a world for children that disqualifies them from participation. The practices of pedagogy locate the children in the schools as 'fitting/not fitting' the embodied norms of reason and of reasonable people. Thus, while this study did not begin as a theory about the racism in schooling, its focus is on the pedagogical technologies by which schools inter and enclose children who, in this study, are predominantly people of color and poor.

My concern with the governing practices of pedagogy inverts Marx's concern with the productive characteristics of labor into a concern with the productive characteristics of knowledge itself (Dumm, 1987). The study of Teach for America considered how the knowledge embodied in schooling produces an unequal playing field. But my interest in the production of an unequal playing field is not in who participates, although that is an important question.[6] Rather, I am concerned with the principles that normalize and classify how participation is recognized, divided, and compared.

Reconstructing a Biography

As I tell this story of the construction of *Struggling for the Soul* and its post-modern turns, I will backtrack somewhat and say something about my own intellectual background. This history is a reconstruction that has no linear development or rational ordering of my life. It 'makes' sense only in this story writing.

I went to an undergraduate liberal arts college where it was not possible to major in education. Teaching was a professional course of study and therefore not a legitimate major. I majored in history (English Constitutional History, of all things with a name like Popkewitz) and minored in elementary education. My masters' degree was in teaching and learning, and intellectually of interest only because of what it assumed. I taught in a Harlem elementary school and my professional education responded to the political and academic educational slogan of the day: 'Learn to read and get a job'. The circulating assumption was that to eliminate inequities, people of color and of poverty had to learn how to read. It seems so naive today, but it was the common sense at that time.

My doctoral studies introduced me to a whole different range of scholarship. My immediate focus was on social studies curriculum and problem-solving. Four years after my masters' degree, the new slogan of educational change was getting children to discover and inquire through the reform movements of the 'new math', 'new social studies', and 'new science' curriculum. There was Jerome Bruner's *Process of Education* telling us that we needed to focus on the structure of disciplines to provide a more adequate understanding of science, mathematics and social studies. And then there was Philip Phenix who talked about different modes of knowing in constructing curriculum. And, of course, there were the range of educational psychologists, including Bruner, Suppe, Shulman, among others, who rang the bells of curriculum as a problem of critical thinking and strategies of discovery.

My dissertation carried forth this concern with discovery and inquiry that was on the main table of educational reform. In one sense, I took the Bruner idea of the structure of the disciplines as a central theme in curriculum development. My particular slot in the debate was to look at political science as a curriculum problem. Others had already considered sociology, anthropology, and history. Political science became my intervention. My concern was to engage children in political inquiry using a discovery approach.

But my relation to the main table of discovery curricula ended there. My intellectual mentor shrewdly guided me during my doctoral studies towards a whole range of literature about the sociology of knowledge rather than to the reigning psychologies of discovery approaches. I say shrewdly because I did not know what hit me until I was deeply involved in writing the dissertation and I am still thinking about how this literature radically restructures the questions and problems of research. It was a literature that I did not know existed from my previous undergraduate and masters' education; in fact, I asked of my doctoral advisor, in a somewhat an angry voice why no one told me about this literature. Courses that I took in history had been about information. Research methods told about the formal logic of research procedures (how to construct variables and the differences between internal and external validity in historical analysis), techniques of interview construction, and so on. There had been no history of the human sciences as social endeavors, just a logic of the development of knowledge.

As I later came to understand, my reading in the sociology of knowledge was more of a 'European' tradition than an American one. Where American positivism and analytical philosophical traditions separate questions of philosophy from history and social theory, the sociology of knowledge combined them. Even the American critical literature of the late 1960s and 1970s that was related to the sociology of knowledge was strongly influenced by emigres who fled Nazi Germany.

My reading of the sociology knowledge was directed towards curriculum models of political science. But that reading compelled me to think about the social construction of knowledge. This thinking was very different from the current vogue in teaching about the social construction of knowledge. While the current discussions draw on psychological lenses, my reading was about the historical and social spaces in which thought is constructed. I read, for example, about the writing of Mark Twain's *Tom Sawyer* as a social 'fact'. The narrative of the novel was understood as reflecting and responding to the tensions of industrialization with those of a Protestant pastoral image that dominated American society.[7] When Tom Sawyer went down the Mississippi River and saw a train, it reflected the felt social tension of the coming of the machine with that pastoral image. My reading also directed attention to the social/moral conditions and disciplinary histories in which the knowledge of historians, sociologists, anthropologists, among others, was constructed and changed.

I began to think about an oddity of the English language and curriculum studies. Our words for thinking about history and physics, among others, are nouns — words that treat the disciplines as objects of knowledge and information. One studies history! There is no word to talk about doing history. Yet once we look closely at the disciplines, we realize that they have a verb sense. One does history and physics, and this doing changes over time, as does the knowledge that is viewed as central to disciplinary thought. Further, the changes are not evolutionary or developmental but occur from changes in the relationship between internal and external factors of disciplinary fields. The US War on Poverty in the 1960s produced new subfields of economics and sociology, for example, in which issues of the poor and differential wealth were empirically emphasized.

The idea of knowledge as socially constructed guided my dissertation about curriculum. It also compelled me to think about different intellectual traditions of the human sciences as socially produced. I thought about how the concepts, methods, and procedures of science act as 'steering' mechanisms that organize our perceptions and actions. I thought about the historical conditions and social/political spaces in which disciplinary knowledge was developed (Popkewitz, 1984). I began to use the sociology of knowledge to think about the spate of reform efforts to improve both the quality of teaching and the social mobility of groups that have been marginalized in US society (Popkewitz, 1976).

As I think about these studies, my interest in the sociology of knowledge is recast and renewed. For convenience rather than historical accuracy, I can trace this interest in a literature that begins to appear (in my thoughts, at least) during the late 1980s. Its American variations are called post-modern feminist literature, certain sociological and anthropological literatures about the issues of representation, and the writing about social science as rhetorical constructions. The band of literature pays its intellectual debt to French historiography, a post-modern sociology, and feminism, such as the works of Foucault, Bourdieu and Butler. The American variations, however, are historically related to American movements in feminism, post-colonialism, and an historicizing of social-political theories about liberalism (and neoliberalism). I came to explore the post-modern literatures as not only a means of interpretation but also an expression of the changing politics of knowledge — post-modern social theory about the relation of power/knowledge both expressed and interrogated the conditions in which it existed.

Thinking about Data and Writing Narratives: Language and Power

My thinking about power and schooling also involved thinking about the methods of data collection and analysis in an ethnography. I often meet people who think that ethnography is a substitute for those who do not want to use quantitative methods, and that the problem of an ethnographic research methods is 'merely' going into classrooms to describe how people talk and act as teachers or students. But the collection and analysis of data is a theoretical problem in the sense of the principles by which phenomena are thought of and classified.

Think for the moment about two different orientations and what they enable us to see in classrooms. When I think about classrooms as a negotiated order among children and teachers, or when I approach schools as places that structure gender or class relations, I select different 'things' to see, interpret and explain. The first directs me to the interactions to consider how meanings are constructed and changed. The second directs me to consider how social forces enter into and organize what occurs in the interactions.

But theory is not only about what is conceptually defined to organize research. Theory is also bound into our conceptions of methods. Often, conventional ethnographic studies 'speak' about triangulation, but the idea of triangulation itself derives from certain theoretical assumptions that function in the construction of the data analyzed. Triangulation is an approach of finding three related incidents to support the conclusions that are stated. Triangulation is to make the qualitative data seem as objective as statistical data. It is based upon a concept of positivism that assumes that one can reach an objective, unmediated explanation. It takes no account of the singular, unique but critical event; nor does triangulation focus on the adequacy of the categories of description as the data are assumed real and unproblematic. My point in discussing triangulation is that what seems as an 'objective' method is fraught with social assumptions and it the theoretically frames what are to be considered as 'data'.

Further, we do not think about the relation of method, data, and theory, but it is something that we need to be more conscious about in educational research. It is easy, for example, to focus on the procedures of data collection to discuss research without considering the assumptions and rules of inquiry that underlie the paths taken. For example, at one level, I could discuss the field procedures of the current study in the following manner. Three graduate students and I visited different school districts in which the corps members were placed during the year. During at least three different times of the year, we visited a school district for a week. Approximate 70 corps members were observed and interviewed in semi-structured approaches. Administrators and other teachers were also interviewed. The approaches were consistent with the methodological literatures in education and anthropology.

But this description would ignore the difficulties in making observations into data. At one level, the observational data have to respond to the theoretical interest in the study. This was difficult even though guidelines were drawn to direct classroom data collection. One graduate student, for example, wanted to give attention to the interactional processes that organized corps members' time. As a consequence, less attention was initially given to the categories and differentiations through which the teachers' practices were constructed. At the same time, the field notes did not distinguish between the actions of boys and girls which meant that when the data were analyzed, I could not systematically analyze gender. In the first place, the observation were changed. In the second place, I realized this lack of distinctions too late to correct.

I speak of these events in data collection, however, to recognize a complex relation. What is written as data relates to 'theoretical' dispositions, which enable certain 'things' to be explored and other 'things' removed from scrutiny. Our observations place boundaries on what is possible to interpret. Data collection and theory are bound.

After collecting data (about 400 pages of description), a sorting procedure was needed to make the data manageable. The data were read and sets of themes or ideas (coding words) constructed to order the analysis and writing. About 100 categories developed in this way, from words to signify teachers' language about 'school as management' to expressions which defined psychological characteristics of the child and views of school subjects. A different level of categories distinguished the language practices by who said it: corps members, staff, teachers, and school administrators.

The categories were not determined before data were collected; yet the categories were related to the theoretical outlook of the research study. As the material was read, for example, the ideas of student potential and hands-on learning became categories. They were coded as separate categories in the data analysis because they were viewed as potentially important distinctions in classifying the objects of teaching and learning. Some of the materials were coded in multiple ways: The phrases/descriptions about children's 'self-esteem' might appear under categories about teaching physics as well as in distinctions about the children who were taught.

Technology became useful in the analysis. I started with a commercial program but found it was cumbersome when sorting the coded field notes. It took a lot of computer memory, was slow in sorting the material according to the coded words, and was not formatted according to the word processing program. I finally switched to a sorting system that worked with our word processing program. Its purpose was to pull up all the coded sections of the observations/interviews within a single file, such as all references to teaching mathematics or to African-American children. From these files, I could begin to examine the distinctions and construct a logic around the distinct elements of the study's narrative.

The task of writing was to take the multiple categories of description and place them into a narrative that explored the nuances of power inscribed in pedagogical practices. This was arduous. I starting writing within some general categories, that seemed important as I played and 'interacted' theory with the empirical data. One such category was the psychology of teaching. From this beginning, I organized themes and subthemes to describe and elaborate. This occurred through reading through the data to identify various distinctions that would help to flush out a logic to the ideas. For example, the ideas about children's 'self-esteem' and 'self-motivation', or the ideas about the wisdom of practice emerged as I sought to work through the data. In thinking about the data, it became evident that an important theme was 'the wisdom of practice'. I 'noticed' in reading the observations of an inservice program and other data that discussions focused on the correct procedures and techniques that the teacher would follow. A different element in the wisdom of practice was the control functions of the lesson plan and the supervisor's observations of the corps members. Through these different sets of practices, I was able to construct sets of relations about the ideas about 'experiences' as establishing boundaries about what was reasonable actions for teaching.

The writing, then, analytically explored and weaved the data into themes/subthemes that were to tell the story of the teacher who administered the child. Here, we can understand how theory relates to data. Theory was constructed (reconstructed) through a continual interrogation of the data at-hand.

A different problem then emerged. I can call this the politics of writing. In the early drafts, I continually focused on the corps members 'as talking about' this aspect of teaching or stating that this or that was in thinking about their successes and failure. This particular organization of data gave reference to the corps members' intent and purpose in teaching. Through the structure of writing, the focus implied that the problem in teaching was that the corps members had not thought sufficiently about what they had done. The remedy, implied in the writing style, was that all that had to be done to reform teaching was to make teachers wiser. This was not my intent although it was the message embodied in the writing.

A major task of the rewriting, then, was to redirect the narrative towards the 'making' of the teacher rather than the teacher's 'making' of teaching. Let me provide an example. A first draft, as I discussed earlier, focused on the sense of mission that the corps members had towards teaching. The argument was how the practices of the first year changed that conception of mission. In the final version, the importance of the idea of mission was theoretically rethought. I placed it historically within a discourse of social engineering that had emerged in the late nineteenth century and was now being reconstituted as 'rescuing' the inner-city and rural child from the evils of their community and own 'self'. By revisioning the data in this manner, I could think about the daily practices of the teacher as an amalgamation of practices that are historically sedimented in schooling as the common sense of teaching and school learning.

The rethinking of the interpretation played into the title of the study itself. The original title of the study was: 'Teach for America: The Privatization of Social Policy in Urban and Rural Education'. This version was a mixture of different stories about the reform program. At one level, it focused on the 'children of Reagan', a phrase ironically used by a staff member to ironically position herself with the political conservative landscape. The draft also focused on the different conceptions of pedagogy held by the students. But as I discussed earlier, these different foci repeated well-founded but well-worn sentiments about the inequalities of schooling and previous theoretical conclusions about the repressive elements of schooling.

Such an approach, I felt, was also ahistorical. It took a particular policy initiative in the political arena and inscribed it as the categories to shape and fashion educational science. Privatization is part of a political discourse. To accept it as a category of investigation is to take others' definitions as the distinctions of research. This way of organizing the research would lose site of the historical set of relations that make a political discourse 'reasonable'. This assuming what needs to be questioned can have drastic and negative results. A recent discussion in poverty research, for example, has pointed to how poverty research since the 1960s has used official state definitions to organize research.

Further, and related to my uneasiness was my pushing towards understanding the concrete, productive elements of pedagogy in constructing an unequal playing field. I rewrote the book, and the title moved to *Constructing the teacher* and then *Struggling for the Soul*. This was to place emphasis on how the discourses that circulate within produces its objects of scrutiny and observation — the child in the inner city schools. In the final version, the soul was emphasized. The selection of the final title was, in part, to emphasize the ways in which norms are produced to divide and differentiate children's being through the linguistic patterns of pedagogy. But the title also responded to a comment of a colleague who said, 'Oh no, not another book on constructing.' Such is the politics of differentiation within academics.

Conclusion

The writing of the study was one of the more interesting projects in my professional career. Its interest lies in my thinking about a number of different strands of scholarship as a way of playing with the empirical data collected. At the same time, the empirical data provide a way in which to play with the different theoretical outlooks that guided my understanding of the phenomena of teaching and teacher education. The outcome of the writing is, for me, a better way to think about school reform, the problem of inequity in schooling, and the difficulties and possibilities of a more progressive institution. None of these is an easy problem. None of them are solved in this study but represent a terrain struggled over.

Here, I think about the task of intellectual life is somewhat like the life of Sisyphus who continually sought to roll the rock up a hill, and who never succeeded in keeping the rock in place once he had reached the top. While we always need to seek better and more humane solutions to our conditions, that work is an imperfect and perpetual struggle. In a sense, this is my struggle as there is always, what Lundgren (1983) has called, a tension between our hopes and happenings as we live in world of ambiguity and uncertainty.

Notes

1 I use the pronoun's 'I' and 'my' here in an historical sense that while it is 'me' speaking, the ways in which I am talking about experience and reflection are also historical phenomena which make such talk possible. I explore these traditions in Popkewitz (1996) and Popkewitz and Brennan, 1998).

2 This is less accurate for studies of gender. See, e.g., Walkerdine, 1988, for example.

3 There are some examples of literature which does push empirically/theoretical beyond the general framing of the sociology of curriculum of the 1970s; see, e.g., Wexler, 1987; Walkerdine, 1988, 1990, Ladwig, 1996; Gore, 1998.

4 The chronologies of my 'stories' would appear as if: there are discourses of racism embodied through the structuring of the federal program to improve the education of American Indians (Popkewitz, 1976), the cultural and social differentiation produced in the reform program (Popkewitz et al., 1982), and the way instrumental rationalities of reform leave unchallenged the teaching assumptions and gender implications of teacher professionalization (Popkewitz and Lind, 1988).

5 The work of Michael Shapiro (1992) political science, Judith Butler (1993) and Denise Riley (1988) in feminist philosophy, Robert Young (1990, 1995) and Nikolas Rose (1989, 1996) in sociology have helped me in thinking about this problem. Also, the Wednesday Group at the University of Wisconsin which over the past decade has continually read across fields and introduced me to a range of scholarship that often remains invisible in the field of education. In this respect, the work of Henry Giroux (1992) and Peter McLaren (1994) is important in their engaging a range of disciplinary literature into conversations about education.

6 It is important because there has been the systemic exclusion of different groups of people in social, economic and political arenas. But at the same time, we need to consider the systems of knowledge that generate principles for participation for two important reasons. First, the focus on who participates while addressing certain categorical systems of exclusions, does not help to understand the principles through which systems of inclusion and exclusion are generated. Second, as I will argue later, systems of exclusion occur through the inscriptions of dispositions and sensitivities towards action. It is at this level of governing that this study is concerned.

7 More recent writing has also enabled us to consider the racial binaries inscribed in such writing. See, e.g., Morrison, 1992.

References

BUTLER, J. (1993) *Bodies That Matter: On the Discourse Limits of 'Sex'*, New York: Routledge.

DUMM, T. (1987) *Democracy and Punishment: Disciplinary Origins of the United States*, Madison: University of Wisconsin Press.

GIROUX, H. (1992) *Border Crossings: Cultural Workers and the Politics of Education*, New York: Routledge.

GORE, J. (1998) 'Disciplining bodies: On the continuity of power relations in pedagogy', in POPKEWITZ, T. and BRENNAN, M. (eds) *Foucault's Challenge: Discourse, Knowledge and Power in Education*, New York: Teachers College Press.

HUNTER, I. (1994) *Rethinking the School: Subjectivity, Bureaucracy, Criticism*, New York: St Martin's Press.

KOZOL, J. (1991) *Savage Inequalities: Children in America's schools*, New York: Crown Publishers.

LADSON-BILLINGS, G. (1994) *The Dreamkeepers: Successful Teachers of African American Children*, San Francisco: Jossey-Bass.

LADWIG, J. (1996) *Academic Distinctions; Theory and Methodology in the Sociology of School Knowledge*, New York: Routledge.

LUNDGREN, U. (1983) *Between Hope and Happening: Text and Contexts in Curriculum*, Geelong, Australia: Deakin University Press.

McLAREN, P. (1994) *Schooling As a Ritual Performance* (2nd ed.), Boston: Routledge and Kegan Paul.

MORRISON, T. (1992) *Playing in the Dark: Whiteness and the Literary Imagination*, Cambridge: Harvard University Press.

POPKEWITZ, T. (1976) 'Reform as political discourse: A case study', *School Review*, **84**, pp. 43–69.

POPKEWITZ, T. (1984) *Paradigm and Ideology in Educational Research: Social Functions of the Intellectual*, London: Falmer Press.

POPKEWITZ, T. (1996) 'Rethinking decentralization and the State/Civil Society distinctions: The State as a problematic of governing', *Journal of Educational Policy*, **11**, pp. 27–51.

POPKEWITZ, T. (1998) *Struggling for the Soul: The Politics of Schooling and the Construction of the Teacher*, New York: Teachers College Press.

POPKEWITZ, T. and BRENNAN, M. (eds) (1998) *Foucault's Challenge: Discourse, Knowledge and Power in Education*, New York: Teachers College Press.

POPKEWITZ, T. and LIND, K. (1989) 'Teacher incentives as reform: Implications for teachers' work and the changing control mechanism in education', *Teachers College Record*, **90**, pp. 575–94.

POPKEWITZ, T., TABACHNICK, B. and WEHLAGE, G. (1982) *The Myth of Education Reform: A Study of School Responses to a Program of Change*, Madison: University of Wisconsin Press.

RILEY, D. (1988) *Am I That Name? Feminism and the Category of 'Women' in History*, Minneapolis: University of Minnesota Press.

ROSE, N. (1989) *Governing the Soul*, New York: Routledge, Chapman and Hall.

ROSE, N. (1996) 'The death of the social? Re-figuring the territory to government', *Economy and Society*, **25**, 3, pp. 327–56.

SHAPIRO, M. (1992) *Reading the Postmodern Polity: Political Theory as Textual Practice*, Minneapolis: The University of Minnesota Press.

SLEETER, C. and GRANT, C. (1994) *Making Choices for Multicultural Education: Five Approaches to Race, Class, and Gender* (2nd ed.), New York: Merrill.

WALKERDINE, V. (1988) *The Mastery of Reason: Cognitive Development and the Production of Rationality*, London: Routledge.

WALKERDINE, V. (1990) *School Girl Fictions*, London: Verso.

WEXLER, P. (1987) *Social Analysis of Education*, New York: Routledge.

YOUNG, M. (ed.) (1971) *Knowledge and Control; New Directions for the Sociology of Education*, London: Collier-Macmillan.

YOUNG, R. (1990) *White Mythologies: Writing, History and the West*, New York: Routledge.

3   Multiculture in the Making

Elizabeth Ellsworth

Power is the ability not to have to learn. Catherine Bateson

What would be the value of the passion for knowledge if it resulted only in a certain amount of knowledgeableness and not, in one way or another and to the extent possible, in the knower's straying afield of himself? There are times in life when the question of knowing if one can think differently than one thinks, and perceive differently than one sees, is absolutely necessary if one is to go on looking and reflecting at. . . . Michele Foucault

Central to the technologies of the self is an attention to the passion of knowledge, a passion which does not reify knowing but rather entails a probability that one occasionally will lose oneself, only to find it in another place, caught up with other knowledge and people. Elspeth Probyn

'Multicultural' is an adjective. 'Multiculture' is a noun. But the difference isn't just grammatical. Framing my work in terms of 'multiculture' instead of 'multicultural' has changed that work and my relationship to it. 'Multiculture' makes approaches to research and teaching possible and intelligible for me that are otherwise impossible and unintelligible when I frame my work in terms of 'multicultural'. I'm going to try to explain here how and why the differences between these two terms have taken on larger theoretical, methodological, and political meanings for me as an educator.

I didn't study the field of education in graduate school. I studied movies. Hollywood movies, mostly. But because I was a teaching assistant from the first day of grad school, I was also trying to figure out how to teach.

It took me a long time to write my dissertation. I kept telling myself it was because I was working half time and sometimes more than half time as a teaching assistant, and that's why it was just going on and on. But from here, 15 or so years later, it's obvious that I couldn't finish the dissertation until that rather bad Hollywood film came out: *Personal Best*. Here's why.

Grad School in the War Years

I got a Masters in Communication (documentary films) during the Vietnam war. My mentor/thesis advisor was a guy whose attic walls were covered with huge sheets of paper, forming a 50-foot long timeline of the war-to-date. Particularly important events were highlighted in color and urgently huge lettering. Along the walls on the floor under the timeline were meaningfully stacked *Newsweeks*, *Times*, newspaper clippings, video-tapes, documents, notes — all corresponding to their place on the timeline. On my one and only tour of this shrine/staging area/combat zone/data base, my advisor told me that *his* dissertation advisor was, as we spoke, in the process of videotaping every network's every newscast every day to archive and analyze their coverage of the war — and had been doing so for years.

My advisor was obsessed. His advisor was obsessed. I haven't followed in their methodological footsteps. I don't, for example, do research by trying to achieve a one-to-one correspondence between the data I collect or the analyses I make and the phenomena they represent.

But there's something else about the way both of them did research that I haven't been able — or wanted — to shake. While their data-philia may have been the most striking thing about their research — driving all their hoarding of videotapes, articles and clippings were unshakable convictions that the ways people were making sense of the Vietnam war were as much a part of the war as was the napalm and fraggings. Both of these guys were trying to prove, through their academic research, that a war over the meanings of this war was going on in the hearts and minds of the people involved in it. They were trying to prove that the ways that things, people, and events were 'made to mean' in that war bore heavily on the actions of governments and of individual soldiers and civilians.

In other words, the ways that the Vietnam war was being made to mean in the US media were as important to carrying on — or ending — the war as were the military dimensions of the conflict or the domestic anti-war movement. Media representations of Vietnamese culture, history, and people weren't neutral reflections of some prior reality of each of those things. They were strategic maneuvers that affected simultaneously both the discursive war of meaning and the material war of agent orange and relocation. The government's use of the media to manipulate meanings made about the war was as much a battlefield maneuver as the bombing of the Ho Chi Minh trail. There was a politics to representation. Lives could be won or lost depending on what meanings were being won or lost.

Dissertating in the (White) Women's Movement

But it wasn't the Vietnam war that shaped my dissertation most directly. By the time I started my PhD around 1980, it was the Women's Movement that was setting the theoretical, political, and daily life terms for my graduate study, and that of most of my peers. And within the context of that 'movement', it was the release of *Personal Best* — the first Hollywood film that was 'really' about a lesbian relationship — that tied my dissertation to my life.

Before PB (as I called it in all my notes and drafts) came out, so to speak, my dissertation was stuck at the end of Chapter 2. I thought it was going to be about feminist documentary films. The first two chapters were about feminist documentary films and documentary film making as a social and political practice in the women's movement. I wanted to 'prove' that film making and film viewing had something to do with social change — that the shaping of films by their makers and the shaping of interpretations of films by their viewers could be effective strategic maneuvers in the struggle for 'women's liberation'.

But, to paraphrase Brenda Laurel, 'intelligence without passion is merely rationality' (1993, p. 214). Sure, my first two chapters were very rational. But they had no passion. They weren't intelligent. It was only Chapter 2 and I was having trouble remembering why I was putting myself through this thing called writing a dissertation. I was forgetting the point of it all.

Then I started noticing pin-ups of actors Patrice Donnelly and Muriel Hemingway appearing on refrigerator doors at potluck dinners in lesbian households. Suddenly, it seemed that every last lesbian I knew in Madison was talking about, analyzing, arguing over, breathlessly waiting for, nervous about, disappointed in, angry about and/or erotic-ally involved in *Personal Best*'s production, advertisement, appearance at the Strand Theater, and/or the film's broader cultural and political fallout. So too, it seemed, were a lot of non-lesbians. PB was sending tremors across the popular cultural landscape: journalists writing in *Time* and *Newsweek* spoke of PB and Title Nine in the same paragraph, and *The New York Times* magazine discussed PB in relation to recently spotted trends toward 'gay-friendly' advertising campaigns by Calvin Klein and others.

Could it be . . . ? Was this an instance of . . . ? Was this movie — the ways it was made and the ways people were 'reading' it — actually having something to do with social change? And could I 'prove' it in my dissertation?

Well, of course I 'knew' PB was 'changing' things. I was living out those changes in (what we used to call in those days) 'my lesbian body' — picking up reverberations and rumblings from the eventness of PB as they moved through both the 'lesbian community' I hung out with and the popular culture that surrounded it. I 'knew' that I and my friends were consciously and unconsciously 'seeing' ourselves and each other 'differently' after seeing PB and experiencing its 'eventness' in the larger culture than we had before. And I 'knew' that I and my friends were being seen and being made sense of 'differently' in the larger culture after the event of PB than before. I don't mean that our or their 'attitudes' towards lesbians changed from, for example, negative to positive, or negative to more negative, or positive to more positive. And I don't mean that misperceptions or stereotypes were either simply 'corrected' or 'reinforced'.

Rather, what I 'knew' from living it out was that the *terms* of making sense of and struggling over the meanings of 'lesbian' had been changed by the event of PB for both lesbians and non-lesbians. Suddenly, the terms for consciously and unconsciously, ex-plicitly and implicitly negotiating the meanings of 'lesbian' among lesbians — and between lesbians and the usually hostile 'outside' world — changed. These meanings were being struggled over, negotiated, and acted out at lesbian potlucks whose contexts of political work and circulations of desire were now (re)formed, in part, by the pin-ups of Patrice Donnelly and Muriel Hemingway looking on from refrigerator doors. What it meant 'to be' lesbian — how lesbians looked, behaved, loved, moved — what counted as 'erotic', what counted as 'attractive', what counted as politically useful to lesbian 'liberation' and what counted as threatening, what counted as authentic representations of lesbians by the popular media and what counted as distortions and lesbophobia — the *terms* in which these things got discussed, framed, and settled even temporarily — were shifted more or less by the event of *Personal Best*.

Remember, this representation of lesbians in the media — no matter how watered down — was new and scary stuff in 1982.

The event of PB pushed me through the looking glass of my academic research. My dissertation no longer had to be merely rational. It could be intelligent. It could be written through what I was living out and through my commitments to working to make 'lesbian' mean differently within both academic and popular culture. I would spend the next five chapters tracing the subtle and not so subtle shiftings in the terms of some of the struggles over meanings of 'lesbian' and 'women's liberation' that PB left in its wake. I would 'prove' that films and the events surrounding them make a difference in struggles for social change. And I would 'prove' that for some lesbians and feminists struggling for social change, films — and PB in particular — became the material they/we used to negotiate the circulation of meanings within their/our own movements and to shape political strategies there.

It was great for awhile. I 'knew' what I knew 'as a lesbian', and I was writing from it. I was finding 'evidence' in published film reviews by lesbians and non-lesbians alike that allowed me to link the ebbs and flows of particular strands in public discourses about lesbians and the women's movement back to the event of *Personal Best*. My dissertation was filled with statements such as 'the lesbian community seemed to agree at this moment that . . .' or 'liberal feminists argued that . . .' and 'lesbian film reviewers writing in lesbian publications used *Personal Best* as a pretext to discuss and negotiate the politics of appearance within the lesbian community . . .'

Gender Almost Meets Race in My Dissertation

Then one of the later drafts came back from one of my committee members. I went to her office to talk. She wasn't happy. All she had to say was something like: 'blah blah blah Community . . .'; 'blah blah blah singular . . .'; 'blah blah blah white. . . .' And a gaping hole tore open beneath my feet, inside my head, through my personal history, back into my graduate coursework, and between my lived experiences 'as' a lesbian and the research tools I had learned in grad school.

It took me two seconds in her office to realize I had written hundreds of dissertation pages as if there were one, unified, locatable, lesbian community — namely, my own conception of 'mine'. I had written hundreds of pages about *Personal Best* as if all lesbians were white. The differences I had located among and between individual lesbian reviewers writing about PB were ideological differences — the standard liberal feminist, socialist feminist, and cultural feminist breakdown of political orientation within the women's movement that everyone writing dissertations had been using. My 'data' contained no examples of writing from film reviewers who were, as far as I could tell, women of color. I had given no thought to how racial and cultural difference within and across lesbian communities rewrote ideological perspectives and audience readings of PB. I had framed none of the questions I was asking about film reviewers' makings of sense about PB in ways that tried to take racial and social difference among lesbians into account. I hadn't problematized the notion of 'being a lesbian' one bit. According to that draft of my dissertation, you either 'were' a lesbian (and there was some unspoken, white, middle class-centric assumption about what that was) or you weren't. And, I hadn't even thought of any of this in the context of writing the dissertation.

Racial, cultural, social class — and even sexual difference — among 'lesbians' had become the structuring absence of that draft of my dissertation. It's what had to be ignored, overlooked, forgotten in order for my dissertation to be what it was as it sat on my committee member's desk. Any acknowledgment of difference (other than those three stereotypical ideological camps) within and across lesbian communities would have made my dissertation, as it was in that draft, unintelligible.

What blew my mind even more, in the days following that meeting, was the deepening realization of how completely I had managed to unconsciously separate 'what I knew', however partially, as a lesbian living in and living out 'the women's movement', from 'what I knew' as a graduate student writing a dissertation. I had been to the Michigan Women's Music Festival's 'Women of Color' Tent and the Iowa University Women Against Racism Conference — I 'knew' about and had participated in lesbian-initiated anti-racism work within lesbian communities and the women's movement writ large. I 'knew' by experience that there were multiple lesbian communities that alternately and often simultaneously both joined efforts and clashed with each other in their political and cultural work. I 'knew' from experience that I myself 'belonged' to several lesbian communities simultaneously, even in Madison, moving in and across communities of academic lesbians, rural lesbians, townie lesbians — using different languages, clothes, knowledges, desires, pleasures, presentations of self, erotics, and political strategies in each. I 'knew' what it was like to have different and often competing levels of comfort, status, economic and political clout in each. I 'knew' what it was like to get tired of, bored, or pissed off by any one of those communities, and to find respite and renewal in one of the others. I 'knew' that in some times and places, I 'was' a liberal feminist, at others a socialist feminist, and yet at others, a cultural feminist — and sometimes, all three.

And I 'knew' something else from lived experience across these sites and perspectives. Much of the motivation within white lesbian communities to lead and initiate anti-racism work within the broader women's liberation movement came not only from the political necessity to forge coalitions among women across race, class, and culture. It also came from the lived experience of women desiring one another and/or falling in love across racial, class, and cultural divides. It came from trying to negotiate and change the social, cultural, and personal fallout of such a multiply transgressive thing.

And yet, when it came to framing and writing my dissertation, I had been capable of sitting for years at a desk and 'forgetting' all of this about myself, the contexts of my life and those of other lesbians. And there was little in my graduate school experience — classes, conferences, journal articles, lectures, colloquia — to remind me, much less provide me with the intellectual and methodological tools for dealing with it.

What did I do with my dissertation? I did what most white academics did in the early 1980s — and many continue to do. I qualified the hell out of it. I went through every page and changed 'Community' to something else like 'communiti*es*' or 'middle-class white midwest academic community in 1980'. I wrote several pages about the 'limitations' of this particular study. I wrote about the need for other studies that would take into account racial, class, and cultural difference within and across lesbian communities. I acknowledged that even the term and identity 'lesbian' is a contested one — it itself is under constant construction, erasure, and reconstruction. 'Lesbian identity' is self-contradictory, partial, multiple, and fractured by repeated, unconscious forgettings not only between individuals and groups — but within selves — like my own forgetful dissertation.

But what I did with my dissertation isn't the point here. More important for this essay is the question: how has this particular moment in my personal history (which wasn't just personal, but also a moment in the academic and political histories of the women's movement, and of film studies as a field) influenced the professional decisions that guide my research, that lead to my choice of subjects and paradigms, and lead me to engage in particular analyses and discussions? The point of this story about my dissertation is to get at the point of this edited book: What guides me during my research and writing in the area of equity, social justice, and power, and what's the interrelationship between my life experience and the theoretical underpinnings of my scholarship? What, in other words, influences a desire to question and/or illuminate privilege and power?

Gender Almost Loses Race in My Teaching

The Hollywood character arc version of this story would end with me being utterly and irrevocably changed by that moment of rude awakening in the writing of my dissertation.

That particular moment in my personal and intellectual history would be a turning point. My desires to question and/or illuminate privilege and power as they play out across race and social class would be solid, unshakable, consistent, and guiding my research and writing. But that's not how consciousness and commitment work.

The year after finishing the dissertation, I was a new assistant professor teaching graduate courses in curriculum and instruction. Going overnight from being a graduate student to a teacher of graduate students was terrifying. I fell back on what I knew best — the ways of thinking, asking questions, framing research, and analyzing data — that I had been taught in grad school. I fell back, in other words, on those very paradigms of research that were themselves partly responsible for me being able to write a complete draft of my dissertation without ever paying attention in it to myriad forms of racial and social difference. Those paradigms were my safety net as I tried to learn the ropes of assistant professorship — paradigms I knew like the back of my hand. But not only that. The paradigms of research I learned in grad school were also safe for me racially. They didn't acknowledge or question the researcher's (my) complicity or implication in racial dynamics. This oversight had of course become a big problem for my dissertation, and for the relation of my academic work to my life as a lesbian. But in the confusion, stress, and disorientation of the next year, that oversight was there as a convenient and institutionally sanctioned safety net. And I used it.

I taught my first two semesters of classes as if the 'turning point' in writing my dissertation never happened. I taught the canon of the field I had come from.

One of my first graduate student advisees came from Puerto Rico to study at my school. Warm, friendly and gregarious, a fighter for Puerto Rican independence and against assimilation, he included me and my partner in his growing family and educated us about the politics and daily realities of being brown in Madison, being bilingual in a school of education with no real bilingual education program and very few students of color, and being the parent of brown bilingual children in Madison public schools. For a white girl growing up in Milwaukee, the city that the government calls, in 1995, the nation's most segregated city; and for an assistant professor teaching in a 'world class' university with one of the worst records of recruiting and retaining students and faculty of color — this friendship was a new experience.

One day he came into my office and closed the door, near tears and angry. He had just come from the first meeting of one of his classes. He had been humiliated, singled out, and infantalized by remarks that the (white, male) professor made to and about him — about his 'latin-ness', his maleness, his ability to play guitar and sing love songs and seduce women, his difference. All this in front of his new classmates who were all women and appeared to be all white. And all this in a class supposedly about cultural difference in education.

Listening to his story, I responded as a friend, a professor, an advisor, and when he filed a grievance — an advocate. But also, listening to him, a gaping hole tore open beneath my feet, inside my head, through my personal history, back into my first two semesters of being a professor, and between my lived experiences as a friend of this student and the research paradigms and tools I had been teaching in my classes. 'As' a lesbian professor, and as a friend, I had been trying to understand the parallels, intersections, and collisions between the unjust social dynamics that shaped my life and those that shaped this student's. But his story shocked me into realizing that once again, I hadn't integrated what I 'knew' (even partially) as a white woman, a lesbian and a friend with what and how I taught and practiced in classrooms and research. Maybe I hadn't been actively harassing students of color in my classes. But I had also done nothing to problematize what and how I was teaching. My classes were not addressing and engaging with the burgeoning literatures written by scholars of color that critiqued the very academic canons I was teaching. And there was little going on at the university to encourage me to do that.

The fields of film studies and curriculum and instruction — as most fields in academe in the early 1980s — had little clue how to reshape the meanings and processes of teaching and research in response to increasing numbers of students of color. Nor, as institutions and fields of study, did they have a clue how to respond theoretically or methodologically to the devastating and burgeoning critiques by people of color of the academy and of western ways of constructing knowledge.

As an assistant professor developing course syllabi and launching what I hoped to be a tenurable 'line of inquiry' — the intellectual and political context for my work in the mid-1980s wasn't the Vietnam war, nor even the Women's Liberation Movement's 'second wave'. It was the social and political construction of a new social and political identity — 'women of color' — through which some of the women who had been marginalized, erased, generalized, westernized, middle classed, white washed, and heterosexualized by feminist discourses of the 1970s, talked back. As a 'third wave', they talked back to feminists who were defining the discourses and politics of the second wave of the women's movement. And they talked back to the academy within which many of those feminists had established Women's Studies programs, effectively institutionalizing those discourses and politics through paradigms of research and teaching.

The point of this story about this moment in my first year of teaching has nothing to do with personal 'guilt' or 'remorse' about what I was and wasn't doing in my classes or research. Rather, I'm telling it here as a way of pointing out how in my life history, I've experienced academe as a context for learning and doing research that splits the personal and the intellectual. And how in my intellectual history, I've experienced intellectual work as never fully conscious, but always and already split by the unconscious — I'm always forgetting something, and those forgettings aren't innocent. And how in teaching and doing research, I have a growing awareness that there is always more to learn, always more than The One Story about anything — despite the fact that for the most part, the academy's *raison d'être* has been to discover and write The One Story. And how all of this adds up to a particular stance I've taken in my work, namely: 'What I know and what I forget always have the potential of being oppressive or exploitative to myself (myselves) and to others — and yours to me.'

Using Post-modernism to Break the Logics of Sameness

So these are some of the ways I'm making sense of my experience, and how my experience has influenced the ways I make sense of what I study and teach as a researcher. The terms in which I've told stories in this essay about those experiences are shaped by the development and influence of post-modernism in academic fields of study in the last 20 years. One of the ways I've responded to those experiences is by turning toward post-modernism as a paradigm to guide my research and teaching practice. And the ways I've turned toward post-modernism, and put it to use in my work, have been shaped by the experiences I tell of here. I'm finding, in other words, that I can use post-modernism to support my engagement with issues of race, class, gender, sexuality as I study and teach the politics of representation in education. I'm finding that I can use post-modernism to break away from the research methods and interpretive frameworks that I grew up with in grad school.

I'd like to give an example of how some of this shakes out in one of the graduate seminars that I teach. It's a way of addressing another goal of this collection of essays — to use material from writing and research to illustrate the choices I've made in the paradigms I use and the questions I ask. It'll also be a way of showing how awareness that all knowledge is partial, limited, and potentially oppressive to self and to others — doesn't leave me paralyzed as a teacher or researcher. I'll try to show how that awareness can support the taking of action through, for example, educational interventions in how power gets connected to knowledges and to processes of making sense.

I'm teaching a graduate seminar called 'Media, Post-modernism, and Education'. And I'm writing a book on the same topic. A big part of the course and of the book is about how post-modernism can be used to frame and pursue research and problems in education.

I start the seminar with a tentative and partial definition of post-modernism, drawn from Brenda Marshall. She says: '[Postmodernism] isn't really an "ism"; it isn't really a thing. It's a moment, but more a moment in logic than in time' (Marshall, 1992, p. 5). 'The postmodern moment is an awareness of being-within, first, a language, and second, a particular historical, social, cultural framework' (Marshall, 1992, p. 3).

Then I talk about how that post-modern 'moment in logic' that Marshall speaks of is really a 'break' in particular, historically constructed logics. As a moment of 'awareness' of being within a language and being within a particular historical, social, cultural framework, the post-modern moment is a break in logics designed to get to universal Truth that is the Same for everyone, every place every time; to One unified vision of the world; to a total and completely adequate account of a problem that leads to a total, predictable, and completely successful solution.

Then, I give students a handout. It's something to go on when I send them out to see if they can find instances of academic research and writing about education that use post-modernism to break such logics. The point isn't to break logics for the sake of breaking logics. It's to show how an awareness of being within a particular language, culture, and historical moment can't exist within logics that drive toward universality, totality, certainty, and unity. And it's to show how, ironically for educators, there is power and positive productivity in finding and putting to use the limits of one's own knowledge.

(You might be starting to sense the connections between this first day of seminar and what I myself needed but didn't have assigned to me when I was writing my own dissertation or constructing my first year's syllabi as an assistant professor.)

The handout I give to students is called 'Interpretive Breaks' (and that's what my book-in-progress is about). It emphasizes how breaks in logic are accomplished when an author shifts his or her interpretive strategies — his or her ways of making sense of a person, thing, or event.

This is what the handout says:

> There's no one way of performing an interpretive break in and through academic writing. Interpretive breaks take many rhetorical shapes and forms. But no matter what the form, in most writings that try to perform interpretive breaks you'll find the following moments:
>
>> There is a moment that testifies to — witnesses — some problem the author sees with the ways sense has been made of a particular circumstance, social identity or positioning, educational or cultural practice, film, video, object, historical moment, etc.

There is a moment when the writer traces that problem to particular practices, ways of making sense, political interests, and shows how that problem has been made possible — socially and historically — by and through those practices, discourses, and interests.

There is moment when the writer takes up the issues and problems at hand from 'somewhere else', from a position of difference. S/he re-interprets, re-writes those issues from some other practice, history, discourse, interest, and attempts to convince us readers that those issues can, and must, be made to mean differently.

There is moment when the writer demonstrates what becomes possible and what becomes impossible, what becomes comprehensible and what becomes incomprehensible, through the re-interpretation and re-writing s/he has performed. In other words, what ways of making sense, and the practices they can be used to legitimize, get shifted by the writer's re-interpretation, re-writing?

There is a moment when the writer tries to produce in me, the reader, a visceral sense of the difference this all makes, of the radical break, breaking of sense, shattering of paradigms, breaking off of relations that their re-interpretation tries to perform. There is, in other words, a moment when the writer uses the aesthetic and rhetorical power of language deliberately and self-consciously. This moment is present in interpretive breaks because the entire project is fueled by the writer's trying to *interrupt* sense-making that has been used to support violence, prejudice, erasure, marginalization, exploitation, hierarchy.

Now, I want to argue that the orchestration of these moments into a piece of academic writing 'counts' as 'research'. It counts as research because it is capable of constructing knowledge. In other words, such writing is capable of constructing changed knowledges — interpretations — of what it means 'to be' x, and therefore is capable of changing how x is treated, how much x matters, how x matters. This change has come about not necessarily because I, the researcher, have discovered 'new' information, but because I have re-framed — re-situated — re-located my-selves-in-relation to old and new ways of making sense of the world.

This seminar explores, in part, how interpretive breaks as a practice of re-locating selves in relation to competing ways of making sense of the world raises implications for what counts as learning. The notion of interpretive break suggests that 'learning something' might be understood as having lost my self 'only to find it in another place, caught up with other knowledge and people, in the reflection of another angle and perspective' (Probyn, 1992, p. 509). If one definition of 'power' is 'the ability not to have to learn', then these moments that compose 'interpretive breaking' are always politicized, because 'learning' is always the refusal of the privilege not to have to learn. In these ways, interpretive breaks are always politicized — never neutral.

End of handout.

Using Post-modernism as an Educator

Now I want to give you a sense of how this notion of interpretive break as a use of post-modernism in educational research can be 'applied' to actual instances of educational research. And more importantly, how and why I use it to elucidate the workings of privilege and power in academic and educational practices.

One of the articles I ask students to read in light of this handout is Paula Treichler's 'AIDS, homophobia, and biomedical discourse: An epidemic of signification' (Treichler, 1991). Here is what such a reading might look like.

Treichler witnesses a number of problems she sees with how meanings have been constructed around AIDS and the HIV virus. In fact, the point of her research is to show that the ways AIDS is made to mean are as important to the work of ending the crisis as are the biological dimensions of the epidemic.

One of the problems Treichler documents about the ways AIDS has been made to mean is the ways it has been 'explained' or 'explained away' by linking it to particular 'kinds' of people — namely, homosexuals, heroin addicts, hemophiliacs, and Haitians.

She traces this problem to particular ways of making sense, and the privileges and power attached to them: It was possible and thinkable for powerful medical and governmental institutions to 'explain' AIDS as a result of exotic, uncommon, deviant behavior, identity or condition because of widely available and actively circulating discourses that stereotyped, demonized, and pathologized the people in these groups. It was (and continues to be) possible to frame AIDS as an issue concerning only marginalized, deviant, different, already sick and expendable people because of the configurations of power and interest around policy making, distribution of economic resources, race, sexuality, media access, religious institutions, and medical research.

Treichler then takes up this particular problem from 'somewhere else' within social and cultural identities, sexual desire, political power, and ways of making sense of lived experience. She rewrites the question: 'who is at risk by virtue of belonging to a high risk group?' to the question: 'who is at risk by virtue of engaging in behaviors that transmit HIV?' This rewriting doesn't only reflect a change in scientific knowledge about HIV, as ongoing research revealed AIDS wasn't 'in fact' 'caused' by 'homosexual' behavior, for example. This rewriting also constitutes an educational and political intervention in ways of making sense of AIDS, and how AIDS was being used to make sense of particular people and social groups. This shift is necessary to ending the epidemic through education — because people must understand that *anyone* can get the virus if he or she participates in particular behaviors — behaviors, like vaginal intercourse (which is no more a Haitian behavior than it is a white Nebraskan behavior), behaviors like anal sex (which is no more homosexual than heterosexual), behaviors like blood transfusions (which are no more hemophiliac behaviors than they are car accident victim behaviors), behaviors like being pricked by an infected needle (risks shared by drug addicts and nurses alike).

Crucial to AIDS education is the interpretive break from framing the disease as a disease of particular marginalized and expendable social groups — to framing it as a commonplace disease transmitted through commonplace behaviors. This makes educational campaigns possible and thinkable that are impossible and unthinkable under the at-risk group interpretation — such as safer sex education for women having sex with men while in what they believe to be monogamous relationships with men whom they believe have had sex only with women. It also makes possible educational initiatives against the discourses and relations of power that make the interpretation and stigmatization of AIDS as a 'gay disease' or 'Haitian disease' viable and thinkable in the first place.

Fueled by passionate commitment and anger against interpretations that lead to discrimination, stigmatization, suffering, death, and the spread of the epidemic — Treichler uses irony, humor, and the non-academic, politicized street language of AIDS activists in this scholarly article. For example, after a lengthy quote from one AIDS 'expert', an immunologist whose attempts to dispel misconceptions about AIDS actually reinscribes ambiguity and uncertainty about how it is transmitted — Treichler asks: 'Would you buy a scientific fact from this man?' (Treichler, 1991, p. 36) She also references works of literature, such as Camus' novel *The Plague*, to bolster her theoretical point that 'Ultimately, we cannot distinguish self from not-self: for "plague is life", and each of us has the plague within us; "no one, no one on earth is free from it"' (Treichler, 1991, p. 69).

She uses rhetorical and aesthetic devices such as these not only to interrupt problematic interpretations of AIDS and social groups — but also, to interrupt the distanced, distancing, supposedly neutral and objective language and stance most often employed in academic writing. She uses them to interrupt and disrupt how we, academic readers, perform our selves as academics when it comes to epidemics and crises of meaning making.

By trying to shift our locations, as readers, in relation to competing ways of making sense of and teaching about AIDS, Treichler invites us to catch ourselves up with other knowledge and people. She invites us, for example, to catch ourselves up with ways of making sense of AIDS that have been constructed by community health and gay rights activists. By bringing the languages and knowledges of these 'other people' into academic research and writing, she challenges her reader's 'ability not to have to learn' — the ability not to have to lose oneself only to find it in another place caught up with other knowledge and people who one's own knowledge has (sometimes unintentionally and unknowingly) marginalized.

So that's one reading of Treichler that I think the notion of interpretive break makes possible.

That's Why I Think in Terms of 'Multiculture' and not 'Multicultural'

This is what I hope this reading of Treichler and the other stories in this essay offer to graduate students in education: a sense of how research about and within social and cultural difference — and we researchers ourselves — are always unfinished and incomplete. What counts as 'the research', and what we as researchers are knowing, forgetting, ignoring, and finding again from a different place — are always in-the-making. And, 'multicultural knowledge' is always in-the-*making* in the sense that what we 'know' about ourselves and others can never be separated from what we are *doing* with that (limited) knowledge. That is, the ways we use the post-modern awareness of being within a particular language, culture, and historical moment as we do research on and within social and cultural difference is actually a part of constructing multiculture.

Research is, in other words, a site of cultural production. It's not just the construction of knowledge 'about' or representation 'of' already existing phenomena. My dissertation, as an act of representation that 'forgot' about race even as it 'remembered' other social and cultural difference, became a cultural artifact through which particular relations of power and social dynamics were materialized and re-enacted in language, rhetoric, and research methods. The question for me becomes, then, *not* 'what *is* multicultural and what *isn't*' when we talk about research practices, but rather: 'What multicultures will we researchers and educators construct in and through the work we perform?'

Thinking in terms of multiculture foregrounds for me the performative power of research and education on and within our lived relations to the politics of difference.

Thinking in terms of multiculture makes particular relationships to the work of research and teaching possible and intelligible for me that are otherwise impossible and unintelligible when I think in terms of 'multicultural'. 'Multicultural' is an adjective, it's a qualifier. It qualifies whatever it appears next to, such as 'multicultural education', or 'multicultural research' or 'multicultural campus', or 'multicultural children's literature'. As a qualifier, it is subordinated to what it qualifies. It's there in the service of what it qualifies. 'Research' and 'education' in other words, pre-exist 'multicultural'. Multicultural education is a particular type of education, multicultural research is a particular type of research. Multicultural is the lesser part, education or research is the center. Education or research are asserted as the thing itself, and multicultural is the modifier that 'butts up against, pushes, nudges, and perhaps shakes the noun' (Marshall, 1992, p. 185).

It's important to ask, I think: Does attaching 'multicultural' to education or research constitute a successful strategy of questioning and destabilizing the terms and parameters already understood to delineate education and research? Is it a crowbar capable of prying open the historically monocultural structures of research and education? When 'multicultural' is added on to pre-existent structures and uses of 'research' — like my dissertation added race in the last draft on to its pre-existent meanings of (singular, homogenous) 'lesbian community'— does it do so only within the terms and parameters already set to delineate 'research' — only within the terms and parameters already set 'before' the invention of the term 'multicultural?' Multicultural research and multicultural education have their origins in research and in education. Research and education remain the originals — the origins? — that multicultural has been invented to modify.

Multiculture, on the other hand, can be given a very different inflection. It can designate 'a culture' in and of itself *and* at the same time multiple-ize and heterogenize the notion of 'a culture'. It resists being used in static, unitary ways — it resists, for example, the designation: The Multiculture. Not subordinated to the job of modifying or fracturing some pre-existing, singular, monolithic, pure, white, homogeneous culture, multiculture can be used to suggest that 'culture' is always already multiple — and in process, in-the-making. Culture never has been anything but the ongoing project of articulating, negotiating, denying, fearing, ritualizing, narrating the self-in-the-other and the other-in-the-self. 'The culture' of the United States is always already a multiculture-in-process. It never has been a fixed, static, original culture into which its 'others' are now being added, which its 'others' are now modifying. The not-so-subtle traces of historical and cultural tension, conflict, multiplicity and difference that appear in America's languages, musics, foods, styles, imagery, stories are the materials and material resources that get worked over in multiculture.

So what is research in relation to multiculture? What is education in relation to multiculture? Instead of multicultural research or education, I'm arguing for re-conceptualizing and re-situating research and education in the context of multiculture. Research and education become particular moments — two among many — in the ongoing processes of multiculture. Research and education become moments in the production and performance of multiculture. And the questions supported by refusing the position of the adjective are not: what is multicultural education or what is multicultural research — but rather: 'What forms of multiculture does this educational practice produce and perform in this classroom?' and 'What forms of multiculture does this research project and process make intelligible and unintelligible?'

I've been trying to use and teach research and education then, as multiculture in-the-making. I've been trying to resituate myself as researcher and educator away from the position of representer and producer of knowledge 'about culture' and into the position of participant in the ongoing process of producing and performing multiculture. The 'validity' or 'worth' of my research and teaching practices then rest not on how accurately I have represented or taught about an already existing culture. They rest instead on the qualities of the multicultures that my writing and classroom relations perform and enact. They rest on the processes of multiculture that my writing and teaching support and extend. And they rest on the leverage that my writing and teaching offer to me and others in the work of prying apart the languages and practices of monoculture that structure research and education.

References

BATESON, C. (1989) *Composing a Life*, New York: The Atlantic Monthly Press.

FOUCAULT, M. (1986) *The Use of Pleasure: Volume 2 of the History of Sexuality*, London: Vintage Books.

LAUREL, B. (1993) *Computers As Theater*, New York: Addison-Wesley Publishing, Inc.

MARSHALL, B. (1992) *Teaching the Postmodern: Fiction and Theory*, New York: Routledge.

PROBYN, E. (1992) 'Technologizing the self: A future anterior for cultural studies', in GROSSBERG, L., NELSON, C. and TREICHLER, P. (eds) *Cultural Studies*, New York: Routledge.

TREICHLER, P. (1991) 'AIDS, homophobia, and biomedical discourse: An epidemic of significa-tion', in CRIMP, D. (ed.) *AIDS: Cultural Analysis/Cultural Activism*, Cambridge: MIT Press.

4 Born to Roll: Graduate School from the Margins

Jennifer E. Obidah

My place on earth means too much to me. *Des'ree*

On 15 May 1995 I graduated with a doctorate in Education from the University of California, Berkeley. I began writing this paper the year that I completed a National Institute of Mental Health (NIMH) post doctoral fellowship at the University of California, Los Angeles. In some academic circles the usual inferences gleaned from this short biography are that I had 'arrived' and that my scholarship was just starting to develop. I take issue with these inferences. If statements of my 'arriving' are based on the assumptions that I have now attained a certain academic pedigree and, consequently, I've moved on up in socio-economic class affiliation, I beg to differ.

It is true that my life had changed as a result of successfully completing graduate school and the promise of an improvement in my financial circumstances loomed on the horizons. It is also true that my work was receiving a modicum of recognition in several academic arenas. However, my 'success' remained couched in ambiguity. At the time of graduation my obvious successes were offers of a tenured track faculty position as well as three post-doctoral fellowships; my first ever published article appeared in the June 1995 issue of the *Harvard Educational Review*, and one publisher had already expressed interest in my dissertation. However, coupled with these successes was my knowledge that, except for the *HER* article, all of my 'success' resulted from my 'AERA hustle'.

I deliberately interrupted my dissertation writing to strategize my attendance at the April 1995 American Education Research Association (AERA) conference in San Francisco. The wonderful owners of the dry cleaning service I used, allowed me to temporarily credit $62 of dry cleaning service for the clothes I used as I dressed to impress at the conference. I tactically maneuvered my presentations, the question–answer periods during sessions, the parties of choice universities, on the spot mentoring by the elders in the field, bold and continuous introductions of myself and my work to professors whose interests were similar to mine, with my resumé on hand to pass on at the opportune moments of these chanced interactions. Ironically, AERA's formal job search procedure, which I paid a precious $34 to participate in, yielded only one interview.

Reflecting on the experience in the weeks following the conference I vacillated between feelings of euphoria at the success of my campaign and resentment mixed with doubt, for if I were indeed as good as I believed and as was proven in my successful campaign, perhaps the campaign might not have been necessary in the first place. Sometimes I assuaged my resentment and doubts by congratulating myself on discovering the 'it's not what you know but who you know' network, but I was not always comforted. I elaborate on this persisting discomfort throughout the rest of this paper.

Nonetheless, my present situation at the time still remained that of a person with dual membership in virtual realities: I was a virtual academic, a post-doc — neither graduate student nor faculty — and I remained a member of the virtual working-class. My parents and friends reminded me that I still did not have a 'steady' job.

Graduate Education

There are practical aspects to completing a graduate program that every student has to go through regardless of race, class or gender. All graduate students to some extent, worry about financing their graduate studies. Once accepted into a program, there are the worries of choosing an advisor and, later, a committee; successfully completing oral exams; and eventually, writing a dissertation (Cambra, Schluntz and Cardoza, 1984).

However, there are sociocultural aspects to these practicalities of graduate life. Cambra, Schluntz and Cardoza (1984) noted that 'even in the theoretically objective academic world, such things as reputation in the community, political preference, personal habits, religion, sex, sexual preference, race, physical handicaps and disabilities, emotional stability, and so forth are very real considerations' (p. 29). In other words, the social, political, and cultural challenges of society penetrate life inside the academy. Thus, the graduate student from a working class background tends to worry more about the cost of graduate school; a female graduate student worries more about completing her graduate study in a male-defined and dominated world; a graduate student from a racial or ethnic background different from her professors' worries more about choosing an advisor she can trust and develop a relationship with — a relationship, I might add, that has implications for many aspects of her future, beginning with success on the academic job market after graduation. That these concerns can conjoin in one student's experience of graduate school illuminates the awesome challenge of such a student successfully completing graduate study.

Though usually thought to be one of the most enabling experiences in a person's life, graduate schooling in the life of some students is primarily composed of unhappy, debilitating experiences laced by self-doubt and insecurity about one's ability to work effectively in one's chosen field. Moore (1985) noted that, though 'all students are made over and acculturated to the ways of academia in graduate school' and that 'part of this change involves giving up your old culture and world view', he concludes that 'while this transition is difficult for everyone, it can be particularly tough for minorities' (p. 81). The present paper details the challenges of graduate school for one student — me, a first generation, working class, black female. Autobiographical reflections of how I developed and maintained my homegrown intellect and passion as I work in the discipline and practice of education contour my analysis of the cultural clashes minority students, in particular, experience in higher education. These cultural clashes, as I have experienced them, revolved around the construction of academic knowledge, the discord that developed between academic knowledge and the knowledge of my homegrown intellect and experience; and, maintaining a self-identity in the face of an imposed 'graduate student' identity.

Knowledge acquired through lived experience can suffer and die at the hands (or should I say 'feet') of hierarchically constructed academic knowledge. Yet there are undeniable parallels between what one chooses to research and write about and one's lived experiences. For instance, the experience of living intimately with frequent homicide that began for me as an adolescent is reflected in my research on the impact of exposure to frequent homicide on adolescents' response to schooling. Similarly, my interest and research on the impact of socially sanctioned authority on the teacher – student relationship has its roots in my experience as a tutor in an afterschool program in Harlem that I detail later in this paper. Ultimately, I argue that a disservice is accorded graduate students who are required, as an integral part of the ritual of academic initiation, to surrender their cultural resources as a prerequisite to successfully completing graduate study. This surrendering comes at the point during the initiation when these cultural tools that had acted in the course of a student's life as resources — resouces that in fact brought them to graduate school — are implicated in a student's potential failure to obtain the graduate degree. This revision of a student's cultural tools from resources to detriments has implications for the high attrition rates among minority student populations. I write this piece to encourage every graduate student whose experiences and interactions with the academy's knowledge constructs have led to self-doubt and passion paralysis. It is my hope that they find a space within my narrative of claiming the marginalization of my homegrown intellect to empower the creation of their own narrative of liberation and to transform pedagogy in their own graduate schooling.

In the following pages I elaborate on experiences that have influenced my present academic interests. I begin with stories from my adolescent years in New York City. Later, I weave my journey through choices of college and employment that led to my decision to pursue first a masters and later, a doctorate. I analyze aspects of my graduate school experiences that locate the cultural clashes earlier mentioned. I conclude with a narrative of liberation in which I claimed my marginalization and developed a pedagogy in which the knowledge from these two aspects of my life, formerly juxtaposed, were reconciled.

The inference that one's scholarship begins after graduate school is one that I address in particular. I am interpreting scholarship as symbolically legitimizing my right to construct knowledge, to develop my own ideas; the ability to infuse my university-acquired references with my own intellectual contributions; to build on this higher degree of literacy. Contrary to the inference that my scholarship has just begun, were it not for the liberating pedagogy I drew from my community and that I continue to hone, my passion for my work might have been lost.

Homegrown Wisdom and Intellect

As I audit the reminisces of my life in the Bedford-Stuyvesant neighborhood of Brooklyn, New York City, I reflect on the themes of poverty, danger, death, life, laughter, and love that composed the rhythm of my life there. These same themes now extend into my work as an educator and a researcher who works with, teaches, and conducts research with the children who live in poor inner-city neighborhoods similar to the one in which I grew up in America.

I was not born in America although my children will be. I was born in Barbados, a small island in the West Indies. As an older adolescent I relocated with my parents to New York City alias the United States of America. I did not experience the K-12 public school system as a student. I had graduated early from high school in Barbados at age 16 and looked for employment once I came to the United States. Growing up in the streets of Bedford-Stuyvesant in New York from Barbados meant a new kind of education. More than school knowledge, I had to first learn street knowledge. I learned the language of a predominantly low-income African-American inner-city neighborhood. I learned how to walk the streets of 'Bed-Stuy, Do or Die!' I learned how to take the subway, sometimes late at night. These were two different lessons — taking the subway during the day and taking it late at night. At night, one had to be twice as alert as one would be in the daytime. At night, once the train reached my stop, Kingston-Throop Station, I learned how to use the strategically placed mirrors hanging above my head in the station to see around the corner of the stairwell where I ascended to street level. When I reached the top of the stairs there was still the five block walk to the brownstone where I lived. I got to know Gilbert the wino on the corner of Fulton and Kingston, not only because he was a permanent fixture on that corner, but also because some nights he was the only reassuring one of the shadows lurking in the dark.

Life had a dangerous edge. I remember my teenage friends Vinny, Sabu, and Elvis. I remember Vinny who I saw one day after not seeing him for a long time, only to learn of his death in a shootout two weeks later. I remember Sabu who was stabbed to death in a fight. I remember Elvis who got shot for two dollars at a gambling table by his friend, our friend, Darrell. Living in the Bedford-Stuyvesant neighborhood of New York City is where my knowledge of living intimately with frequent homicide began.

The potential for emotional explosions was omnipresent. These are the explosions that occur periodically and serve as salves against the crush of oppressions — both external and self-imposed — that permeate the existence of human beings in economically depressed, inner-city neighborhoods. This rage, once exposed, could result at best in a fight or, at worst, in someone getting killed. Living with this potent eruptive anger in poor inner-city neighborhoods might be analogous to the threat of an earthquake for people living in California. For Californians, living with the threat of an earthquake is living with a constant threat of death and destruction. People are aware of it but are never fully prepared for the inevitable earthquake mostly because of its element of surprise. Nonetheless, Californians are respected for their knowledge and awareness of this potential danger and, above all, for their ability to live — and often times very well — in California despite the earthquakes. So too is living with the threat of an anger eruption in urban inner-cities. We lived in Bedford-Stuyvesant with the threat of emotional explosion. In our neighborhood we were respected for our knowledge and awareness of this and of other elements of street life, and we continued to live in spite of the dangers. And we had fun.

I remember summers in New York with my homegirls staying up all night long in the wake of the summer heat that made any attempts at a good night's sleep impossible. We would hang out on the steps of the brownstone where I lived, telling jokes that induced tear-stained, stomach aching laughter. We talked and laughed long into the night. We were often startled by the lightening of the sky and then resigned to the heat and humidity promised by the sun's rising. However, with the windows of our apartments opened, we could snatch a few hours of restful sleep in those early hours of the morning before the heat wave became full blown. My homegirls and I parted company to sleep for a few hours, before meeting once again in the late afternoon.

I remember the block parties, seeing the little girls practice their dance routines weeks and weeks before, to then 'turn it out' at the party. Grandmothers and grandfathers, mothers and fathers, sons and daughters congregated. A block party was a culminating abundance of food, laughter, and fun.

For other recreation, the park closest to my house was a more fearful place than the pool-room, and so I learned how to play pool, and Ms Pac-Man, one of the video games that lined the walls of the semi-dark room in the center of which were two pool tables. I remember night after night of fun in the pool-room — playing pool, video games, listening to music and becoming a member of the spontaneously assembled 'singing groups' that sang along with our favorite records. I remember playing pool with Brandy. When she played, Brandy circled the pool table with the arrogance of the best girl pool player, a position she tenaciously held onto despite many challenges by the other girls. As a rookie homegirl new to the pool room, I learned about Brandy's 'rep' in addition to the reputations of other characters who visited the pool-room. There came a time when I too challenged Brandy. I watched and I learned to play pool. I practiced and practiced. Then I beat her for the first time. It was like winning a major tournament. No trophy, but I got much respect from the pool-room community on that night.

Life in my old neighborhood was not, nor will ever be, one dimensional. Yet, in scholarly writings there is a pervasive tendency to impose narrow, one-dimensional descriptions of the lives of students living in neighborhoods similar to the one of my adolescent years. This was one of the first intellectual assaults I experienced in graduate school, which I will discuss in more detail later. My friends and I did not refer to ourselves as at-risk, impoverished, disadvantaged, or any of the other negatively tinged descriptions pervasive in scholarly education literature. We had full lives despite the circumstances of living in our part of town.

Thus, as I analyze the impact of inner-city public students' lives outside of school on their responses to schooling and on their overall academic achievement, I consistently invoke students' voices into the analysis. Then it becomes difficult to reduce these young people to their occupation of the often unsuccessful roles of students. In reflecting, I remember McDonald, a former student, who skillfully negotiated any reductive impressions of himself as the academically failing student he was in my class or as a child who lived in the dysfunctional foster home he often described to me. I could not reduce McDonald's identity because of gems such as the following name poem he produced in my English class, and which enlightened me to another of his own perspectives of the relationship between his home and school life. In less than 10 of the 50 minute class period, McDonald wrote three name poems, one of which is the following:

Mom look!
Come here quick!
Do you know her
On TV?
No.
And turn off the TV.
Learn your spelling words.
Don't cut it on until you're done.

Students like McDonald act as a constant reminder that people do not only survive in economically disadvantaged neighborhoods, they live as well.

Unlike most of my friends, I started college in 'the city' as those of us from the borough of Brooklyn referred to the borough of Manhattan. Periodically I inquired about my homegirls and others of the pool room community when I visited my mom and other elders that still lived in the old neighborhood. By my sophomore year, all five of my homegirls were pregnant. Three of them were sisters. Tam, who was the youngest sibling and the youngest girl in our group, was 14 when she had her first baby and 16 when she had her second. And Tam could not read. Yogi and Steve were addicted to crack, and Drew and Goofy were in jail.

Others like me left the old neighborhood and lived reasonable lives, but very few of my friends did.

Wary of Being Called on to Know

In my junior year of college I started working at community centers in afterschool programs serving young black youth from Harlem. I worked with these young people in the roles of counselor, tutor, or teacher. I was always drawn to those kids who reminded me of my old crew. Through these experiences, another education began for me. I finally saw what might have been the experience of my friends in junior high school. I would observe the kids with their friends on the playing areas of the center. I would observe students' confidence, their laughter, their quick retorts, dry humor, and spontaneous talk back and forth between friends. Then the time came for the kids to be 'taught' by me. When they entered the classroom, all of the life-liness I observed earlier would be replaced by quietness and/or sullen unresponsiveness. These students became wary of being called on to 'know', to be responsible for the school knowledge lodged in the curricular texts we covered. This was a knowledge that these kids perceived as estranged from the realities of daily life. I became determined to make the teaching and learning environment a different experience for these children.

To these students, I was black like them, but I was also a 'teacher'. As their teacher, I wielded an authority that potentially threatened to impose a student identity on them that they perceived as oppositional to their own senses of themselves. Their sullen resistance indicated to me that authority was inefficient as a premise for effective teacher–student relationships. After working to change the classroom environment, not only was I no longer threatening to my students but I managed to create a safe and motivating learning environment as well.

In summary, I had lived and worked with youth who suffered the debilitating effects of disengagement with their schooling; students who were being taught in school everyday by teachers whom they perceived as so different from themselves and thus un-empathetic and unsympathetic to their daily lives outside of school. My resolve to improve the academic achievement of these children, and my concern about their overall disengagement with schooling, influenced my decision to apply to graduate school.

Underlying my decision to pursue higher education was a desire to enhance what knowledge I already had about the schooling of African-American youth. Born in Barbados and having lived in the United States for only six years at that time, I felt somewhat limited in my knowledge of African-American history. I desired to study more about these people who were black like me, yet very different from me and from the West Indian community transplanted in New York City. These African-Americans were very different from me in their expressions of this blackness. At that stage of my life, I felt the need for a wider, historical perspective of these differences, so I applied and was accepted at Yale University to complete a Masters degree in African-American Studies.

Chosen

I left New York City without a legacy of graduate school wisdom that might have been imparted to me had I had family members who were graduates of higher education: However, no one I knew at that time of my life had ever attended graduate school, and I was 'the first' in my family. My elders only knew that it was 'different'. I was sent to Yale with all that my elders had to give to me: their pride in my acceptance to Yale University, their prayers for me not to fail, and their expectations and hopes that I would graduate. This was the knowledge that I took with me to graduate school.

The sobering reality of difference was the first fact of graduate school at Yale. New Haven was different from New York City, the majority white population at the university, was very different — both in race and socio-economic status — from the majority black population of the Brooklyn neighborhood where I had lived previously. Unhappily, any alliances — from attending the neighborhood clubs, volunteering at the local high school, and getting acquainted with a family through courtship with a local guy — any efforts I undertook as ways to form alliances with members of the black communities of New Haven that surrounded the university were tempered by my transient status and affiliation with Yale. Meanwhile, my actual alienation from other Yalees equaled the alienating nature of the town and gown relationship between the Yale and Greater New Haven communities.

I was even different from the other black people who attended Yale. We were black but they were rich. My 'What's up!?' greeting was as discomforting to them as their formally returned greeting of 'Hi Jennifer, how are you?' was to me. This difference in our styles of greeting one another was the first noticeable wedge of the class differences between myself and other black students who attended Yale.

My Brooklyn talk was even more problematic in the university's classrooms. Compared to other students, it seemed that I spoke with too much passion, too many exclamations, descriptions, and meandering objectives. Patronizing sympathy from both fellow graduate students and the professor usually started with 'So the point you're making is . . .' followed by their version of my comment that never articulated what I originally intended to say. I realized that to these students and professors it was as if I spoke a foreign language with no available instruments for translation to their language. I resorted to reading, writing, and listening as my primary forms of classroom participation.

Differences in uses and forms of language are often pivotal in cultural dysjunctures. In her analysis of cross-cultural confusions, Delpit's (1995) discussion of the academic, middle-class culture lends insight to the former disjunctive classroom experience at Yale. Delpit explains that, in this cultural framework, the content of the lecture takes priority over any other dynamics of interaction, including, for example, the relationship between the speaker and the listener. In this framework the speaker is expected to 'lay out information in a linear fashion, provide background information and guide their listeners to specific conclusions' (p. 148). However, Delpit reasserts the importance of the speaker–listener relationship in her description of the teachers' response to students who are not privy to this cultural framework. She writes:

> Assessors accustomed to this style are likely to suspect that seemingly indirect, highly contextualized or reticent responses suggest that the candidate does not have an answer to a question. Because [the professors] believe they will not be hearing the information requested, they are likely to interrupt the response [from students] in midstream, and as a consequence, prevent candidates from demonstrating competence. (p. 148)

Delpit's assertion explains in part my reception in a cultural framework that was alien to me and one which made me appear as alien to both instructor and fellow students.

As a result of multiple, similar experiences during my sojourn at Yale, I learned to listen more and speak less also due to what I perceived as a near-compulsion operating in the classrooms that made people speak only for the sake of speaking rather than not speak at all. I interpreted this as a way of asserting privilege and familiar comfort with classroom dynamics such as those that existed at Yale. I found listening less taxing on my school experience than always attempting to tease out the most obscure relevance in comments that were made only for the sake of the speaker.

By November of my first year, the university's auspicious buildings of September had become cold inaccessible fortresses surrounded by dungeon-like dormitories. I lived only for the infrequent revitalizing visits to the old neighborhood where self-doubt — the primary emotion I felt within the elm-covered walls of the university — would be replaced with the over-confidence of one that was chosen.

My intermittent visits to the old neighborhood from New Haven rendered a new relationship with the old neighborhood. There, I had also become a transient, a permanent guest. The lives of my friends of old had taken different paths and I no longer felt the need to locate them, but I felt the loss of that need. Gilbert still lived on the corner but the passing years made me unrecognizable to him as the kid who had always rounded his corner as if in flight of pending danger. The neighborhood had changed and I had changed even more. The new lens of awareness acquired through my education at Yale, and with which I began to gaze upon the old neighborhood, dampened my sense of belonging and even my desire to belong. Simultaneously, however, I distrusted the people and the scholarship that engendered this effectual critique of familiar people, places and living conditions. I distrusted this ivy league education that precipitated my discomfort in a place that was central to many adolescent memories. My memories were stained by my education. As time passed, the elders of the old neighborhood became my only motivation for visiting Bed-Stuy.

My second year at Yale was much better than the first. There were sporadic moments when thoughts, ideas, expressions, and events combined into valuable learning experiences. These moments came out of my involvement with the African-American Cultural Center at the university. I became involved at the Center as the director of the Black Graduate Network (BGN), although I confess that, initially, my motives primarily came from my need to alleviate the pain and isolation carried over from my first year. I regained my self-confidence through coordinating events for graduate students. Events such as lectures, discussions, African dance classes, and fundraising parties helped create alliances between the black graduate students at Yale, and they afforded me some sense of community since my former notion of community that was linked to my old neighborhood had become a casualty of higher education.

My success and graduation from Yale was driven by my determination not to disappoint the elders of my old neighborhood. After two years of Yale's ivy league schooling, it was time to move on. I decided to go west to pursue a doctorate at Berkeley. After all, I had survived Yale and I could not foresee a greater sense of displacement than what I had experienced there. However, I miscalculated the stakes of acquiring a doctorate. Since as I said earlier, I was the first I knew who had ever attended graduate school, I had too narrowly equated two years of graduate study for a masters with four years or more of graduate study for a doctorate. They were not the same.

Marginalized: A Public Redefinition of Self

The experience of going to school for a doctorate degree in education re-awakened feelings of living with an omnipotent danger similar to the one in my old neighborhood that threatened my survival; only this time, the danger was more psychological and only indirectly physical. This was the danger of my believing the invisibility that was constantly, and oppressively, imposed on me in graduate school. Ellison (1947) best addresses this imposed invisibility on the African-American existence. He explains it as 'a matter of construction of [people's] inner eyes, those eyes through which they look through their physical eyes upon reality' (p. 7). I learned also that subtlety was a powerful resource in the construction of my invisibility. This is because the use of subtlety has a tendency to render the person threatened with invisibility as paranoid. Ultimately, however, those of us who experience this threat of invisibility are enabled through writing and other forums to combat a reductionist perspective of our experiences to paranoia. As I began this paper, I read the stories of a number of black women who wrote about and articulated similar experiences in their schooling. We all struggle to name the threat, to make its existence visible, for we know this ghost well.

My first contact with this ghost came during my first semester at Berkeley. I was told by the secretary of the division that one of the professors whose class I was taking had expressed concern that I was not participating in class discussions. This course was one of the courses I call a 'classics' course, also known as a 'foundations' course. Foundations courses in education resonate a normalized, privileged ideal associated with the 'classics' in our society, where the question of who and what informs the decision to make the cultural artifact a 'classic', is made obsolete by the designation which also functions as placing the artifact above question. Similarly, in this particular course the professor approached the foundations of education solely from a Marxist perspective and never acknowledged throughout the course that other 'foundations' of education existed. The structure of the class discussions began with a survey of the central texts that addressed various issues and positions regarding the role of education in society. During the discussion we primarily critiqued the limitations of these central texts. I was always puzzled that the texts have remained simultaneously central and severely limited. In addition, alternative texts supplementing these limitations were never introduced by this professor, and, if such texts were introduced by a student, they was dismissed as being even more limited than the texts we were covering. I learned later that this professor had not read or had no knowledge of many of the texts introduced by students, and after experiencing the arrogance legitimized by this professor's 'teacher authority' I saw how it might have been difficult for this professor to admit not knowing, when students, in effect, called on her to know. Unlike my earlier experiences of teaching where I had the opportunity to observe my students in another context before they came to me to be taught, all that this professor knew about us was our status as first semester graduate students. Our former knowledge acquired before entering this new context was screened by our presumed ignorance, which this teacher had a responsibility to undo, sometimes at a cost of devaluing any previous knowledge of the subject. This presumed ignorance is one example of the notions embedded in the ritual of academic initiation earlier mentioned.

Nonetheless, in this professor's class we were told that we were learning the theories central to the discipline of education, and my professor was concerned that I was not 'getting' them since I was not participating in class discussions. There were other students in the class who also were not participating in the discussions, as could be expected in a class of mostly first year graduate students. However, it seemed inconceivable both to the professor and the secretary who relayed the concern — as though it were warranted — that I could merely be *listening*, as opposed to not comprehending texts.

I entered this professor's class choosing to initially listen more than talk because of my former classroom experiences at Yale. However, at Berkeley, my voluntary silence was construed as a lack of comprehension. I was not afforded the possibility of being a listener other than by a fault of ignorance or lack of intelligence. I eventually and successfully asserted myself in the class, utilizing the tactical strategy of 'fronting'.

Fronting is a strategy I learned from my African-American friends in Bed-Stuy. Fronting implies a deceptive aspect to the act of the 'fronter' to assert his or her legitimacy, or rightfulness of position, when challenged. Recall my memories of Brandy, the girl pool player. Brandy's arrogance as she circled the pool table was a part of her front in maintaining her reputation as the best girl pool player. This arrogance, though coupled with expertise, was necessary in and of itself to the legitimation of Brandy's rep. Brandy was very aware that there were other girls, like myself, waiting to usurp her position, and thus she had to utilize tools other than pool playing skills. Arrogance comprised such a tool in fronting. This arrogance, played out in Brandy's loud laughter when she is challenged, and her posturing and bragging at the point of victory — bragging which also continued for days after — dissuaded many of us who entertained the thought of challenging her. This arrogance thereby limited the number of challenges Brandy received and consequently, aided the maintenance of her status as the best.

My employment of fronting in this professor's class was similar to Brandy's arrogance. In the context of graduate school I had began to internalize the imposed position of powerlessness partially embedded in my status as a first semester graduate student, and, unlike Brandy, I did not begin from a position of strength. Nonetheless, fronting was useful in asserting my intellect, my 'getting it'; In short, my legitimation as a student worthy of being accepted in a PhD program in such an esteemed university.

Each graduate student had to present the readings for one class. I chose to present the work of Pierre Bourdieu, since I had been exposed to these writings in a class at Yale. I never spoke in that class. Instead, I took copious notes that not only included the professor's lecture, but students' questions, answers, and other comments. I studied my class notes side by side with the texts, and I learned through this process of teaching myself. By the time I had learned the text, the class had moved on to other texts, but *I* knew that I now knew Bourdieu's theories of reproduction. This class at Berkeley became my time to speak.

I knew that some of the students, regardless of how 'smart' they were, would be having difficulty if this was their first encounter with the French theorist, and so I maneuvered the difficulty of penetrating Bourdieu's dense prose as a tool in fronting. To assert my indisputable comprehension of the text, I diagrammed Bourdieu's systems of relations in his outline of the French educational bureaucracy which I distributed during my presentation. Needless to say, after this presentation my silence was never again questioned and my talk was always encouraged.

Nonetheless, I was angered at having to react to an imposed perception of me that did not begin with me the person, but one that began with my invisibility. Responding to absurd, unfounded, imposed perceptions takes a person into the realm of ghosts where the key to survival lies in constant reminders to yourself that you do indeed exist. The surrealism of the experience is grounded in Dubois' (1953) assertion that America yields African-Americans no true self-consciousness but only lets them see themselves through revelations of otherness.

In *Black and Female: Reflections on Graduate School*, hooks (1989) detailed similar oppressive experiences in graduate school. She wrote that to the white students from privileged class backgrounds, 'tolerating the humiliation and degradations we were subjected to in graduate school did not radically call into question their integrity, their sense of self-worth' (p. 59). She continued that 'white students were not living daily in a world outside campus life where they also had to resist degradation'. She posits that their endurance of certain forms of domination was possible because of a perception of it as a part of an initiation process that would conclude when they became persons of power themselves. Fortunately or unfortunately, *rememories* such as the one captured in the former anecdote informed my graduate school experience more than the usual iconographies of books, journals, classes, and professors. Partly as a buffer from succumbing to an imposed invisibility I started teaching part-time at an urban middle school in northern California where I met more black youth from poor neighborhoods with very similar problems and responses to school learning.

Talking more with mothers as well as kids, I heard stories of kids being suspended in first grade. First grade! One time I gave one of my 8th grade students, Jamila, a grade C for improvement in her class work. Her report card that semester was all Cs except for a B+ she got in PE. She was so happy. She told me 'Since 5th grade up to last year I'd been getting straight Fs. Well I didn't get my report card in 5th.' I heard and saw mothers trying to have their child kept back in school because they knew that the young person could not read or write. And then there was a difficult choice to make because some kids would do worst in the following year. In some instances the choice was not that of the parents. The school would refuse to retain some students because of behavioral problems. They wanted these students to be someone else's problem.

As a teacher I found myself prepared to handle most of any problems with my students right there in my classroom, because I so distrusted the system's way of handling them. I would visit all of the 'alternative classrooms', even teach one myself, and see the students, the majority of whom were most often black youth from the worst neighborhoods in the inner city.

However, as a new teacher, I experienced many troubling moments in my classroom. A version of the explosive anger that existed in my old neighborhood, was also a product of the environment from where my students came. I remember the first time that a fight occurred in my classroom. This was a fight between two boys whom I knew were friends. As the fight erupted and was spurred on by the surrounding group of students, I spontaneously jumped in between the two boys (an action I was rightly advised as a new teacher *not* to do.) I was yelling as I tried to push them apart: 'You will *not* disrespect my classroom this way! This is my classroom! My house! If you want to act like this go to your own house!' The boys' surprise at my taking their fighting so personally, ended the fight faster than any brute strength I had. Then another demonstration of my novice teacher's naiveté aided the unsettling mood in the classroom after the fight.

I lectured the entire class for the rest of the period on how bad I thought fighting was and I voiced my concern about the possible outcomes of uncontrollable anger. I heatedly stressed to the onlooking 14-year-olds:

'In three years it'll be a gun you're using to fight with!'

To my immense surprise the class burst into laughter and one student replied:

'Ms Johnson, it's already a gun!'

I laughed along with the young people and we shared a powerful dialogue that day. As time passed I had few disruptions in my classroom, for as noted by one of my students, 'Ms Johnson don't play!'

The teacher–student relationship of mutual respect that developed between me and my students also helped to create a space for effective teaching and learning to flourish in my classroom. I relished my students' small and frequent steps of academic success.

Still, I was sobered by the fact that the issues I had previously associated only with older adolescents in my day were the issues of the younger adolescents I taught. In moments of despair at this bleak outlook, I remembered my friends from my old neighborhood and resolved to find ways to bring the two worlds of home and school together with more positive results for the children. There was more to my friends, and my students, than the problems that they had and the problem that the structure of the school portrayed them to be. However, also on my mind at the time was a sense of becoming more and more removed from my own schooling experience.

In those first two years of graduate school, unnecessary polarities emerged. I was going to school to learn the discipline of education and at the same time I was teaching in an urban public middle school. I went back and forth from the classroom where I was a teacher of so-called at-risk students to a classroom where I was the so-called at-risk student. Making connections between what could be reasonably referred to as two spheres of the same world was unimaginably difficult. The knowledge I was gaining from my experience as a public school teacher was difficult, even anecdotally, to bring into the discussions in the university classrooms. Phillips and McCaskill (1991) offer an interesting critique of why this might have been the case. In their own experiences they have observed that 'the academy bifurcates our pursuits into two paths — focused (or Tenurable) and scattered (or irrelevant). It puts us in an adversarial relationship that opposes home, family, church and culture.' I penetrated an aspect of the hidden agenda of graduate school training, which is an adherence to knowledge hierarchy, and in my graduate classrooms I was always objecting to the terms and theories of educational discourse that made reference to 'my kids'. These terms and theories often felt assaultive in their analysis of students who attend inner-city public schools similar to the one where I taught. Too often when I read the required texts and in classrooms discussions I felt that the problems in the practice of education were lost or submerged beneath the teaching of the discipline. I became tired of carrying around a knapsack of phony issues — phony in their abstract, theoretical relevance without the accompanying 'how-tos' of implementation. I realized later that I had been struggling against the parameters of *discipline* formation, which, unfortunately, is a major project of graduate school. As Rose (1989) succinctly comments,

> Graduate school forces you to give a tremendous amount of thought to the development
> of your discipline, to its methods , exemplary studies, and central texts. People emerge
> from graduate study, then, as political scientists or astronomers or botanists but not as
> educators. (p. 196)

Rose continues that 'the thrust of graduate training and the professional commitment that follows it are toward the preservation of a discipline not the intellectual development of young people' (p. 197).

As graduate students, our primary contributive role to our learning process was mainly as receptors to the gift of knowledge conveyed by professors. Paulo Freire locates this relationship of teaching and learning in what he refers to as the 'banking concept' of education. Freire (1989) notes that in the banking concept of education 'knowledge is a gift bestowed by those who consider themselves knowledgeable upon those whom they consider to know nothing' (p. 57). Within the university there was little recognition of this student's knowledge and cultural references that I brought to my graduate training. For a student like me — where this source of knowledge is my major strength — this structure of knowledge becomes detrimental to my success in academe. I was beginning to believe and respond to my graduate schooling as a student 'at-risk'. I found myself constantly objecting to professors' teaching of methods and texts as though those that were presented were *the* only, or the best methods and texts, as opposed to them being one set of many methods and texts, all with their own merits and limitations. Rather than credit my objections with further dialogue to know the rationale behind the objection, I was humored — professors would let me speak, pause courteously after my comment, and then continue to teach as though no objection had occurred. At times I was cajoled for being 'too sensitive' and in a variety of other ways dismissed.

Constant struggle with the structured knowledge in graduate school led me to question my place in graduate school. This struggle also dampened the belief in myself as a diamond — in the rough, but a diamond nonetheless. There came a point where I, like Lorene Cary (1991), 'was no longer convinced of the special brilliance I had once expected to discover in myself' (p. 92). Having been a symbol of possibility in my community for so long I was angry at this public redefinition of myself as at-risk. Yet there was more at risk for me than dropping out of graduate school. If I failed, my family failed also; and I would have failed the children to whom I try to give hope with my life's accomplishments. Ultimately this was my responsibility as a chosen one and it continues to be one I gladly shoulder, for it acts as a constant reminder of my place on earth, which — as noted by Des'ree' in the opening quote — means too much to me. Left up to my own sense of my strength and self, I would have been defeated. Once again, it was community love that breathed new life into me at Black Graduation.

Liberation and Transformation

I heard about Berkeley's Black Graduation ceremony accidentally. An African-American teacher who taught at the same middle school as I did knew a student who was graduating from Berkeley. I had not planned to attend the event because I was feeling very removed from life at the university at the time. However, since the teacher was going I decided to attend. I am forever grateful to that teacher for reminding me of the ceremony.

As I entered the doors of Berkeley's Greek Amphitheater on that day, I was awed by the sight of at least a thousand black faces. Grandmothers, mothers, fathers, aunts, uncles, sisters, brothers, children of the graduates, and black children from schools in the area, all gathered for a collective celebration of the graduating students. The ceremony, as is the tradition, began with dance. The procession of graduates danced from behind the stage and out into the crowd. They weave in and out of the collective validation — an audience of smiling faces, camera bulbs flashing, hugs, kisses, tears of joy — before re-emerging and making their way back to the stage. My participation in this ritual celebration re-ignited my connection with my place of earth as a chosen one. I would not be celebrated in this collective way if I did not graduate and be one of this community's chosen.

Black graduation was a ritual tool that began my liberation. I had to reclaim the enterprise of scholarship and research. I had to reclaim my knowledge and curiosity about the experiences of children in education prior to graduate school and integrate relevant academic knowledge as well as the struggles of my graduate schooling (the struggles were valuable lessons in of themselves). I began this process by acknowledging that I had a contribution to make in the discipline and practice of education.

By this time I had completed all of the classics in education courses and I started to seek out the classes of professors who were recommended by other graduate students for their informative and effective pedagogical practices. In addition, I investigated these professors as potential members of my committee. In these classes, I was introduced to knowledge that facilitated connections between scholarship and the realities of every-day schooling. I became a participant in the insightful dialogues that were facilitated by these astute educators, who commanded the art of posing the right question or comment that sparked many thought-provoking intellectual discussions. Out of one such class, some colleagues and I formed a writing group.

We were fortunate at the time to have a professor who did not subscribe to the banking concept of education. He made space in his classroom for us to bring the knowledge of education that others and I had acquired through our practice of teaching. My colleagues and I found our group so helpful to our academic enterprise that we continued to meet in the semester following the one in which the group was formed. We met monthly at each other's apartments amidst dogs, cats, and the occasional husband or child. Even the professor kept in touch and made himself available for our individual or collective consultation. We were no longer his class but we remained his students.

It was out of this experience that I wrote my first work. One year after I finished this paper, 'Life after death: Critical pedagogy in an urban classroom', it was published in the *Harvard Educational Review* Special Issue 'Youth and violence'. This paper described the evolution of my classroom at the middle school into one which the day-to-day realities of students' lives — most significantly their encounters with death — was acknowledged and addressed as central to students' schooling process. I wrote about the transformation of my role as teacher to one which was also student, and students were also teachers, for, as Freire (1989) states, 'real education must begin with a solution to the teacher–student contradiction by reconciling the poles so that both are simultaneously teachers and students' (p. 97). In this paper I also wrote about my academic struggle to combine all of the languages in my life that conveyed different sets of knowledge. I wrote that,

> [This was] my struggle not to subsume the important issue related to my work . . . Thus I have carefully developed a language or re-presentation — written and spoken — that mirrors those language utilized by my students and the teachers about whom I write. As Ngugi Wa Thiongo (1986) asserts: 'From a word, a group of words, a sentence and even a name, one can glean the social norms, attitudes and values of a people' (p. 8). The insistence, pervasive in university settings, on finding one voice, one definitive writing style is problematic in the face of my varied experiences. I claim the languages of all those with whom I teach and work and study as a part of my own ethos and in my formation of a critical pedagogy. (p. 217)

Transforming my pedagogy in this way, re-awakened my passion for my work as an educator. I began to look forward to researching and writing my dissertation.

I conducted my dissertation research in one teacher's classroom at the middle school where I taught. Actually I was invited by this teacher, Karen Teel, to conduct the research. Karen is a white teacher who was having difficulty teaching and relating to her mostly African-American students. She did not know what the problems in her class-room were. She only knew that problems existed, and she wanted to change the teacher–student relationships. Karen and I both graduated from the same doctoral program at Berkeley, but this connection was not the underlying reason behind her invitation. She had observed me as a teacher in my own classroom. In a paper we wrote together, she describes what she saw in my classroom that led to her decision to ask for my help. She wrote:

> Based on my observations I concluded that Jennifer was in fact a very successful teacher with her students. I attributed this to a combination of tight control during lessons and a warm, caring approach during more informal times. Jennifer appeared to have become a strong advocate for her students and they were very responsive to her.

Thus it was my knowledge and authority as a classroom teacher that was the basis of my doctoral research, and the research was very much a collaboration. I did not adhere to a policy of 'conducting research' in classrooms where teachers and students — experts in a knowledge of the everyday rhythms of their classrooms — were recast simplistically as subjects and I as the expert researcher. Karen and I were both teachers and researchers.

Once we agreed to work on the study, I observed Karen's classroom once or twice a week. I observed the students being taught by Karen: their reactions to her, their reactions to the material covered in class, and their reactions to each other. I also observed Karen teaching the students: the ways she sought to engage them both inside and outside of her teaching role. I gave Karen weekly write-ups of my observations to which she in turn wrote written responses. This developed in part because of an earlier decision. Initially we had discussed whether to exchange notes every week or every month. We decided to do it every week, because we both felt that the feedback was invaluable to the practice of teaching and, the more timely the feedback, the better. In this way, the data became a dynamic part of the practice. As well as research data, any immediate findings were used for changes and improvements to enhance classroom teaching and learning. From the outset, this research project was not approached with much so-called 'scientific objectivity'. We were both researcher and researched, and we acknowledged each time we 'interfered' with the academy-sanctioned research process.

After two years of data collection, it was time to write my dissertation. My dissertaton continued my journey of locating my genuine voice as I write about my research. The cornerstone of writing my dissertation was my passion for the subject and people about which I wrote. My passion stemmed from the relationships I built with Karen and the students in her class. I had established relationships of mutual respect with the people in the process of conducting my research, and a result of this was my attempts to capture lives and experiences beyond the research questions that I had brought to the study. In each incident that unfolded in the classroom for example, I tried to record the obvious, the inferred, the implied, the reconciled, and the closure — the hybrid processes through which a particular incident evolved in the social, instructional context. My efforts to be responsible to the friendships that had developed while I was in the field made it necessary to explicate the unexpected and improvised elements, along with those that were obvious, in the context of an event I focused on as part of the study.

Writing my dissertation was an art of synchronicity. I synchronized the knowledge constructed in university classrooms with the knowledge of my homegrown intellect, and teachers' construction of knowledge that I observed in their classrooms. I realized that it was impossible to subscribe to the norm of the academy of finding one voice, one definitive writing style, one hierarchy of knowledge. This was another aspect of the academic initiation that had been detrimental to my learning process. Acknowledging the training and preparation I derived from my life outside the walls of the university propels my resolute conclusion that I *know* what I know.

A Final Note About Being Born to Roll

Each individual writes and performs the script of his or her own life. Neither chance nor a divine being writes the script for us . . . You are the author and the hero. To perform your script well, it is important to pound the script into your head so thoroughly that you can see it vividly before your eyes. (Daisaku Ikeda)

Happily, on 15 May 1995 — also Mother's Day that year, and my mom had flown from Barbados to be there — I was one of many chosen, smiling, crying, laughing, and celebrated faces of black graduates at Berkeley's Black Graduation Ceremony.

In conclusion, there are many issues, people, situations, events, and circumstances that inform the path I have chosen — that is, becoming a professor in education — and the types of research I choose to do. In this paper I focused on my graduate school experience and the impact of that experience on my views about the teaching of the discipline and my notions of what constitutes important bodies of knowledge.

I chose this experience in part because of conversations with fellow graduate students, particularly first generation African-American students. I want these and other graduate students to know that you cannot and should not compromise your passion nor your potential to be effective educators. Today I bring a confidence to my work as an educator and researcher, to evaluations of my experiences, to defining and creating my style of writing. I bring this confidence to the other areas of my work in the academy and to my work with the students and teachers in urban inner-city public schools.

Finally, for those of you who will decide, as I have, to be an educator in the academy, I leave you with the following post-graduate chuckle I was forwarded on the internet.

A Story

It's a fine sunny day in the forest, and a rabbit is sitting outside his burrow, tippy-tapping on his typewriter. Along comes a fox, out for a walk.

Fox   'What are you working on?'
Rabbit   'My thesis.'
Fox   'Hmm, what is it about?'
Rabbit   'Oh, I'm writing about how rabbits eat foxes.'
(Incredulous pause.)
Fox   'That's ridiculous! Any fool knows that rabbits don't eat foxes!'
Rabbit   'Sure they do. And I can prove it. Come with me.'
They both disappear into the rabbit's burrow. After a few minutes, the rabbit returns, alone, to his typewriter and resumes typing. Soon a wolf comes along and stops to watch the hardworking rabbit.
Wolf   'What's that you're writing about?'
Rabbit   'I'm doing a thesis on how rabbits eat wolves.'
(Loud guffaws)
Wolf   'You don't expect to get such rubbish published, do you?'
Rabbit   'No problem. Do you want to see why?'
The rabbit and the wolf go into the burrow, and again the rabbit returns by himself, after a few minutes, and goes back to typing.

Inside the rabbit's burrow, in one corner, there is a pile of fox bones. In another corner, a pile of wolf bones. On the other side of the room a huge lion is belching and picking his teeth.

The end

The moral that accompanied the story when I first read it was, 'It doesn't matter what you choose for a thesis subject. It doesn't matter what you use for data.' However, I have developed another moral for this story in keeping with the main points of this paper. This moral is: 'Be true to your passion, to your work and to *yourself*, and there will always be a way to assert the value of your contributions.'

References

CAMBRA, A., SCHLUNTZ, N. and CARDOZA, S. (1984) *Graduate Students' Survival Guide*, Jefferson, NC: McFarland.

CARY, L. (1991) *Black Ice*, New York: Vintage Books.

DELPIT, L. (1995) *Other People's Children: Cultural Conflict in the Classroom*, New York: The New Press.

DES'REE (1994) 'I ain't movin'', Sony Music Entertainment (United Kingdom Ltd).

DUBOIS, W.E.B. (1953) *The Souls of Black Folk*, Greenwich, CT: Fawcett Publications.

ELLISON, R. (1947) *Invisible Man*, New York: Random House.

FREIRE, P. (1989) *Pedagogy of the Oppressed*, New York: Continuum Press.

hooks, b. (1989) *Talking Back: Thinking Feminist, Thinking Black*, Boston: South End Press.

JOHNSON A.J. (1995) 'Life after death: Critical pedagogy in an urban classroom', *Harvard Educational Review*; **65**, 2.

MOORE, R.N. (1985) *Winning the PhD Game: How to Get In and Out of Graduate School with a PhD and a Job*, New York: Dodd, Mead and Company.

NODDINGS, N. (1997) 'Accident, Awareness and Actualization', in NEWMANN, A. and PETERSON, P.O. (eds) *Learning from Our Lives: Women, Research, and Autobiography in Education*, New York: T.C. Press, pp. 166–81.

NGUGI, W.T. (1986) *Decolonizing the Mind, The Politics of Language in African Literature*, London: James Currey.

OBIDAH, J.E. and TEEL, K. (1995) 'The impact of race and cultural differences on the teacher–student relationship: A collaborative classroom study by an African-American and Caucasian teacher research team,' Unpublished manuscript.

PHILLIPS, L. and McCASKILL, B. (1991) 'Turning the 'who's schooling who?' question around: Black women and the bringing of the everyday into academe', *Signs*, Special issue: 'Post colonial, emergent and indigenous feminisms'.

ROSE, M. (1989) *Lives on the Boundary*, New York: Penguin Books.

5   Between Neo and Post:
Critique and Transformation
in Critical Educational Studies

Michael W. Apple

I began writing this chapter after two recent books on which I had worked for a number of years were completed. One of the books, *Cultural Politics and Education* (Apple, 1996a), was the most recent of an entire series of books that sought to answer some 'simple questions': Whose knowledge is taught? Why? Whose knowledge is not taught? Why? What is the relationship between culture and power in education? Who benefits from this relationship?[1] *Cultural Politics and Education* focused on what I think are the most powerful social movements redefining education today — what I call the conservative restoration. It employed the questions I noted above to critically interrogate conservative proposals for national curriculum, national testing, creating a closer connection between schooling and the economy, and 'choice plans'. It unpacked their economic, ideological, and political assumptions and argued that the ultimate results of such plans will be a society that is considerably more stratified, less equal, and less just.

The second book, *Democratic Schools* (Apple and Beane, 1995), was in many ways a companion volume to the other. Its basis is also in a few 'simple questions': If the conservative restoration is having such a profound effect on what education is for and who it will benefit, what can educators do about it in schools? Are there more democratic possibilities in schools? What concrete practices are *now* going on that provide alternatives to the conservative policies and practices now gaining so much power? Thus, *Democratic Schools* tells the stories of four public, not private, schools that are both socially critical and educationally progressive.

These two books, then, form something of a package, complement each other, and in essence need to be read together. The first provides a critical analysis of the conservative alliance, of its economic and cultural agendas, and of what is at stake if it wins. The second turns its attention to critical practice. Each one gives meaning to the other. Both represent a continuation of my struggle — aided by, and in concert with, others — to comprehend and challenge the dominant ways education is carried on in our societies.

There were a number of tensions that stood behind these books. In this chapter, I want to employ these tensions to take a stand on some of the major conceptual and political commitments that I think are essential in critical educational studies.

I started both *Cultural Politics and Education* and *Democratic Schools* at a time when I had just returned from spending time in a Bosnian refugee camp populated by people (mostly women and children) who had somehow managed to flee the murderous situation there. What I saw in the camp and the stories the mostly Islamic Bosnian teachers told me, left me with a residue of anger that will never be erased. I was also left with a feeling of gratitude and awe as an educator. For in the midst of privations, fear, despair, and uncommon courage, one of the first acts of the people in that camp was to create a school for their children. It was a powerful reminder of how important education is to the maintenance of self and community and to what Raymond Williams so brilliantly called our journey of hope (Williams, 1983, pp. 243–69).

That journey of hope is not made any easier by the fact that these books were written at a time when the Right was (and is) resurgent, when it seems as if we basically have two right wing parties in the United States, and when education and so much else is talked about as if all that counted was either competition and profit or a thoroughly romanticized return to the 'western tradition' (Apple, 1993). As I worked on the two books, rightist religious fundamentalism continued to grow and to have a greater influence on electoral politics, on social policy, and on what teachers will and will not teach in schools. The same was and is true about the growth of racist nativism. Such racist discourse is not limited to public debates about, say, immigration. The fact that the psuedo-science of Richard Herrnstein and Charles Murray in *The Bell Curve* (Herrnstein and Murray, 1994) is currently being treated to such sponsored mobility — even though it is utterly naive in its understanding of genetics and both overtly and covertly racist in its arguments — creates a horizon against which my own writing is constructed.[2] It is also a time when all too many of us seem to have become inured to human suffering nationally and internationally. This is a difficult period for anyone who is committed to progressive social and educational transformation.

This is a complicated and tense period intellectually as well. From the Right, the culture wars rage. Yet, equally importantly, these books were also produced when post-modern and post-structural theories are becoming more influential in cultural studies and in critical educational studies (a label I would prefer to use rather than the more limited one of critical theory or critical pedagogy). There are significant parts of what my friends call 'postie' approaches that are very insightful and need to be paid very close attention to, especially their focus on identity politics, on multiple and contradictory relations of power, on non-reductive analysis, and on the local as an important site of struggle. The influences of some of this are readily visible in *Cultural Politics and Education*. I have no wish at all to widen a divide when alliances are crucial now. However, there are also significant parts of these approaches as they have been introduced into education that simply make me blanch because of their stylistic arrogance, their stereotyping of other approaches and their concomitant certainty that they've got 'the' answer, their cynical lack of attachment to any action in real schools, their seeming equation of any serious focus on the economy as being somehow reductive, their conceptual confusions, and finally their trendy rhetoric that when unpacked often says some pretty commonsensical things that reflexive and activist educators have known and done for years. Let me hasten to add that this is true for only a portion of these approaches, but all of this gives me cause for concern.[3]

Thus, there is a fine line between necessary conceptual and political transformations and trendiness. Unfortunately, the latter sometimes appears in the relatively uncritical appropriation of post-modernism by some educational theorists and researchers. For example, there certainly are (too many) plans to turn schools over to market forces, to diversify types of schools and give 'consumers' more choice. Some may argue that this is 'the educational equivalent of . . . the rise of "flexible specialization in place of the old assembly-line world of mass production," driven by the imperatives of differentiated consumption rather than mass production' (Whitty, Edwards and Gewirtz, 1994, pp. 168–9). This certainly has a post-modern ring to it.

Yet, like many of the new reforms being proposed, there is less that is 'post-modern' about them than meets the eye. Many have a 'high-tech' image. They are usually guided by 'an underlying faith in technical rationality as the basis for solving social, economic, and educational problems'. Specialization is just as powerful, perhaps even more powerful, as any concern for diversity (Whitty, Edwards and Gewirtz, 1994, pp. 173–4). Rather than an espousal of 'heterogeneity, pluralism, and the local' — though these may be the rhetorical forms in which some of these reforms are couched — what we may also be witnessing is the revivification of more traditional class, gender, and especially race hierarchies. An unquestioning commitment to the notion that 'we' are now fully involved in a post-modern world may make it easier to see surface transformations (some of which are undoubtedly occurring) and yet at the same time may make it that much more difficult to recognize that these also may be new ways of re-organizing and reproducing older hierarchies (Whitty, Edwards and Gewirtz, 1994, pp. 180–1). The fact that parts of post-modernism as a theory and as a set of experiences may not be applicable to an extremely large part of the population of the world should make us be a bit more cautious as well.

In *Cultural Politics and Education*, it is clear that part, though certainly not all, of what I say there is based on a critical (and self-critical) structural understanding of education. While not economically reductive, it does require that we recognize that we live under capitalist relations. Milton Friedman and the entire gamut of privatizers and marketizers who have so much influence in the media and the corridors of power in corporate board rooms, foundations, and our government at nearly all levels spend considerable amounts of time praising these relations. If they can talk about them, why can't we? These relations *don't* determine everything. They are constituted out of, and reconstituted by, race, class, and gender relations, but it seems a bit naive to ignore them. There is a world of difference between taking economic power and structures seriously and reducing everything down to a pale reflection of them.

I am fully cognizant that there are many dangers with such an approach. It has as part of its history attempts to create a 'grand narrative', a theory that explains every-thing based on a unitary cause. It can also tend to forget that not only are there multiple and contradictory relations of power in nearly every situation, but that the researchers themselves are participants in such relations (Roman and Apple, 1990). Finally, struc-tural approaches at times can neglect the ways our discourses are constructed out of, and themselves help construct, what we do. These indeed are issues that need to be taken as seriously as they deserve. Post-structural and post-modern criticisms of struc-tural analyses in education have been fruitful in this regard, especially when they have arisen from within the various feminist, anti-racist, and post-colonial communities (See, for example, Luke and Gore, 1992; McCarthy and Crichlow, 1993), though it must be said that some of these criticisms have created wildly inaccurate caricatures of the neomarxist traditions.

Yet, even though the 'linguistic turn', as it has been called in sociology and cultural studies, has been immensely productive, it is important to remember that the world of education and elsewhere is not only a text. There are gritty realities out there, realities whose power is often grounded in structural relations that are not simply social constructions created by the meanings given by an observer. Part of our task, it seems to me, is not to lose sight of these gritty realities in the economy and the state, at the same time as we recognize the dangers of essentializing and reductive analyses (Apple, 1992).

My point is not to deny that many elements of 'post-modernity' exist, nor is it to deny the power of aspects of post-modern theory. Rather, it is to avoid overstatement, to avoid substituting one grand narrative for another (a grand narrative that actually never existed in the United States, since class and economy only recently surfaced in critical educational scholarship and were only rarely seen here in the form found in Europe where most post-modern and post-structural criticisms of these explanatory tools were developed. It would help if we remembered that the intellectual and political histories of the United States were very different than that castigated by some of the post-modern critics). Reductive analysis comes cheap and there is no guarantee that post-modern positions, as currently employed by some in education, are any more immune to this danger than any other position.

Thus, in much of my recent work, it will not be a surprise that side by side with post-structural and post-modern understandings are those based on structural theories. While they are not totally merged, each one serves as a corrective and complement to the other. This is a point I wish to emphasize. Rather than spending so much time treating each other so warily — and sometimes as enemies — the creative tension that exists is a good thing (See Apple and Oliver, 1996). We have a good deal to learn from each other in terms of a politics in and around education that makes a difference (no pun is intended here).

There are a number of other intellectual tensions that swirled around these books as well. As I reflected on the growth of certain styles of doing critical analysis in education, it was also clear that there had been a rapid growth of two other kinds of work — personal/literary/autobiographical and studies of popular culture. The former has often been stimulated by phenomenological, psychoanalytic, and feminist approaches. The latter has arisen from cultural studies. Let me say something about each of these.

Much of the impetus behind personal stories is moral. Education correctly is seen as an ethical enterprise. The personal is seen as a way to re-awaken ethical and aesthetic sensitivities that increasingly have been purged from the scientist discourse of too many educators. Or it is seen as a way of giving a voice to the subjectivities of people who have been silenced. There is much to commend in this position. Indeed, any approach that, say, evacuates the aesthetic, the personal, and the ethical from our activities as educators is not about education at all. It is about training. As someone who spent years teaching in inner-city schools in a severely economically depressed community, I reject any approach that reduces education to mere training or is not grounded in the personal lives and 'stories' of real teachers, students, and community members. Yet something remains a little too much in the background in many variants of the stories written by professional educators and academics — a biting sense of the political, of the social structures that condemn so many identifiable people to lives of economic and cultural (and bodily) struggle and, at times, despair. Making connections between what might be called the literary imagination and the concrete movements — both in education *and* the larger society — that seek to transform our institutions so that caring and social justice are not just slogans but realities, is essential here. Political arguments are not alternatives to moral and aesthetic concerns. Rather, they are these concerns taken seriously in their full implications (Eagleton, 1983). And this leads me to raise a caution about some of the hidden effects of our (generally commendable) urge to employ the personal and the autobiographical to illuminate our (admittedly differential) educational experiences.

For nearly 20 years, until the publication of another recent book of mine, *Official Knowledge* (Apple, 1993), I did not write about my experiences as a filmmaker with teachers and students, in part because I could not find an appropriate 'voice'. It would have required a fair dose of autobiography. I often find autobiographical accounts and narrative renderings compelling and insightful, and do not want in any way to dismiss their power in educational theory and practice. Yet — and let me be blunt here — just as often such writing runs the risk of lapsing into what has been called possessive individualism (Apple, 1990; Apple, 1993; Apple, 1995a). Even when authors do the 'correct thing' and discuss their social location in a world dominated by oppressive conditions, such writing can serve the chilling function of simply saying 'But enough about you, let me tell you about me' if we are not much more reflexive about this than has often been the case. I am still committed enough to raising questions about class and race dynamics to worry about perspectives that supposedly acknowledge the missing voices of many people in our thinking about education, but still wind up privileging the white, middle class woman's or man's need for *self display*.

Do not misconstrue what I am saying here. As so much feminist and post-colonial work has documented, the personal often is the absent presence behind even the most eviscerated writing and we do need to continue to explore ways of heightening the sense of the personal in our 'stories' about education. But, at the same time, it is equally crucial that we interrogate our own 'hidden' motives here. Is the insistence on the personal, an insistence that underpins much of our turn to literary and autobiographical forms, partly a class discourse as well? The 'personal may be the political', but does the political end at the personal? Furthermore, why should we assume that the personal is any less difficult to understand than the 'external' world? I cannot answer these questions for all situations; but I think that these questions must be asked by all of us who are committed to the multiple projects involved in struggling for a more emancipatory education. (And for this very reason, later on I shall end my contribution to this book with a personal story that is *consciously* connected to a clear sense of the realities of structurally generated inequalities that play such a large role in education.)

My intellectual/political tensions did not end here, however. 'Boom times' in academic stocks and bonds come and go (McGuigan, 1992, p. 61). In some parts of the critical educational community, the study of popular culture — music, dance, films, language, dress, bodily transformations, the politics of consumption, and so on — is also big business. And in many ways it should be. After all, we should know by now that popular culture is partly a site of resistance and struggle (Willis, Jones, Canaan and Hurd, 1990; Giroux, 1994; Koza, 1994), but also that for schooling to make a difference it must connect to popular understandings and cultural forms. Yet, our fascination with 'the popular', our intoxication with all of these things, has sometimes had a paradoxical and unfortunate effect. It often has led us to ignore the actual knowledge that *is* taught in schools, the entire corpus and structure of the formal processes of curriculum, teaching, and evaluation that remain so powerful. In many ways, it constitutes a flight from education as a field. In my more cynical moments, I take this as a class discourse in which new elements within the academy in education fight for power not only over school folks but over positions within the academy itself.

In *Cultural Politics and Education*, I talk about the importance of popular culture and make a plea for its utter centrality both in understanding cultural politics and in struggling to institute more socially just models of curriculum and teaching. Yet, many members of the critical educational community have been a bit too trendy about this topic as well. They seem to have forgotten about schools, curricula, teachers, students, community activists, and so on. It's as if dealing with these issues is 'polluting', as if they are afraid of getting their hands dirty with the daily realities of education. Or perhaps they feel that it's not theoretically elegant enough to deal with such 'mundane' realities. While I fully understand the utter necessity of focusing on the popular, as a critical educator I am even more committed to taking the reality of school matters as seriously as they deserve.[4] For this very reason, *Cultural Politics and Education* devotes much of its attention to matters specifically related to the politics of curriculum and teaching, just as *Democratic Schools* is totally devoted to describing how we can make a real difference in the curriculum and teaching that now dominate too many schools.

I do not want to be overly negative here. Many of us have quite ambivalent feelings about the place called school. All of us who care deeply about what is and is not taught and about who is and is not empowered to answer these questions have a contradictory relationship to these institutions. We want to criticize them rigorously and yet in this very criticism lies a commitment, a hope, that they can be made more vital, more personally meaningful and socially critical. If ever there was a love/hate relationship, this is it.[5] This speaks directly to the situation many people in critical educational studies face today and underlies some of the emphases of both books.

The New Right is very powerful now. It has had the odd effect of simultaneously interrupting the progressive critique of schooling while at the same time leading many of us to defend an institution many of whose practices were and are open to severe criticism (Education Group, 1991, p. 33). As someone who has devoted years to analyzing and acting on the social and cultural means and ends of our curricula, teaching, and evaluation in schools, I am certainly not one who wants to act as an apologist for poor practices. Yet, during an era when — because of rightist attacks — we face the massive dismantling of the gains (limited as they were) that have been made in social welfare, in women's control of their bodies, in relations of race, class, gender, and sexuality, and in whose knowledge is taught in schools, it is equally important to make certain that these gains are defended.

Thus, there is another clear tension in these volumes. I wanted both to defend the idea of a public education and a number of the gains that do exist and to criticize many of its attributes at the same time. This dual focus may seem a bit odd at first, but it speaks to a crucial point I want to make about how we should think about the institutions of formal education in most of our nations.

Here I want to say something that may make a number of educators who are justifiably critical of existing power relations in education a bit uncomfortable. The problem I shall point to may at first seem minor, but its conceptual, political, and practical implications are not. I am referring to the discourse of *change*. It stands behind all of those claims about both the autobiographical and popular culture and behind the pressures to connect schools more closely to economic needs and goals. All too often we forget that in our attempts to alter and 'reform' schooling there are elements that should not be changed but need to be kept and defended. Even with my criticisms of the unequal power relations surrounding education and the larger society, we need to remember that schooling was never simply an imposition on supposedly politically/culturally inept people. Rather, as I have demonstrated elsewhere, educational policies and practices were and are the result of struggles and compromises over what would count as legitimate knowledge, pedagogy, goals, and criteria of determining effectiveness. In a more abstract way, we can say that education has been one of the major arenas in which the conflict between property rights and person rights has been fought (Apple, 1993; Apple, 1995a).

The results of these conflicts have not always been settled on the terms of dominant groups. Often, democratic tendencies have emerged and have been cemented into the daily practices of the institution. As William Reese (1986) shows in his history of populist reform in schools, many things that we take for granted were the direct results of populist movements that forced powerful groups to compromise, to even suffer outright losses. Thus, before we give a blanket condemnation to what schools do and turn to what we suppose is its alternative (say, popular culture), we need a much clearer and more historically informed appraisal of what elements of the practices and policies of these institutions are already progressive and should be maintained. Not to do so would be to assume that, say, radical teachers, people of color, women, working class groups, and physically challenged groups (these categories are obviously not mutually exclusive) have been puppets whose strings are pulled by the most conservative forces in this society and have not won any lasting victories in education. This is simply not the case. Not to defend some of the ideas behind person rights that are currently embodied in schools is to add more power to conservative attacks. There *have* been gains. The forces of the conservative restoration would not be so very angry at public schools — at the supposed 'overemphasis' on 'minority culture', on 'feminism', on gay and lesbian rights — if educational and community activists hadn't had at least some success in transforming what was taken for granted in schools. These gains certainly aren't sufficient; but they *are* there.

I do not want to belabor this point, but it does make a major difference in how we approach education. At times, some critical educators have been so critical that we too often assume — consciously or unconsciously — that everything that exists within the educational system bears only the marks of, and is only, the result of domination. It's all capitalist; it's all racist; it's all patriarchal; it's all homophobic. As you would imagine given my own efforts over the past three decades, I do not want to dismiss the utter power of these and other forms of oppression in education or in anything else. Yet, in taking a stance that assumes — without detailed investigation — that all is somehow the result of relations of dominance, we also make it very difficult to make connections with progressive educators and community members who are currently struggling to build an education that is democratic in more than name only. (And there are many practicing educators who have been more than a little successful in such struggles.) It is all too easy for critical educators to fall into this position.

This assumption is problematic conceptually, historically, and politically. It rests on a theory of the role of state institutions that is too simplistic and on an ahistorical understanding of the power of democratically inclined groups (Carnoy and Levin, 1985; Jules and Apple, 1995). It also bears the marks of what seems like a form of self hatred, as if the more we distance ourselves from the history and discourse of education — and turn to other, 'more academically respectable', fields for all of our perspectives — the more academically legitimate we become. The ultimate effects of this are disabling for any of us who wish to continue the long and essential struggle to have our educational institutions respond to the needs not only of the powerful.

This is a difficult tightrope to walk for those of us involved in education. In a time of rightwing resurgence, how do we create the educational conditions in which our students can see (and teach us about as well) the very real and massive relations of inequality and the role of schooling in partly reproducing and contesting them and at the same time jointly create the conditions that assist all of us in empowering each other to act on these realities? Gramsci had a way of saying it: Pessimism of the intellect, optimism of the will. But my point goes well beyond this. Intellect, enlivened by passion and ethical/political sensitivities — and a fine sense of historical agency — will also see victories as well as losses, hope as well as despair. That it seems to me is our task.

Finally, and this is directly related to what I have just said, there has been one other tension behind these books. When I began writing *Cultural Politics and Education* not only did I want to both criticize and defend much that is happening in education, I also wanted to illuminate what it actually *is* that needs to be defended. What policies and practices now exist in schools and classrooms that are socially and educationally critical? Are there what I have elsewhere called crucial 'non-reformist reforms' that need to be continued (Apple, 1995a)? This caused me no end of headaches. While throughout *Cultural Politics and Education* I refer to such policies and practices, for political and ethical reasons (and perhaps for reasons of sanity), I ultimately decided that extensive descriptions of such critical practice clearly deserved an entire book of their own. Furthermore, they should be written by the educator/activists who actually engage in them, in their own words. It is this very reason that at the same time that I was writing the first book, my colleague and friend, Jim Beane, and I produced *Democratic Schools*. As I noted, it details in much greater depth what is possible in public schools now. By focusing on the stories of a number of ongoing socially and education-ally committed public schools run by educators who directly link their curricula and teaching to a clear sense of the economic, political, and cultural relations of power in the world, it gives what I believe is compelling evidence that the journey of hope in education continues in real schools with real teachers, students, and community members. Thus, if you read *Cultural Politics and Education*, and afterwards you still find yourself asking something like 'Okay, Apple, now what? What concrete ideas do you have to practice what you preach? What alternatives would you propose, and what would you keep, to take your critical analysis seriously?' I can only reply that my answers to these questions are provided considerably more fully in *Democratic Schools*.

Memory and Experience

The first section of this chapter laid out the 'balancing act' that I've tried to engage in over the past years. This has involved me (and many others) in the following: criticizing dominant educational practices while defending gains; deepening and defending crucial aspects of structural analyses of education while recognizing a number of the insights in post-structural approaches and incorporating them into my work; engaging in detailed critical analyses of schools while trying to make public more democratic educational policies and practices; and wanting to stimulate a more personal and/or autobiographical appraisal of education but not at the expense of losing our sense of the ways education is currently structured around oppressive economic/political/cultural relations.

Of course, as I have shown throughout this chapter, this 'balancing act' has roots in debates over concepts, methods, and politics in critical educational studies. Yet it roots go much deeper than that. As with most people, they grow out of one's biography in crucial ways. In my own case, they come from a personal history of poverty and from a family who because of this was deeply involved in political action. They come from the time I spent as an activist teacher in inner-city schools and as a president of a teachers union. They come from my early experiences in movements opposed to the racial structuring of this society and from the fact that I am the father of an African-American child, a fact that never lets me forget what race means in this society. And they come from my repeated and continuing experiences over the past three decades working with dissident groups, unions, critical educators, and others who are involved in struggling to create a more just and caring economy, polity, and culture. In essence, it is these early and ongoing activities that provide the impetus behind my work, that constantly force me to confront the fact that education is intimately connected to relations of domination and subordination — and to struggles against them — whether we recognize this or not.[6]

Perhaps I can employ one personal story to illuminate why I think we must never forget such a structural sense of these relations and why the connections between education and the larger structures of inequality need to have a central place in our thought and action in education. In many ways, this story will crystallize and make explicit many of the points I have made here about the political, theoretical, and educational tensions that lie behind my work.

Education and Cheap French Fries

The sun glared off of the hood of the small car as we made our way along the two-lane road. The heat and humidity made me wonder if I'd have any liquid left in my body at the end of the trip and led me to appreciate Wisconsin winters a bit more than one might expect. The idea of winter seemed more than a little remote in this Asian country for which I have a good deal of fondness. But the topic at hand was not the weather; rather, it was the struggles of educators and social activists to build an education that was considerably more democratic than what was in place in that country now. This was a dangerous topic. Discussing it in philosophical and formalistically academic terms was tolerated there. Openly calling for it and situating it within a serious analysis of the economic, political, and military power structures that now exerted control over so much of this nation's daily life was another matter. And we were on our way to a meeting with a group of young teachers in a rural area who were involved in such struggles.[7]

As we traveled along that rural road in the midst of one of the best conversations I had engaged in about the possibilities of educational transformations and the realities of the oppressive conditions so many people were facing in that land, my gaze somehow was drawn to the side of the road. In one of those nearly accidental happenings that clarify and crystallize what reality is *really* like, my gaze fell upon a seemingly inconsequential object. At regular intervals, there were small signs planted in the dirt a few yards from where the road met the fields. The sign was more than a little familiar. It bore the insignia of one of the most famous fast food restaurants in the United States. We drove for miles past seemingly deserted fields along a flat hot plain, passing sign after sign, each a replica of the previous one, each less than a foot high. These were not billboards. Such things hardly existed in this poor rural region. Rather, they looked exactly — exactly — like the small signs one finds next to farms in the American midwest that signify the kinds of seed corn that each farmer had planted in her or his fields. This was a good guess it turned out.

I asked the driver — a close friend and former student of mine who had returned to this country to work for the social and educational reforms that were so necessary — what turned out to be a naive, but ultimately crucial, question in my own education. 'Why are those signs for ***** there? Is there a ***** restaurant nearby?' My friend looked at me in amazement. 'Michael, don't you know what these signs signify? There's no western restaurants within 50 miles of where we are. These signs represent exactly what is wrong with education in this nation. Listen to this.' And I listened.

The story is one that has left an indelible mark on me, for it condenses in one powerful set of historical experiences the connections between our struggles as educators and activists in so many countries and the ways differential power works in ordinary life. I cannot match the tensions and passions in my friend's voice as this story was told; nor can I convey exactly the almost eerie feelings one gets when looking at that vast, sometimes beautiful, sometimes scarred, and increasingly depopulated plain.

Yet the story is crucial to hear. Listen to this.

The government of the nation has decided that the importation of foreign capital is critical to its own survival. Bringing in American, German, British, Japanese, and other investors and factories will ostensibly create jobs, will create capital for investment, and will enable the nation to speed into the twenty-first Century. (This is, of course, elite group talk, but let us assume that all of this is indeed truly believed by dominant groups.) One of the ways the military dominated government has planned to do this is to focus part of its recruitment efforts on agri-business. In pursuit of this aim, it has offered vast tracts of land to international agri-business concerns at very low cost. Of particular importance to the plain we are driving through is the fact that much of this land has been given over to a large American fast food restaurant corporation for the growing of potatoes for the restaurant's french fries, one the trademarks of its extensive success throughout the world.

The corporation was eager to jump at the opportunity to shift a good deal of its potato production from the US to Asia. Since many of the farm workers in the United States were now unionized and were (correctly) asking for a liveable wage, and since the government of that Asian nation officially frowned on unions of any kind, the cost of growing potatoes would be lower. Further, the land on that plain was perfect for the use of newly developed technology to plant and harvest the crop with considerably fewer workers. Machines would replace living human beings. Finally, the government was much less concerned about environmental regulations. All in all, this was a fine bargain for capital.

Of course, people lived on some of this land and farmed it for their own food and to sell what might be left over after their own — relatively minimal — needs were met. This deterred neither agri-business nor the government. After all, people could be moved to make way for 'progress'. And after all, the villagers along that plain did not actually have deeds to the land. (They had lived there for perhaps hundreds of years, well before the invention of banks, and mortgages, and deeds — no paper, no owner-ship.) It would not be too hard to move the people off of the plain to other areas to 'free' it for intensive potato production and to 'create jobs' by taking away the liveli-hood of thousands upon thousands of small-scale farmers in the region.

I listened with rapt attention as the rest of the story unfolded and as we passed by the fields with their miniature corporate signs and the abandoned villages. The people whose land had been taken for so little moved, of course. As in so many other similar places thoughout what dominant groups call the Third World, they trekked to the city. They took their meager possessions and moved into the ever expanding slums within and surrounding the one place that held out some hope of finding enough paid work (if everyone — including children — labored) so that they could survive.

The government and major segments of the business elite officially discouraged this, sometimes by hiring thugs to burn the shanty towns, other times by keeping conditions so horrible that no one would 'want' to live there. But still the dispossessed came, by the tens of thousands. Poor people are not irrational, after all. The loss of arable land had to be compensated for somehow and if it took cramming into places that were deadly at times, well what were the other choices? There *were* factories being built in and around the cities which paid incredibly low wages — sometimes less than enough money to buy sufficient food to replace the calories expended by workers in the production process — but at least there might be paid work if one was lucky.

(Although, as in many instances of this type, it was women who were 'preferred' for these low paid and exploitative factory jobs, since they supposedly were more dexterous, more docile, and were 'willing' to work for less.)

So the giant machines harvested the potatoes and the people poured into the cities and international capital was happy. It's not a nice story, but what does it have to do with education? My friend continued my education.

The military dominated government had given all of these large international businesses 20 years of tax breaks to sweeten the conditions for their coming to that country. Thus, there was now very little money to supply the health care facilities, housing, running water, electricity, sewage disposal, and schools for the thousands upon thousands of people who had sought their future in, or had literally been driven into, the city. The mechanism for *not* building these necessities was quite clever. Take the lack of any formal educational institutions as a case in point. In order for the government to build schools it had to be shown that there was a 'legitimate' need for such expenditure. Statistics had to be produced in a form that was officially accepted. This could only be done through the official determination of numbers of registered births. Yet, the very process of official registration made it impossible for thousands of children to be recognized as actually existing.

In order to register for school, a parent had to register the birth of the child at the local hospital or government office — few of which existed in these slum areas. And even if you could somehow find such an office, the government officially discouraged people who had originally come from outside the region of the city from moving there. It often refused to recognize the legitimacy of the move as a way of keeping displaced farmers from coming into the urban areas and thereby increasing the population. Births from people who had no 'legitimate' right to be there did not count as births at all. It is a brilliant strategy in which the state creates categories of legitimacy that define social problems in quite interesting ways (See Fraser, 1989; Curtis, 1992). Foucault would have been proud, I am certain.

Thus, there are no schools, no teachers, no hospitals, no infrastructure. The root causes of this situation rest not in the immediate situation. They can only be illuminated if we focus on the chain of capital formation internationally and nationally, on the contradictory needs of the state, on the class relations and the relations between country and city that organize and disorganize that country. And they can only be illuminated by recognizing the fact that under prevailing neo-colonial forms, the people of these slums become disposable and invisible — the 'other' — given an international division of labor in which race plays such a large part. 'We' eat; 'they' remain unseen.

My friend and I had been driving for quite a while now. I had forgotten about the heat. The ending sentence of the story pulled no punches. It was said slowly and quietly, said in a way that made it even more compelling. 'Michael, these fields are the reason there's no schools in my city. There's no schools because so many folks like cheap french fries.'

I tell this story about the story told to me for a number of reasons. First, it is simply one of the most powerful ways I know of reminding myself and all of us of the utter importance of seeing schooling relationally, of seeing it as connected — fundamentally — to the relations of domination and exploitation (and to struggles against them) of the larger society. Second, and equally as importantly, I tell this story to make a crucial theoretical and political point. Relations of power are indeed complex and we do need to take very seriously the post-modern focus on the local and on the multiplicity of the forms of struggle that need to be engaged in. It is important as well to recognize the changes that are occurring in many societies and to see the complexity of the 'power/ knowledge' nexus. Yet in our attempts to avoid the dangers that accompanied some aspects of previous 'grand narratives', let us not act as if capitalism has somehow disappeared. Let us not act as if class relations, nationally and internationally, don't count. Let us not act as if what are arrogantly called 'center/periphery' relations that are often based on racial divisions of labor don't exist. Let us not act as if all of the things we learned about how the world might be understood politically have been somehow overthrown because our theories are now more complex. It is this that provides the center of gravity in my work.

The denial of basic human rights, the destruction of the environment, the deadly conditions under which people (barely) survive, the lack of a meaningful future for the thousands of children I noted in my story — all of this is not only or even primarily a 'text' to be deciphered in our academic volumes as we pursue our post-modern themes. It is a reality that millions of people experience in their very bodies everyday. Educational work that is not connected deeply to a powerful understanding of these realities (and this understanding cannot evacuate a serious analysis of political economy and class, race, and gender relations without losing much of its power) is in danger of losing its soul. The lives of our children demand no less.

Postscript

I stared out to do something that I thought was relatively 'simple' in this chapter. My original intent was to put on paper some of the reasons why *Cultural Politics and Education* and *Democratic Schools* took the shape that they did. Yet this seemingly simple task soon got more complex. It caused me to go into more depth into a set of theoretical, political, and educational tensions and to be a bit more of a 'story teller' than I had originally planned.

While a good deal of what I have said here is expanded in *Cultural Politics and Education*, I do want to add one other thing. I ended the 'story' of my drive through that plain with a call for connecting our work as educators to a serious understanding of power, but one that doesn't get so complicated that it forgets that many times it really 'ain't that hard' at times to recognize who benefits from the ways our societies are now organized. Yet, such recognition is not only a theoretic or academic task.[8] This recognition requires that we live our lives differently — for example, that we build alliances with, support, and learn from both the teacher and community activists represented in *Democratic Schools* and those young teachers I was driving to meet on that hot flat plain. No longer eating cheap french fries might help a little too.

Notes

Parts of this chapter appear in Apple, M.W. (1996a) *Cultural Politics and Education*, New York: Teachers College Press and London: Open University Press.

1   The following books made up the series and were written in the order of their listing: *Ideology and Curriculum* (1979; 2nd ed. 1990), *Education and Power* (1982; revised ARK edition 1985; 2nd ed. 1995a), *Teachers and Texts* (1986), and *Official Knowledge* (1993).
2   For criticisms of the conceptual, empirical, and ideological agendas of *The Bell Curve*, see Kincheloe and Steinberg (1996). See also my own critical analysis of some of the reasons such arguments have an impact now in Apple (1996b).

Michael W. Apple

3 See (Apple, 1994). I say *approaches* here because it is too easy to stereotype post-modern and post-structural theories. That would be unfortunate, since the political differences, for example, among and within the various tendencies associated with both are often substantial.
4 That one can deal with popular culture and school culture together in elegant ways is very nicely documented in Weinstein (1995).
5 Ian Hunter in fact argues that critical educational researchers are so wedded to schools that their criticisms function as part of the mobility strategies of an intellectual elite. This is provocative, but essentializing in the extreme. See Hunter (1994). See also my response to his book in Apple (1995b).
6 These more autobiographical details are laid out in more detail in an interview with me published as an appendix in Apple (1993).
7 I shall not name this country here, since to do so could put the teachers and my colleague at risk.
8 I do not want to dismiss the importance of theoretical or academic work, if such work is *overtly* connected to movements for social justice. For further discussion of this, see Apple (1996).

References

APPLE, M.W. (1986) *Teachers and Texts*, New York: Routledge.
APPLE, M.W. (1990) *Ideology and Curriculum* (2nd ed.), New York: Routledge.
APPLE, M.W. (1992) 'Education, culture, and class power', *Educational Theory*, **42**, pp. 127–45.
APPLE, M.W. (1993) *Official Knowledge*, New York: Routledge.
APPLE, M.W. (1994) 'Cultural capital and official knowledge', in NELSON, C. and BERUBE, M. (eds) *Higher Education under Fire*, New York: Routledge.
APPLE, M.W. (1995a) *Education and Power* (2nd ed.), New York: Routledge.
APPLE, M.W. (1995b) 'Review of Ian Hunter: Rethinking the school', *Australian Journal of Education*, **39**, pp. 95–6.
APPLE, M.W. (1996a) *Cultural Politics and Education*, New York: Teachers College Press and London: Open University Press.
APPLE, M.W. (1996b) 'Dominance and dependency', in KINCHELOE, J. and STEINBERG, S. (eds) *Measured Lies*, New York: St Martin's Press.
APPLE, M.W. (1996c) 'Power, meaning, and identity', *British Journal of Sociology of Education*, **17**, pp. 125–44.
APPLE, M.W. and BEANE, J.A. (1995) *Democratic Schools*, Washington, DC: Association for Supervision and Curriculum Development.
APPLE, M.W. and OLIVER, A. (1996) 'Becoming right: Education and the formation of conservative movements', *Teachers College Record*, **97**, pp. 419–45.
CARNOY, M. and LEVIN, C. (1985) *Schooling and Work in the Democratic State*, Stanford: Stanford University Press.
CURTIS, B. (1992) *True Government by Choice Men?*, Toronto: University of Toronto Press.
EAGLETON, T. (1983) *Literary Theory*, Minneapolis: University of Minnesota Press.
EDUCATION GROUP II (eds) (1991) *Education Limited*, London: Unwin Hyman.
FRASER, N. (1989) *Unruly Practices*, Minneapolis: University of Minnesota Press.
GIROUX, H. (1994) 'Doing cultural studies', *Harvard Educational Review*, **64**, pp. 278–308.
HERRNSTEIN, R. and MURRAY, C. (1994) *The Bell Curve*, New York: The Free Press.
HUNTER, I. (1994) *Rethinking the School*, St Leonards, Australia: Allen and Unwin.
JULES, D. and APPLE, M.W. (1995) 'The state and educational reform', in PINK, W. and NOBLIT, G. (eds) *Continuity and Contradiction: The Futures of the Sociology of Education*, Cresskill, NJ: Hampton Press.
KOZA, J. (1994) 'Rap music', *The Review of Education/Pedagogy/Cultural Studies*, **16**, pp. 171–96.
KINCHELOE, J. and STEINBERG, S. (eds) (1996) *Measured Lies*, New York: St Martin's Press.
LUKE, C. and GORE, J. (eds) (1992) *Feminisms and Critical Pedagogy*, New York: Routledge.

McCarthy, C. and Crichlow, W. (eds) (1993) *Race, Identity, and Representation in Education*, New York: Routledge.

McGuigan, J. (1992) *Cultural Populism*, New York: Routledge.

Reese, W. (1986) *Power and the Promise of School Reform*, New York: Routledge.

Roman, L. and Apple, M.W. (1990) 'Is naturalism a move beyond positivism?', in Eisner, E. and Peshkin, A. (eds) *Qualitative Inquiry in Education*, New York: Teachers College Press.

Weinstein, M. (1995) 'Robot world: A study of science, reality, and the struggle for meaning', Unpublished PhD Dissertation, University of Wisconsin-Madison.

Whitty, G., Edwards, T. and Gewirtz, S. (1994) *Specialization and Choice in Urban Education*, New York: Routledge.

Williams, R. (1983) *The Year 2000*, New York: Pantheon.

Willis, P., Jones, S., Canaan, J. and Hurd, G. (1990) *Common Culture*, Boulder: Westview.

6   Writing Gender into Reading Research

Donna E. Alvermann

> In our personal social lives, we tell stories as a way of structuring and giving significance to lived experience, [and] . . . this is not only so for our personal lives. It applies equally to our professional lives and to the stories that sustain us there. We tell stories of our research experiences, stories of the texts we read, stories of our classrooms . . . [and] our stories keep changing as our ways of reading stories (and therefore of making new stories) change. (Gilbert, 1993, p. 211)

An invitation to tell my own story about what historical influences guide my research and writing, why I choose to study the gendered nature of students' talk about texts, where my interpretations come from, and what I hope to accomplish with this line of inquiry came at a time when the University of Georgia's College of Education faculty was taking its first serious look at multicultural education. The College's attention to issues of cultural diversity (beyond the obligatory affirmative action policies that were in place) seemed a milestone, as far as I could determine, and I welcomed the opportunity to think creatively about my role in this new initiative. It was, as Gilbert (1993) alludes to in her statement above, a time for storying — a time for putting into narrative form the frameworks that guide my scholarship and support my values — so that this story, too, might be read, responded to, and changed as I continue working toward writing gender into reading research. But first, before getting into the story, let me set the stage.

Status of Gender in Reading Research

The virtual absence of gender as a category of analysis in reading research has been noted by scholars outside the United States as well as within (Baldwin et al., 1992; Davies, 1993; Orellana, 1995; Patterson, 1995). Like Patterson's findings, my own (Alvermann, 1994) suggest that gender has a low-profile status in the major reading research journals and handbooks published over the last decade. Neither gender nor sex was reported in the majority of these sources.[1] For example, in a hand search of all issues of the *Journal of Reading Behavior* published between 1983–94, I found no mention of either sex or gender in over half (54 percent) of the 209 research articles. In 40 percent of those articles, the terms were used interchangeably as demographic markers to describe the participants (e.g., gender was evenly distributed between the 104 subjects, or the sex of the participants was 24 boys and 21 girls). In only 6 percent of the articles was gender or sex treated as a variable of interest and discussed as part of the findings.

In a similar analysis of *Reading Research Quarterly* (Alvermann, 1994), for the same 11-year period (1983–94), I discovered that less than 2 percent of the articles used gender in ways other than to mark sex differences. The situation was the same for the major handbooks in the field. For example, the index to the first edition of the *Handbook of Reading Research* (Pearson, Barr, Kamil and Mosenthal, 1984) contained no references to gender or sex; the second edition (Barr, Kamil, Mosenthal and Pearson, 1991) mentioned gender on 10 pages spread over three of the handbook's 34 chapters. In the last two editions of *Theoretical Models and Processes of Reading* (Ruddell, Ruddell and Singer, 1994; Singer and Ruddell, 1985), neither gender nor sex was listed in the index.

Although recently a handful of research reports dealing with reading as a gendered social practice (e.g., Alvermann, 1996; Alvermann, Commeyras, Young, Randall and Hinson, 1997; Davies, 1993; Finders, 1996a, 1996b; Orellana, 1995) have begun to make their way into the literacy journals, typically speaking, gender remains a marginalized topic of research in the field of reading education. Part of the reason this is so may stem from the fact gender is viewed by many reading researchers as being synonymous with one's biological sex, and thus of little interest to the reading community. Because the research on individual differences in the 1950s and 1960s generally demonstrated no significant differences between male and female readers, sex as a variable of interest has been downplayed in the decades since then. And, as long as gender and sex are commonly thought of as interchangeable terms among reading researchers, it is likely that gender as a category of analysis will remain a marginalized topic in the literacy field.

The Story Begins

The popular once-upon-a-time opening line in many stories alerts the listener (or reader) to the historical context for a particular narrative. It suggests a sense of place, people, and events to come. It also implies an unfolding of those events. So it is with this story — a brief narrative of some early events in my life that continue to influence what I research and write about today. Born into a working class family, I grew up in the 1940s and 1950s in a small town geographically located in what is known as upstate New York's 'southern tier'. Today it is an economically depressed area, one from which industries have moved in search of better tax breaks or cheaper labor. But I remember the area as thriving countryside dotted by small smokestacks in tiny towns separated by rich farmlands.

My father was a machinist in one of the local Westinghouse plants and the chief organizer of his plant's first labor union. A self-taught man who left school in the eighth-grade to help his family farm the land during the Great Depression, he was not easily intimidated when members of the plant's management team fought viciously and long against unionization. My mother was a full-time homemaker who rented out a few rooms of our house to tourists during the summer. Both of my parents liked to buy old houses, renovate them, and then sell them after we had lived in them for only a short time.

As a child, I found the constant moves (there were five moves in 11 years) a little disconcerting. Later I learned that this buying and selling of houses was how we managed to move to 'better' and 'even better' neighborhoods in a town. Moved from one neighborhood (or one town) to another, I grew to dislike and resist what later I would come to label the pretenses of middle and upper-middle class neighborhoods. At the time, of course, all I knew was the frustration of feeling different from those around me. For example, I can still recall how unfair I thought it was when the girl I considered my 'best friend' in third grade told me that her father, a lawyer, did not want her playing with me after school because my father worked in a factory. I never mentioned this to my father; somehow, I knew even then that it would hurt him. School became my sanctuary. I did well academically and graduated second highest in my senior class.

After college, I taught school in Austin, Texas, in a community that served the largest migrant population in the area. Children from Mexican families would arrive in my room sometime in early October after having harvested the crops in Michigan, and they would leave again in late spring to work their way north again, following the crops. Some 13 years later, after a series of teaching assignments in Houston's inner-city 'white flight' schools, a teaching stint in a small city school system in upstate New York, and considerable work as a Civil Rights activist, I returned to higher education to work on my doctorate in reading education.

My experiences to that point had told me that America was not a classless society; nor was it the melting pot of different cultures that my grade school history texts had led me to believe. Having to move with my family to 'better' neighborhoods, taking refuge in school work when the differences in social circumstances became too painful, teaching children whose schooling was interrupted so families could provide cheap migrant labor, watching white families flee from previously all-white neighborhoods, and participating in the protest movement of the 1960s were evidence enough for me: all was not right with the world. More importantly, these experiences had instilled within me a desire to make the world a better place for everyone.

However, as I look back on my first 10 years in the academy, I can find little evidence that my research and writing were influenced by the social justice issues that continued to occupy my life outside the university. Inside the academy I was a different person. There, I wrote of graphic organizers, schema theory, and comprehension. But the more I inquired into the nature of reading strategies and their effects on students' comprehension of texts (a line of research stemming from my doctoral dissertation), the less satisfied I became with myself, my writing, and the questions that drove each subsequent study. I was searching, but I didn't know for what.

As fate would have it, I met Valerie Walkerdine at a conference held at Mount Holyoke College in the summer of 1991. Although I initially was attracted to her work in *Schoolgirl Fictions* (1990) because of the connections I could make between her working class background and my own, in the end it was her feminist perspective that influenced me the most. *Schoolgirl Fictions*, with its transgressive account of female subjectivity, was my entry into the feminist literature. It was instrumental in my decision to focus on writing gender into reading research, though I did not know it at the time. What I did realize from reading Walkerdine's work and others like her was the immediate application it had for a talk I was preparing to give in front of my peers at the National Reading Conference. It was in preparing for this talk, my presidential address to the NRC audience, that I started to read more broadly in the feminist post-structuralist literature. The paper that resulted from the talk (Alvermann, 1993) questioned our privileged ways of writing and knowing as reading researchers, our hesitancy to share interpretive authority, and the voyeuristic aspects of our research agendas.

Having hit my stride and feeling impassioned once again (as I had in the early days of the 1960s' Civil Rights Movement), I began to focus on the nature of gendered discursive practices (Gilbert, 1989; Mills, 1994; Neilsen, 1994) and their relation to my ongoing study of adolescents' classroom talk about texts. This brings me to the next section of my story and the personal and professional choices I made in deciding to write gender into my research agenda.

Choices I Have Made

Like others before me (Bridges, 1979; Freire, 1968; Lather, 1991), I believed, and continue to believe, that classroom discussion can be a venue for subverting oppressive patterns of discourse and bringing to light the discriminatory practices that make oppression possible in the first place. Although this long-held belief in the subversive possibilities of students' talk about texts — both spoken and written — had prepared me for bell hooks' (1994) 'concept of teaching' to transgress, it was Elizabeth Ellsworth's (1989) work on the repressive myths of critical pedagogy that actually led to my first study on the gendered nature of classroom talk. Finally, the pieces were coming together.

One thing only remained: I needed a rationale for introducing feminist readings into my content literacy course. Because feminist pedagogy is committed to troubling the assumptions that are often taken for granted in our teaching (in order to help us gain insights into practices that have become all but invisible due to their familiarity), I decided to make my own practice, and particularly my role as discussion facilitator in a graduate level literacy course, the site for exploring gendered talk about texts. I believed that studying the give-and-take of such talk would enable both the students and me to appreciate how we position and are positioned by others through the texts we read, write, and talk into being. What I had not foreseen (perhaps because of my naivete in matters related to feminist pedagogy) was how quickly I would be thrust into the role of 'nurturer' or 'caretaker'. I was similarly unprepared for what I learned about myself as I slipped into the role of 'neutral teacher', a position that is untenable among feminist pedagogues (Gore, 1993; Lather, 1991).

In what follows, I provide examples from the self-study that illustrate how my attempts to be inclusive and sensitive to students' needs in my first foray into teaching from a feminist perspective created a struggle laced with self-contradictions. In time, these contradictions led to a fuller understanding of how learning to write gender into reading research is primarily about negotiating power relations.

Interpretive Sources

Setting and Participants

The graduate level course titled Content Literacy, which I taught at the University of Georgia during Spring Quarter of 1994, was designed to teach graduate preservice and inservice teachers in elementary through high school how to motivate *their* students to read and study subject matter texts. In this course, I emphasize the importance of teachers developing an appreciation for students' natural propensity to talk and socially interact with their peers as they learn the content of their subject matter texts. To impress upon the class how seriously I take this socially interactive approach to learning from texts, I devote a large proportion of class time to small- and large-group discussions. Students' final grades also reflect the importance of class participation.

For the first time in the spring of 1994, I introduced feminist perspectives on such traditional topics as reading assessment, ability grouping, and strategy instruction. In introducing them, I relied heavily on a variety of feminist writings, including feminist research, pedagogy, and poetry. All such writings were directly related to the key concepts that I would normally have covered in the course content. With few exceptions, students had not previously been exposed to feminist pedagogy. And, like most of the

Donna E. Alvermann

classes in the College of Education, this class was fairly typical in its composition: 23 females and four males, with all but two (a Taiwanese and a Chinese student) of European American descent.

Researchers' Roles and Procedures

In my dual role as professor and participant observer, I kept a journal and responded in writing to each student's weekly two-page reflections on the course content and the assigned readings. Michelle Commeyras, a colleague in Reading Education, took field notes each time the class met, while Josephine Young, a graduate research assistant, videotaped and later transcribed portions of various class discussions. These primary data sources (my journal, Michelle's field notes, and Josephine's video transcripts) were read and commented on in writing by each member of the research team prior to the weekly analysis sessions. During these sessions, data were triangulated from the researchers' sources, their commentaries, the students' written reflections, and the transcripts that resulted from Michelle's and Josephine's interviews with students in my class. The research meetings themselves were audiotaped and portions were transcribed for use in the ongoing and simultaneous data collection and analysis process.

Findings

In sketching what occurred as a consequence of my efforts to introduce feminist perspectives into the regular course content, I will concentrate on examples involving David Hinson (real name used with his permission). These findings are excerpted from a larger study (Alvermann, 1996; Alvermann et al., 1997) and represent the struggles I encountered as well as the self-contradictions that led eventually to my understanding of how writing gender into reading research entails negotiating relations of power.

One struggle I experienced in Spring Quarter of 1994 as I explored the gendered nature of classroom talk about texts was the self-doubt I felt when class discussions simply reinforced the stereotypes they were designed to critique. For example, when talk in small-group discussions about texts that stereotype men and women prompted some individuals to label others as sexist and their ideas as inconsequential, I had second thoughts about my decision to introduce feminist perspectives into the course. Evidence of this struggle and the degree to which it thrust me into the role of nurturer or caretaker can be found in my numerous references to 'worrying' about one student or another, especially in terms of how these individuals were coping with the assigned readings. For instance, writing about an incident involving David Hinson, I wrote:

> I [am] worried by David's unusual quietness, and . . . whether the topic or the many references to male-dominated Eurocentric [practices] are getting to him. Why do I think that? No tangible evidence, but I guess he has just seemed uncomfortable to me . . . like he is holding something in and that this 'something' would have been volatile if shared. Does anyone else on the research team feel the same way, I wonder. (Journal, 4/13)

When my colleagues and I met the following day for our weekly research meeting, I brought up my concern about David. Josephine noted a similar concern, while Michelle said, 'I didn't notice the frustration level that you are suspecting, but maybe I just wasn't sensitive to it' (Transcript, 4/14). However, portions of a transcript from an earlier interview with David confirmed his growing sense of uneasiness in the class:

> Sometimes I find that when I try to bring what I describe as a dose of reality to the, uh, discussion, that people become uncomfortable with that. I think sometimes the implication is, well, you're the problem, Dave . . . I just think that I am almost put into a situation sometimes where people want me to feel apologetic for the fact that I am white . . . a male . . . [and that] by a lot of standards, I grew up in a fairly privileged environment.

Increasingly, I found myself looking for ways that would signal my neutrality in class discussions. At the time I was not sure why I felt the need to distance myself from such talk. Did I fear coming on too strong? Did I want David and others in the class to view me as a nurturing professor — one who takes care to see that feelings are not hurt and that everyone's voice is heard and respected? Probably. Like Elizabeth Ellsworth (1989), I did not find feminist pedagogy all that empowering, though for different reasons than she has raised. For me, the problem seemed to lie in attempting to straddle the contradictory worlds of feminism and patriarchy. Unlike Hilary Davis's (1992) description of the 'good feminist' (i.e., one who straddles both worlds successfully), I was torn between the two. Although I knew teacher neutrality to be a discursive practice that is at odds with feminist pedagogy, I valued it nonetheless for what I perceived it said about my desire to avoid silencing students, like David, who disagreed with the perspectives I put forth.

In retrospect, I see that by attempting to maintain a neutral stance (e.g., not identifying with a particular position in various class discussions), I had indeed positioned myself — and in a powerful way that involved full use of my authority as teacher. Therein lies the irony, for as Fairclough (1989) would argue, my attempt to downplay my authority as teacher by carving out an impartial or neutral position in class discussions could be interpreted as invoking what he calls 'hidden power'. Simply put, my actions could be construed as disguising and downplaying my authority in order to keep it. By appealing to authority in this way — through the socially sanctioned power relationships that place teachers over students — I came dangerously close to enacting the definition of patriarchy advanced by Lather (1994). This realization has not been lost on me as I continue to think further about what it means to be a feminist teacher.

A New Way of Thinking about Gender/Power

Some fairly ingrained notions about class differences and social injustices, stemming from my early years as a child and extending into my work in the public schools in the 1960s and 1970s, have helped me to understand how gender, like class, is a hierarchical form of power. In coming to view gender in this way, I can appreciate more fully Foucault's (1978/1990) counsel regarding the futility in looking for who has power and who is deprived of it. According to Foucault (1980), the invisibility and pervasiveness of power is exercised *within* the social body rather than *from above it* (p. 39), a development that occurred in the eighteenth century when the power of the sovereign was displaced by a new local form of power. This new form of power, practiced within the social body, 'reaches into the very grain of individuals, touches their bodies and inserts itself into their actions and attitudes, their discourses, learning processes and everyday lives' (p. 39). Increasingly, I see the value of feminist post-structural analyses that expose or lay open patterns in the continual shifts and modifications in gendered power relations. It is through these analyses and similar ones applied to my own research and teaching that I hope to make a difference in the literacy community.

What I Hope to Accomplish

Moving gender as a category of analysis from its current, marginalized status into mainstream literacy research will take the work of many. Although some progress is being made, much remains to be done. How I see myself working toward this larger goal is mainly through three long-term projects that are ongoing and generative in nature. One is the collaborative development of a reading education course with my colleague, Michelle Commeyras. The idea for this course grew partly from our involvement in the College of Education's multicultural initiative. Specifically, the proposed course will engage master's and doctoral level students in exploring the implications of feminist research and theorizing for reading teacher education. It is a course designed for students who are preparing to teach (or already hold teaching positions) in the public/private school sector as well as those who are preparing for positions in higher education. Because this is a new course and the first one ever taught from a feminist perspective in my department, it is likely to generate considerable interest.

A second project expands upon Heath's (1982) concept of what constitutes a literacy event and speaks to my growing interest in exploring the idea that gender is primarily about relations of power. The project involves young adolescents enrolled in a voluntary out-of-school book club that meets weekly at the local library. These adolescents, who come from culturally and economically diverse backgrounds, also keep a daily log of their out-of-school literacy activities. The library setting is an ideal site for observing how, as teenagers, they take up, adapt, and/or resist certain social and gendered discursive practices that enable them to be recognized as members of their particular peer cultures. By exploring how diverse social and cultural practices, including gender, shape and are shaped by the texts that adolescents read, I hope to be able to elaborate upon what Scott (1990) refers to as the 'hidden transcripts' of group interactions. It is my goal to analyze adolescents' gendered talk about texts using Scott's strategy for uncovering the contradictions, tensions, and possibilities inherent in the hidden transcripts by comparing them to the public transcripts.

A third project involves a national survey of 500 literacy professionals in higher education who are engaged in mentoring relationships with master's and doctoral level students. Responses to the mailed survey will be analyzed for descriptive purposes and for insight into which individuals are interested in becoming part of five on-site case studies. The on-site studies will include interviews with the mentor and participating graduate student as well as a shadowing component. The purpose for shadowing the mentor and mentee will be to write a detailed log-narrative of the two people's interactions over a three-day period. This narrative will be used to provide a context in which to interpret the interviews and written survey responses. What I hope to learn from this inquiry into mentoring in the academy is how gendered relations of power influence the capacity for interdependence between reading education mentors and their graduate students.

If my expectations for these three projects are met and their results shared through publications read by those in the literacy community, I will have made some small degree of progress toward my goal of writing gender into reading research. I will also, no doubt, have increased my understanding along the way of how relations of power are negotiated in students' gendered talk about texts. Knowing this is important to me for reasons that extend beyond the academy and my role in it as researcher and writer. For I believe it is critical that we not dismiss students' gendered positionings of each other in their talk about texts as 'natural' or 'just the way things are'. More is at stake than simply an essentialized view of adolescent male and female behaviors. Exercises in power relations spill over to society at large and affect how men and women deal with one another throughout their lives — in political and economic, as well as social, ways.

Note

1 It is impossible to use 'gender' as a term without also addressing its relation to 'sex'. Although some would argue for using the two terms synonymously, Miller and Swift (1991) object. They contend that any such common usage would mistakenly blur what is a biological given with a condition that is socially induced. According to *The Oxford English Dictionary* (Simpson and Weiner, 1989), gender is the appropriate term to use when the intention is 'to emphasize the social and cultural, as opposed to the biological, distinctions between the sexes' (p. 428). Those who take exception to this view (e.g., post-structuralist feminists such as Butler, 1990; Davies, 1993; Weedon, 1987) theorize gender as a discursive practice rather than as a biological given or a social construction.

References

ALVERMANN, D.E. (1993) 'Researching the literal: Of muted voices, second texts, and cultural representations', in LEU, D.J. and KINZER, C.K. (eds) *Examining Central Issues in Literacy Research, Theory, and Practice*, Chicago, IL: National Reading Conference, pp. 1–10.

ALVERMANN, D.E. (1994, April) 'Feminist scholarship and the language of literacy', Paper presented at the annual meeting of the American Educational Research Association, New Orleans, LA.

ALVERMANN, D.E. (1996) 'Introducing feminist perspectives in a content literacy course: Struggles and self-contradictions', in LEU, D.J., KINZER, C.K. and HINCHMAN, K.A. (eds) *Literacies for the 21st Century: Research and Practice*, Chicago, IL: National Reading Conference, pp. 124–33.

ALVERMANN, D.E., COMMEYRAS, M., YOUNG, J.P., RANDALL, S. and HINSON, D. (1997) 'Interrupting gendered discursive practices in classroom talk about texts: Easy to think about, difficult to do', *Journal of Literacy Research*, **29**, pp. 73–104.

BALDWIN, R.S., READENCE, J.E., SCHUMM, J.S., KONOPAK, J.P., KONOPAK, B.C. and KLINGNER, J.K. (1992) 'Forty years of NRC publications: 1952–1991', *Journal of Reading Behavior*, **24**, pp. 505–32.

BARR, R., KAMIL, M.L., MOSENTHAL, P. and PEARSON, P.D. (1991) *Handbook of Reading Research: Volume II*, New York: Longman.

BRIDGES, D. (1979) *Education, Democracy and Discussion*, London: National Foundation for Educational Research Publishing Company.

BUTLER, J. (1990) *Gender Trouble*, New York: Routledge.

DAVIES, B. (1993) *Shards of Glass: Children Reading and Writing Beyond Gendered Identities*, Cresskill, NJ: Hampton Press.

DAVIS, H.E. (1992) 'The tyranny of resistance, or the compulsion to be a "good feminist"', in BUCHMANN, M. and FLODEN, R.E. (eds) *Philosophy in Education 1991*, Urbana, IL: Philosophy of Education Society, pp. 76–86.

ELLSWORTH, E. (1989) 'Why doesn't this feel empowering?: Working through the repressive myths of critical pedagogy', *Harvard Educational Review*, **59**, pp. 297–324.

FAIRCLOUGH, N. (1989) *Language and Power*, London: Longman.

FINDERS, M.J. (1996a) '"Just girls": Literacy and allegiance in junior high school', *Written Communication*, **13**, 1, pp. 93–129.

FINDERS, M.J. (1996b) 'Queens and teen zines: Early adolescent females reading their way toward adulthood', *Anthropology and Education Quarterly*, **27**, 1, pp. 1–19.

FOUCAULT, M. (1978/1990) *The History of Sexuality: An Introduction* (Vol. 1) (HURLEY, R. Trans.), New York: Vintage Books.

FOUCAULT, M. (1980) 'Prison talk', in GORDON, C. (ed.) *Power/knowledge: Selected Interviews and Other Writings 1972–1977*, New York: Pantheon Books, pp. 37–54.

FREIRE, P. (1968) *Pedagogy of the Oppressed*, New York: Seabury Press.

GILBERT, P. (1989) 'Personally (and passively) yours: Girls, literacy and education', *Oxford Review of Education*, **15**, pp. 257–65.

GILBERT, P. (1993) 'Narrative as gendered social practice: In search of different story lines for language research', *Linguistics and Education*, **5**, pp. 211–18.

GORE, J. (1993) *The Struggle for Pedagogies: Critical and Feminist Discourses As Regimes of Truth*, New York: Routledge.

HEATH, S.B. (1982) 'Protean shapes in literacy events: Ever shifting oral and literate traditions', in TANNEN, D. (ed.) *Spoken and Written Language: Exploring Orality and Literacy* (*Advances in Discourse Processes*, **9**, pp. 91–117), Norwood, NJ: Ablex.

hooks, b. (1994) *Teaching to Transgress: Education as the Practice of Freedom*, New York: Routledge.

LATHER, P. (1991) *Getting Smart*, New York: Routledge.

LATHER, P. (1994) 'The absent presence: Patriarchy, capitalism, and the nature of teacher work', in STONE, L. (ed.) *The Education Feminism Reader*, New York: Routledge, pp. 242–51.

MILLER, C. and SWIFT, K. (1991) *Words and Women*, New York: Harper Collins.

MILLS, S. (1994) *Gendering the Reader*, New York: Harvester Wheatsheaf.

NEILSEN, L. (1994) 'Women, literacy, and agency: Beyond the master narratives', *Atlantis*, **18**, 1, 2, pp. 177–89.

ORELLANA, M. (1995) 'Literacy as a gendered social practice: Tasks, texts, talk, and take-up', *Reading Research Quarterly*, **30**, pp. 674–708.

PATTERSON, A. (1995) 'Reading research methodology and the Reading Research Quarterly: A question of gender', *Reading Research Quarterly*, **30**, pp. 290–8.

PEARSON, P.D., BARR, R., KAMIL, M.L. and MOSENTHAL, P. (1984) *Handbook of Reading Research*, New York: Longman.

RUDDELL, R., RUDDELL, M. and SINGER, H. (eds) (1994) *Theoretical Models and Processes of Reading* (4th ed.), Newark, DE: International Reading Association.

SCOTT, J.C. (1990) *Domination and the Arts of Resistance*, New Haven, CT: Yale University Press.

SIMPSON, J.A. and WEINER, E.S.C. (1989) *The Oxford English Dictionary* (2nd ed., vol. VI), Oxford, England: Clarendon.

SINGER, H. and RUDDELL, R. (eds) (1985) *Theoretical Models and Processes of Reading* (3rd ed.), Newark, DE: International Reading Association.

WALKERDINE, V. (1990) *Schoolgirl Fictions*, London: Verso.

WEEDON, C. (1987) *Feminist Practice and Poststructuralist Theory*, Cambridge, MA: Blackwell.

7   Narrating My Life

Mary Louise Gomez

Aunt Stella Lavin's, Winter 1958

Smoke swirls towards the ceiling, enveloping lights and what appear to be the disembodied heads of my aunts and uncles. Their voices are loud, cascading in intensity as
the speakers move swiftly between Spanish and English, from one dispute to another.
Aunt Stella can be heard above the others, rebuking one of her brothers who has dared
to question her views about something. On a formica table in one corner of the room,
amidst bottles of red wine, ginger ale, and plates of cookies lie the remains of a large
platter of *arroz con pollo*.

Janie and I alternate between forays into the crowded kitchen to snatch a treat and
the relative serenity of the folds of our mother's skirt in the adjacent living room. By
10, a few others escape the din of the kitchen and join us in the living room. Uncle
Pepe, Stella's husband, enters silently, sipping his wine, and seats himself next to Mrs
Canas, my Aunt Susie's widowed mother from Mexico City — who has lived with Susie
and my Uncle Fernando and their children for as long as I can remember. They speak
softly in Spanish, shrugging their shoulders in resignation at the length and intensity of
the kitchen conversations. They know, as I do, that resolution is neither a goal nor an
outcome of these frequent noisy gatherings. The argument is process and product,
participation the goal. Acknowledging my mother's presence, Mrs Canas and Pepe
switch to English, and ask about us. How do we like our teachers? Have we made a list
for Santa? Our yawned replies highlight the late hour, and we are sent to the kitchen to
find our father — still in the thick of the shouting — and tell him it is time to go home.

Grandma and Grandpa Butler's, Christmas Day, 1958

It is nearly 5 and we have been promised that soon the gifts will be distributed. Throughout the day, Janie and I conduct a self-appointed vigil over the piles of gaily wrapped
packages lying beneath the evergreen boughs. Seated together on the sofa, we can hear
Grandma, Auntie Dottie, and Mother as they clear the starched cloth, crystal glasses, and
the special ivy-decorated plates rimmed with gold from the table. Grandpa and Uncle
Jimmie sit together in the den, watching Ed Sullivan. Daddy snores in an upholstered
chair that straddles the border between living room and den, his back to the television
and its viewers. Our cousin Debbie whispers on the hallway telephone, sharing confid-
ences with one of her friends back in Boston. We wait and wait. At last, everyone gathers
and Grandma tells Janie that she may select a package to distribute. All — except
Daddy who determinedly dozes — observe and comment as each gift is unwrapped,
opened, and passed about for compliments. Hours later, we gather our gifts for the short
ride home.

Mary Louise Gomez

Clifford Geertz (1995) writes that we cannot understand the history of communities as chronicles in which one event follows another, resulting over time with peace and prosperity in one place and social and economic turbulence in another. Rather, we much consider 'how particular events and unique occasions, an encounter here, a development there, can be woven together with a variety of facts and a battery of interpretations to produce a sense of how things go, have been going, and are likely to go' (p. 3). So, too, must we consider lives. Neither the history of a particular community nor of one individual's life is additive. Rather, I suggest, lives are like the communities of Pare and Sefrou which Geertz studied at various times over the past 30 years. These towns, he writes, always felt as though 'all the really critical things seem just to have happened yesterday and just about to happen tomorrow, [inducing] an uncomfortable sense of having come too late and arrived too early . . .' (p. 2). Geertz concluded that he could not create a text defining these communities as developing in a series of linear and causally-linked events. He writes: 'Change, apparently, is not a parade that can be watched as it passes' (p. 2).

Like Geertz reflecting on visits to two communities over time, individuals can look back and attempt to create a seamless narrative of how we have come to be as we are. In attempting to do so, I have come to understand there is no seamless story to tell, no unitary subject, no bounded, coherent whole to describe and to trace in my becoming. Rather, I see my project as actively seeking my 'fragmented self' (Kondo, 1990, p. 6) that has evolved in relation to the multiple shifting contexts in which I have lived. Toward that end, I present for myself and my readers stories from my past — particular events and unique occasions — and weave these together to develop a portrait of how I came to be involved in education for equity and social justice.

Childhood Memories

In the vignettes with which I begin this text, I contrast two scenes from my childhood. I could say that both stories are 'true' in that I recall these as lived moments in time. Whatever their origins — whether or not these are 'verifiable' experiences in which I participated, these stories are emblematic of the contradictions that I keenly felt between my mother's and my father's families throughout my girlhood. I came to see these contradictions, even as a child, as embodied within me — as alternate ways of being from which I must choose in relation to how I named myself, what I valued, and how I behaved.

As a child, my sister Janie and I often negotiated such terrains of difference in a single day as we ate holiday dinners at Grandma and Grandpa Butler's and drove across town for the evening to Aunt Carmen's, or to the next town to Aunt Stella's and Uncle Pepe's, for coffees, ginger ales made pink with dollops of red wine, and honey-coated pastries. In each place, we were expected to be quiet and 'ladylike' — which meant sitting carefully on a special, not-to-be-sat-on-every-day living room sofa and not spilling anything on it or on our finest — often matching — homemade dresses.

Adults, however, behaved differently on quiet, shady Vine Street where the Butler's lived than on Charles Street, the steep, almost-impassable-in-icy-winters hill where Aunt Carmen's small duplex perched. On Vine, the Butlers maintained a code of politeness that imbued every action and request with portent. Did you ask nicely for the homemade cookies Grandma kept in the jar on her counter? Were your hands washed? Were you quiet playing ball in the yard so that you did not disturb the Lizzari's next door? After dinner, we all retired to the smaller of the two living rooms to watch — in silence — *Gunsmoke* or *Ed Sullivan*, or if it was Saturday night — the wrestling matches featuring Gorgeous George with his exotic bleached hair and gold lame jumpsuit.

On Charles Street, in Aunt Carmen's tiny house, or at Aunt Stella's a few miles away, adults talked loudly and a lot. Politics, sports, the terrible, long Vermont winters, the behavior of neighbors — all were grist for commentary and contestation in English and in Spanish. Food and drink were abundant. Platters of *arroz con pollo*, mounds of *mostaciolli* from the Italian in-laws, pineapple-upside-down cakes, and glass plates loaded with cookies and candies were set out on ancient lace tablecloths as a continuing feast. From a child's eye view, these seemed mystically replenished as quickly as they were consumed. Eating was encouraged. One's empty plate indicated a lack of appreciation for the bounty to which we were privileged or worse — disrespect for the women who had prepared the meal. Other than children, the only persons who were ever seated for any length of time were either very old or were mothers of toddlers whose offspring nestled in their laps. Conversational and eating groups fluidly formed and reformed during each occasion. For these grown-ups, being together was a participative, rather than spectator occasion. My memories of the holiday celebrations of the Butler and Gomez families contrast in size of the gathering, sounds, colors, smells, and movement.

The Butler gatherings were not only quiet, but were nearly always small as my mother had two brothers, both of whom were involved in the hotel management business in other states. One of my mother's brothers faithfully traveled to Vermont from his home in Boston with his wife and daughter each Christmas, Easter, and for two weeks each summer. The other brother and his wife and three children moved to many different places around the United States and rarely returned to New England. So, the Butler holidays were nearly always composed of my grandparents, parents, my sister and I, and my uncle, aunt, and cousin. Most often our get-togethers took place at my grandparents' house where we ate frankfurters, baked beans, and steamed brown bread cut with a string in the winter and shelled beans, corn on the cob, and other fresh vegetables at a backyard picnic table in the summer. My Grandma Butler was a wonderful New England cook; her house often smelled of freshly baked breads, home canned pickles, and sugary cookies. We felt special at Grandma's and Grandpa's as they were always delighted to see us — the only grandchildren who lived in proximity to them.

The Gomez parties were often large and raucous as my father had eight brothers and sisters — four of whom had remained in Vermont to work as secretaries, salesmen, and craftsmen in various industries. They were frequent guests in one another's homes as their social lives revolved around family and extended family relationships. In addition, two of my father's siblings and their spouses and children came home to Vermont each summer from suburban Detroit where they worked in the auto industry. Almost everything was a cause for celebration — each Christian religious holiday, many Saturday evenings, the occasion of an aunt's or uncle's return from Michigan, or a warm summer day called for a dinner of the ubiquitous *arroz con pollo*, a 'cookout' of hot dogs and hamburgers, or a picnic at a nearby lake. Everywhere were adults and children, talking, running, cooking, eating. Each family contributed a dish to share, so to this day I cannot recall any specialties of a particular aunt except that of my Aunt Carmen — who as the oldest child and in the absence of her long-deceased parents — always made the chicken with rice. Janie and I were two of about a dozen children at every outing and I recall my mother frequently scanning the crowd and calling to us to ascertain our safety and place in it.

All of these memories are of a childhood rich in love and family experiences as well as of contrasts in the ways these were offered to me. I recognize that differences such as I describe here do not necessarily foretell a future conflict of identity, or to careers focused in concerns for social justice and equity in schooling. Nor do such experiences lead to inquiry into the ways that the stories we tell and those that are told about us shape our expectations and possibilities as teachers and students.

However, it was not only the cultural differences between these groups of my relations that has led me to choose a particular pathway for my life. Rather, it has been the rarely explicit, yet ever present tensions between these groups of people that guided me to think, at an early age, about language background, social class, and ethnicity. For my sister and I not only negotiated a difference of physical geography in our visits to each place. We also negotiated a landscape of decades-old prejudice and misunderstanding.

Table Settings, and More

The tensions between the two sides of our family were at least a decade old before my sister and I were able to discern them. Even as we began to appreciate that there were not only differences but stresses as well between the Butlers and Gomezes, Janie and I did not speak of what we comprehended. Rather, we watched in bewilderment as these tensions were played out around and through us.

I now appreciate that the sources of stress between the family of Josefa Lavin and Joaquin Gomez and that of Mildred May Mullally and James Thomas Butler were grounded in their social class positions, as well as their ethnic, religious, and language backgrounds. My particular understandings of the social class differences between my parents' families are rooted in the images of two dining tables. One of these tables I have only heard about through my father's and mother's stories of it; the other I helped to set on many occasions during my childhood.

My father told Janie and me many stories of his life at supper time when we were growing up. I think that he did so because he liked to tell stories and because he wanted us to appreciate who he was and where he had come from. His own parents were not around to do this job as both were deceased. My Grandfather Gomez had died when my father was about 14. Joaquin Gomez was a victim of silicosis — the lung disease that many granite craftsmen contracted as a result of long hours in the unfiltered, particle-laden air of granite 'sheds' — places where they carved monuments from stone. My Grandmother Gomez died in her 60s — the year I was born, crippled from arthritis and worn out from raising so many children alone.

One image from my Father's stories that I recall as though I had been there myself was of dinner time at his home. He teased us with it when Janie and I were small and reluctant to eat our dinner. He would say, 'There were so many of us at my house that that platter would come around just once and not a crumb would be left after it went around the table. You only got one chance! *You* would starve if you lived on *our* street!' My image of those meals is enhanced by my Mother's recall of similar dinners served to her at my Grandmother Gomez's house when she and my father were courting. She would laugh and say Dad's story was true. She seemed, even in recollection, surprised by how swiftly everything had moved at those meals and by the numbers of diners all seated together. She also recalled for us that our Grandmother Gomez made wonderful soup, that there was always a lot of it, and that 'not one plate or dish matched' on the table on any night she was there.

The other table of my memory is the one I sometimes helped my Grandma Butler set before we would go to bed when I stayed overnight at her house. My Grandpa Butler had owned a lumber yard — and lost it — during the Depression and afterwards, he worked at another yard until his retirement at age 70. He rose at dawn each morning to be the first there and he and my Grandmother dined together at a beautifully set table each morning before he set off. I think this nightly table-setting lives in my memory because it shows the care my Grandma Butler took with small things like putting everything out for the next morning, arranging the china and silverware just so, and because it shows the rituals that defined her life. Perhaps I also recall this table and its careful setting because it contrasts with the stories my father told us about his family's table and its diners.

The differences between these families were not only variations in living as they have played out for me over my childhood. They also came to signify a preferred way of living — a quiet, more genteel, and orderly way rather than one more uncertain and noisy. How did this happen? Through piecing together snippets of conversation overheard from aunts, uncles, cousins, and from my Father, Janie and I came to know that my Grandparents Butler, and in particular, my mother's brothers, had opposed our parents' marriage. They saw my father's economic prospects — someone who in his 30s worked as a bartender and short order cook, and still helped to support his mother — as dim. They interpreted his sometimes mangled agreement of nouns and verbs in English — his second or third language after Spanish and some Italian and French, as signifying poor social prospects as well.

It is hard to grow up understanding that your mother's family looked down upon your father and his kin. It is hard to grow up wondering if something was wrong with your father and his family. I often asked myself: Why would some of the people I loved not think the others were 'good enough?' They seemed 'good enough' to me. Was there something really 'wrong' that I had not yet figured out? Maybe all that yelling and eating and drinking were bad. Maybe being quieter and always eating sitting down around a table with nice plates and never talking loudly was better. These questions dogged me. They found me when I least expected to ponder replies. Although I did not have the words then to name what they were doing, I now see how early in my life who I was and who I wished to be — my identity — was called into question.

At one time or another during my childhood and adolescence, I consciously chose to identify with one family group or other. For a time as an early teen, I especially did not want to go to those noisy Gomez parties. Trying to be invisible as a teenager was difficult in that company. Later, I found both the strictures of the Butlers and my Father's 'old fashioned, Old World' approach to the safekeeping of teenaged daughters to be equally oppressive and I avoided questions of identity — other than who I was in relation to my peers — who did not seem to have these conflicts and did not appear to care about mine.

Becoming, Away from Home

At 18, I left home to attend a nearby university. It was 1968. Suddenly, everyone seemed to be asking who *they* were and who *you* were. I met young women from the Bronx and from Darien — women who had fought for their place at the university from large, urban public schools and those who had graduated from Miss Porter's. I lived with women whose summers meant waitressing and saving for the next semester and others who lounged on sailboats off the coast of Newport. During those years, I switched my major from sociology to social work and then to political science where I was asked who I was, but only in relation to sweeping moments in time and space in which the 'people' were homogenized.

In the relative anonymity of campus life in the late 1960s when there were so many big questions about civil rights, women's roles, and US foreign policy, I sought solace from questions of my own identity posed as polar choices between genteel New England lady and Hispanic womanhood. Perhaps I could just become someone else all together. If I wore navy blue Pappagallo flats with lime or pink trim, could I 'pass' for one of those private school graduates who wore their insouciance as badges of their privilege? Or, should it be bell bottoms and a ragged t-shirt *sans* bra — to designate my fresh social and political alliances? The Butlers and Gomezes seemed far away as I struggled to cloak myself in a new persona. No one need know where I came from or who I had been — not even myself.

In my junior year, in what I now see as the ultimate act of hiding in plain sight, I married a graduating senior with many academic and social awards, years of graduate school ahead, and an upper class pedigree. In dropping out of school and marrying, I could remake myself. I would wed an identity and avoid difficult choices. This did not last.

Becoming a Teacher

My personal questions returned to haunt me when, newly married and in my 20s, I began to work towards a teaching certificate and a master's degree. For three semesters, I was assigned to various practica and student teaching in Black River, Vermont — a small community where the textile mills had closed, yet the workers and families had stayed on, in poverty.[1] I worked in one kindergarten through grade five school where I taught many children whose grandparents had once been employed in the mills, but whose family fortunes were depleted.

In Black River, I thought I had 'found my calling'. I felt needed and appreciated by children whose lives were visibly difficult. Many wore ragged, soiled clothes and lacked the mittens and hats and scarves that freezing Vermont winters demanded. Several looked perilously thin and had runny noses nearly every day from September through June. Many lived with their siblings and mothers in small rundown apartment buildings by the railroad tracks a block or two from school. Some children had parents who were jailed; many lived in families in desperate social and economic circumstances. My recollections of my Black River children are 22-years-old now. Yet, I still can see their faces, pinched and pink in the cold, running and tumbling into school where the big old radiators hissed away the chill and steamed us dry each morning.

All that year, from fall through the rugged winter to the puddles and mud of a New England spring, I asked myself and everyone I encountered: How can we allow children to live without adequate food and warm housing? How can we ignore the difficulties in which they live and go on about our daily lives? What can one person do? At Christmas time, I made a scene at Grandma Butler's when my aunt and uncle from Boston presented their second-grade grandson a television set for his bedroom. I left my grandparents' Christmas party in tears, thinking about my children in Black River, whose mothers had lined the sidewalks the day that school was out, hoping that they might be one of the lucky recipients of an abandoned classroom tree for their children's celebration.

I could not reconcile the piles of gifts at Grandma's with the bleak holidays facing so many of the children for whom I cared. I asked myself: What did it mean to be their teacher? What kind of person was I — someone who became upset because some other child received a television, yet who did nothing else in particular to make their lives better? How could I act for them? What should I do? And, were these children in some ways like my father and his siblings when they were growing up? My father had been a 'five-year man' in high school and many of his brothers and sisters had dropped out of school shortly after eighth grade to help support my grandmother and one another. Would that also be the fate of the children in my first grade class? What did it mean for my teaching that my father and my aunts and uncles had also lived in poverty?

The only answers I could locate to my questions, either in myself, in the pedagogy of my teacher education program, or in the teaching of other school staff was to create curricula that were child- and activity-oriented. For me, this meant creating literacy and mathematics pedagogy grounded in real books rather than basal readers, in writing lessons that connected children's classroom interests and activities with what they wrote about, and with counting, adding, and subtracting practices supported by manipulatives and problems we created together.

The children in the three primary classes I taught were eager students. They liked me and I liked them. Each day, I read aloud from beautifully illustrated books. Together, we cut and pasted, colored and painted. We made puppets and imagined they spoke to one another and to us. We wrote stories and poems about our cooking and crafts and the trips we took. We counted macaroni, dyed it, strung it, wore it jangling in ropes around our necks. We celebrated every holiday with food and decorations that we made together. We had a grand time. My teaching practices were praised. My answers seemed like good ones — children were happy in school and they learned when the curriculum was exciting and child-centered, when children were 'knowledge-makers'. I could not, for the most part, alter these children's material, every day, sometimes frightening circumstances, but I could make their classroom a wonderful and safe place to be.

During my final student teaching semester in the program, I also became a foster parent to David, a Canadian Indian child in my first-grade class. David's mother was sometimes unable to care for him, and late one Friday afternoon when she was hospitalized in an emergency, the state social services department placed David with me and my husband, Jim. What at first looked like a short-term visit became one of many months and Jim and I settled into new routines that included making snowmen and giving bubble baths.

I set about creating a good albeit (from my perspective) somewhat unconventional home for David. We rode to and from school together, and on the nights I was enrolled in graduate classes, he came along, coloring and playing with trucks in my office, adjacent to the classroom in which I was both a student and teaching assistant. My husband also was enrolled in a demanding graduate program and was infrequently home until late at night. So, my two dogs, and David and I spent our out-of-school time together, taking long walks, playing in the snow, and sleeping as much as possible given our schedules. The dogs, unused to sharing my attentions with another small living creature, frequently met David's good mornings with growls. Yet, by the time toast crumbs fell from David's hands at the breakfast table, both devotedly lay by his feet.

In the late spring, just before Jim and I were to be awarded our graduate degrees, David's social worker called to say that his mother was well enough to care for him. We were sad, yet reconciled to returning David to his mother. David would stay in Vermont. We had new jobs in the Midwest. We drove away and out of David's life.

I would have my own classroom in Iowa. I would try to apply what I had learned in Black River to new children. I did not want to think about David or his classmates as it was painful and worrisome. I buried myself in my new job and its responsibilities and did not write or call David. It had been a painful leave-taking, and I neither wanted to consider the ethics or the efficacy of my teaching nor to think about how deeply I missed one particular child.

Telling Stories about Myself

I confess that I do not know what happened to David and his classmates. It was not until many years later that I witnessed (Felman and Laub, 1992) my time with these children. By then, I was a graduate student again, working on a doctorate in literacy education. Two of my mentors, Bob Tabachnick and Ken Zeichner (Tabachnick and Zeichner, 1991), asked me to write about my teaching of a course in the elementary education program in which we all taught. They asked me to tell how and why I taught a class in Teaching Language Arts in the Elementary School that required students to read narratives of diverse people's literacy learning experiences. In trying to tell prospective readers why I believed that understanding other people's experiences as well as our own was important, I had to remember and reconsider my teaching in Black River, where I first experienced in a classroom setting the confusion of not knowing or understanding the lives of many children and their families.

In writing the chapter for Bob's and Ken's book, I began to see how stories of my teaching were bound up in a search for my identity as a person, as a teacher. I began to see how the various tales I told at different times of my life concerning the same events were like costumes worn for different roles in which I was engaged at the time. Or as Grumet (1991) suggests, stories are 'the masks through which we can be seen, and with every telling we stop the flood and swirl of thought so someone can get a glimpse of us, and maybe catch us if they can' (p. 69). The language of each story I told embodied the discourses, the ideas, available to me at the time. Each story or construction of events was what was possible for me to imagine and understand at the time the tale was told. I saw that none were lies; all were fictions.

In writing and reflecting on my parenting of David, I saw that my caring for him replicated in many ways my classroom practices. I wanted David's childhood and those of his peers to be more like images I carried from my own. At home, each evening, I had fed David hearty, warm meals; I read him bedtime stories. I bought him knitted caps, mittens, and a warm coat, and on weekends, we often drove the 40 miles to my parents' house where we went sledding. At school, we created plays, counted mounds of manipulatives, and baked for every occasion. The classroom my cooperating teacher and I created was a refuge from the world outside of Black River School just as the home I tried to create for David was a sanctuary from the social and economic difficulties he faced with his mother and younger brother.

In each place, I failed to ask: Who are these children and how can I connect my curriculum and instruction to their outside of school interests and lives? Nor did I wonder: How is my caring for David at home or for the group of children in my classroom — connected to their families, their hopes and dreams? Rather, I was what King (1991) calls 'dysconscious' — engaged in an uncritical habit of mind in which ethical judgments about the world and the way it works are made without attention to how the social order is constructed and maintained. At that time, I did not have the words nor the ideas that would have enabled me to critique my practices. So, I suppressed questions about who these children were and how they came to be so. I silenced my personal queries and without a backwards glance, created a vision of myself as savior, a genteel teacher who would help children living in poverty by remaking them into my image of middle-class youngsters.

In my quest to understand and articulate for readers why I taught in the ways I did, I came to new understandings of myself as a young teacher. I found that in telling to myself and my imagined audiences how and why I taught in particular ways, I could see myself anew. I could reorganize my experiences in new ways, making my life history unstable. Simultaneously, I could craft new meanings for who I had been and who I was becoming with the understandings available to me a decade after I taught in Black River (Rosenwald, 1992). I recognized in telling stories to myself and imagined others that I could explore what Kondo (1990, p. 29) calls the 'plethora of available I's' of which we are composed as individuals and how the contexts in which we live and work shape these.

What Now?

Today, I recognize that, as Rosenwald argues (1992): 'Not only does the past live in the present, but it also appears different at every new turn we take' (p. 275). In writing about my teaching two decades earlier (Gomez, 1991; Gomez and Tabachnick, 1991), I have found a way to reconsider my pedagogy and myself. In retelling the stories of my time with David and his classmates, I have also found a way to testify about my own confusions of identity, how these stalked me for more than 30 years, and the ways in which storytelling about my teaching has enabled me to reconcile my uncertainties about a fixed and static self who embodies one set of seemingly polar characteristics or another.

I do not wish to offer the impression that the question of who I am is neatly, tidily, or permanently resolved. I believe, with Kondo (1990) and Narayan (1991, 1995) that the social, historical, and cultural contexts in which we find or locate ourselves play a large role in shaping how which of the 'available I's' in which we live are showcased at any particular moment. As Shotter (1989) has written:

> In other words, in this view, people are not eternal, unchanging entities in themselves (like isolated, indistinguishable atoms), but owe what stability and constancy, and uniqueness, they may appear to have — their identity — to the stability and constancy of certain aspects of the activities, practices, and procedures in which they can make their differences from those around them known and accountable. The aspects in question are those in which, like the authoring of a text, we shape, pattern, and develop, in moment-by-moment changes, as new contingencies arise, the differing relations between our own 'position' or 'place' (who we are), and the positions of those around us. . . . [This is a] concern with the way in which an audience (either a singular or plural 'you') affords, permits, motivates, allows or invites *only a limited* performance upon the part of first-persons. I act not simply 'out of' my own plans and desires, unrestricted by the social circumstances of my performances, but in some sense also 'in to' the opportunities offered me to act . . . (pp. 143–4)

For me, Shotter's words highlight the dialogic relationship between the teller of stories and her audiences. In Black River, stories of my teaching and of my relationship with David were received and shaped in certain ways due to the historical, geographical, and social contexts in which I was located. The audiences for my stories enabled me to develop particular pictures of my practices and did not assist me in imagining others. The audiences for my stories were at once listeners to my tales as well as affirmers of them. As Rosenwald (1992) has written:

> Personal accounts may communicate a speaker's beliefs and commitments to others. They may also reflect these back to the speaker and thereby add to his or her conviction. In this way, accounts bind individuals to the arrangements of the society enforcing the models, whether the accounts feature circumscribed reactions to situations or an entire life course. The political and other arrangements typical of a society are implicated in the conventions of discourse. These arrangements come to be seen as natural and inevitable to the extent that the conventions allow us to communicate (Berger and Luckmann, 1966). Furthermore, these arrangements are renewed and strengthened each time they become manifest in a narrative. (p. 265)

Thus, in recent years, I have aligned myself with people working towards social change. My work reflects my personal beliefs and commitments as well as those of the persons with whom I work and those of the persons with whom I worship. To use Rosenberg's words, the 'arrangements' of my life at work and at home become renewed and strengthened as I labor with like-minded others for equity in schooling and social justice in the world at-large. In conducting action for social change, I also proudly reclaim myself as an Hispanic woman, allying myself with the Gomezes and our kin in Cuba, Mexico, and Spain. I understand that I need not so clearly identify myself with my father's family in order to work for social change benefitting marginalized children and families in the United States. However, what I see this alliance offering me is a means by which to affiliate with those persons and that part of myself demeaned in my childhood memories.

In large part, I attribute this shift in and affirmation of my identity to working here at the University of Wisconsin-Madison where questions of race, class, gender, and sexual orientation and their relations to curriculum and instruction are central to my own and many of my valued colleagues' teaching, service, and research. More recently, I also have become a member of a religious community where action against racism, poverty, and homophobia are central to the mission of the group. The Department of Curriculum and Instruction at UW-Madison as well as my church, then, create social and cultural contexts for my continuing consideration of self that intersects with my professional concerns as a teacher and teacher educator and with my personal concerns as a woman — mother, daughter, wife, and friend. And so, in multiple places, my words and ideas are, as Grumet (1991) suggests, returned to me as the teller in a way 'that is both [mine] and not [mine], that contains [me] in good company' (p. 70).

Stories for Teaching

In these few words, Madeleine Grumet encapsulates my hopes for developing teaching stories as a way for prospective and practicing teachers to reconsider our actions and the grounds on which we have developed these. The goal for this work is that our discourses and our actions will be reflected to us in ways that simultaneously affirm our good intentions and problematize our pedagogy. In the past several years at UW-Madison, I and colleagues (Gomez and Tabachnick, 1991; Abt-Perkins and Gomez, 1993; Gomez and Abt-Perkins, 1995; Gomez, 1996; Gomez, in press) have asked ourselves and teachers at various places in their careers to tell stories about our teaching and its outcomes and to receive responses to these from trusted others.

For the most part, we have worked with prospective teachers who form a cohort group and labor together in classes on campus and in practica in local schools for a period of three semesters or more. The groups meet weekly over the course of their program for seminars that are designed to link and challenge the campus and classroom experiences. The prospective teachers are asked, with the leadership of a faculty member, to tell and critique stories of their classroom experiences to one another. Through telling and responding to these, the teachers explore how and why they create curricula, craft practices, and develop relationships with students. They examine together which children benefitted from their teaching, which ones did not, and why these outcomes were achieved. They reconsider and replan how to reach all learners. They attempt to understand why they feel, think, and act as they do with various children. Through listening to and questioning themselves and one another, they try to imagine and carry out teaching that is academically challenging, socially just, and equitable for all learners.

Critical to the teachers' seminar storytelling is a sense of community and trust developed over time and across various occasions of working together. As a group, we learn to listen to ourselves puzzle through, despair over, and sometimes celebrate our work with children in the good company we have formed. Most often, there are no 'correct' or easy answers to the questions we pose for ourselves and one another. Rather, we offer members of the group time to think through our teaching and the grounds on which it stands. We offer multiple lenses through which our actions and their outcomes can be interpreted as well as multiple strategies for how we might revise our teaching. We offer one another support for the continual re-examination of our pedagogy. As my colleagues at the university and the members of my religious community provide me with a place to tell stories and receive critique and support about myself and my teaching, peers in the cohort group serve similar functions for one another.

For my students, for the children and adolescents whom they will teach, as well as for myself, I hope and plan for continuing opportunities to tell our stories in the service of creating a more just world for all people. In telling stories about my childhood and my adulthood as a teacher here, I have found a way to heal some wounds, to reconsider who I am and how I came to be so, and to articulate the power of our words and the words of those with whom we live and labor in shaping our ideas, our actions, and our possibilities.

Reflections on Writing about Oneself and One's Family

Perhaps Ruth Behar's (1995) words concerning writing about oneself and one's family best express the mixture of trepidation and resolve with which I complete this manuscript. After publishing *Translated Woman* (1993), Behar returns home to a book autographing party her mother has insisted on holding for family and friends. Some hours after the party is over, Behar's parents question both why she has written 'such terrible things about us' (p. 72) and why she has not asked their permission to write about them and their relationships with her and with one another. Behar reflects on their questions:

> In writing about my parents, I also seem to be trying to mark the distance I've traveled, the distance that separates me from them and gives me the power to describe our

relationship. In his memoir *Hunger of Memory*, Richard Rodriguez declares, 'I am writing about those very things my mother asked me not to reveal.' He says he often felt paralyzed by the image of his parents' eyes moving across the pages of his text. But this, he says, didn't weaken his resolve. There is a place, he says, 'for the deeply personal in public life'.[1] On this, if not on most other things, I agree with Rodriguez. Where I differ from him is that, as a daughter, I keep longing for my parents' approval of my writing, even when, perhaps especially when, I'm being 'bad'. (p. 72)

With Behar, I hope, too, for my family's approval. I believe that my now deceased and much beloved father would not feel it is appropriate to write publicly about his personal relationship with my mother and her family. He also might express surprise that his daughter 'the professor' would 'get credit' as he used to say, for writing about her family. Perhaps he would also chuckle that 'now everyone knows' how 'those people' felt about him, and how wrong they were! Nor do I believe that my mother will be pleased to read about what has been unspeakable, except on rare occasions, and then only with anger and embarrassment, in our family. I hope that by sharing this essay, my sister and I can find new ways to talk about who we are and who we may become. I hope also that in reading this, my daughter will understand one construction of how her mother came to be, at this time and in this place. For me, writing these pages has been both an expiation of lingering demons and an affirmation of the power of narrative to teach and to heal.[2]

Notes

1 I thank Beth Graue of the University of Wisconsin-Madison for her usual good humor and sharp commentary on my writing. I thank Jessica Trubek of Long Island University-Brooklyn for her many insightful conversations about narrative and her encouragement to write about myself as I struggled to do so. I thank Carl Grant for the challenge and opportunity to write about my personal life and how it has shaped my pedagogy and research.
2 The names of the community in which I conducted my student teaching and the names of all children in this paper are pseudonyms. I have not given pseudonyms to my family members.

References

ABT-PERKINS, D. and GOMEZ, M.L. (1993) 'A good place to begin: Examining our personal perspectives', *Language Arts*, **70**, 3, pp. 193–202.

BEHAR, R. (1993) *Translated Woman*, Boston: Beacon Press.

BEHAR, R. (1995) 'Writing in my father's name: A diary of translated woman's first year', in BEHAR, R. and GORDON, D.A. (eds) *Women Writing Culture*, Berkeley: University of California Press, pp. 65–82.

BERGER, P.L. and LUCKMANN, T. (1980) *The social Construction of Reality: A Treatise in the Sociology of Knowledge*, 1st Irvington ed., New York: Irvington.

FELMAN, D. and LAUB, D. (1992) *Testimony: Crises of Witnessing in Literature, Psychoanalysis, and History*, New York: Routledge.

GEERTZ, C. (1995) *After the Fact: Two Countries, Four Decades, One Anthropologist*, Cambridge: Harvard University Press.

GOMEZ, M.L. (1991) 'Teaching a language of opportunity in a language arts methods course: Teaching for David, Albert, and Darlene', in TABACHNICK, B.R. and ZEICHNER K.M. (eds) *Issues and Practices in Inquiry-oriented Practices in Teacher Education*, London: Falmer Press, pp. 91–112.

GOMEZ, M.L. (1996) 'Telling and critiquing stories of our teaching: 'For literacy', in GRANT, C.A. and GOMEZ, M.L. (eds) *Campus and Classroom: Making Schooling Multicultural*, Englewood Cliffs: Prentice-Hall, pp. 163–83.

GOMEZ, M.L. (in press) 'Telling stories of our teaching, reflecting on our practices', *Action in Teacher Education*, XVIII, 3, pp. 1–12.

GOMEZ, M.L. and ABT-PERKINS, D. (1995) 'Sharing of teaching for practice, analysis, and critique', *Education Research and Perspectives*, **22**, 1, pp. 39–52.

GOMEZ, M.L. and TABACHNICK, B.R. (1991) 'Telling teaching stories', *Teaching Education*, **4**, 2, pp. 130–8.

GRUMET, M.R. (1991) 'The politics of personal knowledge', in WITHERELL, C. and NODDINGS, N. (eds) *Stories Lives Tell: Narrative and Dialogue in Education*, New York: Teachers College Press, pp. 67–78.

KING, J. (1991) 'Dysconscious racism: Ideology, identity, and the miseducation of teachers', *The Journal of Negro Education*, **60**, 2, pp. 133–46.

KONDO, D. (1990) *Crafting Selves: Power, Gender, and Discourses of Identity in a Japanese Workplace*, Chicago: University of Chicago Press.

NARAYAN, K. (1991) '"According to their feelings": Teaching and healing with stories', in WITHERELL, C. and NODDINGS, N. (eds) *Stories Lives Tell: Narrative and Dialogue in Education*, New York: Teachers College Press, pp. 96–112.

NARAYAN, K. (1995) 'Participant observation', in BEHAR, R. and GORDON, D.A. (eds) *Women Writing Culture*, Berkeley: University of California Press, pp. 33–46.

ROSENWALD, G.C. (1992) 'Conclusion: Reflections on narrative self-understanding', in ROSENWALD, G.C. and OCHBERG, R.L. (eds) *Storied Lives: The Cultural Politics of Self-understanding*, New Haven: Yale University Press, pp. 265–89.

SHOTTER, J. (1989) 'Social accountability and the social construction of "you"', in SHOTTER, J. and GERGEN, K.J. (eds) *Texts of Identity*, Newbury Park, CA: Sage, pp. 133–51.

TABACHNICK, B.R. and ZEICHNER, K. (1991) (eds) *Issues and Practices in Inquiry-oriented Practices in Teacher Education*, London: Falmer Press.

8 Roots and Wings: Conceptual Underpinnings for Research and Contributions Related to Diversity

Eugene E. García

Introduction

In a recent assignment in Washington DC as a senior officer in the US Department of Education, I had the rare opportunity of assessing my professional experience and expertise as an educational researcher and my personal, cultural and linguistic experiences as they related to the tasks of addressing national educational policy. The researcher in me was and continues to be nurtured in some of the best educational institutions of this country. I am at a top-tier university, with excellent colleagues, students and research resources. The non-professional in me was and continues to be part of and nurtured in a large, rural, Mexican-American family — all 10 of us raised speaking Spanish as our native language, all born in the United States like our parents, grandparents and great-grandparents, only four having graduated from high school, only one graduating from college. I found assessing these *personas* (the Spanish term for 'persons') not as difficult as I might have expected and even came to conclude that this intersect was quite helpful to me, my colleagues and the wide variety of audiences that I interacted with in this national role. In fact, I found by bringing together these *personas*, I was able to more clearly articulate why I do the research I do, why I embrace particular theoretical conceptualizations regarding teaching and learning and why my own career has been quite diverse in its evolution. The present article is my attempt to put into writing these intersecting but distinct voices that help me in my pursuits of furthering our understanding of living in a diverse society but particularly as doing so relates to the role of educational institutions who under serve a linguistic and culturally diverse population today and will need to serve them better in the future.

The voices in this article which address these issues of the past, the present and the future recognize the multiple selves that not only makeup my *persona*, but the multiple selves that are a reality for all of us. For me, it has been useful to recognize that I am walking in varied and diverse cultures. But we all do this. Diversity within each individual is as great as diversity between individuals and the many cultures they belong to or represent at any one moment. We are all living with diversity, some of us more than others — but no one escapes this challenge or its advantages and disadvantages. Early Hebrew scholars debated the 'us vs. them' — the Hom and the Goy. Plato and Aristotle differed vehemently on this issue of whether social diversity was good/bad or social homogeneity was good/bad. Plato concluded that homogeneity among peoples in a nation-state minimized political tensions and favoritism. Aristotle, his student, concluded that diversity fostered inventiveness and creativity as well as political compromises in a democracy. Saint Thomas Acquinas professed that likeness in reverence to God promoted unity while Martin Luther opted to promote religious diversity in reverence to the same God. Today within our borders English First is passionately concerned that multilingualism will produce the next significant bloodbath within our country, while indigenous people mourn just as passionately the loss of their languages and cultures. As this country and the world shrink communicatively, economically, socially and intellectually, our diversity becomes more visible and harder to hide. But it has been and will always be there. Our social institutions will need to address it more than in the past, and of specific importance will be how our educational institutions help us address it successfully. At the core of my actions, whether those actions include research, scholarship or community/ political activity, are two presuppositions: To honor diversity is to honor the social complexity in which we live — to give the individual a sense of integrity and where one has developed as an individual the same integrity. To unify is absolutely necessary, but to insist upon it without embracing diversity is to destroy that which will allow us to unite individual and cultural dignity.

The Personas

Eugene

In the discussion that follows I will attempt to address the issues of diversity from the varied voices within me. Those include that voice which often represents my intellectual upbringing and is recognized primarily by my academic credentials — what degrees I received, where and when I received them, how successful I was in those environments, what academic positions I have held, their status in the academic world, the empirical research which I have done, the teaching I have done, and, of course, what articles/ books I have written. They are the educational pedigree indicators of this society. I do not apologize for such indicators or my pedigree rating. But they are more than that. They are a set of experiences and accomplishments that have at their core the attempt to expand in critical and strategic ways our broader understanding of language acquisition, teaching, learning and schooling and their specific relevance to language minority populations — learners who come to the educational enterprise not knowing the language of that formal enterprise — and particularly for a group of students like me who are classified as Hispanic in the present jargon of educators and demographers. I did not begin my academic pursuits with this specific population in mind, but have naturally gravitated to using my professional skills to address issues of relevance to them, but not only to them. These can be best understood as the academic and scholarly accomplishments of Dr Eugene E. García.

The development of Dr García began like most academic careers. An interest in a particular topic in a community college led to some good grades and a particularly solid relationship with a professor who encouraged me to move on to a four-year institution. Another professor at the four-year institution encouraged me to go to graduate school — something my parents, family and I didn't even know existed as a professional opportunity. Having received some excellent counseling and summer research experience in those undergraduate years, I decided I was deeply interested in the emerging human science of psychology and particularly interested in the development of young children — it was fascinating to learn that children acquire as much knowledge in their first five years as they will acquire the remainder of their lives. Moreover, I had a younger brother who I later learned had Down's Syndrome. Growing up with him, and having the responsibility to care for him as our family worked in the fields, I could not understand why he just never 'learned' as I did and why he didn't enjoy the same games my brothers and I enjoyed. I can trace my first interest in psychology to a personal need to understand my brother, a brother institutionalized at the age of 8 because a social worker and a court of law determined that my aging mother and father could not 'handle' him. Poverty, I learned, has its legal and personal consequences. These were the days when institutionalization was an answer to this instance of diversity and long before the days of Special Education and the Individuals with Disabilities Education Act. (Personal note: years later with the help of my family and my own professional understanding of the psychology of mental disabilities, my brother was removed from the institution and now lives in a group home working to earn his own living.)

These personal circumstances and educational opportunities led me to a graduate program in human development where professors and student colleagues encouraged me to take on the responsibilities of research, scholarship and teaching. Thanks to the consciousness created in the early days of Affirmative Action, I was recruited to my first academic position and began the slow but steady academic socialization process related to procuring extramural support for my research, publishing that research and moving up the academic ladder. With this senior status came the opportunity and responsibility to do things right — to ensure that my research and that of my professional colleagues is of the utmost integrity and that it challenges and carries forward an important domain of intellectual inquiry — while at the same time doing the right thing — engaging us in the important theoretical, empirical and broader professional preparation pursuits that ensure equity and excellence in education for all learners.

Gene

The other parts of me are more rooted in the non-academic world, in my social and cultural realities. I'm a son, brother, husband, father, etc. In such social and cultural roles, I have experienced a wonderful family environment, learning much from my father and mother — neither of whom ever had the opportunity to attend school. They taught me to respect them, my elders, my brothers and sisters, others who were not members of my family — such as my teachers — and not like me, and, most of all, to respect myself. They never gave me a formal lesson about these things, they just lived them, in the harsh realities of poverty and the hard work any migrant or sharecropping family can understand. This teaching and learning included environments of outright racism or more subtle institutional racism in which our language, our color and our heritage was not always met with either individual or group respect. It was from these experiences and teachers that the voice of 'Gene' (a name used most often by my family and friends) emerged. It was this *persona* that agreed to work as an undergraduate in the migrant camps, tutoring adults in English and related subjects so that they could pass the GED. The continual membership in community-based organizations like the GI Forum, the League of United Latin-American Citizens (LULAC), the respect and contributions to the Mexican American Legal Defense Fund (MALDEF), the National Council de la Raza (NCLR) and the National Association for the Advancement of Colored People (NAACP) as well as the respect and honor held for Ceśar Chav́ez, Martin Luther King Jr. and the Kennedys are likely attributed to 'Gene' more than 'Eugene'.

It was this *persona* within me that realized early that I was different. I spoke primarily Spanish, my peers only English. I and my family worked in the fields; my peers and their families hired us to work in their fields. My peers enjoyed a much higher standard of living — I recall being embarrassed that my family did not take vacations in the summer nor had running water and flushing toilets. But, quite honestly, most of the time these differences did not weigh heavy on my mind or on my behavior — I had lots of friends, some like me and others quite different than me. It was one of my elder brothers who first signaled something more about the meaning of these differences than the simple fact that they were differences. It seems that someone had called him a 'dirty Mexican'. He appropriately informed me that these were fighting words. Who was I at an early age to disagree? — they sounded like fighting words to me!! But then he went on to teach me a significant lesson — *Do not let anyone ever call you dirty*. He made it clear to me that such a statement implied that our mother did not care about our cleanliness. My mother never sent us to school, church or any other place dirty. All of us were required to shed our school clothes for our work clothes and vice versa on a daily basis. In short, to be called a Mexican was not derogatory, but to be called 'dirty' was cause for defending the honor of our mother. I learned later that many of my peers did perceive calling me a 'Mexican' as derogatory — that lesson came hard and stuck but did not destroy the previous lesson from my brother.

It was 'Gene' who was convinced primarily by non-academic friends to venture into local politics and to seek election to a board of education in a city that was characterized by some as hostile to the language and culture of Chicanos — a label that I and my wife had chosen for ourselves — and who with the help of a broad sector of the community was actually elected, by less than 50 votes out of a total of some 6000 to that body. And it was likely more 'Gene' than 'Eugene' that accepted the invitation to join the Clinton Administration and Secretary of Education Richard Riley in the US Department of Education. I agreed to do so in an attempt to re-authorize a set of legislative initiatives begun in the mid-1960s to assist local and state educational agencies to address the educational inequities which characterized the efforts of our local school with regard to learners who came to those schools from circumstances of poverty and who, like me, did not have proficiency in English when they come to school. It was in these political/policy roles that I realized that policy makers and practitioners of education do not always act upon the very best theory, proven educational practices or even promising educational innovations. They act on purely political interests, many having nothing to do with benefiting the present or future status of children, families or the social institutions we have created to assist them. I realized the importance of the politics of education. 'Gene's' voice is often dominated by these lessons, although 'Eugene' is not totally unaffected by them.

Gino

There is still one other self that will contribute to the analysis of diversity, Hispanics and schooling — one identified best by the endearing name that my mother chose to use for me, 'Gino'. In my large and quite Catholic family, to baptize a child was a distinct honor and in recognition of that honor *los padrinos* — the godparents — were given the authority to name the child. My eldest sister and her husband were selected by my parents to serve as my *padrinos*. My sister was enchanted with the name 'Eugene' and that is how I came to have a Greek name in a cohort of brothers and sisters named Antonio, Emelio, Cecelia, Ciprianita, Abel, Federico, Tiburcio, Christina and born of parents named Lorenzo and Juanita. All these solid Hispanic names adjusted for biblical roots. (My youngest brothers did not escape my fate — he was named Ernest. Why? Because his *padrinos* liked the name.) Of course, my mother could not pronounce 'Eugene' and to her and my immediate family I became 'Gino'.

'Gino' carries a distinct sense of cultural 'Hispanic-ness', 'Chicanismo', 'Latino-ness', 'Raza-ness'. These all reflect a deep regard for the linguistic and cultural roots that foster who he is. Best exemplified by a lesson from my father, again while I was young and not as understanding as I am today as an *educado* — a term my parents used to identify an individual who could distinguish right from wrong. As farm workers and share croppers, winter was a time to prepare for work — there just was not the quantity of work to do during this period. And it was during one farm winter in the high plains of Colorado where I was born and raised that my father pointed to an *árbol* — a cotton-wood tree as I recall — near our home. He asked simply, *'¿Por qué puede vivir ese árbol en el frio del invierno y en el calor del verano?'* (How can that tree survive the bitter cold of winter and the harsh heat of summer?) My father was not a man of many words — he was often characterized by relatives as quiet and shy — but when he spoke we all listened very carefully. I remember struggling to find an answer. I was also characterized as quiet and shy. But I tried to respond to my father — it was the right thing to do. I rambled on for some time about how big and strong the tree was and how its limbs and trunk were like the strong arms and bodies of my elder brothers, particularly the two who were serving in the US Army during the last phases of the Korean War.

Then he kindly provided a different perspective by referring to a common Spanish *dicho/consejo* (proverb/advisory): *El árbol fuerte tiene raíces maduros*. (A strong tree has mature/strong roots). In articulating this significant piece of the analysis that was absent from my youthful ramblings, he made very clear that without strong roots, strong trees are impossible — and we don't even see the roots! In a Spanish class many years later, a teacher extended this lesson further by pointing me to a more elaborate *dicho/consejo: Del árbol caido, todos hacen leña*. (From a fallen tree, anyone/everyone can make firewood.) What became clear to me at that moment was the more substantive lesson my father was framing — if you have no roots, how can you withstand the tests of the environment that surely will come and prey on your vulnerabilities. That without those roots, any tree can be transformed from a beautiful living organism to a fallen entity that can easily be transformed, or more profoundly, destroyed, never to be recognized as the strong tree it once was. For me as an individual with a set of cultural roots: if my roots were to die and I was to be stripped of the integrity that lies in those roots, then I will also disappear along with all that is me.

For many Hispanics in this country, their roots have either been ignored or stripped away in the name of growing strong. Many have been directed to stop speaking Spanish, to perceive their culture as one less-than, and to assimilate as quickly as possible so they can succeed in American society. And, unfortunately, many have suffered the fate of the rootless tree — they have fallen socially, economically, academically and culturally. Like that fallen tree they have been made transformed and have forever lost the individual and cultural integrity that their ancestors once thrived on even in circumstances of greater poverty and social hostility.

But for 'Gino', my mother made very clear, roots and their concomitant integrity and self respect was not enough. As a mother, she wanted the very best for all her children, certainly not the long and painful field work that she had endured for a lifetime. She wanted us *bien educados* — to have a set of formal and marketable skills. She made very clear that children needed wings, like the wings she insisted we children grew every night upon falling to sleep so as to fly to heaven to be with God. All children, she said, were angels. Victor Villaseñor's mother, in recent stories by this Chicano author, elaborates further on this notion. His mother made it just as clear that the children flew to God each night and stationed themselves as stars in heaven. Both mothers express a special regard for the sanctity of childhood and required children to have wings to perform their related roles. My mother made it clear that she could not provide the kind of wings that God and a good education could provide. She knew that the teachers and schools would have to take me further than she could so personally. Education would need to provide the strong and elaborate wings for me to succeed where she often felt she had failed. God can provide you with strong spiritual wings, she reminded us — always go to church and follow His teachings. And, go to school — strong wings like those of an eagle are also what you need in this world to raise your family and provide for them all that we have been unable to provide for you.

For Hispanics in this country particularly, the emphasis on building wings in school has strategically focused on teaching English language skills: 'Teach them English well and then they will succeed.' Yet all educators realize that in today's information age, education must provide broad and strong intellectual wings related to the fundamental linguistic, mathematical, scientific and technological literacy. English literacy is important but it is not enough.

'Gino' listened attentively to a more eloquent account than his own research shared in a recent unsolicited letter from a new teacher in Los Angeles communicating the circumstances of educating students in an urban setting.

A Los Angeles, high school English teacher, unsolicited communication to a previous colleague:

October, 1995
Hi . . .
Here's the report from the Western Front. Please pass it around. What I initially perceived to be innovative use of year-round scheduling seems to be more mechanization run amok. Although they apparently were able to split the kids into three separate tracks with different vacations with little or no problem, the track system has virtually NO academic benefit, at least the way it operates here. There are about 600 9th and 10th graders per track and about 200 11th and 12th graders per track. Look at the dropout rate (near 50 per cent if not more). And the school just received a 3-year accreditation rather than a 7 year so things are pretty bad.

In short, this school and school district are nightmares. For instance, there is no attendance accountability or follow-up except for homeroom. No period-by-period reporting of attendance to the central office. The only phone calls home are for kids who miss homeroom. So kids can — and do — just show up for homeroom and 'ditch' all their other classes, and unless a teacher inquires, but no one bothers, absences are invisible to the central computer and administration. I have about 20 students on my rolls that never saw this semester, even once. Or kids can pick and choose which classes to go to and there is no central administrative accountability.

Reading and writing levels are grotesque. I have only four students who are operating above grade level who could function in an honors program. That's out of 150 on the rolls. Teacher support is nil. I still don't have a stapler or even file folders for portfolio writing assessment. The trash is emptied maybe once a week. The floors are filthier than some bars I've been in, and the bathrooms and stairwells stink. Half the lights are out in most classrooms and every third and fourth light works in the dark hallways. The school, in addition to being year-round, which presents logistical difficulties for a good periodic cleaning, is also used for a night adult school. That means it is being used for twice the time (of) an ordinary building. But it gets worse. Zero maintenance.

Zero, zero, zero. Except for in the main office area, I have yet to spy a custodian doing anything during the day. The dress code is not enforced . . . gangster wear is the norm, not the exception . . . and the administration, besides making occasional announcements, do nothing . . . thus none of the teachers care to stir the pot by even trying to enforce dress codes. Tardies are not enforced. This is LA and despite that kids are wandering through the halls and all over the campus all the time. There is one computer lab for Math, four or five computers in the library and that's about it. The textbooks left for me to use were 1980 copyright 10th grade lit books, and there were only enough for a classroom set. And, of course, all except one of the short stories was about teenage white (male) characters, and these kids just *don't relate* to that. Plus, despite this being a major ESL school, no supplementary resources 'enrichment' materials exist that I can find that contain Black or Brown or multinational short stories or poems . . . They do know the main players in the OJ drama, but one must be careful here when making allusions to that. The Maya Angelou books were in pieces. The book accountability procedures here are non-existent. The administrators don't deal with discipline . . . there is a dean system here. The administrators do assign lockers, handle student picture IDs, write attendance excuses and other similar executive tasks. The principal is an elegant looking woman who looks like an aging movie star . . . and mentally, she is like the 'Sunset Boulevard' movie character waiting for her closeup with Mr DeMille. There is one counselor per 1,000 students, an ESL program for half the students that doesn't seem to be up ticking tests scores or achievement. Half the kids don't bring *anything* to school let alone pens and paper; forget assigning homework. I have twenty-one students with perfect attendance and no discipline problems. Half of them turn in work that is perhaps 4th or 5th grade level; the others don't turn in anything at all. But they are all there every day. I asked other teachers what to do about grades. Well, if they make it every day, pass them with a D even if they don't do anything. Other kids I see one day and then don't see them again for two weeks. The sixth period English class has thirty-seven students on the roll and I have an average of 14–17 in daily regular attendance. There are few AP classes but few students pass the tests. Kids who miss school for field trips and football games are not listed on an excuse sheet nor is there any other official notification. They just tell you they were on a field trip and you mark the grade book accordingly. I guess. Very few — perhaps 10 per cent — of the kids are black and so far the only white kids are from Armenia or Russia with the occasional native white kids spotted here and there. The black kids were jubilant over the OJ verdict; the other (mostly brown) kids were split, but I could see no pattern there. Among grown-ups, middle-class Blacks seemed chagrined or outraged over the verdict but the lower class, high school-educated security guards were also jubilant. Most teachers were outraged over the verdicts, but the white ones were especially quiet about it. On the day of the verdicts, I had an incredible number of absences. Perhaps some stayed home for fear of riots, but the next day, one kid *told me* he stayed home in case of a riot so he could get some *free stuff*. It was a canceled Christmas. This really works my white male middle-class nerves . . . and the other teachers report the same experience. The Rodney King riots were in the immediate vicinity of the school . . . fires burning everywhere, they said, and this is in the mid-Wilshire area which is where all the hoity toity north-west Austin types of buildings and residences are, despite the 'port of entry' school population.

I asked the Union Steward if all the schools in LA were as screwed up as this one. He said that he has taught only at LAHS but that he hears it is the same way but the sad thing is that it doesn't have to be that way. Indeed. The English teachers here are cold, intelligent and superb. But they all tell me to forget everything I know and just do the best you can with what tools you have and forget how it could be. The faculty has rich experience, but I have never seen so many good ideas from attendance to technology disappear into such a black hole of central administrative and school administrative ennui. These kids are sweet. What lives they have led. So many from El Salvador, fleeing the government violence. The native speakers are incredibly poor, but sweet kids. One kid, who works harder than any kid I have every seen, literally just got off the boat from Korea in August. Another kid, from El Salvador, is as bright as the brightest I ever had . . . I would give anything to get that kid out of here . . . I have had the weird experience of having collaborative group work on short stories conducted in spoken languages other than English and then each group reports back to the entire class in English. But kids are kids. It's too bad this system here just processes them through, like the Pink Floyd mechanized conveyor belt 'We don't need no education' song, but on a bad drug trip.

'Gino' feels that Hispanics and others in similar circumstances, like those represented by him and his family, have been educationally short-changed. This is reflected for him in his sister's name change by her teacher, her name changed from 'Ciprianita', the name of her *padrinos*, to 'Elsie', the teacher's favorite name, and the counseling he received against going to a good university because his SAT scores were not very high — in fact told that he would never be a PhD, although he didn't even know enough then to understand the low expectations that were imbedded in that counseling. And, reflected more generally in the absence of individual and social integrity of 'minority' groups, which can account for school underachievement, the high drop out rates from high school, and the low college attendance rates. 'Gino's' voice raises with the plea *ya basta* ('That's enough'). This country can no longer afford these deplorable educational outcomes.

The 'Hispanic' Debate

However, Eugene, Gene and Gino realize that his voices are not alone nor are even his views held by all Hispanics in the US. That is another reason for this book. Most critical of such views of the interactive relationship of Roots and Wings for Hispanics are two well regarded and influential Hispanic authors, refuting the importance of roots and the relationship of those roots to educational development of Hispanics. Linda Chavez, an advisor in the Reagan White House, journalist commentator and author of *Out of the Barrio: Toward a New Politics of Hispanic Assimilation* (1991) suggests that: Every previous group — Germans, Irish, Italians, Greeks, Jews, Poles — struggled to be accepted fully into the social, political, and economic mainstream, sometimes against the opposition of a hostile majority. They learned the language, acquired education and skills, and adapted their own customs and traditions to fit an American context (1991, p. 2).

The key for Hispanic success in America, Chavez argues, is minimizing the public/governmental recognition of Hispanic roots and the individual and governmental promotion of assimilation. She chides the federal government particularly federal bilingual education programs and Hispanic leaders for promoting permanent victim status and vying with black Americans for the distinction of being the poorest, most segregated and least educated minority, thereby entitling them to government handouts. These in turn, her conclusion advances, encourages Hispanics to maintain their language and culture, their specific identity in return for rewards handed out through Affirmative Action and federal, state and local educational policies which thwart assimilation. This doesn't sound like my father's concern for the importance of roots and my mother's wings. Linda Chavez is just wrong — theoretically, empirically, politically and ideologically. It will be up to the varied voices of this author to make that clear in this volume.

Eugene E. García

However, yet another Hispanic author is relevant here: Richard Rodriguez. He is very eloquent in his description of his upbringing in a 'Mexican' home and a private Catholic school where the English-speaking nuns literally beat the Spanish language and the 'Hispanic-ness' out of him. His book *Hunger of Memory* (1985) describes this forced assimilation, painful as it was, that propelled him to new heights of educational achievement. And although he never really articulates the conclusion himself, he leaves open the suggestion that such treatment of Hispanics is exactly what they need to get over their 'problems'. Eugene, Gene and Gino reach a very different conclusion in their contributions to this debate. Some will see these combined voices as an Hispanic response to the views articulated by Linda Chavez and Richard Rodriguez, as another entry into this Hispanic debate. In some respects it is that. But it is mostly one researcher dealing with the diversity within him to address those issues of great significance to him. They are not meant as part of an ideological or political debate, they are meant to be a scholarly, thoughtful, and meaningful contribution to the enhancement of education in this country and around the world. Of course, readers like you can come to your own conclusion.

It Doesn't Have to Be Either/Or

My wife and I joined the 'Chicano Movement' in 1970. She was working to support me while I studied my way through graduate school at the University of Kansas. She was from a little town in southern New Mexico known as Central, near the larger but still small town of Silver City. She had grown up in a 'Chicano' family, and spoke both Spanish and English (although her Spanish was better than mine) and had very strong 'roots' in the culture of that family and community. We were married in 1969. We were both living a long way from our families in Kansas. However, we managed to find family-like support. We found the local Hispanic catholic parish — Our Virgin of Guadalupe Church, of course. And there and through other Chicano acquaintances we had at our jobs and ones I made playing softball, we were adopted by, and adopted, new Chicano families. We became part of the Escobar, Rodriguez, Renteria, etc. families. We joined the 'Chicano movement' far from the heart of that movement in California, Texas and Colorado, because we identified with its cause — equal educational opportunity — as it related to us and our 'new family' in Kansas.

We also had others who were like family and had other causes. The Guesses, the Baers, the Livingstons, etc. These individuals worked with us in pursuit of educational opportunities for mentally retarded children. We all felt strongly that much more could be done. We believed in that cause — equal educational opportunity — for the children we served. We worked to support the Special Olympics and often brought institutionalized, 'retarded' children home with us on weekends.

It was not unusual for us to attend a cocktail party with one group of friends/family on a Friday night and on that same weekend attend a quinceñera — a traditional Mexican celebration of a young girl's entrance into adult society — on a Saturday. At one gathering we would speak mostly English, and at the other mostly Spanish. The music we enjoyed in one gathering ranged from classical to rock and in the other gathering from *Mariachi* to *Norteñas* and sometimes rock, but never classical. We moved comfortably between 'cultures'. While there were similarities across those 'cultures' and significant differences, we did not have to choose between them. We were respected, enjoyed, prospered and received support from each. It was not an 'either/or' situation. In short, this type of existence is the ideal for Hispanics in the United States.

During a time when US Congress holds hearings on 'English Only' laws, proponents of such laws would have us believe that homogeneity in language and culture must be promoted by the government. Some of these same proponents often argue for keeping government out of people's lives, but not on this issue. Yet, individuals like me, representing most Hispanics in this country, move back and forth comfortably between languages and cultures, most of the time, without many problems. Quite often it is a linguistic, social and economic advantage to be able to do so.

I resent it when the Executive Director of the organization English First proposes that citizens must know English before they can vote. My mother does not speak English, through no fault of her own, yet she has been committed enough about her participation in this country's democracy to vote in every presidential election — sometimes for the Democratic candidate and sometimes for the Republican candidate. This is more commitment than 40 per cent of the US citizenship that does not vote but speaks English. She was born in this country as were her parents, worked hard all her life, raised 10 children, and taught us more than anyone else about respecting others. How can someone like this be the target of disrespect in a democracy committed to 'equality and justice for all'. I like to use my mother's experience in this context of the English-as-an-official language debate. Simply, the argument is made that if she had learned English, she would have been a better and more participatory citizen. Yet, my mother votes, contributes to her community, raised four sons who served in the armed forces and no child of hers is on the 'government dole'. I know English-speaking mothers who have four sons in prison and several on welfare. Is English language proficiency, then, a significant determining variable for good citizenship? What my mother could have profited from was better educational opportunities.

I realize that at the center of this discussion are strong personal feelings about my culture. What is exemplified in my work attempts to move beyond that. It is an effort at a more thoughtful, comprehensive and integrated 'complexification' of the issues of 'culture' and its conceptual meaning in today's diverse societies. It is also an overview of how diversity in this country has been treated in the 'culture wars' — from Americanization to Bilingual/Bicultural Education. I'm convinced intellectually, empirically and educationally that it does not need to be 'either/or'.

The Contribution

Ultimately, my own work brings to the surface the many *personas* of this author. What it attempts to do is make clear that both the social/cultural as well as the personal integrity of all individuals in this country are critical ingredients for our future success as a diverse society. Very directly, much of my work addresses the present circumstances of minority children and their families drawing on demographic indicators, quantitative studies and qualitative studies to more fully explore their circumstances in the United States. It sets the stage for understanding why a discussion of education and diversity is important at this time. The work attempts to address the linguistic and cultural attributes of our diverse populations. The concept of culture is critical in understanding present American society and the meaning of diversity not all us are alike — then how are they similar and how are we different? The work attempts to expose society's long-standing efforts to eradicate diversity, and to promote assimilation for many linguistically and culturally diverse populations. It is the story of anti-immigration, ethnocentrism and the prevailing federal, state and local policies born out of the Americanization philosophy — a philosophy leaving our important social institutions culturally and intellectually bankrupt.

An important shift in the work begins a decade ago, beginning with the emphasis from the general to the specific. It focuses on those programs that nourish roots and develop wings for our diverse populations. It is the story of teachers, classrooms, schools and communities that have recognized the significance of who they are and are making educational success a reality — honoring their roots and providing the wings. This research is a set of stories for US 'minorities' with examples of African-American, American-Indian, southeast Asian, Arab-American, Latinos and others often character-ized as 'at risk' populations that provide further the evidence that collective integrity is related to educational success in present day America. The work attempts to articu-late how we can learn from these success stories about the challenges awaiting us in tomorrow's America and in the global village. Where is this work headed? It seeks to enunciate a rationale and guidelines for a new conceptual framework built upon the notion that our future, particularly our successful educational future, depends on our new understanding that in a diverse cultural context, respect for the uniqueness of the individual is not enough. Instead, what must be added is respect for, and recognition of integrity of the culture in which the individual develops and resides.

References

CHAVEZ, L. (1991) *Out of the Barrio: Toward a New Politics of Hispanic assimilation*, New York: Basic Books.
RODRIGUEZ, R. (1982) *Hunger of Memory: An Autobiography*, Boston: D.R. Godine.

In Search of a Method for Liberating Education and Research: The Half (That) Has Not Been Told

Joyce E. King

Groundings

> It was through their unrequited toil that I was educated, while they were compelled to live in ignorance. I am indebted to them for the power I have to serve them . . . (Harper, 1892, p. 176)

As my grandmother and I approached the corner store just before daybreak, a fire flickered in a battered, old steel drum. The people huddled around the fire, their heads wrapped or hooded against the damp morning chill, were our neighbors. Nodding in unspoken, respectful greeting, they stepped aside and opened the circle so that we could take our places beside them. I was about 9 or 10 years old, and my head and shoulders barely reached my grandmother's elbow as I stood next to her. We were in Stockton, California, in the rich agricultural heartland of the San Joaquin Valley. These people and their families, like mine, had come from Oklahoma, Texas, Arkansas, and Louisiana where they had known my grandmother long before I was born. We were there early that morning in the semi-darkness to wait for the rickety bus that would take us to the fields outside of town. Some days we went to 'cut' onions (which meant pulling them up out of the ground, cutting off the tops, stuffing them into burlap sacks, and dragging the sacks over to the weighing stand to be paid a few cents for each sack). This was hot, back-breaking, dirty work that people with no other options were paid very little to do. That day we were going to pick strawberries, and we were in the field working by sunrise. It was a wonderful day for me because I was going to work with my grandmother and share the special status that she enjoyed. I recall how the people stepped aside when we passed because my grandmother, whom everyone called, 'Miss Chicken', was someone special in our community.

Later, I understood some of the reasons why my diminutive grandmother commanded such respect and power in our community. She could read and write but my grandmother did not complete elementary school. Yet, she owned not just her own home — which she had helped to build — but several other houses where our relatives lived as well. Still, we were not prosperous but working people like our neighbors. My grandmother was also one of the best workers around: No matter what crop was being cut, picked, or chopped, she always kept ahead of everyone else in the field. When I was older, my grandmother explained to me how she became such a fast worker. In Oklahoma, when my grandfather was in prison, she was working in the cotton field alone to feed their five young children. Two ex-convicts made up their minds to help her. They used to put her in the row between them and chop alternately in her row and

Joyce E. King

theirs, so she could make more money. Working in coordination with them, she swung her hoe in time with their rhythm and, matching their cadence, she kept up with them. Despite her small stature, she developed the speed, stamina, and accuracy to set the same pace for other workers.

Ironically, in the California strawberry field that day, a group of Filipino men had great fun helping me keep up with her. They put me in the row between them and they kept my baskets filled with berries. All morning we stayed close behind her as she worked her way up and down the long rows of luscious strawberries. (I couldn't resist popping one in my mouth from time to time.) Not only was I proud of how much money I made that day, I didn't know that we were 'poor', or that the work we were doing was looked down upon.

Such memories play an important role now in my work as a sociologist of education. They remind me of ways the actual Black Experience often contradicts representations of black life and culture in school texts, research literature, and images of black people in mainstream American popular culture. The neighborhood where I grew up was very much like an African village: the people who lived there were related by family ties, social bonds, and survival struggles over several generations. The elders had known my mother when she was a girl. These families had migrated more or less together from the same towns in the south before coming to California during the Depression. Mostly they were field hands, share croppers, laborers, and domestic workers. For generations they had followed the harvests doing the work that made it possible for them to survive and for me to be educated and to become a sociologist, teacher educator, and researcher. Like my mother's side of our family, they had come to California's central valley to pick cotton and harvest other crops. Yet they were also skilled in carpentry, plumbing, cooking, sewing, house building, bricklaying, and other forms of knowledge and expertise that ensured our survival. Whenever the older people talked about their lives and their struggles, which was not very often, they would tell us — in that parsimonious and poetic way that they used Bible verses, proverbs, and metaphors to make a particular point without saying it directly: 'The half has not been told.' More often they would tell us to 'Get an education because nobody can take that away from you.' I never knew for sure, and they never told us, just what they thought might be 'taken away' from us. Our dignity and self-respect perhaps? Or perhaps they feared for our very sanity, considering how often I heard someone begin a prayer in church by intoning, 'Thank you, Lord, for waking me up clothed in my right mind.'

Growing up in Stockton, I remember being surrounded by people in my family and in our neighborhood who knew how to do any number of things well. Doing things well was especially important in my family. My mother has often told me stories about Grandma Lena, who, although she was born into the presumed slothfulness of plantation slavery, impressed her high standards upon my mother. Under Grandma Lena's watchful eye, my mother's job as a young girl was to iron the long, starched white aprons the women wore. My mother vividly remembers her grandmother's warning: 'Don't leave no cat faces in them aprons!' That's what Grandma Lena called the almost unavoidable wrinkles and smudges that resulted from using the old-fashioned iron they heated in a fire outdoors. If Grandma Lena spotted any 'cat faces', my mother said she would have to start over: boil the water to wash the apron, then starch and iron it again. In other words, not only was the *ethic* of doing good work highly valued, but the expectation was *excellence*. My mother has passed this expectation on to me and I have done the same with my children. What's more, in my research and writing I am contributing to the growing body of scholarship that documents these kinds of strengths and the cultural knowledge that has been useful for black people's survival (King, 1994; 1995a; b; King and Mitchell, 1995).

In addition to values like these that have grounded me, I, too, observed and participated in processes of economic and cultural production that demonstrated the knowledge, skill, ingenuity, and creativity in our community. When I was a girl, I helped my grandmother make quilts. I watched her re-cycle old garments and create intricately beautiful and useful quilts that we very much prize today. I marveled at the evenness and uniformity of her tiny stitches and the strength in her steady hand. She taught me how to make a knot at the end of the thread with one hand. What a great sense of accomplishment I felt when I could finally lick the thread, twist it just right around my fingers, and produce a neat knot, effortlessly, like she did. My job was to thread her needles and, of course, to keep her company.

I also helped my mother make jams and jellies, 'can' (preserve) peaches, pickle cucumbers, and I watched her make the lye soap that she cooked in a tin tub over a fire outside in the back yard. My mother also tended the roses and lilies that spruced up our yard. She even removed a wall in our small house one day to enlarge a room. My father, who worked as a laborer building roads and bridges, wore khaki pants and shirts that I ironed. He hunted rabbits and pheasants and often he brought home freshly caught cat fish or red snapper. During the hunting season, he took the whole family with him to hunt deer in the mountains each year, so we missed school but experienced another kind of education.

Just about everyone in our community was engaged in some kind of productive work: the Mexican couple whom we called 'Moms' and 'Pops' lived and owned the store next to my grandmother's house. I spent many hours there watching the women grind chillies and corn and make tortillas and enchiladas. A black family owned the corner store where we waited for bus to go to the fields; a blind, itinerant preacher earned money by piercing ears when he passed through the neighborhood. He pierced my ears when I was about 6 years old. Then there was 'Miss Laurine', the lady who took care of me while my mother did 'day's work' (domestic work) on the 'white' side of town.

Although Miss Laurine was different from the other adults around — she had some rather peculiar ways — her presence in the community was not marked by her differentness but by inclusion. Miss Laurine lived alone in a trailer by herself; she smoked a pipe, and she talked with a 'funny', unfamiliar accent. For example, she called me 'Jice'. I didn't know why until Bobby Hill, a young Jamaican scholar whom I met years later at Stanford University, said my name the same way. 'Back home in Jamaica', he said, 'we would call you Jice.' For the first time I realized that Miss Laurine must have come from Jamaica, too. But why? And how did she get to a town in California's central valley? This is a story I will never know. I remember asking my mother why everybody called Miss Laurine 'miss' — including my mother, who was not so much younger than Miss Laurine. My mother explained that Miss Laurine's white hair — a sign of eldership — required showing her that kind of respect. Miss Laurine was another of those powerful black women who commanded immeasurable respect through her life example, her care for the people, her competence, and her courageous spirit in overcoming life's difficulties. I wrote about these qualities of black women in an article on black women's leadership (King, 1988).

It is unfortunate that the know-how, striving, and struggles of the people in my community-family were never reflected back to me in school in any way that enhanced my understanding of either my own life or theirs. Our stories were untold and, therefore, invisible or distorted. The only textbook narrative about us that I remember at all declared triumphantly that 'The slaves were happy on the plantation.' On the other hand, the questions I have pursued and the interpretations that I offer in my research, writing, and teaching are grounded in this community-family reality that is often and necessarily in opposition to the official curriculum of the school and the social curriculum of US culture (King, 1995b; 1994; 1992) which too often depict black people as defective or deficient. The National Alliance of Black School Educators has observed this and notes the consequences such distortions have for the education of African-American students. NABSE reported that:

> African American culture is often relegated to an inferior symbolic universe by schools, thus hiding our group's true historic struggle for survival, liberation, and enhancement. The African American student, then, may view herself or himself and her/his group as inferior and behave accordingly. Ignorance of and disrespect for African American history and culture also breeds low expectations and unhealthy educator assessments of African American students, families, personalities, and potentials. (NABSE 1984, p. 12)

While we didn't learn about the significance of the African presence in US society or much about the histories and cultures of the diverse people around us, our families expected us to respect the human dignity of each person. This included our Mexican neighbors, the Filipino men, as well as different individuals among us, like Miss Laurine or the man who had his hair done every Saturday at the beauty shop and who 'shouted' in church on Sunday morning just like the women when someone sang 'his song'. In other words, we were raised to recognize and respect the worth of people and to value honesty, helping others, generosity, and justice.

From Collective Cultural Memory to Historical Consciousness and Liberating Modes of Inquiry

It is worth noting that I do not have many childhood memories of white people, with the possible exception of teachers who stand out for the special ways in which they encouraged me but not others. I realize that both white and black teachers, in fact, chose to sponsor, promote, and support me but not my cousins or my older brother. In the second grade, for instance, the same black teacher, who didn't form any overt bond with me but who I think sent me a summer subscription for the *Weekly Reader*, dragged my cousin out of our classroom kicking and screaming. I can't remember what he did but he was expelled from school. He has become a casualty of the war against black males.[1] When I was in sixth grade on the first day of school, my former kindergarten teacher, who was white, called me back to her classroom to calm my younger cousin whom the teachers had locked in the bathroom for punishment. When I got there, he was crouching in the toilet, crying and yelling hysterically that he did not want to be locked up like his father, my favorite uncle, who had been sent to prison for possession of marijuana. Nevertheless, he became a professional football player and is now a successful business man. In effect, white people were not really part of our community. At school we discovered that we were different from them: we didn't talk like them and they were unpredictable and even dangerous. This was especially so for those who came into contact with the police or strayed too far from home into 'Okie Town' across Highway 99, which divided us from them. My cousins and I trespassed on a white man's property there once, and he shot at us to chase us out of his cherry orchard. Another white man followed us home from high school for several days. He exposed himself as he drove along slowly beside us with the car door and his pants open. No one thought about calling the police to report this. Instead, my best friend's mother kept a vigil by the window each day, watching for our return from school until this danger had passed.

We had white friends at school but this depended on their behavior and their attitude toward us. For example, one of my white classmates, who lived near our school, Fair Oaks Elementary, invited me home with her one day. I discovered that they had Kool-Aid with dinner just like we did. In the second grade, another white friend said she wished I could come home with her and go to her church, but she couldn't invite me because I was black. Our teachers were oblivious to, or unconcerned about, these kinds of incidents. They concentrated on teaching us 'American' culture: We sang European American folk songs ('Oh, my darling, Clementine . . .'and 'She'll be coming around the mountain, when she comes . . . she'll be driving six white horses, when she comes . . .'); we learned to square dance; and our teachers corrected our speech. Very patriotically we celebrated Hawaii's statehood by dancing the hula in grass skirts.

This hegemony, now called white supremacy/racism, persisted at all levels of our formal and non-formal educational experiences. By the time I went to junior high school, another one of my cousins, who is a year younger than I, still could not read. When we were bussed to the white side of town for summer school in the eleventh grade, the school we attended, Lincoln High, was much better equipped than ours. The wealthy white students could actually speak the language and perform plays in French, while we couldn't say a word in French after three years of study.

The pernicious cultural system that values whiteness and devalues blackness was also evident in the community. Whenever black people expressed admiration for the beautiful cultural center the Filipinos built, they would also say, 'It's a shame that black people can't work together to build anything like this.' Is it any wonder that, like many other black *and* white children who were bombarded with images of whiteness in school books, White angels and disciples on our Sunday School cards, and a blonde, blue-eyed Jesus behind the pulpit at church, I grew up with that nagging suspicion, wondering: 'Is there something wrong with *us*?'

The professional vocabulary that I learned in graduate school, terms like 'tracking', 'sponsored vs. contest mobility', and 'cultural deprivation', did not adequately explain and only partially addressed such alienating educational experiences. Paradoxically, my search for methods of liberating education and research is rooted in the collective cultural memory of the Black Experience that black church and community-family life also produce. Despite the predominate cultural system, affirmations of our humanity were always erupting within various forms of black cultural expression: in the beauty and harmony of the gospel songs we sang when our youth choirs traveled from church to church; or in the 'Sha-na-nah . . . Get a job' doo-wop harmonies we crooned as teenagers; in how 'sharp' we could look on the first or the last day of school or Easter Sundays; in a powerfully moving sermon that made people jump up and shout, 'Preach!' or in a rhythm and blues artist's mesmerizing performance that made us shout, 'Get down!'; in the eloquent prayers of the deacons and deaconesses; in our Easter speeches that we learned 'by heart'; in the precision routines and intricate hand signals the ushers used to direct the congregation at church; in the abundant and delicious 'soul' food served at church and family gatherings; in the talent shows and after school dances where we did the 'Texas Hop', the 'Chicken', and the 'Mashed Potatoes' to James Brown's latest hit song.

In other words, Black cultural expression, which is most often collective, partici-patory, and life-affirming, validated our *being* within an existential social reality where *everyone* could be and do something excellent and worthwhile. This is the power of *blackness* that could not easily be contained, repressed, or simply erased from our collective cultural memory. As CLR James (1970) noted, 'the capacities of men [and women] were always leaping out of the confinements of the system' (p. 136).[2] Reading this kind of critical interpretation of our survival and struggles by black studies scholars, especially after meeting someone like CLR James at Stanford University, made a tremend-ous impact on my thinking. Eventually, I gained the confidence and the historical con-sciousness to pose new questions about the Black Experience from a 'Black Perspective' and to think in new ways about racial justice, liberating education, and liberating inquiry by, with, and for the people (Dubell et al., 1980).[3] This achievement was a victory of collective cultural memory and historical consciousness over alienating education and abductive school knowledge (King and Wilson, 1990) that misrepresents reality, as Carter G. Woodson (1933) showed so clearly in his classic study, *The Mis-education of the Negro*.

The Deciphering Praxis of Black Studies

The critical power of African-American cultural knowledge and thought (King, 1995a) are significant dimensions of the Black Experience that are reflected in my research and the 'practical-critical activity' (Kilminster, 1979, p. 17) that characterizes my teaching methods. Grounded theoretically in the Black Studies intellectual perspective and prac-tically in the participatory, communal, and expressive quality of black life and culture (Gay and Baber, 1987), my theoretical and methodological approach to research and teaching represents a praxis of transmutation that seeks to change both cognitive and affective schema.[4] My focus is on thought and feeling. I use the term praxis to denote more self-consciously reflexive teaching, learning, and inquiry processes than the term 'practice' suggests. Thus, as the knowledge, thought, and abilities of students or research participants change (Carr and Kemmis, 1986, p. 42), a reflexive process of teaching or research also changes, and as I have discovered in my own work, this kind of praxis can enable new forms of competence, collective cultural memory, and consciousness.

According to Karenga, one of the founders of the modern Black Studies discipline, 'Black Studies is critical and corrective of the inadequacies, omissions and distortions of traditional white studies' (Karenga, 1993, p. 18). The theoretical perspective of the discipline of Black Studies consists of an epistemological critique of the social order and its hidden costs and a critique of school knowledge and practices that sustain it. In this regard, Black Studies represents a critical perspective that transcends ameliorative multicultural educational approaches (King, 1995a). Wynter (1992a, b; 1995) uses the term 'deciphering practice' to describe how the Black Studies intellectual perspective can reveal the cultural rules of the 'symbolic representational systems' and the 'conceptual-cognitive categories' (Wynter, 1995, p. 13) of the social order that govern (and limit) our behavior, perceptions, and affective responses. Her culture-systemic analysis also reveals how conceptual blackness and whiteness function in our society (Morrison, 1992), that is, how black people's socially constructed 'otherness' plays the role of alter-ego in relation to the society's normative conception of whiteness (Wynter, 1992a). Consequently, this alter-ego role actually gives black people — or any group put in this position — a perspective advantage of alterity that is not the result of our ethnicity but of our 'liminal' social position. Alterity not ethnicity, therefore, permits critically aware black people to understand and to challenge white supremacy/racism for the benefit of humanity.[5] That is why, as Karenga has observed, it is possible for Black Studies to be 'critical' and 'corrective'. Wynter's culture-systemic analysis enables us to understand and to transcend the societal discourse that regards black identity, intelligence, and ingenuity with suspicion — with the 'taint' of inferiority that results from our supposed 'genetic defectivity'. Hacker (1994) describes the persistence of this founding belief structure of race in American society thusly:

> . . . at the heart of the matter is a belief once freely voiced, but no longer openly aired, that African genes do not provide a capacity for complicated tasks. (p. 459)

In sum, Wynter's 'deciphering practice' of Black Studies (Wynter, 1992b) aims to advance human freedom from the 'specific perceptual-cognitive processes by which we know our reality' (Wynter, 1995, p. 13). Her analysis builds on the work of Carter G. Woodson, Frantz Fanon, Ralph Ellison, and others who laid the groundwork for the new studies that emerged in the 1960s, as well as scholars like Elsa Goveia and Asmarom Legesse, whose work contributes a Caribbean and African perspective on these matters.

Building a more just society and world is a task that involves re-writing the knowledge in school curricula and the academic disciplines, as Wynter's work suggests, and re-thinking the narratives that are embedded in our minds and bodies (that limit our cognitive and affective capacities). Thanks to the Black Studies Movement I developed greater understanding of, and I remain dedicated to, helping others understand the significance of the African presence in the history and development of this society — and indeed of all humanity (King and Wilson, 1990). Therefore, I have devised research methods that function pedagogically in culturally relevant ways to recuperate the truth of black life and cultural knowledge from America's myths, including the narrative of 'race'. Hopefully, my work is contributing to the kind of education in which people need to know their own special cultural truths, that is, as Karenga suggests, to know themselves in order to live better and to make a better world. Thus, the research contexts and methods I have constructed for recovering the collective cultural memories of African-American women, in particular, are designed to use our memories, knowledge, perceptions, and feelings to analyze and change our social and cultural condition.

My research has examined the educational and social practice of black women as mothers and as teachers, racism in the curriculum, and black student alienation. In the early 1980s I began a series of group conversations with black and white mothers about their social practice or pedagogy (Reeves [King], 1983). This experience led me to investigate the specific 'emancipatory pedagogy' of black teachers who were known to be particularly effective and dedicated to liberating education. I undertook these inquiries in response to the puzzlement that black women — both mothers and teachers — expressed to me about the education and survival of black children. The research that is reported in *Black Mothers to Sons: Juxtaposing African American Literature with Social Practice*, and in several other publications analyzing black student alienation and black teachers' emancipatory pedagogy (King, 1991b, 1992; King and Mitchell, 1995; King and Wilson, 1990; Reeves [King], 1983), illustrates the way in which I have involved the participants in my research in reciprocal and reflective dialogue with me and with each other. This line of inquiry began with listening to women who were trying to understand their own practice in relation to the predicament of black students and families.

My research documents the social practice/pedagogy of black mothers and teachers and contradicts the (mis)representation of their work in the education and social science literature and popular culture as well. Vivid memories of the remarkable women in my community-family have inspired me to search for and to construct liberating research methods and contexts to challenge the images of black women as inadequate mothers or emasculating matriarchs that I read about in graduate school, the popular stereotype in fiction, print, television, and film of black women as maids, mammies, and Jezebels, and the invisibility of black teachers in the research literature. That black women have been more honestly and accurately portrayed in black fiction and poetry is indicative of the 'communicentric bias' in the conceptual paradigms and research methodologies that Gordon and his colleagues identified and critiqued (1990). About the same time that Carolyn Mitchell and I were working on our study of black mothers and sons using African-American literature, these researchers suggested that a marriage between the 'arts, humanities and social sciences' is needed 'in order to understand the lived experiences of Blacks, Latinos and Native Americans' (p. 18). In fact, we used African-American literature in *Black Mothers to Sons: Juxtaposing African American Literature with Social Practice* (King and Mitchell, 1995), in the way Gordon and his colleagues suggested.

Also, in part as a result of methodological and ideological bias, my research and writing challenges positivist claims of a special, detached status of researcher 'neutrality' and 'objectivity' (King, 1995a, 1996a). I have advocated and modeled a more publicly partisan role for the researcher (and teacher) as a participant in the cooperative generation of 'critical consciousness and forms of knowledge that serve social action' (King, 1991b, p. 265). Further, I argue that this is a 'legitimate task of social research' (King and Mitchell, 1995) and education, a position that is perhaps more acceptable now that qualitative research and critical pedagogy have found a stronger foothold in the academy.

The inquiry processes I have developed conclude by focusing participants' attention on thought and action for changing the predicament of black people. This pedagogical role for research that has evolved includes reciprocal group conversation (among participants and with the researcher/s) followed by the 'practical-critical activity' of reflecting back on and co-analyzing our experience. This mode of inquiry helps participants recover and value their collective cultural memories and to develop historical consciousness. Critical, collective awareness of our history, centered in one's cultural reality, as well as knowledge and awareness of systemic factors, our own complicity in our predicament, and of our potential as change agents is what I am referring to as historical consciousness. One of my studies, which was undertaken in 1986, is a participatory investigation black teachers' emancipatory pedagogy (King, 1991b). The study concludes with the following observation regarding the pedagogical nature of this kind of participatory and liberating mode of inquiry:

> The discussion [with the Black teachers] that took place at the end of the research seminar suggests that this experience of reflecting on and sharing their thinking and practice holds some promise for supporting teachers in their professional development . . . [and] suggest[s] that the opportunities for reflective analysis and the supportive group experience that the study provided contributed to the teachers' conscious awareness of *system* factors that affect their teaching. (King, 1991b, p. 264)

The participating teachers found support in this research experience for their emancipatory pedagogy in opposition to alienating education. This study, which illustrates the research-as-pedagogy approach that I have been developing over a number of years, demonstrates the process of constructing a specific site of memory, which Clark refers to as *lieux de mémoire* (Clark, 1991; King, 1992).[6] I concluded that this kind of 're-search that involves [teachers] in learning with other teachers in this way can also help them gain the confidence and insight to work together to invent educational solutions for the problems of student alienation, professional disempowerment, and societal oppression' (p. 265). The search that led me to develop this kind of liberating research (and education) began when I was an undergraduate at Stanford University in the 1960s and we were awakened by reading Fanon's (1963) *Wretched of the Earth*, Freire's *Pedagogy of the Oppressed*, and other writers who privileged the collective cultural memory and historical consciousness of those for whom education (or research) has been a deadly weapon (King and Wilson, 1990). This contradictory dialectic of alienating schooling and resistance which has influenced my research is discussed below.

Education and Research: Deadly Weapons or Tools for Liberation?

> Some of our citizens will have large amounts of money spent on their education, while others have none. Those who receive this privilege, therefore, have a duty to repay the sacrifice which others have made. They are like the man who has been given all the food available in a starving village in order that he may have the strength to bring supplies back from a distant place . . . If he takes his food and does not bring help to his brothers he is a traitor. Similarly, if any of the young men and women who are given education by the people of this Republic adopt attitudes of superiority, or fail to use their knowledge to help the development of this country, then they are betraying our Union. (Mwalimu Julius K. Nyerere, Tanzania)

Alienating schooling annihilates or co-opts those who are unable to resist. Although I was not aware of it when I entered Stanford University in 1965, the cultural knowledge and the values that grounded me in my community-family also prepared me to resist schooling for alienation and annihilation. This was not necessarily a conscious and deliberate process of resistance but a journey of discovery and recovery of cultural memory that was aided by the Black Studies Movement, the 'new scholarship' of the 1960s, and mentoring by older scholars who showed us the way. The social movements and the climate of the 1960s as well as my family's socio-economic circumstances launched me on an inexorable search for the intellectual autonomy that is necessary to understand our special cultural truths and our social reality 'in order to change it'. I was the first and 'only one' to go to college but I had also been selected for this privilege, that is, for 'sponsored mobility' by the first grade when, for example, I was chosen to play the lead role of Jane in the school play. My mother has helped me remember that I learned the lines for all the characters not just my own. Certainly, the teachers appreciated my abilities. As the years passed, however, I watched as my family members and peers were utterly destroyed by the same alienating schooling that promoted and enabled my 'success'. Without consciously rejecting this unsettling reality, I nevertheless, began searching for something better than education for assimilation, alienation, or annihilation.

When I entered Stanford University during the height of the black liberation movements and the Black Arts Movement in the Diaspora and in Africa, black students had the opportunity to be inspired and challenged by black scholars, artists, and activists throughout the Black World. Amiri Baraka brought his revolutionary vision to the campus. In a riveting recital of his revolutionary poetry Baraka's challenge was: 'Who will survive America? Black people of course, very few Negroes and no colored people at all!' Karenga chided us to remember that the names of the workers who had built the buildings where we were studying would never be memorialized in placards on the walls. Reading James Boggs's book, *Pages from a Negro Worker's Notebook*, was also inspiring. Angela Davis, Gwen Patton Woods, and Sonja Sanchez were some of the women who moved us to more critical thought and action by their heroic example. We read Fanon in a community study group that St Clair Drake invited us to attend. Drake, as he was fondly known, introduced us to the black intellectual heritage in the large Black World, as we struggled to overcome our miseducation in our courses.

The dialectic of alienation and resistance that propelled me toward forms of consciousness and self-possession as an African-descent person also included particular community-family-church experiences that helped shape my identity, education, and my idea of work. I distinctly remember, for instance, a thunderous sermon a visiting minister delivered at our church one night. 'You are *black*, people. You are a *black* people!' he roared, putting extra stress on the word '*black*' each time and pounding the pulpit with his huge hands to punctuate this heretical message. We knew this minister; he was from a church in Oakland and he was a laborer like my father. His rugged hands, like my father's, were chapped, swollen, and calloused from digging ditches and shoveling wet cement. The church sat in stunned silence. At home later that evening, as my mother and I exchanged furtive glances, we laughed nervously and we whispered these heretofore unspoken words again: 'You are *black* people!' It felt good. Never had we heard such a fearless declaration of racial pride. A study of black history, of course, shows the powerful role of black ministers and the church in the black liberation struggle.

Just as the Black Panthers were organizing in the community, we black students were struggling for change on our campuses. By the time black students at San Francisco State launched the Black Studies Movement, I was ready to reject the idea that education should help us escape our community, family, identity, and the role and responsibilities of being black. I was one of the student leaders at Stanford who demanded changes in university admissions and the curriculum and the university's relationship to the community as well. An indication of the miseducation against which we were struggling is that, before I began to study with St Clair Drake, I discovered the Harlem Renaissance and the writing of WEB DuBois in Europe, when I was studying at Stanford's campus in Florence, Italy. No teacher in high school or at the university had ever mentioned this watershed of black intellectual history and culture. A poem by the Harlem Renaissance poet Waring Cuny (1923) titled 'No Images', that I read for the first time in 1968 in an Italian library, spoke directly to my predicament.

When I visited the Louvre in Paris, I was amazed to learn that the Egyptians were actually black like me. What I saw was the unmistakable black color the Egyptians used to depict themselves. I stood there dazed, motionless, and speechless in front of the wall sections taken from the Egyptian tombs.

Other memories of my awakening historical consciousness are more painful. While I was in Florence enjoying the privilege of studying the Italian language, absorbing European art and architecture and the glory of the European Renaissance (and recovering my African roots), black communities back in the United States were under siege. I felt helpless and betrayed. Black people were dying in the streets as cities burned and tanks rolled through our communities. I could barely express my anguish and distress to my fellow students. When I returned home, my older brother described how he sat up throughout the night with a loaded rifle across his lap trying to decide if he should go out in the streets and use it. As far as I am concerned, my consciousness, my educational privilege, and my opportunity to make a contribution to the 'race' have been bought at a terrible price. Although I excelled in school with the sponsorship of teachers at every grade level, many of my relatives and classmates, who were alienated from school were expelled, failed, jailed, and some were killed. I have never ceased to be in awe at the totality and brutality of their destruction. The disproportionate number of black men, women, and youth in prison today, the so-called 'war on drugs', and the criminalization of black men in particular are manifestations of alienating schooling for annihilation. Therefore, alienation, a central focus of sociological analysis, is not an abstract concept for me. I understand very well the distinction that Wynter makes between the supposed nihilism of black existence today and our *nihilated (néantisé)* identities (Wynter, 1989). My freshman class at Stanford in 1965 included the largest group of black students that had ever entered the university at one time. There were 25 of us and fewer than a dozen black students were already enrolled. Earl, a brother from Watts in inner-city Los Angeles, used to wear his 'stingy brim' hat and brightly colored 'Bossa Nova' shirts that stood out against the stark whiteness of White Plaza in the center of the campus. Before the end of our second year, Earl was dead. I believe that I became a sociology major to seek answers to save our lives.

It wasn't sociology but the 1960s that saved *my* life by making it possible for me to question the predominate research paradigm and the prevailing body of knowledge about black folks in this society that I was introduced to in my study of sociology and other courses. The process of becoming educated not merely schooled (Shujaa, 1994) included participating in the student-led, community-inspired movement to transform the university and use our knowledge in service to the community. We were deeply involved in the black community of East Palo Alto located at the opposite end of sedate, palm tree-lined University Avenue, the main thoroughfare in the city of Palo Alto that leads to Stanford.

Real community problems and the reality of oppression sharpened my understanding of the need for, and the possibility of, liberating education and research. For example, in my junior year I asked my sociological theory professor how this course could help me address the life and death issues I was confronting in East Palo Alto, where I lived at that time. He asked me if I ever worked crossword puzzles, which he described as an intellectually challenging past-time. Somewhat taken aback by this, I explained that I was too busy tutoring high school students who couldn't read and who were dropping out of school. So, I said, 'No', I had not spent any time working puzzles. Quite matter-of-factly he said, 'Perhaps you are not intellectually capable of succeeding here at Stanford. Maybe you should go down the road to San Jose State and study social work.' I excused myself and that was the last time I sought his assistance. Fortunately, I was developing other standards by which to measure my intellectual abilities and my potential for success at Stanford. My response to his assessment of me was to do good work on my own culture-centered terms. When I was a senior in the Sociology Honors program the next year, I began to critique the theoretical assumptions and the research methodology taught in my sociology courses as objective, neutral, and universal knowledge.[7]

I was both disturbed and challenged in another sociology course that used Native American Indian Coyote tales to illustrate achievement motivation theory and to demonstrate a statistical procedure for quantitative content analysis. The professor presented research that purported to show that Native American people have a low level of motivation to achieve, as demonstrated by an analysis of their folktales. I found the analysis to be culturally biased and offensive, so I devised a different statistical procedure. Mine showed that Coyote, the protagonist in the Native American tales, as well as 'High John the Conqueror' and 'Stack-o-lee', folk heroes in African-American tales (Lester, 1969), demonstrated more motivation to achieve than characters like 'Humpty Dumpty', 'Little Miss Muffet', and 'Jack and Jill' in European Mother Goose nursery rhymes. Although the TA asked me if I had done this work myself, I received an 'A' on the assignment. My collective cultural memory and my engagement with the black intellectual tradition enabled me to think such autonomous, oppositional thoughts.

Research with/for the Community:
From Cultural Knowledge to Social Action

. . . No one ever thinks that Duke Ellington might well have been a classical composer, but [that] he was looking for something better. (Ellison, 1972, p. 408)

The Black Studies Movement also called for both research and service in the community. As a result of my experience tutoring barely literate black high school students, I developed an honors thesis research project that focused on generating new knowledge related to the problem of student alienation. This project, which I completed at Ravenswood High School in east Palo Alto, focused on how black students understood and interpreted their own alienation and school failure. Working with a sympathetic school counselor, I developed an innovative qualitative research design that permitted me to talk with black students about these problems using examples that reflected their own lived experience of schooling. The counselor and I invented a group of fictitious 'cases', including photographs, school records, and family backgrounds for students who were failing, doing poorly academically, or were not achieving their full potential in school. I presented these cases in interviews with a group of black high school students whose records were similar to those of the ones we had invented. My purpose was to invite these students to help me understand their own behavior (e.g., cutting class) and 'lack of motivation' as well as how they perceived the fictitious cases. One student in this study offered a perceptive observation that I will never forget. This young black woman said, 'If he [the student in the case] knew *why* his parents are the way they are and *why* he is the way he is, maybe he could do better.' Her observation has been a guiding focus of my work since then.

My doctoral research a few years later involved a behavior change/decision-making curriculum intervention for black high school students that extended and built upon this honors thesis project. Since then, the research that I have conducted on the emancipatory pedagogy of black teachers, the social practice of black mothers, as well as analyses of alienating curriculum and racism in textbooks (King, 1992), reflect the importance of 'knowing why' in order to enable students, teachers, and parents to 'do better'. My research and writing focuses on alienation and consciousness, culture-centered knowledge, ideology, and hegemony, and bias in research, curriculum, and school knowledge. In short, I have been searching for ways of doing sociology better — in a way that does not serve oppression. My research and teaching can be seen as an ongoing, systematic study of how collective cultural memory, which is a form of folk knowledge, and historical consciousness can be mobilized to address problems in education and society. One premise of my research and teaching is that liberating methods of inquiry that use the cultural knowledge or lore of black people can support social action that serves human freedom and emancipatory education, including transformative, culture-centered pedagogy and curriculum. According to Robinson (1990), the word 'folklore' is a composite of 'folk' . . . meaning 'people' . . . and 'lore,' meaning 'knowledge' (p. 212). Robinson continues:

> Thus, it is the knowledge of the people, not just any knowledge but a particular knowledge that has proved to be valuable within a community because it has passed the test of time, a lore that people have found to contain important representations of themselves as a group. (p. 212)

My work is grounded in black lore or cultural knowledge, the Black Studies epistemology, and dialectical social theory (Fay, 1975; Giddens, 1979). This theory holds that people develop particular forms of knowledge (e.g., black cultural knowledge) which, like class consciousness, reflect 'a political and social awareness that grows out of a common experience; perceived common interests and shared self-knowledge and self-definition' (Eyerman, 1981, p. 283). I referred to such cultural knowledge as 'the survival structure of black life' in my doctoral dissertation (Reeves, 1974) and as 'diaspora literacy' (Clark, 1991) in a more recent publication (King, 1992). In *Black Mothers to Sons* I describe the need for a 'dialectical research strategy' to recover these forms of knowledge, that is, a research strategy 'which aims to help people discover more about their own lives in a culturally relevant way' (King and Mitchell, 1995, p. 67). Here is the description of my approach to this kind of liberating social science:

> This methodology recognizes that particular knowledge of the world contained in people's daily cultural practice and social experience is not merely distorted by the dominant ideology. Rather, knowledge generated from and grounded in people's culture and experience can be liberating as well. Illuminating the conditions which produce this kind of liberating, culturally relevant knowledge is the long-term theoretical and practical goal of the Afrocentric method. This methodology is the outgrowth of a conviction (and theoretical perspective) that social science inquiry can be a liberating process which simultaneously fulfills certain conditions of science. From this perspective what differentiates this partisan (non-neutral) mode of inquiry from a mere ideological exercise in self-deception is that it generates knowledge using procedures that are systematic and public, that is, knowledge that is subject to verification or refutation. (p. 67)

Although I had long since graduated, I sought Drake's reaction to this chapter because these were issues we had discussed many times over the years. It was very gratifying when he read it and told me that my position was 'well argued'. In fact, since this book was first published in 1990, other liberatory and critical approaches have evolved among Afrocentric and feminist scholars and researchers in the decolonized world (Bellenger, 1992; Collins, 1991; Dubell et al., 1980). In a chapter in the *Handbook for Research on Multicultural Education*, I discuss several exemplary educational models, which I refer to as 'culture-centered', that value community knowledge and 'redirect learning [and research] toward community needs' (King, 1995a, p. 281). These models include Maiga's (1995) Gao School Museum, a pedagogical innovation that was developed in Mali, West Africa; Fasheh's (1990) critical community based approach to mathematics that is responsive to the Palestinian revolt; and the critical, culturally grounded teaching interventions MacLeod (1991) developed working with black students in rural Mississippi. Both Maiga's Gao School Museum and MacLeod's culture-centered critical pedagogy, which builds on the freedom schools of the Civil Rights movement, 'get students directly involved in studying their culture and emphasize the need for social action through collaborative research that enhances their academic learning' (King, 1995, p. 281).

As my research evolved, I also resolved certain contradictions and criticisms of critical pedagogy and research grounded in critical theory. For example, opponents of these approaches argue that there is an inevitable element of coercion or indoctrination involved in critical theory/pedagogy, whether used in the classroom or the research process. In addition to concerns about ideological imposition, however, black researchers have experienced the countervailing positivist admonition that researchers should be objective and, therefore, detached from the 'object' of study as a particularly burdensome dilemma. I experienced this dilemma in graduate school and addressed it my doctoral dissertation in the following way:

> Social science research as a vehicle of the oppressor's ideology and consciousness, which the black [graduate] student must internalize to be accepted as a full-fledged member of the profession, conflicts with the values, goals, and experiences all oppressed people necessarily share. (Reeves, 1974, p. 87)

The Dean of the School of Education at Stanford at the time, Arthur Coladarci, suggested that I address such concerns by including an additional chapter in my doctoral dissertation called 'The Black Sociology of Knowledge'. At first, I believed I was given this assignment as a sanction for having taken a public (and political) position that was critical of the cultural deficit paradigm that was prevalent in the School of Education at that time. Actually, the assignment helped me tremendously: It challenged me to review the literature systematically and to critique the prevailing paradigm in writing. Consequently, in this chapter I expressed my understanding of the partisan role of the researcher and the socio-cultural foundations of research (and teaching) by, for, and with the people (King, 1990; 1994; 1995a, b; 1996; 1997). Affirming my cultural groundings in this way was an invaluable lesson, for as CLR James understood so well, culture is also a form of political expression (Hamilton, 1992).

With the assistance of professors like St Clair Drake and Elizabeth G. Cohen, who listened to me, challenged me, and encouraged me to express and develop my views, eventually I was able to articulate an alternative to the theoretical, epistemological, and methodological orthodoxy of the time in sociology and education. In the process, I also discovered the scholarship of other black and Third World scholars who were raising these issues in other fields, including the humanities. For instance, the black essayist Mel Watkins emphasized the importance of using our own lens to view and interpret black life and culture. I cited his critical essay on James Brown's lyrics in my doctoral dissertation to make the point that 'the black alternative to the "meaningless and fragmented existence" of mainstream American culture [and education] has been an intense concentration' on the personal in social relationships (Watkins, 1971, p. 30).[8] Scholar-activists like Grace and James Boggs provided incisive readings of reality. In fact, an essay by Grace Boggs analyzing the educational crisis facing black youth that I cited in my doctoral thesis, is still urgently relevant today. In this essay Grace Boggs noted that:

> The overwhelming majority of black youth see no relationship between this type of education and their daily lives in the community or the problems of today's world which affect them so intimately . . . (Boggs, 1974, p. 69)

My point is that in graduate school I experienced a similar kind of alienation. However, our predecessors in the black intellectual tradition had demonstrated ways to 'marry their thought' in Wynter's words (1995) to the plight of the oppressed (Childs, 1989;

Fasheh, 1990; King and Mitchell, 1995; MacLeod, 1991), and sometimes asking my mother or grandmother their views on a particular subject also kept me grounded. That is to say, the collective cultural memory of the lived realities of the Black Experience aided my search for ways to recover and to use the knowledge and cultural practices that have been of value to black people's survival. Thus, both critical scholarly analyses and the folk or traditional wisdom of our 'living thinkers' (James, 1993) have been central to my development as an activist scholar and educator.

Though challenging, graduate school was part and parcel of my continuing journey of discovering a larger and ongoing black intellectual tradition of struggle. In the process I questioned the concepts, methods, and world view that research terms such as 'informant', 'collaborator', 'control group', 'target population' as well as labels like 'drop-out' and 'culturally deprived' connote. I rejected methods and concepts that disempower people by making them 'objects' rather than 'subjects'. Eventually, I resolved the contradiction between the conflicting interests and the culture of the social science profession and the needs and culture(s) of oppressed people by creating opportunities to include those whom I am studying *with* as full-fledged partners in the research process (and in my pedagogy). Although I use methods like participant observation in my research, I accept without ambivalence the responsibility and leadership involved in modifying this methodology in order to do research in partnership with people in ways that serve the community's interests (King, 1988).

Despite the psychic holocaust of racism (King and Mitchell, 1995), in my community-village we lived and worked in respectful solidarity; upheld the ethic and dignity of good work; and demonstrated racial solidarity while valuing cultural democracy. As a result of a deepening understanding of this cultural legacy, my commitment to a liberating mode of culture-centered research and education for all people also deepened. My recent research and pedagogy in teacher education opposes society's obsessive valorization of whiteness and challenges ideological distortions in the curriculum and the culture. The experiences described in this chapter have helped me to build a pedagogy for (mostly white) credential candidates that responds to a form of racism that I have identified and defined as dysconsciousness[9] (King, 1991a; 1995c; 1997).

Conclusion

Malcolm	. . . The greatest mistake of the movement has been trying to organize a sleeping people around specific goals. You have to wake people up first; then you'll get action.
Miss Nadle	Wake them up to their exploitation?
Malcolm	No, to their humanity, to their own worth, and to their heritage. The biggest difference between the parallel oppression of the Jew and the Negro is that the Jew never lost his pride in being a Jew. He never ceased to be a man. He knew he had made a significant contribution to the world, and his sense of his own value gave him the courage to fight back. It enabled him to act and think independently, unlike our people and our leaders. (Breitman 1965, p. 198)

My work as a sociologist of education and teacher educator in both university and community contexts relies on reflective, experiential, community-based inquiry methods that evoke and use black people's collective cultural memory in order to awaken people's historical consciousness of oppression and agency. During a recent group interview that

I organized with several black women who wanted to start a community women's group, for example, we shared memories of women who had exerted a strong, positive influence on our lives. This group conversation led us to rediscover ourselves in contrast to the negative image of black women represented, for example, by the hideous aunt Jemima stereotype ('Ain't cha mammy, black? Ain't cha mammy on the pancake box?'). By listening to each other's stories, we discovered that black *and* white people had called our foremothers 'aunt' as a sign of profound respect for their special status and power in the community. The realization that 'aunt Jemima' could symbolize black women's power rather than our degradation was so compelling and energizing that it became the generative theme for the women's leadership development group. We called our group: 'The Jemima Circle'. The experiential curriculum I developed involved a culture-centered examination of our skills, cultural knowledge, and lived experience. I have used this kind of community praxis or research-as-pedagogy to recover our cultural knowledge, to keep us from forgetting who we are as African-descent people, and to enable us to realize what more we are capable of achieving. As the African proverb says, 'Knowledge is another name for strength' (King, 1992). The analysis of this learning experience will focus on the use of African-American cultural knowledge in adult learning, women's development, and community change.

In conclusion, the community-family values and cultural expression of the black folk tradition that have kept our humanity in tact and the black intellectual critique of white supremacy/racism have been integral to my search for ways to make education and research tools for liberation. This chapter illustrates my liberatory praxis of education and research, yet it is well to remember that 'the half has not been told'.

Notes

1   Urban black males, for example, face a '... 10 percent chance of death by homicide (for whites, it's 1 in 80); 27 percent decline in average real income for black men in their 20s from the early 1970s to the mid-1980s; during roughly the same period, they filled just one out of every 1,000 new jobs created; white life expectancy is still rising, but life spans for black males declined four years in a row in the 1980s, dipping below 65 ... Black males account for one in four cases of AIDS, 46 percent of all prisoners in the United States; they are jailed at a rate four times higher than in South Africa ... In Milwaukee, black males account for less than 30 percent of the students, but they face 50 percent of the suspensions and over 90 percent of the expulsions. Less than 2 percent of black males maintain an A or B average and less than 20 percent sustain a C average or better' (S. Karp, 1991, *Z Magazine*, p. 87).

2   Trinidadian scholar-activist and organizer, CLR James lived for a time in the US. A culture and social change theoretician and revolutionary strategist and thinker, he wrote a history of the Haitian Revolution, *The Black Jacobins*, from the perspective of the enslaved Africans.

3   St Clair Drake (1987) explicated the importance of the *Black Experience* and studying it from a *Black Perspective* in *Black Folk Here and There* (Los Angeles: UCLA Center for Afro-American Studies). Drake was one of my mentors at Stanford University. As head of the African and Afro-American Studies Program, he introduced a generation of black students to the black intellectual tradition and to rigorous, independent thought in our *own interests*. See the dedication to his memory in, 'In search of African liberation pedagogy: Multiple contexts of education and struggle,' which I wrote as guest editor for this theme issue of the *Journal of Education* (Volume 172, number 2, 1990, pp. 3–4).

4   A schema is 'a mental codification of experience that includes a particular organized way of perceiving cognitively and responding to a complex situation or set of stimuli' (*Webster's New Collegiate Dictionary*.) I discuss this pedagogy in greater detail in: 'Thank you for opening

our minds: On praxis, transmutation and Black Studies in teacher development', in J.E. King, E.R. Hollins and W.C. Hayman (eds) (New York: Teachers College Press, 1997).

5 Sylvia Wynter discusses the meaning of alterity in several publications, including the *Dictionary of Multicultural Education* (Grant and Ladson-Billings, 1997).

6 In an article that describes my analysis of and involvement in California's controversial history textbook adoption in 1991, I use the term *lieux de mémoire* to refer to the practical-critical research context that I constructed to investigate parents' and teachers' understanding of the Black Studies critique of racism in these texts (King, 1992).

7 A number of publications during this period questioned the bias of the social science disciplines, particularly sociology and psychology. See Alkalimat (1969) and J. Ladner (1973).

8 Space does not permit me to discuss the significance of interpersonal relationships and values such as reciprocity and respect, for example, with regard to the communal nature of black life. See the discussion of mutuality and reciprocity in black family relations in *Black Mothers to Sons* (King and Mitchell, 1995) and the discussion of Alasal-Tarey, a Songhay (West African) cultural concept, in 'The purpose of schooling for African American Children: Including cultural knowledge' (King, 1994). Also, urban anthropologist Elijah Anderson's research demonstrates the importance today of respect among black youth, whose 'code of the streets' emphasizes not being 'dissed' or disrespected (Anderson, 1990) *Streetwise: Race, Class and Change in an Urban Community*, Chicago: University of Chicago Press).

9 Elsewhere I define the 'limited and distorted understandings my students have demonstrated about inequity and cultural diversity' as 'dysconsciousness': that is, '. . . an uncritical habit of mind [including perceptions, attitudes, assumptions, and beliefs] that justifies inequity and exploitation by accepting the existing order of things as given' (King, 1991a, p. 134).

References

ALKALIMAT, A.H. (1969) 'The ideology of black social science', *Black Scholar*, **4**, 2, pp. 28–35.
ANDERSON, E. (1990) *Streetwise: Race, Class and Change in an Urban Community*, Chicago: University of Chicago Press.
BALLENGER, C. (1992) 'Because you like us: The language of control', *Harvard Educational Review*, **62**, 2, pp. 199–208.
BOGGS, J. (1963) *The New American Revolution: Pages from a Negro Worker's Notebook*, NY: Monthly Review Press.
BOGGS, G. (1974) 'Education: The great obsession', in Institute of the Black World (ed.) *Education and Black Struggle: Notes from the Colonized World, Harvard Education Review*, **2**, pp. 61–81.
BREITMAN, G. (ed.) (1965) *Malcolm X Speaks*, New York: Grove Press.
CARR, W. and KEMMIS, S. (1986) *Becoming Critical: Education, Knowledge, and Action Research*, London: Falmer Press.
CHILDS, J.B. (1989) *Leadership, Conflict, and Cooperation in Afro-American Social Thought*, Philadelphia: Temple University Press.
CLARK, V. (1991) 'Developing Diaspora literacy and Marasa consciousness', in SPILLERS, H. (ed.) *Comparative American Identities*, New York: Routledge, pp. 40–61.
COLLINS, P.H. (1991) 'Black feminist thought: Knowledge, consciousness, and the politics of empowerment', New York: Routledge.
CUNY, WARING (1923) 'No images', in JOHNSON J.W. (ed.) *The Book of American Negro Poetry*, NY: Harcourt, Brace and Company, p. 283.
DRAKE, S.C. (1987) *Black Folk Here and There* (Volume I), Los Angeles: Center for Afro-American Studies, UCLA.
DUBELL, F., ERASMIE, T. and DE VRIES, J. (eds) (1980) *Research for the People: Research by the People*, Linkoping, Sweden: Linkoping University.
ELLISON, R. (1972) 'Remarks at the American Academy of Arts and Sciences Conference on the Negro American, 1965', in CHAPMAN, A. (ed.) *New Black Voices: Criticism*, New York: The New American Library, pp. 402–8.

EYERMAN, R. (1981) *False Consciousness and Ideology in Marxist Theory*, Atlantic Highlands, NJ: Humanities Press.

FANON, F. (1963) *The Wretched of the Earth*, NY: Grove Press.

FASHEH, M. (1990) 'Community education: To reclaim and transform what has been made invisible', *Harvard Educational Review*, **60**, 1, pp. 19–35.

FAY, B. (1975) *Social Theory and Political Practice*, London: George Allen and Unwin.

FREIRE, P. (1970) *Pedagogy of the Oppressed*, New York: Continuum Press.

GAY, G. and BABER, W.L. (eds) (1987) *Expressively Black*, NY: Praeger.

GIDDENS, A. (1979) *Central Problems in Sociological Theory*, Berkeley: UC Press.

GORDON, E.W., MILLER, F. and ROLLOCK, D. (1990) 'Coping with communicentric bias in knowledge production in the social sciences', *Educational Researcher*, **19**, 3, pp. 14–19.

GRANT, C. and LADSON-BILLINGS, G. (1997) *Dictionary of Multicultural Education*, Phoenix, AZ: Oryx Press.

HACKER, A. (1994, April 4) 'The elusion of equality', *The Nation*, **258**, 13, pp. 457–9.

HARPER, F.E. (1892/1992) 'Iola Leroy or shadows uplifted', in ANDREWS, W. (ed.) *The African American Novel in the Age of Reaction*, NY: Penguin Books.

JAMES, C.L.R. (1963) *The Black Jacobins*, NY: Vintage Books.

JAMES, C.L.R. (1970) 'The Atlantic slave trade and slavery: Some interpretations of their significance in the development of the United States and the western world', in WILLIAMS, J.A. and HARRIS, C.F. (eds) *Amistad 1*, NY: Vintage Books, pp. 119–64.

JAMES, J. (1993) 'African philosophy, theory, and "living thinkers"', in FARMER, J.J. and FARMER, R. (eds) *Spirit, Space and Survival: African American Women in (White) Academe*, NY: Routledge, pp. 31–46.

KARENGA, M. (1993) *Introduction to Black Studies*, Los Angeles: University of Sankore Press.

KARP, S. (1991, June) 'Is black male all right?', *Z Magazine*, pp. 86–8.

KILMINSTER, R. (1979) *Praxis and Method*, London: Routledge and Kegan Paul.

KING, J.E. (1988) 'A black woman speaks on leadership', *Sage*, **5**, 2, pp. 49–52.

KING, J.E. (1991b) 'Unfinished business: Black student alienation and black teacher's emacipatory pedagogy', in FOSTER, M. (ed.) *Readings on Equal Education, Volume 11: Qualitative Investigations into Schools and Schooling*, NY: AMS Press, pp. 245–71.

KING, J.E. (1991a) 'Dysconscious racism: Ideology, identity, and the miseducation of teachers', *Journal of Negro Education*, **60**, 2, pp. 133–46.

KING, J.E. (1992) 'Diaspora literacy and consciousness in the struggle against miseducation in the black community', *Journal of Negro Education*, **61**, 3, pp. 317–40.

KING, J.E. (1994) 'The purpose of schooling for African American children: Including cultural knowledge', in HOLLINS, E.R., KING, J.E. and HAYMAN, W.C. (eds) *Teaching Diverse Populations: Formulating a Knowledge Base*, Albany: SUNY, pp. 26–44.

KING, J.E. (1995a) 'Culture-centered knowledge: Black studies, curriculum transformation, and social action', *The Handbook of Research on Multicultural Education*, NY: Macmillan, pp. 265–90.

KING, J.E. (1995b) 'Nationalizing the curriculum or downsizing citizenship?', in EISNER, E. (ed.) *The Hidden Consequences of a National Curriculum*, Washington, DC: American Educational Research Association, pp. 119–44.

KING, J.E. (1995c) 'Race and education: In what ways does race affect the educational process: A response', in KINCHELOE, J.L. and STEINBERG, S.R. (eds) *Thirteen Questions: Reframing Education's Conversation* (2nd ed.), New York: Peter Lang, pp. 159–79.

KING, J.E. (1996a) 'Bad luck, bad blood, bad faith: Ideological hegemony and the oppressive language of hoodoo social science', in KINCHELOE, J.L., STEINBERG, S.R. and GRESSON, III A.D. (eds) *Measured Lies: The Bell Curve Examined*, NY: St Martin's Press, pp. 177–92.

KING, J.E. (1996b) 'Race/ethnicity', in JONES, F. et al. (eds) *Encyclopedia of African-American Education*, Westport, CT: Greenwood Press, pp. 380–4.

KING, J.E. (1997) '"Thank you for opening our minds": On praxis, transmutation and black studies in teacher development', in KING J.E., HALINS, E.R. and HAYMAN, W.C. (eds) *Preparing Teachers for Cultural Diversity*, NY: Teachers College Press, 1977, pp. 156–69.

KING, J.E., HOLLINS, E.R. and HAYMAN, W.C. (eds) (1997) *Preparing Teachers for Cultural Diversity*, New York: Teachers College Press.

KING, J.E. and MITCHELL, C.A. (1995) *Black Mothers to Sons: Juxtaposing African Literature with Social Practice*, New York: Peter Lang (First published, 1990).

KING, J.E. and WILSON, T.L.W. (1990) 'Being the soul-freeing substance: A legacy of hope in Afro-Humanity', *Journal of Education*, **172**, 2, pp. 9–27.

LADNER, J. (ed.) (1973) *The Death of White Sociology*, New York: Vintage Books.

LESTER, J. (1969) *Black Folktales*, NY: Grove Press.

MacLEOD, J. (1991) 'Bridging street and school', *Journal of Negro Education*, **60**, 3, pp. 260–75.

MAIGA, H. (1995) 'Bridging classroom, curriculum, and community: The Gao School Museum', *Theory into Practice*, **34**, 3, pp. 209–15.

MORRISON, T. (1992) *Playing in the Dark: Whiteness in the Literary Imagination*, Cambridge, MA: Harvard University Press.

NATIONAL ALLIANCE OF BLACK SCHOOL EDUCATORS (1984) *Saving the African American Child*, Washington, DC: Author.

NYERERE, J.K. (1967) *Education for Self-reliance*, Dar-es Salaam, Tanzania: Author.

REEVES, J.K. (King, J.E.) (1974) 'An experimental evaluation of a behavior change curriculum for black high school students', Unpublished doctoral thesis, Stanford University.

REEVES, J.K. (King, J.E.) (1983, April) 'A comparison of mothers' and teachers' educational practice by race and social class: A dialectical research strategy', Paper presented at the American Educational Research Association annual meeting, Montreal, Canada.

ROBINSON, B.J. (1990) 'Africanisms in the study of folklore', in HOLLOWAY, J.E. (ed.) *Africanisms in American Culture*, Bloomington: University of Indiana Press, pp. 211–24.

SHUJAA, M. (1994) *Too Much Schooling, Too Little Education: The Paradox of Black Life in White Societies*, Trenton, N.J. Africa World Press.

WATKINS, M. (1971) 'The lyrics of James Brown: Money won't change your lickin' stick', in WILLIAMS, J.A. and HARRIS, C.F. (eds) *Amistad 2*, NY: Random House, pp. 21–43.

WOODSON, C.G. (1933) *The Mis-education of the Negro*, Washington, DC: Associated Publishers.

WYNTER, S. (1989) 'Beyond the word of man: Glissant an the new discourse of the Antilles', *World Literature Today*, **63**, pp. 637–48.

WYNTER, S. (1992a) *'Do Not Call Us Negros': How Multicultural Textbooks Perpetuate Racism*, San Francisco: Aspire Books.

WYNTER, S. (1992b) '"No humans Involved": An open letter to my colleagues', *Voices of the African Diaspora*, **8**, 2, pp. 13–16.

WYNTER, S. (1992c) 'Re-thinking aesthetics: Notes toward a deciphering practice', in CHAME, M. (ed.) *Ex-iles: Essays on Caribbean Cinema*, Trenton, NJ: Africa World Press, pp. 237–79.

WYNTER, S. (1995) '1942: A new world view', in HYATT, V.L. and NETTLEFORD, R. (eds) *Race, Discourse, and the Origin of the Americas*, Washington: Smithsonian Institution Press, pp. 5–57.

10 Finding My Life's Work

Mildred J. Hudson

Getting from There to Here

It seems natural as I reflect today why I have a PhD in Educational Administration and Organizational Behavior. My dissertation (Hudson, 1985), and later book, *How Educators Get Top Jobs: Understanding Race and Gender Differences in the Old Boy Network* (Hudson, 1991), focus on the inequities of the nation's educational and employment systems. I feel pleased with these studies, knowing that I have added two more pieces of research to the store of literature on race relations and discrimination. The studies were conducted to help counter the lies, misconceptions and stereotypes that are so entrenched today in universal thought.

But feeling a certain measure of satisfaction with this early research did not just happen by chance. It was a process that began when a friend and colleague, Harvard researcher Sondra Kathryn Wilson, asked me a question that I could not immediately answer:

'How could you have pursued a PhD given the circumstances of your early life?' she asked.

I had never thought about the question in depth and gave her a rather glib answer:

'I am not very different from all the other African-Americans born in the South during World War II. My family were poor farmers who lived in the backwoods; I learned the value of hard work, loyalty and family tradition.'

My friend was skeptical: 'Lots of people live on farms, work hard and love their families', she said, 'but they don't earn PhDs. They never become researchers and writers. How did you get from there to here?'

I tried again. I told my friend that the secret probably lies in the birthplace — that the world is full of displaced Mississippians who once lived a nightmare. It is probably the memory of the nightmare that is the motivating factor: I know what America once was — and what it sometimes yearns to be.

My friend persisted, reminding me that even at the age of 18 I demonstrated little if any, real academic promise; nor was I a typical 'late bloomer' in my mid-20s. 'And', she added, putting the final touches on her argument, 'you never even met a person with a PhD until you were an adult!'

I told my friend that there is probably more to it than I wanted to admit; and even I know that describing the harshness of Mississippi never really reveals the full story of my family, my life, what motivates me. I grew up in a segregated black world in the backwoods of Mississippi in a world filled with cotton fields and canebrake. It was a racy world of rich soil, pungent in gospel flavor and swinging in the rhythm of the blues.

The juxtaposition is always there when thinking about that birth land. My childhood included a generous and loving black community, but also a world teeming with white supremacists, white sheets, and red-faced white men with rancor dripping from their hearts.

In this chapter, I hope to share with the reader how my present goals, beliefs, interpretations and aspirations evolved from an early age through personal experience. I explore ways in which I have utilized such experiences not only to conduct better research, but in my other professional positions as well. I hope that those new to the field of research and writing will do the same as I have and make a commitment to work within issues of equity and access for all people.

The Early Years: A Stranger in the Family

Shortly after *How Educators Get Top Jobs* was published, my mother and I shared memories from my childhood. We laughed as we recalled my struggle in our big, rambunctious family of 10. We remembered my feelings of isolation, even with four brothers and three sisters.

At the age of 4 I had walked a short distance from our home to sit alongside the dirt road that passed in front of the family farm. Sitting there, I felt so small against the tall weeping willows and thick growing weeds. I worried as I watched the darkening sky, encircled by high cotton and corn fields. Could a rattlesnake be slithering nearby? Would another mad dog come searching for chickens?

As I sat there, I allowed my young mind to escape. I imagined that my 'real' family would rescue me and take me to a world embraced by tranquillity. Growing up in my lively family, I felt a keen need for peace and quiet. But the sun receded and the sky turned black and my mythical family never arrived. Sometime later, however, my real mother did. She repeated what she had said to me on so many other evenings: that I *was* home; that this was my real family; and that I needed to prepare for bed.

Later as two aging adults, my mother and I would remember these earlier patterns and concerns — and laugh with a certain relief that we both made it through that period in our lives.

'Frankly, I would have wondered about your family origin myself', my mother chuckled, 'had I not felt the pain of your birth. You were so different, but always a wonderful addition to the family and a comfort to us all. We tried hard to understand your special needs. We knew you had the makings to write this wonderful book.'

I was the first in my immediate family to earn a high school diploma. My five brothers and sisters before me wanted to attend school but, because there was farm work to do, it was nearly impossible.

My oldest sister, Mildverta, told me recently that by the time my father allowed them to register for school in late November, the first semester was almost over.

'Imagine trying to learn a full semester's work in a few short weeks', my sister said, 'and add to that the fact that we never learned to read well — never really had any books. In school, the teachers didn't know what to do with us, and we didn't know what to do with ourselves.'

It was easier for me to attend school. Being one of the younger siblings, by the time I began school my parents had acquired additional land and the family finances had improved. I never really experienced the hard farm work that extracted so much of my family's time and energy. I also began doing something early-on that excused me from most chores, and I took advantage of it. I learned to read at the age of 4.

I am not quite sure how it happened — or even if I read well — but I received enormous attention from everyone for trying. I also discovered that some members of the family would move about quietly when I picked up reading materials. Whenever I could, I used these materials to send a strong message that everyone should be quiet. I would climb up on a kitchen chair, spread the written symbols prominently before me and read out loud with great aplomb. Such performances almost always lowered the level of the other noise in the house.

I loved reading, and still do today. As a child, it was a way to discover the world outside of the farm. There were no public libraries or school libraries, so almost everything I read was inappropriate for a young mind. I read magazines like *True Love*, *Sepia*, *Love Stories* and other monthlies that extolled stories of love, romance, and 'immoral' sex. My brothers and sisters also occasionally brought home a few old books, which I eagerly explored. There was also a weekly newspaper, black magazines like *Jet* and *Ebony*, *Reader's Digest* and the Bible.

In 1954, at the age of 11, I read many stories written by whites about how the Brown vs. Board of Education of Topeka, Kansas decision would destroy the white race, and civilization. I also followed the Rosa Parks case in the newspapers in 1955. It was sometime during those pre-adolescent years that I decided I would have to leave the South: that I would need to seek a bigger world. I began to pay particular attention to news of cities like Chicago, New York, Los Angeles, even Paris.

Being the first in my family to earn a high school diploma was a proud moment for our family. I could never, however, avoid thinking about my older siblings and how they (certainly as capable, if not more, than I) had been shortchanged in their education. I am sure this inequity inspired me to want to bring about equal access to education for all children. I wanted every child to learn to read, and be able to grow intellectually. Nothing in life seems more dismal than to think the odds are against you — that one is predestined to live a hopeless existence.

The Impact of Racism

My family and I experienced a level of racial discrimination in our early years that, even today, feels like an open wound. Without planning, I have somehow been able to transfer this pain and fear into a body of research that, hopefully, will continue to help others. During the 1940s and 1950s, when I was growing up, the country seemed relentless in its discriminatory practices. I think there were two incidents that made me vow to try to do something about race in America.

I can still remember the pain in my father's face when he vowed never again to speak to my mother's uncle, Mose Wright, for allowing the white mob to murder my 14-year-old cousin, Emmett Till, and dump his body into the Tallahatchi River.

'He [Mose Wright], my father would utter with great sadness', should never have been without his gun. He should have shot those men at first sight and died before he allowed them to take his grandson.' In my father's eyes, my mother's uncle was not a real man. He had let the family *and* the race down.

There in *Jet Magazine* is my cousin's mangled body rumpled in a casket for all the world to see. I feel fear and shame as I read the article. I try to understand how his smiling brown eyes (a trait of the Hudson clan) could now look like big black holes. 14 years old and dead, dead, dead: His tortured face now like rotting gravy on black, moldy biscuits.

The article in *Jet* states that this is what happens when a black boy whistles at a white woman. Could this happen to me? Could a 12-year-old black girl like me be killed, too? I thought about all the standards of behavior I had learned from the family, the black community, the broader white society. I could not remember any rules for whistling. I wondered what white people wanted from us: From what I had learned, they already owned almost everything. Years later, I came across some words from the poet, James Weldon Johnson, that resonated in my thoughts of Emmett's murder:

> Undoubtedly, some people will find it difficult to understand why a supremacy of which we have heard so much, a supremacy which claims to be based upon congenital superiority should require such drastic methods of protection. (1995)

My father was a man who tried hard to protect his family, yet, I can never remember a day as a child when I felt safe. If not for us, then for someone we knew who might be threatened or killed, beaten, robbed or forced to flee terror in the middle of the night.

Even before my cousin's death, there were other experiences that instilled in me a hunger for understanding and eradicating racism. I understood that Whites had power that my family and friends did not, except perhaps, for my father — and his guns. There were guns everywhere that we were taught from an early age to shoot: BB guns, 22's, and shotguns (if we lived long enough to use them). I sensed early-on that guns are dangerous, but crucial to our survival.

There was a gun in the 1949 Hudson that my father was driving. My relatives marveled at the new car, particularly because it carried the family's name. But on this day heading south from nearby Clarksdale to Greenwood, Mississippi, my preoccupation was with trying to keep my freshly starched clothes from being wrinkled. As usual, there was little room in the car.

We were on the two-lane rather bumpy highway on our way to visit relatives, and despite the fights in the car's back seat, I loved these family outings. We would usually arrive at one of our relatives' houses, begin eating the moment we arrived and continue eating until the late afternoon. But not long after embarking on the trip, I sensed that something was wrong. The teasing in the car's back seat was unusually harsh and unrelenting. Then everyone's voice soon became too loud, even for our family. The heat became unbearable, especially because the windows were all closed.

Trying to relax in my mother's lap, my shoes accidentally landed on my brother's clean pants, but he did not yell at me as he usually did. Like everyone else in the car, my brother seemed preoccupied, looking toward the rear of the car. Everyone, except, that is, my father, who was driving and looking straight ahead.

I still remember the stiffness of my mother's arms as she tried to comfort me, but hearing shouting from all around me, I picked up on the fear in the car and joined in shouting orders to my father. That was how my family was (and still is) — always acting like a pack of lemmings, responding in unison in times of joy and in times of pain — always coalescing and together.

We were moving faster down the road than I had ever experienced, and my father was reaching into the glove compartment for his gun.

The children were all shouting, 'Go faster, Daddy!' My mother was crying for my father to stop.

My mother's pleas finally won out, and the car came to an abrupt halt. My father placed the gun in his pocket, got out of the car and walked back to the car that was following us. In the blue car were four white men with their siren screaming and scroll light flashing. As I watched my father walk toward their car, one man stayed behind and three of the men walked toward him. I remember thinking that the numbers seemed unfair: four men against one man with a car full of young children and a pregnant wife. As the men met my father halfway between their car and ours, I could hear my father's words, but not theirs, and he was shouting:

> I said, what do you want?
> (Pause).
> I wasn't driving too fast!
> (Pause)
> What you scaring my wife and children for? You can take me to jail, but don't scare my children.
> (Pause)
> Well, take me to jail then, but I'm not giving you a penny 'til we get to the police station.

Then my father abruptly returned to the car and followed the four men toward whatever destiny had been decided. We trailed behind the men for quite some distance, but they moved at a speed difficult for us to keep pace with. My father slowed down. The men soon disappeared.

In the next town, we learned that the men were not policemen as they had claimed, but highway robbers, who spotted a black family in a new car, and suspected easy prey.

I cannot remember now if we continued our trip. It does not matter. But it was at that age that I began to think seriously about the life we were living. I wondered why we had been forced off the road. I saw the fear in my father's eyes and remembered being enormously grateful to him for risking his life for his family. There, in that car, I wanted to help my father and family for making my life bearable. I vowed to find new ways to help protect my family; to pick up the torch where my father left off. But back then, at the age of 6, I could not yet know how.

Looking back, the answer to my friend's question, 'How did you get here from there', became clearer. It is not very difficult after considering my early life to see how I got here — to understand how the values, influences and experiences of my family are represented in my research and writing. My parents taught me the value of hard work. Racism was pervasive in my life. In all of my research — whether I am the author or whether I am responsible for commissioning the author — there are always three major themes:

- The search for ways to eradicate racial discrimination.
- The study of obstacles to employment for African-Americans, women and other people of color.
- The examination of the inequities that poor and minority children face in public schools, including the search for ways to improve the education and skills of adults who serve them.

Back then, as a young child, I think I picked up my family's torch in the only way I could — by being a good student. I graduated second in my class from elementary school. In high school, besides doing quite well, I also worked full-time and embarked on a life of self-study that went far beyond what my teachers required.

I read the work of African-American scholars like WEB DuBois, James Weldon Johnson, and another of my mother's cousins, Richard Wright. I read all of Shakespeare's tragedies, and gained additional insights into the state of the world from Dostoevsky,

Tolstoy, Marx and Ghandi. I spent my early years looking for ways to understand the commonalties among people. I graduated from high school, then I left for New York.

Gaining a Broader Perspective

I took the Trailways bus to New York, arriving with only $8 in my pocket. I chose New York for no other reason than it was how far my money could take me by bus. I found a place to stay one night and (with the advice of rooming house neighbors about how to find temporary work in the city) landed a job the next day. I lived in the rooming house on 89th Street and Columbus Avenue and worked as a temporary clerk at Macy's, the department store on 34th Street. I worked at Macy's five days a week and cleaned other people's apartments on weekends.

I liked living in the rooming house, but it was hot and dirty and dangerous. Sometimes drug deals went sour. People were shot. Once I volunteered to ride in an ambulance with a neighbor who had slipped into a diabetic coma. The most common denominators among us were our poverty and jobs that led nowhere. Perhaps it was my age (or later, the man in my life), but I felt happy back then. New York was a laboratory for understanding many of the questions I had puzzled over for years. I loved the fact that my neighbors had descended on New York from all over the world. I eagerly sought to understand their histories.

When I was not working or exploring the city, I read almost anything. Now, I could borrow up to four or five books from the library at once, and the variety was endless. In the summer, almost everyone in the rooming house either sat outside or tried to find other ways to keep busy and remain cool. Central Park West was only a block away, and I often sat on a park bench with books in hand, near the bridle path, watching women and men my age gallop by.

Besides working and reading and getting to know my neighbors, I also loved visiting museums. Museums in the city were free back then — free, quiet, safe and mostly within walking distance from my room. I eyeballed the gigantic displays and read plaques that told me what museums felt I should know. I kept torn yellow pages listing museum addresses, visited each one of them what seemed to be hundreds of times and tried hard to make sense of how the world worked.

In Mississippi, I had wanted to know about these things, but there were few opportunities to learn. Here in New York, I carried on the family's tradition of hard work, thirst for knowledge and the desire to be free.

It was through my visits to museums that I first met a person with a PhD. He was white and male and from a New York family of medical doctors. The second PhD I met was also white and male. I was in my early 30s before I met a black person with a PhD. By then I was well on my way to earning my own.

I met the two PhDs because one of them knew an African-American artist I knew slightly. This artist had stopped in New York briefly on his way to Ghana. We bumped into each other at the Museum of Natural History on 79th Street and Central Park West. Through him, I met friends who introduced me to the two PhDs.

I have remained associated with these friends and other like-minded people throughout my adult life. Although few had doctorate degrees at the time we met, most, like me, were struggling to become educated. Back then, in the early 1960s in New York City, there also seemed to be a genuine interest in getting to know people across racial, cultural and economic lines. I was a high school graduate often working two jobs and attending school at night, but that did not deter friendships at every level. I still have friends who are millionaires and others who barely survive on welfare.

The Need for Formal Study

I met my future husband soon after I arrived in New York. He had reluctantly come along as a blind date for one of my roommates. That night, he heard me say that I was now working for the New York Telephone Company, and the next day he called the personnel office and found me. I married at the age of 20. My husband, who had earned a degree in history from Columbia University when I met him, later received his MA in social work from the University of Chicago. There is no question that he was instrumental in my deciding to return to school. He and his friends spent every weekend arguing about world issues at our home, and I recognized the need to take classes to sharpen my debating skills and knowledge base.

We had our daughter, Jill, in 1966, when I was 23. Holding my child in my arms, I felt so inadequate. What could she learn from me, a high school graduate? How could I ensure her a superior education that would free her to compete in an imperfect world? How could I protect her from experiencing the racism I felt so scarred by? Lying there in great pain after a very difficult birth, I thought about the conditions of my life for many hours. I made a promise to Jill that I would set her on the path to the highest levels of education.

Over the next 18 years, I raised my daughter while also working and attending college. Her father and I also enrolled Jill in private schools and made it a matter of pride not to accept any scholarship support. I will always treasure the morning we packed the car and drove Jill off to Harvard/Radcliffe College for her undergraduate studies. It was a stellar moment for Jill, for her father, for me, and my parents, because it was that same week that I would successfully defend my PhD dissertation.

I earned five degrees while Jill was growing up, one in history, three master's degrees and my doctorate. Jill's Harvard degree is in history. She earned her master's degree in business administration from Cornell University. I believe that our degrees and hard work can be attributed to our family's dream — of my attempting to pick up the torch for my father at the age of 6, and now my daughter and I carry it forward.

Work and Dignity: The Family's Signature

One thing my family and I can agree on is that we are hard workers. This is our signature, whether we are still doing farm work or writing books.

'I used to say', my older sister, Mildverta, reflected recently, 'that we were just taught to be slaves. But looking back now, I am grateful for our training. We know how to take care of ourselves. I can always make money for myself — and for two or three other people, if necessary.'

Nearing the age of 60, my sister, who is now financially secure, still often works 16-hour days in a hospital's pediatric ward in Chicago. I tell her that she is working too hard, but I am from the same cloth. I have sometimes worked until I fainted. Once, in my 20s, I worked two jobs and took 16 credit hours per semester. I earned straight As that semester. When several friends expressed concern about my schedule and health, I would say that I was at a movie or in the library reading some popular book just to get them not to worry. My New York friends did not know that hard work and long hours were a part of my family heritage.

During this time one of my friends warned that if I continued my work habits, I would soon die. I almost did die, but I have since met many successful people from poor families who work like me. Out of habit as a farmer's daughter, I still wake up at four in the morning and wait for the world to get up.

It seems as if I have held a hundred jobs in my lifetime: shoe repair woman, cook, housekeeper, nurse's aide, computer operator, secretary, community organizer, teacher at every educational level, proofreader, indexer, antique clothing store owner, teacher trainer, school administrator, researcher, foundation worker, and now a scholar and writer.

These experiences, mostly at the lowest level in organizations, have helped me to meet all types of people, sharpen my skills as a researcher and prepare me for a way to help others. I, for example, know how it feels to work under the most difficult conditions in organizations, and to be treated with the greatest disrespect.

I keep my previous work experiences in mind as I conduct research, particularly in the area of employment discrimination. In the various positions I have held as a manager, I have tried to seek alternatives to current workplace conditions, to institute policies to ensure that the workplace meet the needs of employees. Always on the lookout for ways in which organizations can be used to liberate, rather than oppress; to empower, rather than disable, my research examines not only how people find work, but also how they are treated once they are employed.

Encouraging Organizational Change

I cannot remember a single experience I had as a young woman with predominantly white institutions that did not discriminate against me based on race. Today, we African-Americans often refer to this form of prejudice in a matter-of-fact way as 'institutional racism'. In my early years, for me this meant being:

- oppressed by all formal authority, particularly policemen;
- barred from schools where Whites attended, and when begrudgingly admitted, told that we were dumb, then resegregated at the classroom level;
- excluded from participation in all organizational activities, except in very narrowly defined roles, e.g., sitting in the balcony of a movie house or in the back of a bus;
- unable to find food, go to the bathroom, walk on a sidewalk or pray in a church where Whites attended.

I asked my mother several years ago about another incident that I recalled from my childhood. Shortly after my sixth birthday a group of policemen dragged my father from our house, beat him until he screamed in terror, then took him off to jail. My mother said that the incident had been primarily precipitated by the recognition of local Whites that our family had become too prosperous, and too independent. When my father refused to sell his cotton to the local cotton gin owner for an inequitable price, he was then accused of stealing it. Jail followed.

Eventually, the charges against my father were dropped. He was declared innocent, but I have never been able to erase the incident from my emotions. Almost a half-century later, I still feel the policeman's words, 'Goddam fucking Niggers trying to take everything.' Even today, my own body still contorts while remembering the pain of nightsticks landing on his blue-black, bloodied skin, his strong, cracking bones.

That was Mississippi in the 1940s. My father had followed the formal rules, yet he was still punished by the system. The laws have changed to provide some relief from those racist practices, but here is one question that arises out of my father's experience that continues to guide my research: How can organizations — often born out of racist practice — (sometimes established for such purposes) be expected to liberate?

In my work I start with the assumption that organizations do not willingly change their behavior — at least not very often nor very fast — not unless there are mechanisms in place that will punish them severely for their wrongs and reward them for their enlightened ways. Even then, organizations can be expected to find ways to revert to their old patterns; to oppress, humiliate and enslave.

In my efforts to understand the early discrimination that my family endured, I elected to study pre and post Civil Rights organizational behavior as a part of my dissertation topic: *Job Contacts in Educational Administration: How Usual Informal Job Contacts May Affect the Hiring of Women, Men, Blacks and Whites* (1985). I wanted to understand how, and if, the old anti-black bureaucracy had changed: what mechanisms were being put in place to protect rather than oppress African Americans. My dissertation suggested that many practices in organizations have not changed; rather, they have merely become more informal.

Let me offer an obvious example: One has only to pick up a newspaper in almost any large city today to understand that many black men still experience what my father did in the 1940s. All of America witnessed the beating of Rodney King by the Los Angeles Police Department a few years ago. The same authority/institutional structure that allowed policemen to terrorize my father in the 1940s still allows for the beating of Rodney King. Such barbaric behavior is rarely sanctioned today in the formal organizational system; yet, policemen continue their practices through informal systems. Most African Americans are not fooled by the new semantics which simply mask ongoing discrimination.

My research would suggest that informal, brutal practices by formal authority today is not really very hard to conduct. Many illegal behaviors are now considered 'traditional' — within the norms of police culture. I try to ferret out these forms of discrimination — these silent systems operating to continue oppression. I want the world to understand that discrimination based on race remains enormously painful to those of us who are the targets of the attacks and bear the brunt of the pain. I use the updated language of research to present the evidence — to convince the country of the hardship. I want America to again become more aggressive in its commitment to freedom, to equality. Our very survival is at stake.

The Importance of Credentials

Upon reflection, most of my education has been devoted to understanding how the majority culture operates, particularly what motivates it in its rancor toward people of color. That is why I earned my first degree is in American History. I wanted to understand, as Derrick Bell (1992) also pondered: what is it in the nature of this culture that gave it permission to snatch 50 million black babies and teenagers from our families, declare us to be less than human, and use our bodies for profit and pleasure? (p. 11).

As my studies progressed, I realized that I could not only help myself understand the problems of race in society, but I could also help my family understand how we, of African background, got to Mississippi. We had a right to know why our lives have been so oppressed, our family so complex, and how we have spun miracles out of a nightmare.

While graduate students at Columbia University, many of my black colleagues were upset with our professors for encouraging us to select dissertation topics that concentrated on African-American issues. There was a feeling that our white male professors were limiting us to such matters — ghettoizing us even at the highest levels of intellectual pursuit. Perhaps this was the motivating factor of a few, but as our research topics began to emerge, we learned how little viable research had been conducted in our disciplines and willingly chose topics which contributed to a greater understanding of our history. I wanted my doctorate to contribute to research on African-American issues, yet, I was equally interested in understanding the motivation of those in power.

When, for example, I examined job search literature as a possible dissertation topic, I found that 99 percent of all research in the area had been conducted only on white males. Where women and minorities were mentioned (usually in the *implications of the study* section), it was assumed that women and people of color did the same thing as white men to get jobs. My research suggested that this was not necessarily the case.

I soon learned that research on African-Americans was not only desperately needed, but it also presented opportunities to push at the traditional boundaries of the field. If, in fact, women and minorities do not get jobs in the same ways as their white male counterparts, how do they get jobs? What has the discipline failed to consider? How must we now reorient our thinking to ensure that the best research will be conducted in the area?

I enjoy my work immensely. I want to examine issues of equity and access — but sometimes I wonder what else might I have been able to think about had so much of my life not been prescribed by the color of my skin. I try not to allow myself to be angry — to worry about the lost opportunities because I played the cards that were dealt me.

Like all mothers, I think that my daughter is beautiful and brilliant and generous of spirit, yet, I am also keenly aware that I studied organizational behavior and linkage theory, and applied it to our lives. I am glad to have access to a bit of powerful information about how America works — both formally and informally — and I have tried to help my daughter leap over the obstacle course.

I am capable of working on more than America's race problems, but this is a promise I made a long time ago to my father, when he faced the fake white policemen and told them not to frighten his children. I have been blessed with the skills, education and desire to fulfill this promise to my father, my family; and as James Weldon Johnson so stated, 'This is a work so glorious.'

The author currently lives in New York City and is a University Scholar-in-Residence at Morgan State University. As a program officer for the DeWitt Wallace-Reader's Digest Fund for seven years, she was responsible for developing and implementing roughly $100 million in educational programs designed to increase educational and career opportunities for poor and minority youth. Her teacher recruitment and preparation program at the foundation, Pathways to Teaching Careers, was adopted by President Clinton as part of a $350 million national educational initiative for the nation's public schools.

Mildred J. Hudson

References

BELL, D. (1992) *Faces at the Bottom of the Well: The Permanence of Racism*, New York: Basic Books.
HUDSON, M.J. (1985) Job contacts in educational administration: How usual informal job contacts may affect the hiring of women, men, blacks and whites, PhD Dissertation: Columbia University.
HUDSON, M.J. (1991) *How Educators Get Top Jobs: Understanding Race and Gender Differences*, Landam: MD University Press.
JOHNSON, J.W. (1995) 'Lynching and mob violence,' in WILSON, SONDRA K. (ed.) *The Selected Writings of James Weldon Johnson, Volume I*. New York: Oxford University Press, p. 53.
MATTHEWS, B. (1995) 'Fifty years and other poems,' in WILSON, SONDRA K. (ed.) *The Selected Writings of James Weldon Johnson, Volume II*. New York: Oxford University Press, pp. 363–4.

11　The Professional Is the Personal: Personal Identity and Research Agendas

Michael C. Thornton

There once was a society containing two groups, the sraloks and the masses. The sraloks (a.k.a., the knowledgeable ones) claimed they could successfully discover the inner most experiences of outsiders. Further, the knowledge they uncovered, they argued, was complete in all important ways. They were so sure of their skills in this matter that they spread the idea far and wide of the benefits of these abilities for the good of society. When asked by the masses how they achieved such a remarkable feat, the sraloks responded by saying that they did so with the aid of a special wand. Not anyone, they hurriedly warned, could employ the wand effectively and properly, for its use required special training and special procedures must be followed. But when used appropriately, the wand allowed one to become free of personal bias and overcome one's own limited experience when examining others.

But without their apparent knowledge, the wand also created a bubble around the sraloks such that they could but see only part of the outsider's world; the bubble distorted the sraloks' vision and hearing. In reality, the wand failed to give a true portrait of the others. When the outsiders told them this, the knowledgeable ones of course argued that since the others were not sraloks they could not know of what they spoke. Further, because they refused to believe in the irrefutable magic offered by the wand (when used appropriately), the sraloks argued that the outsiders proved the soundness of the wand's magic. For like their responses, the wand had too shown them to be lesser beings than even the masses in the knowledgeable ones' society.

Introduction

As observers of social life, social scientists describe and also develop strategies for understanding our changing environment. One of the most important of these recent changes has been the immigration of expanding numbers of ethnic and racial minorities to the United States. Perhaps galvanized in part by the resultant impact on American life, many observers began to write of a more complex social environment, some emphasizing the intersections of race, gender and class, while others elevated attention brought to so-called mixed racial families and people (Root, 1992; 1996).

Nevertheless, this increased appreciation of the complexity of the social landscape is guided by anachronistic assumptions of bygone eras. Racial ideology provides powerful and unseen frames to these discussions. Despite some major changes in the spectacle of race relations in the United States, most debates are abbreviated to two colliding and irreducible elements at odds (Martinez, 1992). Unfathomably, phenomena with more than two racial groups are generally ignored (Thornton and Shah, 1996); truly multiracial discussions are rare. The conversation remains fixated on black–white, and usually black–white in conflict. This oversimplifies a complex situation, and denies reality, often with severe consequences.

Moreover, even when Whites are compared to some other group, such as Blacks or Asian Americans, most dialogue is fixated on white views. In treating Whites as subjects, others become mere objects of discussion. This has led, in some cases, to treating white perspectives as universals. A famous Buddhist saying recalls: 'To point at the moon the finger is needed, but woe to those who take the finger for the moon' (Suzuki, 1949, p. 1). While recognizing the growing complexity of the racial make up to society, social scientists remain more absorbed in whites' feelings toward racial minorities and rarely about how the rest of the world feels about those who are not white. In that they do the 'pointing', they also bring their own experience to discerning others — an experience that colors how others are depicted, with little recognition of that fact. Further, we are subjects of this discourse only when we are a problem, or when we write the treatises.

The Construction of a Professional and Personal Agenda/Identity

We are a mixture of our society's and our own histories and desires. I owe my existence to individuals who braved a hostile world to force open doors of opportunity, an effort that ultimately was for us all. I am here as a result of a struggle to expand immigration to include more than just Europe. I am one of many offspring of Asian-American couples who came as part of the Asian immigration to the United States during and after the Korean War.

The dynamic changes occurring during this era gave me an experience that underlies the kind of research I do and how I examine issues within this research. Perhaps most dominant was my growing up with the 'truism' of the 1950s and 1960s that race is dichotomous, that racial identity is either/or, a view of race that remains a legacy today. This dual way of decoding life, mainly racial life, had a special effect on me because I did not fit the traditional racial patterns. That my mother was Japanese only complicated matters. This concept of race strongly exhorted that crossing of racial boundaries had dreadful social and personal repercussions. In wrestling with this view and the inconsistencies it pointed to in my life, in exploring my place in America, I could not know that I was preparing myself for my professional life.

Despite my graduate school training, I realize that there is no such thing as objective research, work that is somehow 'above the fray' of human existence. By definition, research involves personal choices, which we have a vested interest in. Furthermore, in today's world we do not have the luxury of standing on the sidelines of world and domestic events, for by doing so one contributes to making a maddening situation worse. Thus my own life provides the impetus to what I find important enough to examine. For me this is not that far removed from my connection with communities of color and their endeavors to overcome an often hostile environment.

To highlight the link between research and personal identity, I will use myself as an example. In this essay I wish to explore how I came to discover my 'take' of social events of the past 20 years and how this view influences my work. Specifically I will first talk about my experiences as I see them framing the kind of work I do. Knowing something about my past makes it easier to discern why I choose to deal with certain issues in my work, and why I conceptualize them the way I do. Secondly, I then connect this foundation to my professional life. I wish to show how my experience colors my research. Thus the theme here is not how one keeps personal experience out of the research process, but how one uses it to better inform that process and those who read the research. This does not negate the results, as traditional research suggests, but instead makes them more honest. If you know my biases, the better you are able to evaluate the results.

My Early Socialization

In my early life, I felt confused about where I fit into society; my identity was disjointed. Perhaps this is not surprising. I was born in Kobe, Japan, in 1952, the child of a black American father and a Japanese mother. This was a time in which America's view of racial minorities was at best neutral and at worst filled with overt hostility and perceived racial superiority; Whites, even wartime enemies (e.g., German POWs), were treated better than Americans who were of color. Having just completed a war with the Japanese a few years earlier, my mother being Japanese further complicated how I was perceived. So both of my heritages were ill-received.

But bringing them together was perhaps most problematic for the time. Interracial marriage was frowned on in most circles. This can be seen in part in legal and social convention. Many states outlawed interracial marriage; that would change only in 1967, when the United States Supreme Court made these laws illegal. Initially, immigration policy enabled European but not Asian war brides to immigrate to the United States. While this policy would later be amended to allow entry of the latter, these laws reflected the belief that races were distinct and meant to stay so.

Mass media and academic communities of the time were both adamant about the nature of Asian-American marriages. Newspapers and popular magazines predicted their doom. The *Saturday Evening Post* of 19 January 1952 described them in the following way:

> Nothing much but time and bitter experience can overcome great hazards like language difficulties, racial question marks, and the separation of truth about America from dreams of America expounded by homesick soldiers and distorted movies.

Many academics reinforced an oversimplified view of these unions. Examining the issue in the early 1950s, one anthropologist described males who were maladjusted, for the women 'still behave in a manner to make a man feel he can maintain feelings of masculine self importance yet at the same time can expect to be indulged in his dependent needs' (De Vos, 1973, pp. 2–3). Later studies contended that people entered these marriages because of psychological or economic inadequacies (e.g., Kim, 1972).

On occasion, the other side to this portrayal did appear, suggesting that the unions were normal (Schnepp and Yui, 1955; Strauss, 1954) and as stable as any American marriage (Connor, 1976). Walters (1953) found all his sample making successful adjustments.

Although I only read these accounts while in graduate school, the themes coming out of them — that these marriages were either good or more likely bad — were very common to me. To me the outstanding nature of this debate was that it ensued in public. This was also a time when America was starting to grapple openly with our stance on racial equality, coming on the heels of the defeat of the despotic regimes of Japan and Germany. The propaganda of the time suggested that the war against Germany was fought to free people, in part, from a belief in racial supremacy. That the United States in practice often acted as if a racial hierarchy existed was at the time often contrasted with the *cause celèbre* of the war.

One result of this open debate was that race relations had begun a small thaw, at least in terms of rhetoric and some policy. Surprisingly, this thaw was no more articulated than in the military, where, because of pressure in part from black constituencies, there was a move to make the black presence overseas representative of their presence in America. My father's being in Japan at the time was due in part to an official policy which stated that 10 percent of military personnel in Japan were to be black. In practice this meant that soldiers were assigned by racial background. My father was assigned to a base in Kyoto, one that was mostly black.

My father's military career had a profound impact on my views of the world both then and now. The military has few peers; it is a complete institution, dominating every aspect of life. As a dependent (the term used for members of military families), I had little individual identity, for I was cataloged by my father's rank. The military moved us wherever, and whenever, the need. For my first 18 years, I lived in five states (involving some 20 moves, once three times in one year) and three foreign countries.

While moving so much was traumatic in ways I'm still detecting, the regimentation of the military perhaps limited the impact. We knew what was expected of us. America (and things American) was superior, any deviations from such beliefs were unacceptable. We would live in quarters with other families who were of similar rank and lifestyle, living spaces that were exactly alike. We knew our behavior reflected on our military parent, and directly influenced promotions; so we behaved, or else. Because of constant movement, it was understood that close friendships were inadvisable, so courteous and surface-level relations were most common.

At the time, the regimentation was comforting because it was predictable — with our moving so much that was a good thing. However, looking back I see that this environment was also unsettling. One thing stands out. The military is well known for its patriotic underpinnings: apple pie, mom and the flag. There was also something racial minorities should expect. The ideology was that the military, unlike other institutions of the time, was color-blind. The military was argued to be the best place for them, because it was on the forefront of racial integration and harmony.

In many ways, my chosen career in academia parallels the military careerist's lifestyle: geographic mobility, status based on rank and an ideology of racial equality. Reinforcing this belief was the meritocractic idea that we were evaluated by our father's efforts, i.e., his rank. Thus, one's race was not primary. I was not in the league with officer's or civilian's kids (who were usually white) not because of my race but because I was the child of an NCO. Among civilians, a similar argument would be to say that one is less because your parent works on the line and not in the office. I accepted the argument at the time.

But this motivated dichotomous thinking about the world: you were patriotic/unpatriotic, an officer's/non-commissioned officer's child, for America/against America. You were an American or a foreigner. This latter label became singularly important to me. When overseas we lived in little Americas, protected literally by a gate with armed guards keeping non-Americans out and my education was sponsored by the Department of Defense. In the United States, there was a we (the military) and a they (civilians). In my world primary identification was unrelated to racial heritage and my class background. I was an American — period.

Thus, my identity held no racial allusions. At the time, I argued that this was the best country in the world, that I could become whatever I wanted if I were willing to sacrifice. I wanted Vietnam in my future. I was so blinded by my patriotism. For most of my early life I could not escape this indoctrination that focused on ideology more than reality.

Despite the years of work spent in bringing me to this view, one small event would lead me to begin to question where I fit in this picture. Well through high school, I lived for a military career. I had my heart set on West Point, only in part because my parents could not afford to send me to college otherwise (at the time, West Point was free except for an obligation to serve several active duty years). But a school counselor suggested I take the National Merit Scholarship Test. I refused initially, telling my father that it was too costly to register (it was one dollar and he paid it). After becoming a semifinalist and then an alternate, I began to see myself differently. I began to think that maybe I did not have to limit myself to a military life; especially as I began to see that careerists were often very conservative about many issues but especially race.

The year before, I was glued to the television watching as the selective service draft numbers were called. That year I got a number low enough that if I had been of age I would have been drafted; I believed that I would also have gone to Vietnam. That I might be able to go to college without going to West Point, and that I might die in Vietnam caused me to rethink my short life. College became a more comforting thought.

The College Years

College for me was like it has been for many — an eye-opening experience. I fell in love for the first time, I weathered true personal responsibility and I began the journey of exploring whom I was.

I went to college right after the great student protests closed down campuses (the semester before I arrived in 1970). It was a time of social unrest, as they called it then, especially around issues of race and roots. In that environment, my badge as an American was quickly challenged. In all honesty, prior to my arrival I usually denied my blackness, often, when asked what I was, I would mention that my mother was Japanese or that I was Puerto Rican. That in many circles PRs were no more accepted than Blacks should tell you how I felt about being black — that anyone was better. But most often I tried not to bring up my heritage.

Nevertheless consistently confronting new messages about whom I was forced me to consider other options, in a way that would later bring about a fundamental change in what groups I would feel a part of. I began to consider alternative reference groups to America (i.e., Whites).

The most pivotal event was that I fell in love. This was my first significant romance and it was with a white woman. In part, her being white fulfilled the need to have myself validated as a person (although at the time I don't know if I really understood this). Ironically, she had a very strong interest in Africa, an interest I soon began to mimic to try to impress her. This was at a time when the idea of 'roots' was taking hold in the wider society. My interest in Africa became, after a while, more than a means to impress, leading me to take several classes on Africa. But one in particular, a class entitled the 'African Diaspora', taught by Professor Ruth Sims Hamilton at Michigan State University, would be most important. We explored how African peoples went to places in the world I never would have believed. I missed class the day we were assigned regions to explore in more detail. Thereafter, the only available region was the diaspora to Asia. I complained that this was not of interest to me — but I had no choice. Dr Hamilton, and this chance event, changed my life.

I grew up hearing that people like me, of mixed racial heritage, are born with an inherent limitation: with two racial groups built into them, the internal conflict is unavoidable and inevitably debilitating. The only way out was to choose one identity and stick with it. But in reality there was no real choice given to me, for in this society I could not identify as Japanese. Here, I was told, being black was the only way to my salvation.

But for most of my life Blacks were depicted as less desirable characters; they were the last group I wanted to be identified with. However, in exploring my African roots, I came to examine myself more closely. Coming to college I was American. But I soon began to question what that meant. My classes on Africa led me to be more critical of a country with such a checkered history when dealing with people who only differed from them by skin color. Could I respect such a world? The growing disillusionment with my world led to a fundamental change in my identity. I was becoming 'black'.

Concomitant to this development, I did what many undergraduates do: looked to answer the broader question of 'who am I?' I looked to Psych 101 answers. I learned that because of the personality traits I had, I could be described as immature, too reliant on my mother, etc. In other words, I was a spoiled little boy! What I did not realize, engrossed in my 'American' identity, was that I would not find myself in texts that failed to examine the psychology of racial minorities, but notably those with my up-bringing. I only began to appreciate how inadequate these texts were to my life after the class on the diaspora and my look for my African roots.

One evening, tossing and turning in bed, I shot upright with a great insight: I was brought up by a Japanese woman! In hindsight, this revelation was obvious, but it became the key for me to understand what was missing in my only looking at my African roots. Growing up in a world that saw race as an either/or phenomenon, it did not dawn on me to consider the multiple aspects of my being. Making the link between my Africanness *and* my Asianness was to be the foundation to my dissertation, where I examined how black and Japanese couples socialized their offspring for ethnic identity.

A by-product of this project was my decision to take the road less traveled. I now describe myself as both black and Japanese American (in particular, a 'blap', a term coined by the sister of my soul mate). Though I still grapple with what that term means to me, I would have it no other way.

My Research Agenda: Strategies of Resistance

In my youth, I became captivated with the ideas of bravery and sacrifice. I am still in awe of people who give their lives for others — the ultimate sacrifice. Notably majestic to me is when this action is taken when the individual ostensibly had more to lose than to gain, when not acting would have been acceptable behavior. Like when someone jumps on a grenade to save comrades, though escaping would have been a justifiable act. For a while I failed to realize that my interest in this subject had to do with my being impressed less with dying than with living — living a life that extends beyond oneself. And while I fail at this all too often, I know that my privileges would not be possible without others' sacrifices, sometimes with their lives.

These sacrifices are part of overall strategies of resistance, overcoming the odds. Some level of dignity and self-determination is possible through resources that are available in everyday life. In my work I assume that communities, families and individuals possess assets that, while remaining unappreciated by the larger society, contribute immensely to survival, to the abilities to counteract stifling forces. These sorts of resources are unexplored because they are often manifest in day-to-day activities. These mundane struggles of life that form the foundation of the overall effort of resistance are unspectacular, they are average. Yet, placing these average life events at the center of analysis reveals empowered people within structures of domination. I believe that exploring forms of power by historically marginalized groups is a way to rethink social change and the politics of empowerment.

This requires that one presumes that communities have constructive legacies, which are in part related directly to family and its cultural, organizational and racial group footing. Cultural heritage provides a repertoire of resources, familial lifestyles and patterns of social involvement. Ethnic/racial heritage creates a tradition of mutual aid strategies changing the nature of community and family life. These in turn reflect norms and values of standard behavior by which families operate, including how family members identify, define and try to solve problems.

Pauli Murray wrote: 'A system of oppression draws much of its strength from the acquiescence of its victims, who have accepted the dominant image of themselves and are paralyzed by a sense of helplessness' (1987, p. 106). People of color are often rendered as overwhelmed by racism. We are commonly seen as impotent, to be pitied/blamed, for we are resigned to our fate.

The reality, of course, is that people of color have persistently fought oppression, both overtly and always covertly. Social change in the US has occurred because of black activism, civil rights movements among the most obvious examples. We have never been powerless.

The key to grasping how people of color forge powerful group and family ties lies in the adaptive skills we have constructed from culture and experience. We do not merely react to abuses by the institutions in our lives or lay down to await the inevitable. Instead, we choose from several options. The elements of adaptation, culture, and choice are important in understanding how people of color resist oppression.

Of course, this resistance is shaped by the wider social locale. In particular, resistance involves an interplay between how the larger setting affects everyday lives and how these experiences help shape the larger context. Agency is how interpersonal activities influence larger contexts and vice versa. It concerns events of which an individual is a perpetrator. For Giddons (1993) agency is 'the stream of actual or causal interventions of corporeal beings in the ongoing process of events-in-the-world'. These actions occur despite other options, the individual 'could have done otherwise'. These acts are deliberate because 'the agent knows (believes) [the act] can be expected to manifest a particular quality or outcome, and in which this knowledge is made use of by the actor in order to produce this quality or outcome' (1993, p. 83). While effects of this act may be uncertain, agency implies that people are not simply passive onlookers in their own lives, for they make choices and act to change their world. Agency is about events that would not have transpired if the individual had not intervened.

I see my work as tagging these forms of resistance, in contrast to mainstream conjecture about the 'essence' of communities of color. My focus reflects my experience, it is the foundation to my work; because of my early experience, perhaps it could be no other way for me. I see how difference, whether in color, gender or world view, is used against those who differ.

I identify with these communities because I have a stake in their survival. I believe that they have much that this society could learn from. Because our communities are seen to be a drain on the wider society the contributions we have and will make are belittled, resulting in relegating us to the margins of society. Because of this view, our real essence is that we often overcome despite the odds, despite an often unsupportive society. In assigning us to the margins, resistance becomes more difficult, a fact we see in declining conditions for notable portions of our citizens.

I see my work supporting the struggle to resist oppressive forces in two ways: I choose topics others typically describe as esoteric and marginal, and I use them as examples of how people of color alter their environments in meaningful ways, overcoming obstacles, making something new (at least different from what would 'normally' be expected), changing their environment to better work in their own interests. In the remainder of the essay I'd like to show how my work does this.

Racial Attitudes: The Crossing of Boundaries

I view race and culture as the foundation to resistance. My work reflects the role these phenomena play in two arenas: Black bonds with other groups of color, and the organization to black family life. Group (racial) identity is typically viewed as bonding with only one ethnic group. Rarely do we consider concurrent ethnic attachments. The common assumption is that such ties are rare given clear racial divisions; in some circles, embracing two groups at once is characterized as unhealthy. My work on intergroup attitudes explores this angle and reveals that customary commentary on group identity fails to reveal the unique linkages Blacks have with other racial groups. I explore this subject with what has been termed the common fate model of race relations; the popular model of race relations is realistic group conflict theory.

Most commonly relations between communities of color are described as inherently conflict-ridden (Zinsmeister, 1987; Shah and Thornton, 1994). The realistic group conflict model (Bobo, 1988; Glaser, 1994) supports this assumption. Its advocates suggest that intergroup discord is not due primarily to frustrations between people (i.e., not to personal prejudice). Instead conflicts are the result of differences that become highlighted when respective groups have incompatible goals, where the gains of one are at the expense of the other (Rabbie, 1993). The normal course of events in the US, in this view, is that racial minority groups have goals inherently at odds.

However, the evidence for this as is related to relations among groups of color is mostly anecdotal. Few works examine these relations. Most historical accounts point to a rapport between them (e.g., Grinde and Taylor, 1984; Katz, 1986; Littlefield, 1977; Forbes, 1984). However, much recent evidence on black relations with Asian-Americans and Hispanics seems to support the conflict view (Dyer, Vedlitz and Worchel, 1989; Franklin, 1981; Lee, 1987). For example, Oliver and Johnson (1984) argued that because Latinos and Blacks in LA compete for the same jobs, their affiliation is innately confrontational, a view we've found to be reinforced by the mass media (Shah and Thornton, 1994; Thornton and Shah, 1996).

In contrast, the common fate perspective (a.k.a., common bond and racial solidarity) suggests that those with similar backgrounds have a bond with one another. Kurt Lewin (1948) described a group's essence to be the interdependence of, and not, the (dis)similarity of its members. Some research suggests that when members of a social category face exclusion from outsiders based on their membership, they feel a common fate with other groups with similar experiences. This feeling of interdependence may induce emotions of group belongingness and identification that cross social categories (Horwitz and Rabbie, 1989; Rabbie, 1993, 1992).

Accordingly, minority groups which are objects of prejudice and vilification should be attracted to each other. Most commonly these bonds cross ethnic lines, such as in the creation of Latino ethnic identity in Mexican-American and Puerto Rican communities and the emergence of panethnic systems among groups such as Latinos, Asian and Native Americans (Nagel, 1995). In these instances, in order to effectively compete with the majority, disadvantaged groups come to realize the utility of forming a coalition rather than fighting each other. A number of studies focusing on racial differences lend support for this argument (Yoon, 1995; Borus, 1973; Stanton, 1972; Fiman, Borus and Stanton, 1975; Maykovich, 1971).

The common fate model holds that competition may not necessarily lead to antagonism between Blacks and other racial minorities; it may be more likely to lead to animosity toward a common adversary — Whites. Because racism has hindered Blacks, they may have a profound sensitivity to how it can be a detriment for the social and economic well-being of other groups. Thus Blacks may have more complex views on the context of competition than a group conflict model would suggest. Although acknowledging the presence of economic competition among racial minorities, Blacks may see the conflict from a broader outlook. That is, Blacks may regard such rivalries as minorities being pitted against each other by Whites. In this sense, they lose by competing with each other.

Much of my recent work is an attempt to elaborate on this idea of the common bond thesis. When asked if they worried about their ability to pay their bills, we found that Blacks in a national sample who were felt *closer* to other minority groups than those who were not (Thornton and Mizuno, 1995; Thornton, working paper). Traditional models cannot explain this sort of response. Further, we examined how respondents felt toward Mexicans and other minority and immigrant groups who they believed were taking black jobs (Mizuno and Thornton, under review). Black respondents who felt competitive with these groups did not feel any special feelings toward them but definitely *did not* distance themselves from them as the conflict model would predict. The same questions did elicit strong feelings about Whites. Respondents who agreed with the belief that immigrants were taking their jobs, felt significantly distant from Whites. This suggests that economic competition among racial minorities may not necessarily lead Blacks to draw lines between themselves and other minorities as 'us' versus 'them'. It is equally likely that Blacks include racial minorities on one side of the line, with Whites on the others side of the line.

We also discover other factors traditionally considered anathemas to good relations do not tell us much about black attitudes (Thornton and Taylor, 1988a, b; Thornton and Mizuno, 1995). Religion, economic well-being, and group solidarity are all traditional predictors of blacks' feelings toward other people. We find that those who identify themselves as very religious are most likely (compared to those who are not) to feel a bond with various groups, such as West Indians, American Indians, Asian-Americans and Hispanics. While primarily true among black women, that religious connections bond one to outside groups is rarely found among Whites — the effect is usually the opposite. Likewise, we discover that Blacks who support efforts at community development (e.g., advocating buying only in black-owned stores, or voting for black candidates) feel bonds with ethnic minority groups mentioned above. Moreover, those who support these development efforts distance themselves from Whites. Thus, so-called black nationalism/separatism is in reality addressed at primarily Whites.

Part of discerning why these links are not more obvious is related to what we learn from the major source of information about race relations — the mass media. We have explored how this institution explains the connections Blacks have with Asian and Hispanic Americans (Shah and Thornton, 1994; Thornton and Shah, 1996). We found that mainstream news magazines used immigrant and model minority cliches to explain group conflicts. It was commonly asserted that Blacks should model their actions after Asian-American and Latino efforts at joining the mainstream. Omitting structural and broad economic conditions, the magazines argued that Blacks will succeed economically only after they have acquired the immigrant credo of hard work. In a current book project, a colleague and I have begun to examine how the mainstream (e.g., *Newsweek* and *New York Times*,) and the minority press (e.g., *LA Sentinel* and *KoreanAm Journal*) covered the LA, DC, and Miami riots, and the West Indian boycott of Korean groceries in New York. Preliminary analysis indicates that, for example, the Asian-American press coverage diverged notably from that of the mainstream press. One sign of this is their emphasis on natural links between Blacks and Asian-American communities, an affinity rarely mentioned in other presses.

I see my work on the experience of people of mixed Asian and African heritage as an extension of this resistance to essentialist precepts (Thornton, 1983, 1992; Williams and Thornton, 1998). I examine the nature of identity development, how these individuals create their own identities from a number of possibilities; in so doing they go beyond the identities typically given to them by society (usually monoracial). They cross racial boundaries and do so to create often mentally healthy self-concepts, in ways unpredictable by traditional models of identification. This work also suggests alternative models to what is meant by blackness and Asianess.

Caregiving and Resistance

Another area I address is social support among ethnic elderly (White-Means and Thornton, 1996; Thornton, White-Means and Choi, 1993). The work I do in this area examines the nature of networks that Blacks form to help their elders cope with later life, particularly when they become physically frail. We compare these networks to those of white ethnics (English, German and Irish Americans). Several patterns highlight the silent work of resistance within black communities. The first is that home health care is more time-consuming for Blacks than for these other groups. On average Blacks spent more than 29 hours per week caring for elders. This is, on average, four hours more *per day* than provided by the other groups! The greater time spent in care by Blacks is in part related to greater physical depreciation among black elders (White-Means and Thornton, 1990a, b). But it also reflects something about the bonds many Blacks have with their elders.

Secondly, black women gave the most time to this endeavor, spending 9 to 12 hours more per week in care than was true of the white ethnic women. While women generally are the primary caretakers, we found that black males gave about 20 hours per week to care, placing them behind black and English-American women and Irish-American males, but ahead of all other groups, including German- and Irish-American females.

Blacks with substitutes to perform these duties actually spent more time caregiving (about 30 hours per week) than those without substitutes (about 29 hours a week). While it is unclear why this pattern exists, it may be related to greater frailty among black elders and thus they may need more assistance than do their white peers. Some of these duties might conflict with other caregiving tasks there is no time to perform. The resultant 'free time' may be used to complete neglected caregiving obligations.

Finally, we found that Blacks reach out beyond traditional family boundaries to assist others. Reflecting the cultural tradition of extended families, an interesting pattern is observed when contrasting the time spent in caring for elders who are part of an immediate (e.g., spouse, siblings, children or grandparents) versus non-immediate (distant kin, neighbors, friends, e.g.) kinship circle. Black caregivers to immediate family members spent on average 28 hours a week with their duties. This figure rose by two additional hours per week when caring for non-immediate members. What is done with this additional time is not clear.

This sort of bond cannot be assessed through prescribed models of family and community life that focus on nuclear families. It is clear, nonetheless, that devotion to elders is extensive regardless of whether the kinship link is legal or extralegal. Efforts to cope in black communities often involve people outside of traditional family circles. One wonders what these communities would look like without the kindness of friends and neighbors (as well as family). These indigenous resources are often taken for granted or, most often, ignored. But they epitomize the strategies of resistance found at all levels of life within communities of color.

Conclusion

The themes of my work reverberate with those of my life. I strive to examine the resources intrinsic to our communities, that allow us to persist and resist an often hostile and unforgiving environment. Reflecting the more general efforts to resist, my work on caregiving points to the family as being the foundation to agency. Family members help others to lead more fulfilling and functional lives. Without this agency, our communities would be much worse off, unable to stem the tides at the flood gates.

They do this in part by using alternative conceptualizations of the world, in this case, of family. Not the entity of American and Western lore, but instead these are families that cross boundaries to include people normally excluded as members of traditional families. This kind of family is well-known in black and other communities of color. The wider society chooses to describe these families as distorted and, more often, deviant versions of the real thing. Other Americans often do not appreciate the foundation these families provide, that these 'distortions' are in fact the backbone to most of these communities.

Reflecting on my own experience, my work also explores how people of color respond to race relations in unique ways. Blacks are often able to see through the false dichotomy of racial divisions promulgated by the wider society — one in which we all are pitted against each other, but especially against other people of color. While this conception of the world is far from universal in black communities, my work indicates that many Blacks understand that white supremacy is the frame to decipher relations among groups of color. This implies that there is also a discernment that a dichotomous view of race and race relations reinforces our own domination. Indeed many comprehend this in that they distance themselves only from Whites, even as they recognize that groups such as Mexicans and Asians compete with them for scarce resources. This scarcity is understood not to ultimately reflect minority group desires or interests, but instead whites' profiting from a belief in competing interests. Through their highlighting underlying bonds between Blacks and their communities, my work on media also suggests that Asian-American newspapers appreciate the role of white machinations. Mixed racials make this connection even more explicit, behaviorally bridging groups expected to feel enmity toward each other.

These sorts of insights are not often appreciated by traditional work. My work clearly shows how Blacks (and to a lesser degree, Asian-Americans) perceive their world, make something of their often marginal positions in it, and how, in so doing, change society. One cannot understand the strengths these communities bring to everyday life without examining the social landscape from their perspectives. Once one does this, agency is seen in everyday efforts of survival and struggle.

There is a move to essentialize most people, trying to find that crucial element believed to epitomize the group (Thornton and Shah, 1996). This process is part of the electronic, post-modern world, a process that has led, via film, television, and mass media more generally, to forcing information into increasingly standardized modes. I think my task as a scholar is to oppose this trend, instead I must advocate for an increasingly diversified conception of who we are as people. Not to do so, would be to suggest that those who sacrificed before me, so that I would have an greater chance to live my life in the way I choose, gave of themselves in vain. And while I often fail at this effort to do their lives justice, often because of my own shortcomings, I know that my own fate is just as much tied to those who came before as those who will follow. We are in this together. I have come to believe even more strongly as I age, that resistance is the only healthy choice, frustrating any effort to make us into stereotypes — the very essence of contradiction of the human spirit.

References

BOBO, L. (1988) 'Group conflict, prejudice and the paradox of contemporary racial attitudes', in KATZ, P. and TAYLOR, D. (eds) *Eliminating Racism: Profiles in Controversy*, New York: Plenum, pp. 221–48.

BORUS, J. (1973) 'Reentry: Adjustment issues facing the Vietnam returnee', *Archives of General Psychiatry*, **28**, pp. 501–6.

CONNOR, J. (1976) *A Study of the Marital Stability of Japanese War Brides*, San Francisco: R and E Research Associates.

DE VOS, G. (1973) *Personality Patterns and Problems of Adjustment in American-Japanese Intercultural Marriages*, Taipei: The Orient Cultural Service.

DYER, J., VEDLITZ, A. and WORCHEL, S. (1989) 'Social distance among racial and ethnic groups in Texas: Some demographic correlates', *Social Science Quarterly*, **70**, pp. 607–16.

FIMAN, B., BORUS, J. and STANTON, M. (1975) 'Black-White and American-Vietnamese relations among soldiers in Vietnam', *Journal of Social Issues*, **31**, pp. 39–48.

FORBES, J. (1984) 'Mulattoes and people of color in anglo-North America: Implications for Black-Indian relations', *Journal of Ethnic Studies*, **12**, pp. 17–61.

FRANKLIN, J.H. (1981) 'The land of room enough', *Daedalus*, **110**, pp. 1–12.

GIDDONS, A. (1993) *New Rules of Sociological Method* (2nd ed.), Cambridge: Polity Press.

GLASER, J. (1994) 'Back to the black belt: Racial environment and white racial attitude in the South', *Journal of Politics*, **56**, pp. 21–41.

GRINDE, D. and TAYLOR, Q. (1984) 'Red vs. black: Conflict and accommodation in the post civil war Indian territory, 1865–1907', *American India Quarterly*, **8**, pp. 211–29.

HORWITZ, M. and RABBIE, J. (1989) 'Stereotypes of groups, group members, and individuals in categories: A differential analysis of different phenomenon', in BAR-TEL, D. GRANMANN, C., KRUGLANSKI, A. and STROEBE, W. (eds) *Stereotyping and Prejudice: Changing Conceptions*, New York: Springer Verlag.

KATZ, W. (1986) *Black Indians*, New York: MacMillan Publishing.

KIM, B.I. (1972) 'Casework with Japanese and Korean wives of Americans', *Social Casework*, **53**, pp. 273–9.

LEE, L. (1987) 'International migration and refugee problems: Conflict between Black Americans and Southeast Asian refugees', *Journal of Intergroup Relations*, **14**, pp. 38–50.

LEWIN, K. (1948) *Resolving Social Conflicts*, New York: Harper and Row.

LITTLEFIELD, D. (1977) *African and Seminoles: From Removal to Emancipation*, Westport, CT: Greenwood Press.

MARTINEZ, E. (1992) 'Beyond black/white: The racisms of our time', *Social Justice*, **20**, pp. 22–34.

MAYKOVICH, M. (1971) 'Reciprocity in racial stereotypes: White, black, and yellow', *American Journal of Sociology*, **77**, pp. 876–97.

MIZUNO, Y. and THORNTON, M.C. (1996) *Perceived Economic Well-being and Black Attitudes toward West Indians, Hispanics and Whites*, Working Paper.

MURRAY, P. (1987) *Song in a Weary Throat: An America Pilgrimage*, New York: Harper and Row.

NAGEL, J. (1995) 'Resource competition theories', *American Behavioral Scientist*, **38**, pp. 442–58.

OLIVER, M. and JOHNSON, J. (1984) 'Inter-ethnic conflict in an urban ghetto: The case of Blacks and Latinos in Los Angeles', *Research in Social Movements, Conflict, and Change*, **6**, pp. 57–94.

RABBIE, J. (1992) 'Effects of intra-group cooperation and intergroup competition on ingroup-outgroup differentiation', in HARCOURT, A. and DE WAAL, F. (eds) *Cooperation in Conflict: Coalitions and Alliances in Animals and Humans*, Oxford: Oxford University Press, pp. 175–205.

RABBIE, J. (1993) 'Determinants of ingroup cohesion and outgroup hostility', *International Journal of Group Tensions*, **23**, pp. 309–28.

ROOT, M. (ed.) (1992) *Racially Mixed People in America*, Newbury Park, CA: Sage.

ROOT, M. (ed.) (1996) *The Multicultural Experience: Racial Borders As the New Frontier*, Newbury Park, CA: Sage.

SCHNEPP, G. and YUI, A. (1955) 'Cultural and marital adjustments of Japanese war brides', *American Journal of Sociology*, **61**, pp. 48–50.

SHAH, H. and THORNTON, M. (1994) 'Racial ideology in US magazine coverage of Black–Hispanic relations, 1980–1992', *Critical Studies in Mass Communication*, **11**, pp. 141–61.

STANTON, M.D. (1972) 'Understanding the Vietnam veteran: Some social-psychological considerations', in SHERMAN, L. and CAFFEY, E. (eds) *The Vietnam Veteran in Contemporary Society*, Washington, DC: US Government Printing Office.

STRAUSS, A. (1954) 'Strain and harmony in American Japanese war-bride marriages', *Marriage and Family Living*, **16**, pp. 99–106.

SUZUKI, O. (1949) *An introduction to Buddhism*, NY: Philosophical Press.

THORNTON, M.C. (1983) 'A social history of a multiethnic identity: The case of Black Japanese Americans', Unpublished doctoral dissertation, University of Michigan.

THORNTON, M.C. (1992) 'Is multiracial status unique?: The personal and social experience', in ROOT, M. (ed.) *Racially Mixed People in America*, Newbury Park, CA: Sage, pp. 321–5.

THORNTON, M.C. (1996) Group solidarity, racial settings and black adult feelings toward American Indians, Africans, Hispanics, Asian Americans and West Indians. Working Paper.

THORNTON, M.C. and MIZUNO, Y. (1995) 'Religiosity and black adult feelings toward Africans, American Indians, West Indians, Hispanics and Asian Americans', *Sociological Focus*, **28**, pp. 113–28.

THORNTON, M.C. and SHAH, H. (1996) 'US news magazine images of Black-Asian American relationships, 1980–1992', *The Communication Review*, **1**, pp. 1–30.

THORNTON, M.C. and TAYLOR, R. (1988a) 'Intergroup perceptions: Black American feelings of closeness to Black Africans', *Ethnic and Racial Studies*, **11**, pp. 139–50.

THORNTON, M.C. and TAYLOR, R. (1988b) 'Intergroup attitudes: Black American perceptions of Asian Americans', *Ethnic and Racial Studies*, **11**, pp. 474–88.

THORNTON, M.C., WHITE-MEANS, S. and CHOI, H-K. (1993) 'Sociodemographic correlates of the size and composition of informal care networks among frail ethnic elderly', *Journal of Comparative Family Studies*, **24**, pp. 235–50.

WALTERS, L. (1953) 'A study of the social and marital adjustment of thirty-five American-Japanese couples', Unpublished master's thesis, Ohio State University.

WHITE-MEANS, S. and THORNTON, M.C. (1990a) 'Ethnic differences in the production of informal home health care', *The Gerontologist*, **30**, pp. 758–68.

WHITE-MEANS, S. and THORNTON, M.C. (1990b) 'Labor market choices and home health care provision among employed ethnic caregivers', *The Gerontologist*, **30**, pp. 769–75.

WHITE-MEANS, S. and THORNTON, M.C. (1996) 'Well-being among informal caregivers of indigent black elderly,' *Journal of Comparative Family Studies*, **27**, pp. 109–28.

WILLIAMS, T. and THORNTON, M.C. (1998) 'Social construction of ethnicity versus personal experience: The case of Afro-Amerasians', *Journal of Comparative Family Studies*, **29**, 2.

YOON, I-J. (1995) 'Attitudes, social distance, and perceptions of influence and discrimination among minorities', *International Journal of group Tensions*, **25**, pp. 35–56.

ZINSMEISTER, K. (1987, July/August) 'Asians: Prejudice from top and bottom', *Public Opinion*, **59**, pp. 8–10.

12 'Funny, You Don't Look Puerto Rican', and Other Musings on Developing a Philosophical Orientation to Multicultural Education Research

Sonia Nieto

Who we are as individuals, the values we hold dear, our particular identities, and the work that we do — all these need to be understood in tandem. Nevertheless, academics for the most part have avoided discussing such connections because we have been taught that our scholarly work needs to be 'objective', with no hint of bias and based solely on scientific and rational thinking. However, without taking into account the background and experiences of scholars, and the forces that drive them to do the work that they do, I believe we are left with an incomplete understanding of the work itself. The result is a less honest history because it supports the claim that scholarship is largely unaffected by forces outside the purely scientific realm, factors such as personal life stories, social structures, and political ideologies. In effect, the view of scholarship as unaffected by anything other than just scientific inquiry has resulted in a separation of intellect from affect, and in an image of the scholar as totally divorced from the everyday world of social and political life.

An experience that I had several years ago epitomizes this kind of bifurcation: I had been asked to address a group of high school students, all of them Latino and African-American young people who were potential applicants to my university. The administrator in charge asked me to speak with them about my work as an academic and of 'the life of the mind'. Being a visual person, I couldn't help but imagine a disembodied brain bending over a computer, with the rest of the body unaccounted for! This was a comical image, to be sure, but it was also disturbing to me because I would never have described the work that I do in those terms. On the contrary, I had tried throughout my professional life to combine my scholarly interests with larger, social issues, a commitment to social justice, and advocacy and activism to help improve the educational opportunities of all children, but especially for those who have not had access to such opportunities. To speak of my work as separate from these commitments would make it, in my mind, meaningless. In addition, to address 'the life of the mind' with a group of young people might further have hindered their understanding of the fuller purposes of scholarship and inquiry; it might also have discouraged them from pursuing an academic life themselves. I chose, instead, to speak with them about the excitement of doing research, about how it connected with my life as a Puerto Rican woman and as a mother and teacher, and about how we needed the passion, hard work, and intellect of young people such as themselves to help make a better world. I believe it was a more successful presentation than discussing the work of academics as simply abstract and theoretical endeavors.

The 'value-free' perspective of scholarship has undergone important changes in the past decade or so, and one is now likely to find more academics freely discussing theories within the context of their lives and experiences rather than as having developed them full-blown out of the blue. Granted, many academics are still reluctant to place themselves in their research in this way because doing so seems to violate the neutral ground they feel they are meant to inhabit. However, I find it refreshing and also more useful to learn about the context of the work of other academics, and to understand why they have chosen certain paths and not others. It is within this framework that I have written this chapter.

My purpose here is to reflect on the experiences I have had as an 'insider/outsider' in the educational establishment, and to describe the results of this role on my philosophical approach to multicultural education. First, I will discuss a number of pivotal, personal experiences in my life, and how these influenced me to become an educator. I will discuss three specific political assumptions that I have derived from my experiences that guide the work that I do. Throughout this discussion, I will refer to research I have done and to some of my writing, as well as to a number of texts that had a profound effect on my evolving philosophy of education. I then explore the implications of these political assumptions, especially for my work in teacher education.

Life as a Puerto Rican Student in US Schools: The Insider/Outsider

As a person born and raised in the United States, I should have felt at ease and accepted in schools and in society in general. But this was not always the case for me or for many others like me. Not really an immigrant (first, because I was born here, and second, because all Puerto Ricans are US citizens, regardless of birthplace), yet not fully accepted as 'American' because I was different from the images I saw reflected on television and billboards and movies, I found myself in what Gloria Anzaldúa (1987) has described as the 'borderlands', spaces inhabited by those who live their lives in two cultures and invariably create a third in the process. As a young girl visiting Puerto Rico and certain that I would find there the total acceptance I could not find in New York City, I was astounded to be called an 'American' by my cousins. How could that be? In Brooklyn, when people knew my background, I was called 'Puerto Rican' or 'Spanish' (or even 'Spic' on a couple of occasions). When people did not know my background, they were often surprised to find out that I was Puerto Rican. I suppose it was the freckles, maybe the olive skin (too light, in their minds, to be authentically Puerto Rican), perhaps the fact that even though I did not speak English when I started school, I had little trace of a Spanish accent by the time I was in third grade. Whatever it was, this is how my odyssey with 'funny, you don't look Puerto Rican' began. It is an experience that I have had to live with for many years, and it has undoubtedly influenced the work that I do. Ironically, many years later, I discovered that virtually every Puerto Rican I met had had the same experience in spite of their varied backgrounds. They also were 'different from the others', or 'didn't really look Puerto Rican', perhaps because they were too light-skinned or too dark-skinned, too tall, too educated, or too 'something' that made them appear to challenge the limited picture of what Puerto Ricans were supposed to be like.

Even very young children pick up societal messages about cultural superiority and inferiority, and I was no different. I had learned at a young age to be embarrassed by the thick accents of my parents and by their *jíbaro* (peasant) ways. Thus, when I first heard 'funny, you don't look Puerto Rican', which was invariably meant as a compliment by well-intentioned people, that is exactly how I accepted it. The message that being

Puerto Rican was not such a good thing was clear, and if I behaved or looked different from other Puerto Ricans, I had learned that this was an asset.

In school, I was a very good student, often the 'teacher's pet' because I listened, paid attention, did my homework, and studied. I was an avid reader, and even during recess, I could be found poring over my basal reader to get a head start on the stories we would read in class. Although I loved to have my mother hear my teachers' praise, and I begged her to come to 'Open School Night', I also cringed when she showed up because she was not the young, sophisticated, slim, blond, English-speaking mother of the television shows we were just beginning to see in the 1950s.

My parents were not the models we saw in our basal readers either. They were considered foreigners; they were also older than most parents, uneducated, and certainly not middle-class. My mother at least had almost a high school education, having dropped out in 11th grade, a great accomplishment in the Puerto Rico of the 1920s. My father, on the other hand, had left school in 4th grade. Being the second oldest of 10 children, he needed to work in the fields to help support the rest of the family when his mother was widowed at a young age. Although he had already lived in the States for over 20 years by the time I was in school, his English was, at best, skimpy, and I often thought that because he had learned to communicate more often with some of our neighbors who were Jewish immigrants than with native English speakers, he knew more Yiddish than English.

When I was about 9 years old, my father bought a tiny *bodega* (a grocery store that sells Latin American and tropical foods) in the basement of a tenement in our neighborhood. I spent many hours there, helping weigh and sell *plátanos* (plantains) and other Caribbean vegetables, as well as the penny candies and sodas and canned goods he sold there. I think my first experience with 'funny, you don't look Puerto Rican' began there. One day a vendor came in and asked me where Tito was. When I told him that my father was in the back room, he was taken aback. 'You're Tito's daughter?' he asked incredulously. 'Funny, you don't look Puerto Rican. And you speak English so well.' I blushed appreciatively, and in that moment, I understood that I had been allowed to become an 'insider', and 'American' in a community of foreigners with accents or darker skin than mine.

Over the years, I heard and saw this same reaction many times, but my own reactions have changed. At first I was happy to hear the comment, feeling that somehow I had overcome the disability of difference. In this, I was not very different from Richard Rodriguez (1982), the 'scholarship boy' who learned to be ashamed of his parents and accept the dichotomy of the 'public' language of English and 'private' language of Spanish. In the process, he largely discarded Spanish and his Mexican heritage, and he became an opponent of such policies and programs as bilingual education and affirmative action. His is a tragic story; in a sense, it is the quintessential American story of millions of immigrants who have felt the pressure to conform to one language and one culture in order to fit in and succeed in our society. It is also, in many ways, an understandable response to the pressure to assimilate.

As I got older, however, I began to question this response. In junior high school, for instance, I was frequently called to the main office to translate or interpret for some of the many Latino parents in our community who could not speak English. Obviously, I began to reason, being able to speak two languages must be a good thing if I was needed for this assistance. A few of my teachers also began to comment on how fortunate I was to speak Spanish as well as English. I began to reconsider my reaction of pride at not being recognized as Puerto Rican.

I also started to react critically to some of the stereotypes I heard around me. By the time I was in high school, my family had moved to a largely middle-class community and I attended a school in which I was one of a handful of Puerto Ricans in a student body of over 5,000. A discussion in a civics class stands out as particularly meaningful during that time. The Cuban revolution had just taken place, and a young man in our class was concerned about our country having to accept the many Cubans who might now want to emigrate. He expressed the fear that they would bring gangs, crime, and other social ills to our city, just as the Puerto Ricans had! Being the only Puerto Rican in the class, I was stunned into silence, and our teacher said nothing to counteract his view. After class, I went over to him and said, 'I'm Puerto Rican, you know?' And he said something else that I have heard many times over the years: 'Oh, really? Well, I don't mean *you*. You're different from other Puerto Ricans.' Rather than accept it as a compliment this time, I told him that I was in a Puerto Rican girl gang (my mother would have died!), and said, 'And if you're not careful with what you say, we're going after you.' On that day, I probably reinforced all the negative stereotypes he had of Puerto Ricans; after all, here I was, a quiet, serious, good student, and even *I* was in a gang! At the time, it was all I could think of to say.

By the time I got to college (where, again, I was one of a handful of Puerto Ricans), I no longer accepted automatically the 'compliment' of being different from others in my community. But the sense of not quite belonging, of being the proverbial 'outsider', was something I could not shake. Seemingly accepted and liked by my peers, nevertheless I was still reminded that I was different from them. Once, when rushing off to a dance with a group of my sister's friends, who was attending the same college, one of them looked at herself in the mirror horrified at the amount of make-up she had hurriedly applied, and said, 'Oh my God! I must look just like a Puerto Rican!' When she realized what she had said, she looked sheepishly at my sister and me and said, 'I don't mean you, of course. You're different.'

It became clear to me that being Puerto Rican (or being of any other ethnic group that was considered marginal) carried with it a great deal of negative baggage. It also meant that there was only *one model*, that is, that being Puerto Rican meant being slightly dark-skinned (not white, but not black either) and short, with somewhat curly, dark hair; it meant speaking English, if at all, with an accent; being a poor student and a troublemaker in school; wearing only bright colors; speaking very loudly; and having many, many children. For young men, it also meant carrying switchblades. And here I was, 5′7″, fairly light skinned, with freckles and straight hair, and a good student to boot. Where did I fit in?

I have come to understand that the problem with such stereotypes is that they allow so little room for divergence. Puerto Ricans, on the other hand, are extremely diverse: we are black, brown, and white, and everything in between; tall, short, fat, and skinny; we speak Spanish and/or English, and all sorts of combinations of these; we wear bright colors and dark ones; we are good students and not so good students; and we are factory workers and professors, housewives and scientists, welfare recipients and secretaries. But no matter what we look like, what we do, or the life situation we live in, we all deserve to have a sense of dignity and to be treated with respect. Consequently, now when people tell me, 'Funny, you don't look Puerto Rican' (yes, many still do), my response is generally, 'Funny, you *do*!' This usually gets their attention, and I go on to explain that anybody can 'pass' for Puerto Rican, from the darkest to the lightest, from the most highly educated to the least, and from the monolingual English speaker to the monolingual Spanish speaker.

Choosing Education

My experiences in school, as well as those outside of school, led me to choose teaching as a career. I don't claim that I consciously thought about becoming a teacher because I wanted to counteract the assimilationist messages I myself had heard as a student. However, I have no doubt that my great desire to become a teacher was largely motivated by my commitment to make school more meaningful, more comfortable, and therefore, more enabling for other students facing the kinds of dilemmas I had faced. Having always felt like an outsider, I wanted to become an insider so that others could be insiders also.

The 'insider–outsider' dichotomy has been very similar to the 'borderlands' metaphor. Being an insider meant that I could now claim a measure of expertise and knowledge in an arena that was important to me. I could help effect changes in schools, or at least in a particular classroom, with a number of specific children. By my mere presence, I could bring up issues of language and culture that had never been broached in my school before. I was the outsider who had insisted on getting on the inside.

However, while becoming an insider in education, I also became, in some ways, an outsider in my own community. Those Puerto Ricans who were fortunate enough to get a college education were few indeed in the 1960s. We were held up as examples, to be sure, but we were also held at a respectful distance because we had been given privileges that most Puerto Ricans could not even dream of. Consequently, although I have at times felt that I belonged in both places, other times I have felt that I belonged in neither.

I have learned the rules of the game, but I do not always play by them. I have tried to resist both extremes, the 'Horatio Alger Syndrome' so favored by the English-speaking and dominant European American community, or what is at times the defensive nationalism of the Puerto Rican community. I am no longer flattered when those who are not Puerto Rican fawn over my achievements as a vindication of the 'American Dream', and who see my accomplishments as the epitome of 'pulling yourself up by your bootstraps'. There are too many others in my community who have not been given the chance to reap the benefits of the educational system, and to insist that it is a solitary and individual enterprise is to be blind to institutional barriers that get in their way. On the other hand, although I am fluent in Spanish, I am impatient when a group of Puerto Ricans insist that everyone must speak only Spanish, as if that made us somehow more authentic. There are many Puerto Ricans raised in the United States, especially young people, who speak no Spanish, yet who are no less Puerto Rican than others who do. I have become, in other words, both an insider and an outsider in both communities, and this has undoubtedly influenced the political assumptions that underlie my work as a Puerto Rican academic.

Political Assumptions of My Work

The United States has always been a multicultural and multiracial society, although this reality has not always been admitted. Layering the 'melting pot' concept over the racial and ethnic diversity of our country allowed little room for acknowledging differences, especially when the majority of those immigrating were from Europe and, therefore, more 'meltable' than those with darker skins and non-European cultures. The fact that the growing diversity of the United States has become a subject of great concern and debate in the past two decades is due to at least three interrelated issues: the dramatic growth of certain communities of color, the radical restructuring of our economy and subsequent squeezing out of the middle class, and unprecedented immigration from South America and Asia. This growth has been well documented and is expected to increase. For example, it is projected that by the year 2010, the white population will increase by only 9 percent, while the black population will increase by 29 percent, and the Latino population by nearly 80 percent. Furthermore, by 2040, the population of Asian and Pacific Islanders is expected to more than quadruple (O'Hare, 1992). Language diversity is also growing. More than 31 million people, or 14 percent of the nation's population, age 5 and over, speak a language other than English, including nearly 10 million school-age children (US Bureau of the Census, 1993; Waggoner, 1994). Add to this the fact that 50 of the largest 99 school districts serve primarily students of color, while the nation's teaching force is becoming *less* diverse, and we begin to understand the enormity of the problem of matching the knowledge and expectations of educators with the social and learning needs of the students they will teach (NCES, 1994; Yopp, Yopp, and Taylor, 1991).

These statistics face me every day as I work with teachers, teachers-to-be, and other educators. I am concerned on a daily basis with how teachers learn to negotiate cultural differences in ways that both affirm their students and prepare them to become critical and productive members of our society. How I make myself visible to these educators so that they understand 'where I'm coming from' without unduly intimidating them in the process, and what this means in terms of my approach to professional development, are also of concern to me. There are at least three political assumptions that I bring to my work every day. I will describe these and explain what I mean by them, especially as viewed from the research and writing I have done.

Education is a Political, Social, and Pedagogical Process

When I started teaching, I viewed the profession as it is often portrayed in the media: as the realm of selfless and charismatic teachers who transform the lives of their children through individual effort and by dint of hard work and high expectations. This was the kind of teacher I wanted to be. I worked hard to become known as a strict but affectionate teacher, and as one who accepted no excuses for laziness or failure. I often think of those first students I taught, and I wonder where they are now. I believe I made a difference in the lives of some of them, but I know now that I could not singlehandedly have changed their life options because there were too many other barriers working against them. I did not pay very much attention to structural barriers and institutional inequality because I had absorbed thoroughly the ideals of meritocracy ('hard work will get you what you want', 'anybody can be President of the United States', and so on). These are indeed worthy ideals, but I began to understand that they were often impossible in a society that castigated those who lived in poverty, spoke languages other than English, or had the misfortune to attend poorly equipped, overburdened schools. I saw that many of my students were capable of brilliance, but that they had not been given a chance to demonstrate it, and I began to understand that there were often huge gaps in their education because they had not been taught some skills that were basic to academic success. In a word, I began to question the truths of the meritocracy.

This was a gradual process, of course, and one that is still developing. A dramatic juncture happened when I became a doctoral student and was introduced to such books as *Pedagogy of the Oppressed* by Paulo Freire (1970), *Teacher* by Sylvia Ashton-Warner (1963), and *The Rise and Fall of the Corporate State* by Joel Spring (1972). Then I took an economics seminar at the University with Sam Bowles and Herbert Gintis where we used as the text the manuscript of their forthcoming book, *Schooling in Capitalist America* (1976). An article by Annie Stein (1971), a scathing attack on the failure of the New York City Schools to educate black and Puerto Rican youngsters, the very same schools that I had attended as a child, provided me with further reflection. Reading these books and articles was a riveting experience for me. Here were texts that questioned not only teaching methods, but the very foundations of education. These books provided a hodge-podge of interrelated theories based on economic barriers, cultural mismatch in classrooms, and structural inequality, and they gave me a partial answer to the dilemma of school failure.

At the same time, as a student of multicultural education, I was fortunate to study with Bob Suzuki, one of the first scholars in the country to focus on this field and whose seminal article, '*Multicultural Education: Who Needs It?*' (1979) had a profound effect on my thinking. We used James Banks' *Teaching Strategies for Ethnic Studies* (1975, 1st ed.) as the text and we read everything else that we could get our hands on that was related to multicultural education (Gay, 1971; Cortés, 1973; Grant, 1977). These pioneers in multicultural education were considerable sources of inspiration for me and for my peers. Slowly, my thinking on multicultural education evolved from viewing it as a nice way to make the curriculum more relevant, to a profound awareness of the political, social, and pedagogical underpinnings of *all* education. These ideas simmered for many years, and although I began teaching courses in multicultural education in 1980, I did not write about it for a long time.

In 1983, my ideas started coming together on paper when I was asked to give a keynote speech at an early childhood conference sponsored by the YWCA in Boston. It was there that, for the first time, I outlined some of the characteristics that I felt were central to a critical understanding of multicultural education. I believe I discussed five such characteristics, but they were the foundation for the definition of multicultural education that I eventually included in my book, *Affirming Diversity*, which would not be published until 1992. In 1984, at a conference sponsored by the Traprock Center, a peace studies and teacher resource center in western Massachusetts, I was again asked to give a keynote speech on the topic of multicultural education. I called it 'Affirming Diversity', the first time that I was to use the phrase that later became the title of my book. Here, too, I spoke about the importance of developing a perspective of multicultural education that went beyond ethnic tidbits and considered larger contextual questions of inequality. That is how the subtitle of my book (*The Sociopolitical Context of Multicultural Education*) came to be.

Through the years, I have come to understand that teachers and other educators need to be introduced formally to this concept of the sociopolitical context of education. Very rarely is it explicitly taught, yet realizing that education is a political, social, and pedagogical process is absolutely essential if we are serious about educational and social reform. Teachers need to be provided with examples of what this means in practice; otherwise, they can fall back on easy answers to complex problems. They may either cite genetic or cultural differences and, therefore, blame the children and their families for educational failure; or they may blame environmental conditions such as poverty and lack of English skills as the culprit. At the other extreme, they may latch onto any number of techniques or approaches (multicultural education, cooperative learning, bilingual education, whole language, and so on) as the sole answer and indeed the panacea to all the educational ills found in our schools. Just as I did, they may sing the praises of a meritocracy that makes it possible for some to succeed, but they will not question why others do not. That is, unless teachers have the opportunity to study the sociopolitical context in which education takes place, they will not grasp fully the complex reasons for educational success and failure. This is a primary political assumption of my work.

All Students of All Families Bring Valid Experiences, Insights, Talents, and Skills with Them to School

I began my formal studies in multicultural education in 1975, but I had been a bilingual teacher since 1968. Although I had my doubts about the efficacy of bilingual education (after all, I had never been in a bilingual program myself), I became convinced of its power and by its results shortly after I began teaching my fourth-grade class at PS 25 in the Bronx, the first bilingual school in the northeast. Not only were children learning in two languages, but they were also learning to respect and use their own culture and experiences in the service of their learning. This was a new idea for me because before this, I had accepted the notion that those of us who were not from the dominant culture had to leave our identities at home in order to have a chance at educational success. Here was a new proposition: we could become not only bilingual, but also bicultural, and we could bring our home and community experiences into our classrooms with us.

In 1968, this was a radical idea. Our society had spent a couple of centuries trying to expunge the linguistic and cultural differences of enslaved Africans as well as those of Asian, Latin American, and European immigrants, and even of those who were conquered in their own lands (American Indians throughout the country, Mexicans in the Southwest, and Puerto Ricans on the island). The thought that people from these communities might have something to contribute to their own education had rarely been considered, except where there was cultural congruence as was the case with segregated black schools before court-mandated desegregation (Walker, 1993).

My own teaching experiences confirmed that students had a lot to build on. First, there was their native language. I began to see that we had often treated language ability in a language other than English as a liability. Even in bilingual programs, it was often viewed as a bridge that could be burned once English was acquired. Bilingual education, when viewed in this way, became one more vehicle by which young people moved from native language monolingualism to English language monolingualism. This idea, first expressed by Jim Cummins (1979), became the basis for defending the language rights and legacy of the growing numbers of children whose native languages were disrespected and maligned by schools. Rather than a liability, we began to understand that native languages other than English could provide the needed foundation for developing skills important for academic learning.

Based on that concept, it was a simple matter of viewing culture in the same way. I have tried throughout my academic career to bridge the gap between bilingual and multicultural education and I began to ask questions such as: What can I learn from my students? What cultural references do they have that can be used effectively in the classroom? What skills and talents do their parents and other community members have? How can schools become places where these can be affirmed? At the same time, I began to think of the importance of the student voice in general, and how it is usually kept silent, and I was inspired by such books as Michelle Fine's *Framing Dropouts*

(1991) and Luis Moll's (1992) work in using students' funds of knowledge. My work in multicultural education thus began to focus on the important insights that students have about their own education, and this was reflected in the case studies I did in my book (Nieto, 1992, 1996) and in my subsequent article in the *Harvard Educational Review* (1994b).

Students are not simply walking sets of deficiencies. But teachers, especially those from the majority culture, may not recognize the skills that students come to school with. It is essential that my work with teachers take this principle into account by helping them see the gifts that students bring to their learning. This realization led me to another closely related concept, namely, that teachers also bring with them particular insights, talents, and ways of understanding reality.

All Teachers Bring with Them a Particular Way of Looking at the World

Everybody comes to the schoolhouse door with particular, and therefore insular, experiences, and these influence what and how we think about our students. Sometimes the result is behaviors that reward or punish some students simply for their social class, race, gender, or native language. On the other hand, especially if they are from the dominant culture, teachers and students can be blind to their own culture while accepting it as the norm against which all others are measured (Tatum, 1992). Teachers from dominated cultures, however, also have an incomplete perspective about their students because all of us, regardless of background, have been educated in a monoculture way. Therefore, all teachers need to be helped to learn about other ways of looking at the world by leaving the comfort of their own particular and incomplete experiences. That is, teachers need to be aware of their own position in society and learn to view it critically.

In my teaching, I have used this concept by building on the skills and experiences that teachers have, and then I try to move them to understand the experiences of others different from themselves (I have recently written about the need to do this in multicultural education courses; see my chapters in the book by Rudolfo Chávez Chávez and Jim O'Donnell and in the forthcoming book by Donaldo Macedo). In addition, my courses in multicultural education provide students with many perspectives of others that they may not receive in other professional development experiences, whether through articles written by those from marginalized cultures or videos about particular communities. In addition, I encourage educators to read novels, historical accounts, and biographies of people they may not be familiar with, but who have important things to say. 'Decentering', a term used by Suzuki in his classic article on multicultural education (1979), is thus also a necessary process for teachers, not simply for students. It is a process that helps teachers understand that nobody can have all the answers to the perplexing and complex problems of education.

Finally, in order to challenge schools as they are, I ask teachers to think critically about institutional policies and practices that may jeopardize some students, including tracking, testing, pedagogical approaches, and a rigid and ethnocentric curriculum. By reflecting on how schools could be otherwise, teachers can develop a more creative stance in their own teaching, and they can learn to view educational reform in more complex ways. But envisioning change is not always easy, and there are few examples of multicultural schools in action. Therefore, in one of my courses, I use the excellent teacher-developed resource, *Rethinking Our Classrooms* (1994), and I recommend a number of teacher-support networks (a full resource list is available in the 1996 edition of *Affirming Diversity*). In addition, the lack of practical examples in multicultural education served as the rationale for an article I wrote focusing on five vignettes of imaginary schools engaged in different levels of support for multicultural education (Nieto, 1994a). Thus, my writing often emerges from problems or dilemmas I am having in my own teaching, and they are one way I have of addressing what I consider some substantial needs of my own students.

Some Implications of My Political Assumptions

I believe that the political assumptions of my work can be seen in everything I do, whether in teaching, writing, or research. The topics I choose to study, or the courses I design, all result from the three assumptions I have described above. Let me list a number of the implications specifically for the way that I approach teacher education that I think result from my assumptions:

1 *Providing teachers a context for understanding racism and other forms of institutional oppression*
Unless I do this, multicultural education can become yet another superficial approach to very serious problems of inequality. Through readings, relevant videos, and discussions in both large and small groups, as well as through particular assignments that I give, I challenge teachers to understand how institutional oppression is a barrier to equity in schools.

2 *Focusing on the importance of holding consistently high and rigorous expectations for all students*
Teachers frequently expect too little of their students, and this is an understandable, but unacceptable, response given the many obstacles placed in the way of student learning. In my work with teachers, I emphasize that raising the expectations we have of all students is one way to counter these obstacles, although this alone cannot result in academic success for all. Nevertheless, I often have them think and write about how they communicate their expectations to their students, and what the hidden or unintended messages may be.

3 *Understanding that what goes on in school can add or detract from student learning*
That is, the curriculum and instructional approaches used in schools can have a profound effect on students, either motivating or alienating them from the educational experience. If they feel connected to, and inspired by, their learning, students can soar to great heights. In working with teachers, I ask them to develop curriculum and pedagogy that are motivating, challenging, and relevant to the lives of their students. This means, first and foremost, to learn about their students' lives, interests, and skills.

4 *Appreciating that what goes on outside school can also either add to or detract from student learning*
Parents and the community can have a strong influence on student learning, and as educators we need to find ways to help bring the contributions of families to school learning. This means using students' languages, cultures, and other experiences in the service of their learning. Because educators have often heard only about negative influences that families have on their children, I focus

instead on the aspirations and dreams they have, and I ask teachers to take these into account in their classrooms and schools.

5 *Achieving social justice cannot take place in schools alone*

This is a hard lesson for teachers to learn, as it was for me. But I have learned that our work needs to be both inside and outside schools, challenging policies that benefit some at the expense of others. Undoubtedly, schools can do much in the struggle for social justice, especially at the level of individual success and triumph. But they cannot do it all. My work with teachers stresses that unless we wage a struggle at both the micro level of schools, and the macro level of society, little will change.

Conclusion

Just as any other scholar, I have been influenced by my personal and cultural experiences, by the studies I have done and the people from whom I have learned, by my life as a wife, teacher, and mother, and by the students I teach. Fitting together like the pieces of a puzzle (although not always perfectly aligned), these parts have combined to help me develop a philosophical and political orientation to my work.

My own struggle with identity was no doubt one of the factors that led me to teaching. 'Funny, you don't look Puerto Rican', a generally innocent statement made with the best of intentions, became for me a catalyst for questioning my own identity as well as those conditions in our society that make that backhanded compliment so acceptable. The statement itself is a symbol of that most basic of tensions in a pluralistic society: the need to reconcile diversity and unity. This tension has led me to ask other questions: Why has it been seen as necessary to eradicate differences in order to create harmony? What does it mean to be an American? Can being an American mean being different from the majority? Can being Puerto Rican fit into the definition? And, finally, how can we make American identity more inclusive and welcoming of all our people?

My questions began with the experiences I had, but, of course, they transcend the particular reality of just one person. In my teaching and research, I keep questions such as these foremost because it seems to me that the way we answer them as a society will either doom some students to continue to question their worth and limit their chances for effective learning; or it will provide them with an impetus and support for becoming a new kind of American, one that challenges limited notions of belonging, importance, and dignity.

References

ANZALDÚA, G. (1987) *Borderlands/La Frontera: The New Mestiza*, San Francisco: Spinsters/ Aunt Lute.

ASHTON-WARNER, S. (1963) *Teacher*, New York: Simon and Schuster.

BANKS, J.A. (1975) *Teaching Strategies for Ethnic Studies*, Boston: Allyn and Bacon.

BIGELOW, B., CHRISTENSEN, L., KARP, S., MINER, B., and PETERSON, B. (eds) (1994) *Rethinking Our Classrooms: Teaching for Equity and Justice*, Milwaukee, WI: Rethinking Schools.

BOWLES, S., and GINTIS, H. (1976) *Schooling in Capitalist America: Educational Reform and the Contradictions of Economic Life*, New York: Basic Books.

CORTÉS, C.E. (1973) 'Teaching the Chicano experience', in BANKS, J.A. (ed.) *Teaching Ethnic Studies: Concepts and Strategies*, Washington, DC: National Council for the Social Studies, pp. 181–99.

CUMMINS, J. (1979) 'Linguistic interdependence and the educational development of bilingual children', *Review of Educational Research*, **49**, pp. 222–51.

FINE, M. (1991) *Framing Dropouts: Notes on the Politics of an Urban Public High School*, Albany: State University of New York Press.

FREIER, P. (1970) *Pedagogy of the Oppressed*, New York: Seabury Press.

GAY, G. (1971) 'Ethnic minority studies: How widespread? How successful?', *Educational Leadership*, **29**, pp. 108–12.

GRANT, C. (ed.) (1977) *Multicultural Education: Commitments, Issues, and Applications*, Washington, DC: Association for Supervision and Curriculum Development.

MOLL, L. (1992) 'Bilingual classroom studies and community analysis: Some recent trends', *Educational Researcher*, **21**, 2, pp. 20–4.

NATIONAL CENTER FOR EDUCATION STATISTICS (1994) *Characteristics of the 100 Largest Public Elementary and Secondary School Districts in the United States: 1991–1992*, Washington, DC: Author.

NIETO, S. (1992/1996) *Affirming Diversity: The Sociopolitical Context of Multicultural Education*, New York: Longman.

NIETO, S. (1994a) 'Affirmation, solidarity, and critique: Moving beyond tolerance in multicultural education', *Multicultural Education*, **1**, 4, pp. 9–12, 35–8.

NIETO, S. (1994b) 'Lessons from students on creating a chance to dream', *Harvard Educational Review*, **64**, 4, pp. 392–426.

NIETO, S. (Forthcoming) 'From claiming hegemony to sharing space: Creating community in multicultural courses', in CHÁVEZ CHÁVEZ, R. and O'DONNELL, J. (eds) *Speaking the Unpleasant: The Politics of Non-engagement in the Multicultural Education Terrain*, Albany: State University of New York Press.

O'HARE, W.P. (1992) *America's Minorities: The Demographics of Diversity*, **47**, 2, Washington, DC: Population Reference Bureau.

RODRÍGUEZ, R. (1982) *Hunger of Memory: The Education of Richard Rodríguez*, Boston: David R. Godine.

SPRING, J. (1972) *The Rise and Fall of the Corporate State*, Boston: Beacon Press.

STEIN, A. (1971) 'Strategies for failure', *Harvard Educational Review*, **41**, pp. 133–79.

SUZUKI, B. (1979) 'Multicultural education: Who needs it?', *Integrated Education*, **17**, 97, 98, pp. 43–50.

TATUM, B.D. (1992) 'Learning about race, teaching about racism: The application of racial identity development theory in the classroom', *Harvard Educational Review*, **62**, pp. 1–24.

UNITED STATES BUREAU OF THE CENSUS (1993) *Foreign-born Population in the United States*, Washington, DC: US Government Printing Office.

WAGGONER, D. (1994) 'Language-minority school-age population now totals 9.9 million', *NABE News*, **18**, 1, pp. 24–6.

WALKER, E.V.S. (1993) 'Caswell County Training School, 1933–1969: Relationships between community and school', *Harvard Educational Review*, **63**, 2, pp. 161–82.

YOPP, H.K., YOPP, R.H. and TAYLOR, H.P. (1991) 'The teacher track project: Increasing teacher diversity', *Action in Teacher Education*, **8**, 2, pp. 36–42.

13 Personal and Intellectual Motivation for Working from the Margin

Carl A. Grant

> The genesis of my research questions lay deep in the tensions and conflicts of my
> everyday life . . . There was no split between my personal and intellectual dilemmas . . .
> I was inside my own questions and methods, positioned within the object and process
> of my inquiries. (Middleton, 1993, p. 65)

There are several reasons why I do the research and scholarship that I do. These reasons
are grounded in the principles of social justice and multicultural education, and they are
guided by my personal and intellectual commitment to improving education for students
of color and other marginalized students. These reasons also come out of my respect for
African-American and other scholars who have sought to make a positive difference in
the world for all people.

My work is also driven by the belief that things can be better. For years, a poster
with a statement by George Bernard Shaw has been mounted on my office door. This
statement illustrates my belief in possibilities for change, it reads:

> You see things as they are; and you ask 'Why?' But I dream things that never were: and
> I ask 'Why not?'

In this chapter, I discuss four experiences that have helped to shape my scholarship
— teaching in Chicago, attending graduate courses for my Master's degree at a Chicago
University, conducting research for my dissertation as a graduate student at the University of Wisconsin-Madison, and working with Teach for America. Of these four experiences, it is teaching in Chicago that has had the greatest impact on my research and
scholarship.

Teaching in Chicago

As a former student of the Chicago Public School System, I never experienced (or
recognized) overt racism in the elementary (K-8) and secondary schools (9–12) that I
attended. However, as a teacher in Chicago in the 1960s, I learned that many of the
policies and practices of schooling, and why and how they were enacted, were detrimental to the needs and well-being of African-American students.

This learning began when I was hired as a new teacher and assigned to George
Washington School. My specific assignment was to teach science and/or social studies
as a member of an eighth grade team. There were five of us on the team: two first-year
and three second-year teachers. Our rooms were on the third floor of a fairly modern,
well-maintained (i.e., clean) building. Our classrooms were next door to one another

and/or across the hall from each other. We quickly developed a spirit that was based on our desire to become good teachers and to help our students. We believed that, if we worked as a team, our students would become aware of this unity and we would be more effective. We were inexperienced but enthusiastic and teamwork and hand work became our hallmark. Three African-American men and two African-American women made up this departmentalized teaching team. Each of us had a homeroom and my responsibility in the team was to teach science. I was a biology major in college and personally and professionally enjoyed science. I was excited about the opportunity to teach students the importance and value of using science as a tool and passport in their lives.

Our students were intelligent and obedient, and the few who were gang members did not bring that behavior on school grounds. The students looked forward to their graduation from eighth grade the following June but a good number of them were vague about what to study in high school and the importance of four successful years in high school to their future career and life circumstances. Unlike the characters in the movie 'Risky Business', very few of these students had a design for the future that included a high GPA, high school honor classes, or college-track courses. This realization about our students caused us to engage in many activities and projects to help them understand the significance of a good education and to learn how to acquire a good education. We often discussed the personal and professional opportunities that come with an education. In these discussions we appealed to the students' responsibility as African-Americans to take advantage of the sacrifices that their ancestors had made when they risked life and limbs to learn to read and write during the time of enslavement and that their parents were making to support their education. We wanted them to understand that achieving in school was not just a 'white thing', but a proud people thing. More importantly, we pointed out the obligation they had to themselves to be the best they could be. We discussed the hard choices they had to make to be successful and we explained to them that education was their only real legal option to a productive life.

At the practical level, we gave them insights and suggestions on how to prepare for and take standardized tests, and how to interview for part-time jobs. We discussed the importance of being able to code switch and function in both black and white America. We gave them cultural information that would foster their ethnic pride. We did not have an articulated theoretical framework, nor were we using action research, journal writing, or any research method and/or procedures to study this problem. What we had was the motivation from lessons learned and lessons being learned about racism and other social injustices to direct us in helping our students.

Many of our students had never left the south side of Chicago, and the ones who had were never encouraged to take advantage of the many opportunities a major city provides for the education and welfare of its young people. Few students had been downtown to see and visit the high-rise buildings, the public library, city hall, the up-scale department stores, theaters, and concert halls. We organized after-school clubs and, on Saturday mornings, often took students to museums, the Art Institute, and to movies. We also attended the few available exhibits and art fairs by African-Americans and other racial and ethnic groups. We wanted our students to see this work and become further convinced that Blacks were contributors to the US culture. However, exhibits by people of color were rarely on display. Some of the Saturday morning excursions were often followed by lunch at a downtown restaurant where they practiced their code switching skills and other social skills needed to navigate through mainstream society.

The education and life experiences that the Chicago city center could offer were less than a 30-minute subway train ride from where the students lived. Yet, for all practical purposes, it could have been hundreds of miles away. Why didn't our students take this subway train ride? They were old enough, they didn't have a great deal of money but they had enough money to treat themselves to a city center excursion, a downtown movie, popcorn and a hot dog. There was no overriding worry of personal harm, the gangs were not as violent as they are today (besides, the gangs did not come to the downtown area) and there had not been a race riot or any major racial disturbance in Chicago for decades.

The students and their parents gave us some reasons for their actions. They were recent arrivals to Chicago and never heard about all of the free or inexpensive events in the city center (at that time, many of the museums and the Art Institute were free or the cost was minimal). Also, most of their new friends did not go downtown and their community was fairly large with a variety of stores and other community needs. An additional reason, one that the parents and students did not explicitly voice but was nevertheless implied, was that the city did very little to attract our students to take that 30-minute train ride to the center of town.

It was not long into our teaching experience that my teaching team colleagues and I realized that we were getting our students 'late'. Late because the effects of several years of poor schooling (both poor teaching and poor achievement), poverty-line income living and socialization, and racism are difficult to turn around. For years our students had been taught both implicitly and explicitly that they were not intelligent, their educational career would be short (one to two years of high school), the positive development of their personhood was their problem, and their full participation in the American dream was a very, very long shot and not really desired by the dominant group. IQ and achievement tests confirmed, although falsely, these ideas on a regular basis. Furthermore, the results of these tests were presented as an accurate predictor of the life chances of our students and their parents. When students did have good teachers and received good grades on teacher-made tests, they learned that these successes did not really count in the larger scheme of things. Their teachers' statements of beliefs in their ability could not accompany them like one can carry a passport. Also, a teacher's statement would not count as much as their achievement and IQ test results. For the students who did excel, in spite of the formal and informal racism embedded in school, they still had to be prepared for racism in the world outside of their neighborhood and community. A world that frequently showed that it did not regard the ideas and lives of African-American children highly.

The curriculum and textbooks we were assigned to use ignored African American people. When African American people did receive attention, they were treated like second-class citizens or in a stereotyped manner. I recall meeting with my principal to discuss ordering some different textbooks. The science textbooks that I was using were outdated, worn, and included few, if any, science activities that took into account the students I was teaching. I was politely refused. My principal offered two reasons: one, we needed to spend the money on a new reading program; and two, he observed that, although it had nothing to do with my teaching, my students would probably not be doing too much with science in their future. He suggested that if I was really concerned I should consider developing my own science activities to supplement the science program we were using. I recall replying that according to the budget committee there was enough money for both reading and science textbooks and that I bet the students on the city's north side had both — teachers who related their science teaching to the students and textbooks that took the students into account. My principal just stared at me and walked away. Of course, I didn't get new science textbooks.

Amazingly, the library in our school had an excellent collection of books written by African-American authors and stories of high interest to African-American students. This was a feat accomplished by the school librarian, an African-American woman who had acquired a city-wide reputation as an outstanding librarian and who had been at the school for several years. However, the books and materials that the students saw in the library were, to many of them, both a contradiction and/or a put down since the 'official' books — their textbooks — had no or limited information on African-Americans when the 'unofficial' books — the books in the library — had information on African-Americans. For the students this reinforced the idea that information about African-Americans was unimportant and that they, as African-Americans, were unimportant in US society.

Observations like these were the critical incidents in teaching that made it difficult for the students to believe in what we were saying to them about the importance and self-fulfillment an education can provide. Also, for some students who came to George Washington after completing the first five or six grades elsewhere, the collection of African-American books in the library was both a source of confusion and frustration. The students were confused and frustrated because it brought into question the knowledge that the African-American teachers at the feeder school had about their own history as well as the teachers' willingness to take action to change the status quo. To this day, I still remember Marion asking:

> Why does the librarian at this school know about books by and about African-Americans? Why is the librarian at this school able to have these books in the library? And why is it that the librarian and teachers at my other schools, many of them African-American, did not have these books?

The students' queries were not presented in a mean-spirited manner and many of them were not presented in a polished manner. However, they were powerfully insightful evidence that the students had passed 'Critical Thinking 101'. Our responses to them were also not polished or based upon research evidence. We too were learning about the many dimensions of the racist educational system, and the many ways defacto desegregation throughout the city harmed African-American students. We also came to realize that in spite of the discussions that were occurring across the nation and within Chicago on issues such as white flight, school boundary changes and plans to achieve school desegregation — in other words, how to make assimilation work — the devastating impact that has accrued from years of school segregation was not receiving the quality of attention needed to correct these injustices.

The stated rhetoric by the school system was: 'equal opportunity and a good education for all students'. The unofficial policy was the legitimacy and importance of the Eurocentric tradition. Leadership at the city level was predominately white and the intent of the city leaders was to make certain that the city's institutions, such as the schools, reflected a Eurocentric theme. Most of the school leadership was white as well. The African-Americans who were leaders were expected to operate within a Eurocentric paradigm. Although it was not unusual for students to have an African-American teacher, African-American students soon learned that their teachers lacked the political and social means necessary to change district and school policies. The most that teachers, who genuinely cared for their students, could do for them was to teach them, explain to them the importance of an education, explain how they 'made it' through the racist educational system, and discuss the hopes and possibilities that could come out of the

Civil Rights Movement. For most students these were inspirational and interesting discussions. For only a small number of students, however, did these discussions provide enough information and incentive to make a difference in their educational achievement. Racism and poverty were/are tough wardens of our 13–15-year-old students.

The informal or hidden curriculum supported the beliefs and values espoused in the overt curriculum. This curriculum argued that African-American students should model their way of living and behavior after the dominant group. Even in a city as large as Chicago, with a good portion of the population being African-American, it was difficult to identify locations (e.g., museums) and events to take students on field trips that celebrated their history and culture. Field trips were important, even necessary, because they exposed the students to greater Chicago. However, in taking students on field trips, we further exposed them to white domination and privilege. To compound this problem our critiques of these events and places, while bluntly accurate about the racism, were often narrow and limited because we (teachers) had been educated under the same system and were trapped in what DuBois in *The Soul of Black Folks* refers to as 'double consciousness'.

From my teaching in Chicago I learned first hand about the many faces and sneakiness of racism and classism. I learned that many of the policies and procedures offered to combat racism and to help poor children were simply rhetoric — tigers without teeth or claws. I also learned about how students believe they are trapped in a world of hopelessness, and that it takes a good deal more than pretty speeches and tough lectures to help them see an escape or even survive.

Teaching, Not As We Were Taught

During the time we (the eighth grade team) taught together — late 1960s to early 1970s — three of us started graduate school and two started law school. I attended one of the downtown universities and began pursuing a master's degree in curriculum and supervision/administration. My thinking, along with a number of my teaching colleagues and friends, was to acquire the school administrator credentials so I could become a school principal and proceed up the Chicago School System's administration ladder. This way, we thought, we could set about changing the educational system. A major hurdle to this line of reasoning was that very few African-Americans passed the Chicago Principal Exam. We acknowledged this racist barrier but believed that if we studied and worked together we could figure out the racist nature of the exam and then figure out a way to pass it.

Besides attending graduate school, funding from Johnson's Great Society Program supported staff-development meetings that teachers were expected to attend. Numerous sessions were devoted to the 'inner-city child'. However, what we heard in most of our graduate courses and many of our staff-development sessions contradicted what we knew from working with our students.

Most of the graduate courses were taught by professors who seemed to have little, if any, experience working in an urban school or any first-hand knowledge about students who lived in an urban area. In most cases, professors relied heavily on the assigned readings to carry the discussions about students attending schools in urban areas. These readings for the most part were written by authors who also lacked any substantive experience teaching in an urban classroom or real understanding of African-American experiences. When race, socio-economic class, and gender were considered as variables in much of this scholarship they were interpreted in a narrow and limited manner, e.g., comparing black and white students' achievement scores and parents' educational attainment. In class we rarely analyzed the readings for conceptual or methodological basis, or for limitations and inaccuracies. A newspaper article on urban schools or a news reporter's (brief) experience in a large urban dwelling provided the professors' teachable moments — that is, something provocative to discuss outside of the assigned reading materials.

The education canon for graduate students espoused several related themes: students who attended school in urban areas were culturally deprived, and urban students were culturally different and needed compensatory education grounded in white, middle-class experiences; the urban community is a 'ghetto' and most urban schools are in 'depressed areas'; the influence and significance of the school is minimal, it is the home that 'really counts'; and due to their lack of self-discipline and underachievement, African-American students, especially males, need placement in special education classes.

These ideas collided with what we were experiencing in teaching African-American students. Students were not culturally deprived nor did they see themselves that way. As African-Americans their culture had a rich history full of pride. Their communities had numerous houses of worship, they were very civil and had several different kinds of small businesses. The houses and the apartment buildings (2–16 units) were modest and clean. Lawns and gardens — a good deal of them contributed and cared for by community residents — filled the landscape in the spring and summer time. Some of the students came from single-parent homes but many came from two-parent families or extended families. Money was a concern but people were not poverty stricken. The students were lively, inquisitive, and anxious. They were comfortable with themselves and each other wherever they were: at the Chicago Art Institute, a downtown restaurant, or the DuSable Museum of African American History and Culture.

What our students needed was an educational system which not only actively endorsed equal opportunity and equity, but also held educators responsible for delivering the same accountability. They also needed classroom teachers who had excellent content and pedagogical knowledge, who respected their students' cultural heritage, and who had an active interest in their students' present and future welfare. For many of our students, having five young African-American teachers was unusual. Also, to have three males who were approximately 10 years older than the male students was uniquely and positively different.

For a graduate class assignment I conducted a case study with two of my students. Conducting case studies seemed to be a favorite assignment for a good number of our college professors during the late 1960s. Two of my teaching partners who were attending other graduate schools were also engaged in conducting case studies. As a group, we used these case studies to inform ourselves more about the life and experiences of our students. We learned that two reasons a good number of our students had major difficulty achieving were because they had ineffective teachers (black and white) in grades 1–3, and because the home and school had not been communicating. The importance of good home–school communication became vividly clear from an incident that began as I was leaving school one day:

> Leaving school late one evening, I saw Robert, a student who was in my science class but not in my homeroom painfully limping off the playground. I asked him what had happened and he replied that he had twisted his ankle. I bent down to take a look and saw it was severely swollen. I didn't think it was broken but nevertheless he was in a good deal of pain and in no condition to walk home. I asked if I could call his parents

to come pick him up. He said, 'No' and then embarrassingly replied, 'We don't have a phone'. Then, in the same breath he said, 'Can't you give me a ride?' I knew it was against school policy to put students in your car but calling the police for assistance was against both of our ways of thinking. Also, it would take forever for the police to arrive. So, I got Robert into my car and we drove to his home. When we arrived, I helped him up the stairs to his apartment door. When he knocked, the woman who opened the door looked at him, then looked at me, and then returned her gaze to Robert. She asked, 'What wrong, are you hurt? Who is he?' Robert told his mother what had happened to his ankle and introduced me to his mother as his science teacher, Mr Grant. She responded, 'It took my son getting hurt to have you teachers show some feeling.'

The incident above played an important role in my teacher education and in establishing me as a teacher who sincerely cared about his students. Throughout the semester, I had several opportunities to talk with Robert's mother, Mrs Ingate. She became my ally and friend. She told the parents I was a teacher who cared and could be trusted. She and several other parents shared with me the community's view of the school. It was not very pretty. Many community residents, especially those with children in the school, believed that the principal and most of the teachers were indifferent toward them and their children. I will never forget a parent saying, 'It's only a paycheck for them.' Mrs Ingate told me that, although two of her kids had graduated from the school, she knew very little about what was going on and how they (parents) could develop greater school–parent/community participation. I told her that a number of new teachers had come to the school and were dedicated to seeing that the students received a first-class education. I also told her that we needed their help to make this happen. Mrs Ingate and the other parents were not like the parents we were hearing about in our graduate classes. They were friendly, respectful, and wanted their sons and daughters to receive a good education and become productive members of society.

During my years of teaching I never met any parents who did not want the best education possible for their child. Furthermore, the parents were willing to do their part to help their children achieve their education. Nevertheless, it is important to understand that some of the parents had developed a mistrust towards school in part because of a lack of communication or poor communication between the home and school, and because schools (the educational system) had marginalized many of these parents when they were students in the educational system.

The canon for those preparing to become teachers stated that urban students lacked self control and that their classroom behavior required constant regulation and strict codes of discipline. During my years of teaching I have found this belief to be greatly overstated, and in my classroom research, I found this idea to be exaggerated. Yet, this belief was accepted and believed so widely that it produced a self-fulfilling prophecy. The students in our team were responsive to our requests and very capable of managing themselves. The science activities in my classroom involved a good deal of group work and out-of-your-seat work to get reference books and other materials. In other words, absolute classroom silence was not the order of the day. The classroom policy the students and I developed included students having the liberty to move about the classroom and to discuss their science work with one another until a different behavioral response was needed. My one request of the students regarding discipline, which they respected and upheld, was if and when I was absent or away from the room, they should work more quietly, in case the substitute teacher's noise-level threshold and expectations for discipline were different than mine or the principal should come in and misinterpret their behavior and punish them for not working quietly.

My ideas and beliefs about the students were not always received well in my graduate classes. My comments were often ignored or dismissed. I was told that my school was an exception or that I was only talking about my class or team, and the assigned readings were based on research. Also, the comments from a number of my classmates supported those found in the readings. Some of the African-American teachers in the class told me I was wasting my time, to keep quiet, get my grade, and not to p . . . off the instructor. I often left my graduate classes frustrated and angry. Some of the anger was in part born out of how I was treated but mainly I was angry because of the neglect and unfairness that the students in my classmates' classes must have been experiencing. I was frustrated because these teachers were not evil or mean spirited, they had not been taught or learned any better. They too were the victims of a mis-education and an ethnocentric socialization. Their education had taught them to support white privilege and a melting-pot ideology. In addition, their present education was teaching them that the Civil Rights Movement had come a long way in producing an equal playing field for Whites and Blacks so most social inequities were based upon the laziness and indifference of African-Americans toward education.

The staff development sessions were pretty much based on the prevailing ideas espoused about urban students as portrayed in the teacher education canon. It seemed to be assumed that the information on culturally deprived children fit most, if not all, African-American urban students. In a good number of the staff development sessions, the organizers would devote a small amount of attention to African-American history and culture or provide some ethnic studies information — a book by an African-American or the success story of a contemporary African-American. I recall at the conclusion of one staff-development session where we had received information on how to use a reading program, which basically deskilled us because much of what we were instructed to do was to explicitly teach from the manual. The workshop leader presented *Before the Mayflower* by Lerone Bennett, Jr. She then suggested that we may wish to get the book and read excerpts from it to our students. She further added that along with getting the book we should probably get the issue of *Ebony Magazine* that contained a photo essay on the book because it would enable our students to better appreciate the story. A number of us had already read the book and seen the photo essay because the book had been published several years before in 1962. Nevertheless, we respected the suggestion as coming from someone trying to 'help'. However, when Larry innocently asked her a question about the book, we discovered that she had not read it. Furthermore, as she continued to respond, it became obvious that the suggestion had been made only to try to demonstrate that the workshop organizers were sensitive towards African-American history and culture.

Both our graduate classes and the staff-development sessions by and large dismissed the personhood of African-American students and their ability to achieve academic success. Also, these instructional sessions offered minimal help to teachers who were serious about educating students who lived in urban areas. While I was not thinking about a teaching career at the university level, I knew that if that opportunity came my way, I would never teach as I had been taught.

Cultural Affirmation in the Eyes of Children

Even when you believe you are on the right track, signs that confirm this belief are a welcome sight. This is especially true when I was constantly told by professors and classmates that what I saw taking place in my classes was an exception. Although I tried to dismiss their comments, they tended to hang on. An incident that went a long way in affirming my beliefs about students in urban areas occurred when I was doing research for my dissertation. My study included examining the influence of a social studies/reading program, 'We are black,' on the self-concept, attendance, and reading achievement of 10 classes of third and sixth-grade African-American students. Important to this account is the way in which the students in all 10 classes responded to the 'We are black' program. The classes selected for the study contained only African-American students. Overall student achievement was low and teachers complained about the students' lack of response to their assignments and school in general. However, I will never forget the joy and respect of students in each of the classes in the experimental group when I arrived and gave the social studies/reading program to the teachers. They were excited. I had never witnessed such a reaction from students over instructional material. The 'We are black' program immediately captured their hearts and imagination. In each of the 10 classes the students 'ohh'-ed and 'ahh'-ed as they eagerly read the materials. The eyes of the students grew larger as they looked at all of the stories about black people in the program. The students shared information with one another as they read, usually whispering to each other. It was as if it was secret information, something that could not be made public for if it was, it might be taken away. I learned from my observations and discussions with the teachers that the students were not sharing answers but sharing excitement. They handled the material as if it was fine jewelry. They enjoyed it, took delight in looking at the pictures, and showed a respect and admiration for text material that was astonishing. Most of the teachers shared special stories with me about the students' 'love affair' with these materials. Several of them pointed out that when the students were using the materials, classroom discipline problems disappeared. The sixth-grade students wanted to know where I had gotten this material. They said they had never seen an entire social studies/reading program designed around African-Americans. They wanted to know if there were other materials like this that I could bring.

The students in the control group were angry with me because they could not use the material. It was very difficult explaining to them why some classes received the material and other classes did not. The only way I was able to satisfy these students was to promise that later in the semester I would bring a set of the materials to their classroom.

Those students supported what I knew to be true about African-American students: they wanted to learn and they took pride in their learning, especially when it was about them. They wanted to know about their history and culture. They were suffering academically and socially as well as being suffocated educationally by being denied such information. By their actions they affirmed my ideas about the significance of a culturally relevant curriculum. This experience also taught me the importance of conducting educational research, especially research that takes the students' interests and needs into account.

Teach for America

In 1990 I served as the Dean for Teach for America's (TFA) Summer Institute. This institute was designed to help prepare 500 TFA corp members to teach in rural and urban areas in the United States. The corp members were touted as the best and brightest graduates from the best colleges and universities in the US. These young people joined TFA because they wanted to help students in rural and urban areas of the US achieve educational success and have productive lives. Unlike times in the past when young people performed national service to avoid the draft, it was said that corp members joined TFA 'to make a difference'. The 500 members consisted of a more balanced ethnic and gender representation than what is usually found in most teacher education programs.

One of the major policy and curriculum components of the Summer Institute was diversity and multicultural education. Interestingly however, the corp members at the very beginning of the institute advocated a nationalistic or ethnic perspective rather than a diversity or multicultural perspective. By this I mean that corp members (e.g., African-American, Latino, white American men, gays and lesbians) were primarily interested in making certain that the Institute's curriculum addressed their group. Some members were mainly interested in learning about how to educate their group — that is, acquiring the knowledge that would help to teach their own group. Others believed that, as members of a particular social group, they were, for the most part, already prepared to teach the young people of their group. These corps members believed that all that was needed was the 'legitimacy' to teach which they would receive from being a corp member in TFA and attending the institute. I was amazed that such an intelligent group of young adults were so primarily concerned about a particular group of students when most of the classes in which they were teaching, and possibly would be teaching were multiracial, and they could see that all students, especially those from marginalized groups, needed help. Also, they knew that one of the qualifications for joining TFA was to help students which meant more than just their own particular ethnic or social/cultural group.

The reasons behind this 'group centeredness' appeared to be based on past socialization and schooling. African-American corp members believed that African-American students had gotten the shaft in life and they needed to concentrate on educating them; gay and lesbian corp members believed that both gay and lesbian students and teachers had to remain 'in the closet' in school and therefore were being unfairly treated both psychologically and emotionally and needed their help; and white male corp members believed that the Civil Rights Movement and affirmative action legislation had made them second-class citizens on the job market and subjected them to unfair attention because of deeds performed by their foreparents decades ago — they argued that they didn't know and therefore should not be held responsible for their ancestors' deeds.

I came away from the Teach for America experience appreciating the importance of teachers having excellent content knowledge and the need for teachers to have excellent pedagogical knowledge and skills. However, I learned that we cannot take it for granted that teachers are willing to teach all students. The Corps members needed to get beyond their own group membership; they did have particular knowledge about the group(s) that they had membership in, but they also needed a multicultural knowledge base that could be used to help all students. Also, they needed to realize that just because they were a member of a particular group, they still had much to learn about how to teach students of that group, for no group is a monolith. Simply put, the corps members in TFA taught me that educators need to continually examine their own belief systems and classroom practices, otherwise the larger vision of making changes in society will be reduced to little goals of only helping those who look like us.

Conclusion

These experiences, along with others, have played a major role in the kind of research and writing that I do. I am struck by the power of societal socialization (including schooling) to influence intelligent people (especially educators) to rarely question issues of race, class, and gender, or to only question those issues that are of particular interest to them. Very often education is seen as neutral or not as a tool that enables one to analyze and critique societal structures. Also, because of these experiences I remain steadfast in my dedication to helping those who plan to teach or become teacher educators to understand that all students can learn and most students want to learn. And, as teachers and teacher educators we must be responsive to all students. Similarly, I am dedicated to helping those starting their career in educational research to understand how the intersections of race, class, and gender impact educational problems and our understanding of educational problems.

Finally, a statement from Gary Okihro's (1994) book, *Margins and Mainstreams*, captures my beliefs about why what I and others like myself do is important. Okihro writes:

> [The] core values and ideals of the nation emanate not from the mainstream but from the margins — from among Asian and African Americans, Latinos and American Indians, women, gays and lesbians. In their struggle for equality, these groups have helped preserve and advance the principles and ideals of democracy and have thereby made America a freer place for all. (p. ix)

This poignant statement brings me full circle from where I began this essay and is an excellent reminder to those of us who work from the margins that it is we who inspire and make real the core values (e.g., liberty, equality, justice) of our democratic way of life.

References

BENNETT, L. (1964) *Before the Mayflower: A History of the Negro in America, 1619–1964*, Baltimore, MA: Penguin Books.

DU BOIS, W.E.B. (1993) *The Soul of Black Folks*, New York: Random House.

MIDDLETON, S. (1993) *Educating Feminists: Life Histories and Pedagogy*, New York: Teachers College, Columbia University.

OKIHRO, G.Y. (1994) *Margins and Mainstreams: Asians in American History and Culture*, Seattle: University of Washington Press.

14 The Educational Researcher As Critical Social Agent: Some Personal Reflections on Marxist Criticism in Post-modern Times of Fashionable Apostasy

Peter McLaren

The future isn't what it used to be. It has disappeared into the realm of commodity exchange to be promoted as something that's already arrived, a type of Baudrillardean *hypertélique* slight-of-hand that has produced the present as a future dystopia — a utopia that has been lost in advance. As captured in Edward Kienholz's assemblage artwork, *The Future As an Afterthought* (Hopps, 1996), we are faced with the consequences of our historical choices. On the other hand, we are told by the custodians of family values that the past is something that we can look forward to, once the present is swept clean. Sweeping clean the present in this context means getting rid of those pernicious and short-sighted liberals whose youthful rebellion in the 1960s was responsible for the present disintegration of the social order. Intellectual life is on the demise. Within universities the link between intellectual life and revolutionary praxis has been relegated to the dustbin of institutional memory. Theory has become a dirty word as the pure scientists stage their attacks on the academic left in books such as *Higher Superstition* by Paul Gross and Norman Levitt (1995).

As educational researchers we can no longer count on the future and past to provide us with the necessary perspective to help guide our activity as social agents. We are even made to wonder whether history has ever taken place — anywhere. We are continually being displaced from our historical location and relocated into a subjectivized world without history or possible landscapes — we are, in other words, being reinvented by the retroaction of history for a world of instantaneity, of interminable repetition.

Having made these remarks, it should come as no surprise that the invitation by Carl Grant, requesting a paper addressing the theoretical contours of my work in the form of a first person account, was intriguing to me. After all, it is rare in this climate of simultaneity to be asked to connect one's theory to one's social and historical formation. Of course, personalizing or humanizing the scholar is not without its attendant risks. Some might reason, for instance, that an autobiographical style is similar to writing in neon and could too easily expand into a spectacle of academic self-indulgence. The academy, critics might argue, is already situated far too forbiddingly and securely within promotional culture (in LA especially where scholars grapple with meaning in a surreal post-Simpson-trial millieu). In such a hyperreal climate scholars risk sacrificing their scholarly accomplishment to fetishized self-indulgence, to the cult of personality, and to subordinating their political concerns to the media-generated world of popular fandom. One thinks immediately of Camille Paglia, the self-proclaimed 'greatest feminist of the twentieth century' and the 'Madonna of academia', whom Teresa Ebert (1996) describes as 'being at the forefront of the cultural shock troops carrying out the backlash against feminism in patriarchal capitalism' (1996, p. 25). Her burlesque retro feminist sojourns into prime time television and major newspapers — not to mention the crackpot extremism of her books — is enabling her ideologically to renaturalize late capitalism's gender divisions of labor and unequal access to social resources (Ebert, 1996). Witnessing scholars revealing details of their sex lives while celebrating theories ludicrously and luridly transmuted into sound-byte simplicity is enough to keep a self-respecting academics from ever leaving the world of arcane discourse. On the other hand, we now have academic figures boldly entering the realm of mainstream US culture who are speaking out in profoundly autobiographical terms about social issues and in so doing are contributing as public intellectuals in important ways to the struggle for liberation (bell hooks and Cornel West are two emblematic figures that come immediately to mind). The point is that for those of us who work in the academy, there are many good reasons for us not only to revisit our commitments to the public, but also to reflect upon the historical formation of our own ideas and agency.

I recall, for instance, a question posed to sociologist Pierre Bourdieu by the distinguish Marxist scholar, Terry Eagleton, in an issue of the *New Left Review*, where Eagleton asked Bourdieu if the subtext throughout all of his work — that of the 'common life' — was influenced by Bourdieu's biographical circumstances of being a first-generation intellectual. Bourdieu replied:

> I try to put together the two parts of my life, as many first-generation intellectuals do. Some use different means — for instance, they find a solution in political action in some kind of social rationalization. My main problem is to try and understand what happened to me. My trajectory may be described as miraculous, I suppose — an ascension to a place where I don't belong. And so to be able to live in a world that is not mine I must try to understand both things: what it means to have an academic mind — how it is created — and at the same time what was lost in acquiring it. For that reason, even if my work — my full work — is a sort of autobiography, it is a work for people who have the same sort of trajectory, and the same need to understand. (1992, p. 117)

Bourdieu's response helped me not only to gain some purchase on why his work has always had some intrinsic appeal to me, but additionally to reflect upon biographical connections to my academic research. Ben Agger (1992) sounds an important warning for academics when (in the context of cultural studies), he writes:

> Cultural studies must write for those whose gazes have been regulated by the culture industry and who thus live their lives in terms of the quotidian existences scripted for them and for the cultural heroes with whom they identify. It must aspire to a public accessibility without which one cannot say that theory has political impact or relevance. (p. 160)

Because, as Agger says, 'Stupidity is socially engendered through culture in order not to endanger the dominant quotidian' (1992, p. 160), educators need to work against the grain in order to forge a genuinely counter-hegemonic praxis in our work. As Todd Gitlin points out:

> To paraphrase Marx, men and women think, but not in a language or concepts or even emotions utterly of their own making. To paraphrase Marshall Berman paraphrasing Trotsky, you may not be interested in philosophy, but philosophy is interested in you. (1995, p. 200)

To work as an educator against the intellectual and cultural grain of the dominant quotidian has meant discovering why philosophy is interested in us, even as we may be motivated and rewarded to find such a question irrelevant to our lives. Writing books and articles that are decidedly academic (in order to make a living and survive within hegemonic academic institutions such as UCLA) has a purpose that goes beyond scholarly fetishes taking up space on library shelves or accumulating credentials in arenas of scholarship. I have always found experimenting with critical discourse to be an important act of intellectual subversion. Subversion also means writing books and articles that more easily lend themselves to critical appropriation by constituencies of educational activists. The work of Paulo Freire is a good example of such writing. Occasionally (but not occasionally enough) I have tried my hand at writing for different audiences: for teachers in columns penned monthly for a Canadian teachers' union; for prospective teachers in my introduction to critical pedagogy, *Life in Schools*; for academics and teachers in my quarterly interviews in the *International Journal of Educational Reform*; or for artists and cultural workers in an East LA Chicano/a journal such as *Alchemy* or *Razateca*.

These are, admittedly, meager attempts at counter-hegemonic strikes when compared to the public forays of other researchers and I readily acknowledge I need to do more. Whilst I agree that researchers must actively resist opacity in much of their work, this must not translate into the elimination of critical meaning and certainly should not give license and legitimacy to the cultural hegemony that creates the lexicons, systems of intelligibility, and interpretive schemes of our white Anglo heterosexist 'plain talk'. There is an exactingness to theoretical reading that should not be abandoned nor compromised. Since the language of criticalists themselves is not, as Agger maintains, 'presuppositionlessly representational', he is correct in asking that it be vigorously interrogated for its polemical and perspectival authoriality. This is not a call for a simplicity in our writings that can assist verifiability, but a call to recognize when theory occludes its own political, ontological, and epistemological foundations, when it can remain trapped in 'its own hermetic self-isolation' (p. 161).

Language helps us reflect the world — partial truths about the world — but also refracts the world, distances ourselves from it, and dispossesses us as agents as much as it enables us to act in and through history. Language puts us on an encounter with more than ourselves; it confronts us with history, a history that always exceeds who we are in terms of the ethical and political dimensions it calls into question, dimensions (cultural, social, legal, etc.) which predate our emergence into subjectivity. Language puts us on a collision course with life, instituting a trajectory to our own death even as it gives us a vehicle for constructing our encounters with the living. My experiences as they relate to my work as a social theorist cannot be adequately articulated through language but language can at least bind me (albeit provisionally) to my responsibility to connect my scholarly work to an ethical domain that resides outside of myself. This is because the 'self' that I wish to claim as my own is created only at the agonistic moment of moral tension between agency and responsibility. The responsibility to which I refer is that of becoming a critical agent/critical citizen since it is my belief that only critical agents can exercise the cautious and resolute responsibility necessary as democratic citizens to struggle effectively against social and economic injustice.

For these reasons and others, the challenge that Carl Grant set out for his contributors — to chronicle their own self-formation as researchers — began to appeal to me for a number of reasons that heretofore I had not considered. Reflecting on the political and moral dimensions of one's work can possibly serve as an important act of political advocacy and can act as a counter-hegemonic articulation of urgent social issues. This is no small feat, especially at this historical juncture of 'fast capitalism', of de-industrialization, union-bashing, economic dislocation, wide-scale unemployment resulting in part from a transition to a post-Fordist phase of friction-free casino-style capitalism, and moralistic, ideological cant surrounding family values. At a time when wealth is swiftly transferred upward while the state tells us that our systems of production are under assault from global competitors employing unfair trade practices. At a time when science is waging a war against aging and surplus, untoned flesh and the over-ambition of human genes to rebel against immortality; when affirmative action has been generalized by the white media into the fictive absurdity of reverse racism; when many African-Americans and Latinos occupy fractal zones of economic violence and social terror while the white Anglo male bourgeoisie, in a repugnant act of motivated amnesia that permits them to deny their role as the most privileged group in history, are demanding that they be recognized today as the most forsaken and vulnerable constituency of the oppressed in the United States; when in places like South Central LA, hope for children of color is far removed from the evocative appeal of a Jessie Jackson exhortation — 'Keep hope alive' — but rather takes on a depressingly ecstatic value captured in the words of a 12-year old African-American girl whom, when I asked her how she was doing, replied, 'I'm still alive, so I guess I'm OK.'

Humankind has already become extinct and we have passed into a type of post-human cyborg state. We live in an era where the dream of a reconciliation of capitalism and democracy is not likely to be realized. Where the exploitation of the labor of the many by the few remains relatively uncontested. Where millions of children throughout the global starve to death even though, for the last 30 years, food production on an average has increased 16 percent faster each year than population size; where starvation is the result of capitalist overproduction for profit; and where, in the United States (to give only one example) thousands of tons of dairy products are put in storage to artificially maintain a certain level of profit on diary items (Ebert, 1995–6). Where, in a political climate of economic terrorism, we find politicians such as Newt Gingrich accusing the welfare state of driving people to murder their children (Susan Smith) and to rip babies from mothers' wombs. It is hard to imagine, even in this country, that the shutdown of the United States government could in fact be precipitated by the anger of the House Speaker at being slighted by Clinton during a flight on Air Force One or that the poor could be sacrificed to such an extent for the welfare of the rich; or that affirmative action could be considered by such large sectors of the general public as nothing more than reverse discrimination; or that the tentacular and hydra-headed beast of capitalism could be naturalized as a unquestioned backdrop to everyday global life, to *das Allgemeinmenschliche*.

When the Republican Congress preaches less government and more local control of resources and policies, I am reminded of the old Citizens Councils of Mississippi — the Ku Klux Klan in silk ties and gabardine suits writ large — operating, as in the 1950s, with the tacit endorsement of the FBI and using black informants as *agents provocateurs* in the civil rights movement and I can't help but think of Clarence Thomas and UCLA Regent Ward Connerly as present-day examples of such agents.

The United States is fast becoming a Christian fundamentalist Sunday school taught by blood-hungry Texas pastors who pack Colt .48s and sport citizen militia camouflage uniforms. Senator Phil Gramm has received nearly half a million dollars throughout the course of his career from the National Rifle Association by adopting strong pro-gun stance and recounting how his elderly 'Momma', who carries a .38 special, asked: 'Phil, you reckon with all this meanness out there, I ought to get me a bigger gun?' And this from recent Presidential contender (Sipchen, 1996). Comments made by California's infamous Governor, Pete Wilson, in his sixth State of the State Address, typifies the way in which retrograde government policies have been increasingly naturalized, and their maliciousness incrementally normativized, such that they are rarely marked for what they really are: class and race warfare. The *Los Angeles Times* reported Wilson placing the blame for social decay on 'welfare dependency, permissive courts and deadbeat fathers' (Lesher, 1996). Children of unwed mothers, Wilson tells us (echoing Charles Murray, co-author of *The Bell Curve*, and mentor to many conservative politicians), have become expendable burdens to society.

All these rhetorical slanders against society's victims are coming at a time when the federal government is under attack — even under terrorist assaults, as the Oklahoma bombing ominously reminds us — and people are crying for the salvation of privatization. Whilst individuals on welfare are demonized by the politicians, those same politicians strive to maintain welfare for the rich in forms of tax breaks and other incentives. In my opinion, the perspectives of Wilson and Gingrich lurch perilously close to being sinful. I am using the term sin as it defined by theologian James H. Cone. According to Cone:

> The sin of whites is the definition of their existence in terms of whiteness. It is accepting the condition that is responsible for Amerindian reservations, black concentration camps, and the rape of Vietnam. It is believing in the American way of life as defined by its history . . . This country was founded for Whites and everything that has happened in it has emerged from the white perspective. The Constitution is white, the Emancipation Proclamation is white, the government is white, business is white, the unions are white. What we need is a destruction of whiteness, which is the source of human misery in the world. (1986, p. 107)

Those words were first sounded by Cone in 1970, and in my view they are as relevant today as they were then. We need to destroy Whiteness. But the destruction of whiteness is not the same thing as the destruction of white people. Whiteness is a construct that is not absolute but relative. It is a situated narrative that needs to be understood historically in the context of its invention through the colonial imagination and the blood of empire.

Recently, I read with disheartening interest the results of a study conducted by one of my colleagues, Sandy Astin, of UCLA's Higher Education Research Institute, which was discussed in the *Los Angeles Times* (Wallace, 1996). The study surveyed 240,000 college freshman. While 70 percent believed college officials should give race some special consideration when deciding who to admit, over 50 percent of freshmen said that affirmative action in admissions should be abolished (which in my mind can be linked to the neoliberal attack on 'special interests' such as issues raised by African-Americans and organized labor). Eight-six percent felt that citizenship status was an important criterion and more than 84 percent felt that children of alumni should receive special consideration. Only 28 percent of freshmen felt that keeping up with political affairs was an important goal in life and only 15 percent indicated that they frequently discussed politics. No more than 59 percent of freshmen felt that abortion should be kept legal. The survey appears to support other evidence that suggests a neoconservative political imaginary is holding sway. Witness the growing taxpayer antagonism towards welfare recipients and a government stress on recipient obligations rather than entitlement, the pronouncements on single-mothers as not wage laborers, a greater stress on personal moral responsibility (changing the characteristics of the poor — i.e., the supply side) than structural unemployment due to macroeconomic factors (creating more jobs

— i.e., the demand side), leading to blaming the victim ideologies and the marginalization of the poor to the system of social labor, the demonization of the economically disenfranchised as parasites and the exclusion of domestic, undocumented and part-time workers from social insurance benefits; the privileging of consumer ethics in the political imaginary; and the enforcement of a neoliberal stress on partnership between government and business, anti-union sentiment, the reproduction of the division between contract and charity in social welfare, and the blurring of the distinction between commodities and public goods (Fraser, 1993). According to Nancy Fraser, the government appears to be suggesting that 'all that is required for a decent standard of living is an adequate cash income, low taxes, and a full-time wife and homemaker' (1993, p. 14). In many ways conditions have worsened for the poor and people of color than when we took to the streets in the 1960s, when we marched for civil rights, when we occupied campus buildings, when we fought for better working conditions, when we disrupted school board meetings.

Under these conditions it becomes clearer why it is vitally necessary for the contemporary scholar to serve as a political advocate when so much of daily life is in upheaval. I agree with Fraser that we should struggle towards what she calls a 'democratic socialist-feminist political imaginary' that entails among other things, the following: expanding the vision of a fully social wage; defending the importance of public goods against commodities; challenging the technocratic discourses of the state that reduces citizens to clients and consumers; agitating for the importance of unwaged domestic work and the child raising labor of women; enlarging the view of entitlement; criticizing 'the hyperbolic masculinist-capitalist view that individual 'independence' is normal and desirable while 'dependence' is avoidable and deviant' (1993, p. 21); insisting on a view of public provision as a system of social rights; rejecting the idea of 'personal responsibility' and 'mutual responsibility' in favor of 'social responsibility'; and promoting social solidarity through confronting racism, sexism, homophobia and class exploitation. Consequently, I feel that scholars need to overtly connect their research to both to their manifest and tacit political concerns and interests. Only then can they exercise their social responsibility as public servants for the common good. Only then can they develop a sense of shared responsibility in the face of global interdependence that does not necessarily require or depend upon shared identity (Fraser, 1993).

Younger scholars and especially newcomers to the field of critical educational theory will, I believe, benefit from attempts by *veteranos* in the academy to connect their research and writings to their personal motivations, interests, and experiences. Readers can judge the extent to which such political agendas contribute both to the research in question and the political imaginary that either implicitly or explicitly informs it. The challenge of this invitation by Professor Grant was additionally complicated by the fact that, since I am a transdisciplinary scholar, I work in a considerable range of disciplinary fields, perhaps too many in order to give a fair, or at least an informative accounting of my work. Consequently I have chosen to discuss only the very broad sweep of some areas of my work, concentrating of that which most directly speaks to my work on issues of multicultural education and critical pedagogy.

My scholarly work is that of an educational researcher and theorist working at the intersection of anthropology, sociology critical social theory, and curriculum studies. My work is best characterized under the broad rubric of critical educational studies and in the context of four general headings: critical pedagogy and curriculum studies; the social context of literacy; ethnographic research; and, more recently, multiculturalism.

My work has largely been influenced by the writings of Paulo Freire, a name which encrypts the contested encounter among capitalism, schooling and democracy, and whose work is traversed by a call to rethink the concepts of education and liberation. Like Freire, I do not consider human subjects to be empirically transparent beings. In other words, what we assume ourselves to be as individuals is fundamentally at odds with our constitution as subjects, the latter constituting a process of which we are only partly cognizant. The complex social forces and relations of which we are a composite are only dimly, if at all, understood by us. I also believe that our subjectivities do not antedate our entrance into the world of social relations and practices but are fully conditioned by social reality. Of course, the question of how this occurs is still largely unexplored in the educational literature. The work of criticalists, like Freire, has helped to explain — if only in a rudimentary way — how subjective consciousness can be constructed within the objective terrain of social relations. In other words, they have helped to explain how our practical consciousness often misrecognizes experience as the effect of the senses when in fact it is conditioned by the historical laws of motion of capital.

The spirit of my work in educational research is similar to that of the contemporary criticalist: to develop languages, models, and practices of empirical and conceptual analysis and to create both spaces and opportunities in social and institutional sites for constructing a language of possibility and a pedagogy linked to the practice of freedom. Such a task can be challenging to educators and scholars uneasy with new languages of analysis and new approaches to understanding everyday social life. Now I should here qualify what I mean by the term 'new'. As a Marxist cultural theorist, I am certainly indebted to a wide range of Marxist (and non-Marxist) theoretical traditions. What is new about much of the new criticalist endeavors is that the very best of them attempt to cross borders — whether they are borders of militant dogmatism, hierarchy-building, boundary-maintenance, or epistemological privilege.

During the 15 years that I have served in the academy, my work has been guided by the following question: What is the relationship among schooling, the production of ideology, and the formation of subjectivity within larger cultural logics of post-industrial capitalism? Attempting to answer such a question has brought for me some successes and many failures. It has meant discovering various scholarly procedures for investigating and transforming textual and material practices of everyday life, especially as these practices implicate the student pedagogically in specific histories and modes of address that both limit and enable human possibility. Attempting to answer such a question also predisposes me to work towards an understanding of the principles and practices of democratic culture that enable students and educators to refuse received identities, to subvert given roles and behaviors, and to invent new narratives of identity, new pedagogical and social formations and affiliations in the interest of a democratic imaginary that speaks in the tradition of history's great struggles for emancipation.

The theoretical orientations of my research — for better and for worse — can be traced to my early undergraduate work in Elizabethan drama, theatre arts, and from there to my graduate studies and to my modest excursions (often informal but always energetic) into symbolic anthropology, critical ethnography and social semiotics. As a young man, one to whom Dylan Thomas might have affixed the term 'a windy boy and a bit', I had always been drawn to the *avant garde*, to bohemia, to flirtations with the Beat Poets, to music, to art, and to literature. Like Derrida and Ewald (1995), I feel that a certain 'madness' must watch over all thinking processes and this perhaps explains why my work does not result from some apocalyptic engagement with a canonic corpus of writings within a single tradition but rather constitutes weird encounters between Baudelaire and Freire, between Nietzsche and Spinoza, between Baudrillard and Levinas, between Marx and William Burroughs, between Jean Genet and Sor Juana Iñes de la

Cruz, between the occult and Catholicism, between the Christian sacraments and the rituals of Santéria, between Edward Kienholz and social realist painters, between Deep Forest and Lightning Hopkins, if the geometry of these juxtapositions can be imagined. Yet I have come to realize that the Marxist project of class struggle needs to underwrite the project ahead.

Perhaps because I passionately hated school and emerged from both high school and my undergraduate years in university in a zombified, half-sensate state, I was especially drawn to what I believed constituted alternative ways of confronting the Mount Olympian iterations of North American identity structures: conformity to texts of bourgeois authority, a repulsively triumphalistic nationalism, and a sacerdotal dedication to the self-generating logic and self-reifying tendencies of capitalism. I hated capitalism more than school — its tongue-wagging holy servant — and even at a young age I felt that capitalism possessed a self-generating and decontextualizing logic, although I would have used different terms then to describe it. It was, I felt, an exceptionally malevolent and pernicious disease and I could never understand how anyone with even a dysfunctional moral conscience could tolerate it. I believed that trade unionism was the social vaccine that could defeat it. Today's tycoon capitalism with its culture of speed has coupled consumer capitalism and military power, producing as offspring a species of violence so frightening and formidable, we have yet to name it, let alone destroy it.

Never a *littérateur*, but never the less a serious student of the arts, I found the seedbed of my resistance in surrealism, Data, and the situationist movement. A Data evening in Zürich, hosted by Hugo Ball and Emmy Hennings and held in the Cabaret Voltaire would have been an inspiration like no other. The formative years of my political development occurred during the Vietnam War and the birth of the North American 1960s counterculture. As a Canadian living in Toronto, I participated in the anti-war movement and many US draft resistors became friends and associates in the burgeoning radical youth movements of the decade. Inspired by the Cuban revolution through Cuban Third World solidarity organizations and Cuban protest art, I began to take an interest in Marxist revolutionary politics. Not content with remaining far from the youth cultures proliferating at the time, and inspired by the teaching and example of Che Guevara and Malcolm X and what I felt the May Movement in France in 1968 would eventually contribute to the *Lebenswelt* (although I did not go to Europe at that time so I cannot lay claim to being a '*soixante-huitard*'), I made several excursions to San Francisco and Los Angeles in my late teens and early 20s, hoping to work with the Black Panthers, and to make a living as a writer or sculptor. I believed then, as I do now, that white people needed to form alliances with people of color in the interest of anti-colonialist an anti-capitalist struggles. The centuries-old anticolonialist pronouncements of Denis Diderot, a radical renegade among the *philosophes*, taught white students like myself that not all Europeans were imperialist monsters. In a recent book, Shohat and Stam (1994) have described his statements as inverting the trope of barbarism and the colonialist metonym of beast and savage by considering the colonizers to be the real barbarians. Diderot wrote:

> Barbarous Europeans! The brilliance of your enterprises does not impress me. Their success does not hide their injustice. In my imagination I have often embarked in those ships which bring you to distant countries, but once on land, and witness of your misdeeds, I separate myself from you and I join your enemies, taking arms against you, bathing my hands in your blood. (Benot, 1970, p. 172, quoted in Shohat and Stam, 1994, p. 89)

I do not wish to repeat the early influences on my political life as an elementary school teacher which are chronicled in *Life in Schools*, and in discussions that have followed in the educational literature. I will therefore emphasize my work as a cultural worker in the university. Perhaps I can give some explanation for the contradictory subjective formation inscribed by my desire, by revealing *en passant* that I was greatly interested in theology and considered becoming a member of the priesthood, possibly a Paulist or Passionist. Whilst some people have (half-jokingly) remarked that they can trace the gravitational pull of my rhetoric backwards in history all the way to my short six-month stint in an evangelical Christian group at 18, and to my conversion to Catholicism at 25, coupled with my early interest as an undergraduate in Trotsky, Malcolm X, and the Marx of the *Gundrisse*, I have always resisted such frequently misguided attempts at articulating historical determinations with respect to my own work or the work of others in the sense that 'causes' for our actions can never be known in a definitive sense, especially if we acknowledge, as I do, the passionate recalcitrance of the unconscious which makes it unrepresentable to us except through archetype, myth, symbol and metaphor.

When my industrial arts teacher hacked away at my hand with a heavy metal ruler because I had used the wood chisel incorrectly, the punishment taught me not to be a better carpenter but rather to despise school. Being jailed by police (who later beat me with metal flash lights) during an instance of political rebellion in my teens instilled in me an insane loathing for the police, whom I came to believe (and still do) largely serve the interests of the dominant political/economic class.

The firing of my father as manager of an international electronics firm (a managerial position highly coveted because it brought my family from working-class life to a lower middle-class existence) created in me a strong aversion for commercial life in general and an absolute hatred of multinational corporations in particular (no doubt accounting for some of the historical pessimism and jaded liberal skepticism of my early adulthood). The avant-grade became a resource for me to nurture an oppositional creativity just as later Marxism became a weapon not only for analyzing social relations but for changing them.

My growing disenchantment with Catholicism as an ideological servant of the rich opened the door to the writings of Latin American liberation theologians. Frequent visits to Latin America and the Carribean followed (and continue to this day). I became interested in folk religions and religious practices such as Santéria and Umbanda. Named in Brasil by Umbanda practitioners as a son of Oggún (conceived of the uníon of Obatalá and Yemmu) the Yoruba god of war and iron, I received some insight into why throughout my life I have been drawn to warrior traditions of shamanism and social struggle. My colonial subjectivity was shattered by images at the National History Museum in Chapultepec Park, Mexico City, which I first toured with a Zapoteca professor from the National Autonomous University of Mexico City in 1987. The art of Frida Kahlo, Diego Rivera, and José Clemente Orozco ripped through my psyche and tore it asunder and I am still picking up the pieces and attempting to put myself together again as a de-colonized spirit. The point I am underscoring is that all of my work is influenced by my experiences and their imbrication with my political unconscious and by the fact that, as Derrida and Ewald put it, we are all born into and inscribed by *a certain preference*:

> I . . . *happen* to have been *born*, as we were saying, *into the* European *preference*, into the preference of the French language, nation, and citizenship, to take only this one

example, and also into the preference of this era, of those I love, of my family, of my friends — and of my enemies too, of course, and so on. At every moment, and it is our daily experience, these preferences can contradict and threaten the imperatives of the universal respect of the other, but neutralizing them or denying them would also be contrary to any ethico-political motive. For me, everything is 'drawn' from experience (live, daily, naive or well thought out, always thrown against the impossible), *from* this 'preference' which *I must both affirm and sacrifice*. For me, there is always, and I believe that there *must be more than one language*, mine and that of the other (I am greatly simplifying) and I must try to write in such a way that my language does not make the language of the other suffer [*souffrir*]. That he/she puts up with me [*me souffre*] without suffering [*sans souffrir*] [because of it], receives the hospitality of my language without losing or integrating himself/herself in it. (1995, p. 290, italics in original)

As a teenager, my preferences as an Anglophone were solidified in masculinist peer bonding in hockey and curling rinks and would provoke racist attacks on French-Canadians as my friends and I challenged them annually to fights at the winter carnival in Québec City. Yet earlier years in Winnipeg had brought me Métis friends whom I would defend against attacks by Anglophones. Perhaps this 'split-I' could best be accounted for in Lacanian terms, but in brute political terms, I was being formed out of the discursive economies of white supremacist patriarchal capitalism. I lived the confusing, contradictory and hate-filled world of white racism that was under assault from views of liberation that were reaching me only occasionally and eventually turned my world into turmoil as I began to read Malcolm X, Frantz Fanon and Paulo Freire.

Growing up as a working-class youth, and then 'making' it to a middle-class neighborhood when my father got a job as a manager of an electronic firm, gave me a sense of two languages of interpreting and living in the world. In a sense, this early code-switching among life experiences perhaps helped to shape my preference in academic heroes that privileged the transdisciplinary scholar. I had always admired the life and work of William Morris — author, poet, artist and craftsman, printer and calligrapher, formidable socialist and activist, businessman and private individual, and certainly the example of his life contributed to my interest in transdisciplinary scholarship. At the time that I enrolled in doctoral studies at the University of Toronto's Institut d'Etudes Pédagogiques de L'Ontario, Victor Turner, the world-renowned symbolic anthropologist, was conducting path-breaking transdisciplinary work at the University of Virginia, bringing dramaturgical theory and anthropology into close collaboration, particularly as this applied to the study of ritual. I soon became a scholar of Turner's work. I found a rich (albeit elitist) transdisciplinary milieu in which to conduct my studies at Massey College, University of Toronto. I was fortunate to be one of the few education students elected through competition as a 'Junior Fellow' of Massey College, University of Toronto. Massey College is the only private college in the University of Toronto, and is composed of graduate students selected by merit from English literature, medieval studies, sociology, economics, anthropology, philosophy, history, medicine, law education, and other disciplines throughout the university. It was here that I first encountered in a powerful manifestation the high culture of the bourgeois academy.

Modeled after Balliol College, Oxford University, England, Massey College facilitates interdisciplinary collaboration among high-achieving graduate students from various departments on campus. Weekly lunches (which required gowns, Latin prayers, and attending 'high table' dinners with the Master, Robertson Davies, and senior fellows such as Northrop Frye) brought together professors and graduate students in a spirit of pretentious bourgeois civility that smelled of stale cigars and bad sherry. Looking back at my educational experiences at Massey, it is not surprising that the work of performance theorists, political economists, anthropologists, dramaturgical theorists, literary critics, and symbolic interactionists largely informed the theoretical basis of my early works.

Although I was interested in Marshall McLuhan's theories, and gave serious consideration to working with McLuhan as a graduate student, I eventually decided to throw myself into the anthropological literature. Whilst working on my dissertation, I requested the opportunity to audit a doctoral seminar in the Department of Anthropology, University of Toronto. In addition, I had the good fortune to observe some lectures at the Toronto Semiotic Society's summer institute which helped to deepen my framework for engaging the anthropological literature. It was during lectures by professors Michel Foucault and Umberto Eco nearly two decades ago that my scholarly interests began to shift from Saussurean semiotics, the linguistic anthropology of Lévi-Strauss, and the cultural anthropology of Victor Turner, to the discursive production of power and privilege, to Baudrillard's architectonic reconstruction of sign systems as hyperreality, and to neo-Marxist studies that explored the relationship among race, class, gender, and sexuality. These interests were further heightened through engagements with traditional Marxist theory, the neo-Marxism of the Frankfurt School, the Birmingham School, social semiotics, discourse theory, feminist theory, and critical post-structuralism. My experiences at the institute helped to account for the 'critical linguistic turn' in my ethnographic investigations that brought a distinctly 'post-structuralist' perspective to my work.

From 1983 until 1986 the major focus of my scholarship was ethnographic research in urban educational settings which I pursued while teaching at Brock University (Canada) and my first year at Miami University of Ohio. My work at Miami University from 1986 until 1993 frequently shifted in focus, eventually spanning diverse intellectual and theoretical traditions. To a large extent it was exercised from a grounding in critical social theory, in particular materialist feminism and the work of the Frankfurt School. The work of Henry Giroux was foundational to my development as a social theorist at that time. Writing in the educational fields of critical pedagogy, curriculum studies, the social context of literacy, ethnographic research and multiculturalism, my work engaged theoretical debates involving the politics of the canon, race relations, postcolonial politics and pedagogy, national educational reform proposals, gender, sexuality and the curriculum, media literacy, critical ethnography and action research, and teacher education reform. Some of my writings were quite conceptually oriented at that time, dealing with issues such as the relation between language and subjectivity and the role of ideology in language. Since 1993, I have shifted focus to issues in multiculturalism and multicultural pedagogy in urban school settings. I am presently trying to understand what makes social agents consent to their own domination and the exploitation of others through hegemonic cultural, social, and institutional relationships. (I am using the term hegemony to refer to the production of agency through dominant forms of ideological persuasion rather than physical coercion.) In order to accomplish this, my interpretive work continually is imbricated in a theory of meaning, identity-formation, and agency which is based on the concept of intersubjective understanding. Intersubjective understanding is mediated through language and through extra-linguistic modes of knowledge grounded in a theory of the body. Intersubjectivity must always be understood in relation to social structure. Sometimes my writings emphasize macrostructures such as the globalization of the economy and in other instances they highlight the microphysics of meaning such as those that can be expressed extra-discursively such as individual gestures. Yet always the focus in two-pronged. In what follows, I will attempt to elucidate in very broad strokes the specific claims and problematics, successes and failures, of my research.

Although labeled (by myself as well as others) in some of the recent literature as a critical post-modernist, I prefer to consider myself a Marxist social theorist — at least in my own eyes (this is not to deny my flirtations with 'post-Marxism' in some of my work in the late 1980s). In response to critics of my work who remark that Marxism represents a form of empty idealism that speaks to an imagined but unattainable future, I maintain, to quote Terry Eagleton, that 'Marxism is not a theory of the future, but a theory and practice of how to make a future possible' (1990, p. 215). Marxism is in my view the single most important form of political analysis and transformation available. I began to write as a Marxist in 1985 and concentrated in the area of critical theory, having engaged orthodox Marxist studies that in my opinion failed to adequately engage issues of culture and representation. I directed my interest to the work of the Frankfurt School, and was especially intrigued by the work of Walter Benjamin. I felt at the time that the empirical work that I was doing in ethnography limited my ability to be sufficiently versatile in theoretically challenging those larger structural relations of exploitation that have millenially impeded or brought to a halt struggles for democracy throughout the globe. I felt then as I do now — even more so — that progressive scholars in the academy need to take a stronger stand against educational policies that simply serve corporate needs and that are masterminded by Republican legislation which reduces taxes through cuts in education. Over the years, my interests have grown more 'macro' as I have sought a more critical understanding of the changes in and consequences for education within the context of global capitalism — a capitalism in which students are being regularly trained for the degraded practices of corporations while the profits of such corporations continue to be directed away from the public and the earnings of wage laborers on a global basis continue to diminish.

Approaching educational reform from a Marxian perspective, brought me up against a daunting inheritance. This was especially true when my interests turned to the Frankfurt School. Frankfurt School Critical Theory developed from Marxist social theory and was, in effect, a critical response to Marxist thought. The work of Frankfurt School social theorists (Horkheimer, Adorno, Marcuse, Habermas, etc.) has made major contributions to the understanding of cultural (superstructural) phenomena (social practices, systems of intelligibility, cultural formations, economic arrangements, institutional structures) in its emphasis on the production of consciousness and the role of human agency in affecting radical social change. The Frankfurt School of Critical Marxism has focused on the ways in which dominant social groups in capitalist societies negotiate and maintain political hegemony by appropriating, co-opting, exploiting, and diffusing the transformative potential of the culture of the subordinate classes. Whilst I found the disdain for the popular among theorists such as Adorno to be distasteful as well as theoretically confounded, I found that a great wealth of understanding could be had through a protracted engagement with critical theory. Critical theory has the practical intent of fostering a critique of the existing social order — the repressive, alienating, and dominating social reality — in order to further the struggle for, and realization of, human freedom and happiness. Critical theory utilizes a negative dialectics. Negativity is used here in the sense of exercising critical judgment within the tension between the demands of reason and the positivity of a distorted social reality or existing fact. Social reality contains its own opposition; all existing facts are contradictory in themselves. Negation helps reason and freedom to be realized. A negative dialectics, simply speaking, means revealing how the given facts of commonsense reality which appear as the positive index of truth, are in reality the negation of truth, so that truth is established only in the destruction of facts. This negativity is not mere denial (abstract negativity) but rather determinate negativity.

In my work in critical educational theory I attempt to explore the dialectical tension between theory and practice. Such a dialectic operates in two registers: The minor key dialectic operationalizes hermeneutic and socio-analytic mediations while the major key dialectic operationalizes theory and practice at the level of history. In other words, my work attempts to understand the production of student agency and identity within schools, institutions, and within popular cultural formations by utilizing critical theories that enable me to problematize the lived experiences of students in school settings (critical hermeneutics, existential phenomenology, and negative dialectics) while at the same time respecting the macro structures of social and economic life by situating my micro analysis within the framework of a Marxist political economy. As our categories for understanding the world change, as we engage in a re-politicization of the political, so will our understanding of what it means to change the world and make it a more just, humane, and democratic place.

Occasionally I do make Spinozistic and Reichian excursions into monistic accounts of subjectivity that challenge dialectical approaches to the mind/body split. In this regard the book, *Anti-Oedipus*, made a special impact on me. According to its authors, Deleuze and Guattari, the Oedipus complex has become a colonial social mechanism in our society which represses the flow of desire. Desire is not a psychic process but a psychic recodification of repressive, capitalist, and colonial social structure. Furthermore, psychoanalysis operates as an instrument of social control and a policing agent for capitalism (Young, 1995). In this view, the social field is historically determined through the flow of desire. Capitalism, linked to ambivalent desire, is the determining motor of colonialism and operates as a territorial writing machine.

Historically, my research follows a shift away from the early Frankfurt School emphasis on critical emancipatory consciousness, self-conscious reason, and the centrality of non-identity thinking towards a non-essentialist view of revolutionary consciousness grounded in a theory of intersubjective understanding through language. Following Habermas, I have modified the dialectic of domination and the dialectical primacy of the object with a conception of subjectivity as constituted within linguistically mediated intersubjective relations. Yet I am aware that Habermas largely ends up with a subjectivist standpoint, despite his efforts at intersubjectivity. At the level of practice, my work attempts to create an oppositional cultural politics and transformative praxis that enables teachers and students to analyze how the dominant and negotiated meanings that inform classroom texts are produced and to uncover the ideological and political meanings that circulate within them. Of course, a politics of subversion must be accompanied by concerted efforts to establish a revolutionary praxis. And this can only be brought about through a direct challenge to the globalization of capital.

Whilst the Frankfurt School theorists developed analyses of twentieth century culture, they generally were concerned with understanding the production and consumption of aesthetic culture — art, music, poetry, literature — and the way in which such culture could produce transformative moments even in the light of increasing economic rationalization and bureaucratization of social life. Since the Frankfurt School theorists in their culture-industry thesis failed to take seriously the politics of popular culture — preferring instead to problematize 'high culture' — I was drawn to the work of British cultural studies, (mainly the Birmingham Center for Contemporary Cultural Studies) which centered around Gramscian post-scientific Marxism and its attempt to 'culturize' Marxian theory. I considered the work of Gramsci to be an important correct-ive to economistic versions of Marxism, without realizing just how far cultural Marxism would eventually remove itself from issues of the economy altogether. Drawing on a dialectic of unity and diversity developed by Marx, and employing the concept of dialectical unity in a historical-political sense, Gramsci was able to articulate social and historical contradictions with a framework that brought theory and practice together in a non-tautological unity — in a philosophy of praxis. Hegemony, in Gramsci's view, is always a contradictory unity, the product of both force and consent. The work of David Harris (1992) has chronicled some of the dilemmas that an embrace of Gramscianism had created for contesting global economic restructuring and for building a viable leftist political movement.

Recognizing the importance of the Frankfurt School's culture-industry thesis, I came to realize, along with other social theorists, that while they were anti-Stalinist, the polit-ical articulations of the Frankfurt School theorists were filtered by the gilded haze of mandarinism, failing in many instances to phenomenologize or ground their analyses in the lived experiences of oppressed groups (Agger, 1992) — an oversight which prevented sufficient groundwork for a liberatory politics of education or critical pedagogy.

During this time I had also failed to recognize sufficiently the extent to which British cultural studies had downplayed Gramsci's call to dismantle capitalism (Sears and Mooers, 1995). I also greatly over-emphasized the role of ideology in the practice of hegemonic domination and in doing so failed to adequately consider the fact that, following Scott (1990), subordinate classes are less constrained by the dominant culture at the level of thought and ideology and more constrained at the level of political action and struggle. In other words, the oppressed are not too zombified to critically strategize techniques and practices of resistance. Whilst most acts of power from below appear to observe the rules, and reinforce hegemonic appearances at the level of what Scott calls 'the public transcript', considerable resistance takes place within 'the hidden transcript' of the powerless.

Cultural theorists such as Stuart Hall — whose work has been profoundly instru-mental in my formation as cultural critic — tends to view transformation largely as a practice of ideological contestation and a counter-hegemonic movementism. Of course, Hall's attempt to describe how popular culture is replete with hidden advocacies and arguments that are ideologically coded has inspired important new analyses of pop-ular culture as forms of representation and practices of interpretation that counsel our conformity, authorize and narrativize the quotidian events in which we habitually and thoughtlessness engage, and provoke our embrace of consumerist imageries and ideo-logies. In my view, however, Hall's emphasis on indeterminacy and the conjunctural and agonistic field of ideological forces does not sufficiently challenge the objective conditions of global capitalism (Sears and Mooers, 1995). Certainly, I had never believed there to be an objective correspondence between class position and ideology, but British cultural Marxism and the work of other theorists such as Laclau and Mouffe — while often brilliant — went too far, I thought, in de-emphasizing the determining role of the economy in the production of hegemonic relations of domination and exploitation and failed to address a revolutionary praxis that included workers as wage laborers. In retro-spect, I believe that many of us attracted to cultural studies' clarion call to form new social movements and strategic alliances were initially attracted to the idea of freeing up cultural spaces that were not already overdetermined by economic relationships. In other words, at some level we were as convinced of the omnipotence of semiological structures and the sovereign imperatives of the code as we were fearful that too strong an emphasis on political economy could indeed provoke many of us to duplicate the very bourgeois world we intended to supplant. Of course, this meant succumbing in our research to a politics of singularity, micro-contexts, and parochial revisionism and failing to take seriously enough the concept of social totality which would have enabled us to challenge with more exigency those processes that sustain relations of exploitation across contexts (Hay, 1995).

What is motivating my recent work is my continual frustration with textual resistance, even as I am attracted to and contribute regularly to much of this work. Admittedly, bourgeois leftist practice is seductive, and some of it is undeniably important. But much of it unwittingly supports current regimes of wage labor and capital. Part of my concern with over-emphasizing textual analysis is perhaps due to the fact that, as I watch my own children and graduate students struggling to survive, I am continually reminded that things are getting worse, not better, and that capitalism has mutated, as it always has, in invidious ways that mandate more than just epiphenomenal forms of counter-hegemonic struggle.

Los Angeles is a city of fierce intensities. As I walk the neighborhoods in Los Angeles, as I travel through West Hollywood, Beverly Hills, Watts, Compton, and East Los Angeles, and notice how people have been variously inserted into complex and intermingling networks of power and sociality, and the resulting disparity between rich and poor, my rage grows and my loathing for the capitalist order becomes frighteningly unabated. How could any educator whose work is informed by a praxis of resistance and transformation not be aroused to action after the recent clubbing of undocumented Mexicans by Riverside County sheriff's deputies? Or after the protest of former Chief of Police Darryl Gates, who defended the use of police batons since the police could no longer apply choke-holds? How could any educator, after the savage beating of Rodney King, escape the visceral reality of police horror that confronts us in our cities and towns? We are living the nightmare of Kienholz's *Five Car Stud* (Hopps, 1996) where white men in rubber Halloween masks are castrating a black man. We are living in the apocalyptic choke-hold of Western civilization. Darryl Gates sits at home grinning. The race war he secretly desires will come. He and his salivating minions will be able to beat as many African-American and Latino/a men, women, and children as they want and the white public will cheer them on. While I believe that theories are weapons, and words the swords of revolutionary praxis, I also feel that much of what passes for political resistance on the part of post-structuralists is a case of mistaken identity. Mistaken for revolutionary praxis are attempts at destabilizing, softening, or subverting the certainty of sign systems, epistemological perspectives, or the 'always already' of the trope which are erroneously assumed by many of the high priests of deconstruction to exist prior to the history of capitalist production. For instance, I believe that Latino/a populations, African-Americans, and working-class Asians and Whites are struggling against more than the way that they are positioned in the field of hierarchical social relations in terms of a dominant cultural politics. That is, I believe that they are fighting more than the nominalism of linguistic imperialism. Rather, they are advocating the very right to signify, to name, to narrate, not only as the indentured, the displaced, the subordinated, the immiserated, or the nameless but in the context of acquiring a new identity through a critique and an overthrow of colonial and capitalist social relations. In my deepest moments of depression and despair, I fear that my long-term commitment as an educator to the most revolutionary expressions of transformative praxis has been compromised in my commitment to interrupting the type of agency necessary for the current transitions and flows taking place within global capitalism. For me, this project highlights the fact that stressing the signifier over the signified or executing a critique of binary oppositions as contributing factors of white supremacist patriarchal capitalism won't necessarily destabilize in any fundamental way the asymmetrical relations of power in ways that one might have once felt possible during those epiphanic moments when post-structuralism was briefly heralded as the revolutionary theory par excellence for the future and perhaps the new *grande époque* of revolutionary politics. I am not saying that my work or that of other post-structuralist educators has been a waste of time. Cultural critique will always be important. Yet whilst I am still drawn engagingly to analyses of superstructural arrangements — popular culture (most recently hip hop) — in particular — I am taking greater pains to situate my analysis of racism and multiculturalism within the context of larger structural mediations, and not just the 'upper circuits' of capitalist superstructural relations (i.e., the realm of cultural politics).

As I mentioned earlier, I trace some of my interest in superstructural arrangements to an early interest in the hallucinatory politics of madness and my fascination with the counterculture. Of course, the boundless paradox of Nietzschean intelligibility and my interest in the undecidability and extra-linguistic aspects of meaning provoked my interests in painting, sculpture and performance as a means of understanding the unbearable anguish of being within capitalist social formations. These interests still burn in my secret thoughts at the back of my mind (referred to by Baudrillard as *arrière-pensées*). One such influence is the work of the anarchist-artistic movement from 1957– 72 known as the Situationist Movement. This group was influenced by the work of post-symbolist poets, Dadaists, and Surrealists and developed strategies of refusal that are premised upon a rejection of the assumptions behind the universal structure of capitalism. The Situationists rejected the alienation that today not only is located in capitalist production but has shifted into the capitalist technocentrism dazzlingly present in all aspects of everyday life. Responding to the ways in which capitalism has turned contemporary life into a spectacle and individuals into passive and powerless spectators in a world constructed through an endless succession of images, the Situationists and the Zurich Dadaists encouraged the recreation of everyday life through *détournement*. *Détournement* consists of exposing objects of everyday life as products of alienation. For instance, my work has variously attempted to reveal everyday school life as a form of perversion (*Critical Pedagogy and Predatory Culture*, 1995a); as a culture of pain (*Schooling as a Ritual Performance*, 1993); and as an agency of normalization (*Life in Schools*, 1994). The work of Leon Golub and especially the tableau assemblages of Edward and Nancy Reddin Kienholz have taught me more about the physiognomy of alienation and the poetry of destruction than any bourgeois theorist.

My interest in cultural politics is also reflected in the Foucaultian materialism of much current critical social theory as well as the New Historicism that emerged in 1980s literary scholarship, and the New Pragmatism and anti-foundationalist philosophy. Here the scholarship — even though it was often not sufficiently cited — of Raymond Williams and Cornel West figured prominently in influencing my work. The work of philosopher Gilles Deleuze has played an important role in my thinking, especially his appropriation and rethinking of Spinoza. The critical post-structuralist influence in my work extends and deepens the critical theory framework that guided my earlier scholarship, even as I attempt to refigure it within a more Marxian problematic.

Post-structuralist approaches to the concept of truth have been as prominent in my work than Marxist concepts of, say, false consciousness and yet I would still argue that the concept of false consciousness has the strongest valency for a revolutionary praxis. In other words, whilst a version of the truth may in fact turn out to be a textual fiction

Peter McLaren

(Baudrillard believes not in truth but obviousness or evidence), people do live out their lives in material contradiction to the multifarious ways in which they understand their lives. In other words, they live their lives in a false relationship to their material existence. Viewing truth more in terms of its sociohistorical and pragmatic articulations than in terms of its ontological status, and influenced by Foucault's notion that knowledge is what is socially recognized as knowledge (truth is what a particular culture counts as true or what functions as true), my work attempts to understand everyday life as an ideologically inscribed enactment in which there is only one single truth: the truth which tells us that there is no truth, only the mediations of various representational and economic structures. But post-structuralists need to be called to task by Marxists who uncoil the following question: Is exploitation therefore mainly a textual mediation? In my view — no. Exploitation is very real. It is related to the exploitation of the labor power of the many by the few. Consequently, I wish to maintain that despite its limitations, mine is not the apolitical and ahistorical post-structuralism of ludic postmodernism. It is decidedly Marxist, rejecting the neoliberal and reactionary incarnations that sometimes accompany post-structuralist accounts. Regrettably, yet in many ways understandably, liberalism and consumerism have enthroned themselves as the twin ideologies of many postmodern and post-structural forms of theorizing. I believe that some of what this liberalism (in the best, left-liberal sense) is all about — that of claiming a preferential option for disenfranchised, peripheralised, marginalized, and exploited social groups — is important but could be deepened and in important ways refigured and revalued by a Marxian perspective. Consequently, I believe that insights from both left-liberalism and Marxism (with a greater emphasis on Marxism) are important in forging a praxiological dimension to critical pedagogy, a dimension that assumes counterhegemonic and liberatory positions. The key point here is that much liberal social theory occults the materialist contradictions of wage labor capitalism and it licenses its claims by concentrating its analysis on the consumption of images and the outdatedness of wage labor (Ebert, 1995). Walking through Watts, Compton, south central or east Los Angeles can give you a sense of the exploitative nature of wage in a way no book or theory can and so can a visit to the favelas of Rio De Janeiro and São Paulo or the barrios of Mexico City, Guadalajara, Juarez, or Mexicali.

My recent move from Cincinnatti to Los Angeles has been accompanied by an interest in the Chicano movement and the ongoing struggles of the Chicano community, especially in east Los Angeles. In addition to uncovering the existence of sweatshops where Asian workers were held in virtual bondage, recent investigative reporting by *The Los Angeles Times*, has revealed the conditions for Latino/a immigrant workers to be equality as horrific in the global factories of LA. One woman was reported to be doused from head to toe with boiling oil when a laminating machine exploded, one man was drowned in a glue vat, another was struck in the head by a 50-pound chunk of flying metal while tooling a chrome wheel; other Latino/as have been electrocuted, crushed by hydraulic presses or pulled into the gears of giant machines (Valle and Torres, 1994). Latino/as count for more than half of Los Angeles County's manufacturing workforce although they comprise only approximately a third of its population. We are witnessing the Latinization of the country's largest manufacturing center, and the emergence of a majority working class in the greater Los Angeles area. The status of many of these workers as undocumented places them at special risk to exploitation, as they are blamed for lowering wages and spoiling the bargaining power and social benefits of unionized workers. Under initiatives such as privatization, the social wealth of local communities has been co-opted by capital as capital has been able to appropriate more and more of local government's economic planning and regulatory (resource allocation) functions. Community participation needs to increase in terms of micro-industrial and micro-economic policies for the Latino/a community in east Los Angeles. But such a community is often regarded as just a marginalized pool of surplus labor for local industries and people lose the opportunity to recreate their own neighborhoods.

As Valle and Torres have pointed out, the de-industrialization of central Los Angeles has been accompanied by a re-industrialization of the greater East side. Single-use industrial cities like Vernon resemble the *maquiladoras* that line Mexico's northern border. On the other hand, you have Santa Fe Springs, a middle-class Latino enclave sustained by post-Fordist manufacturing (Valle and Torres, 1994). Single use cities such as the City of Industry, the City of Commerce, Irwindale, and Azusa, are examples of economic government that uses a municipality's authority to expropriate private property, draw municipal boundaries and subcontract private firms to provide public services. Single use cities do not enjoy citizen rule. City boundaries are created to exclude voters and to include vital assets such as rail lines, freeway access or mineral rights. Here, private monopolies run public services. Economic government transfers public capital into private hands development, often causing high municipal debts, chronically under-funded schools and social services in the greater eastside. The city has become, as Torres and Goldberg (1996) note, balkanized, fragmented, and cartelized. The workforce is racialized, ghettoes have become more isolated, and the political economy of prisons is fast replacing the political economy of military bases. Torres and Goldberg see Proposition 187 as proposing 'waged slavery' in its refusal to educate immigrants and its plan to cheapen the labor supply by privatizing its associated costs.

I live in a city of invisible workers, a city of privatized apartheid — what Torres and Goldberg refer to as an unspoken reserve army of labor made up of people of color who are keeping unskilled wages and the minimum wage in check. You can see the containment and territorialization of Los Angeles in its highways which have been likened to those of Johannesburg. Los Angeles has a greater commitment to prisons than to schools — the Governor wants to privatize schools but use public funds for prisons. California's commitment to de-education is profound. California is spending a larger percentage of its state budget on prisons than on higher education (Torres and Goldberg, 1996). Statistics show that individuals with less than an eighth grade education commit significantly fewer crimes than those with an education ranging from eighth grade to one year of college (Torres and Goldberg, 1996). So it seems obvious that California is investing in two major social practices: keeping its poverty-stricken workforce uneducated and, if possible, locked up behind bars. There is a profound sickness in the air, the scent of death and the perfume of despair. Racism is the lifeblood of this city. Racism — that structured ensemble of social and institutional practices and discourses, that pernicious system of genealogical self-rejection (Shohat and Stam, 1994) — informs the collective subjectivity of the city. It has become the tain of our mirrored selves. We must construct another axiomatic for the researcher, one that speaks not only to the particularities of abjection, but to political agency as transformative praxis. Nothing less will suffice. Or we shall be swallowed by our creations. Any progressive educational project that takes place in Los Angeles must have at its center of concern the plight of the excluded, the immiserated, the scorned, the wretched of the earth. But concern is not enough. We must have the appropriate tools of social analysis and the will to act upon our analysis.

If we are not prepared to spend time in struggle with our Chicano brothers and sisters and our African-American brothers and sisters then ours is a pedagogy of hollow hope. To claim that educational research needs to identify itself with a preferential option for the poor is not just an idealistic desideratum written in nostalgia by Che or Amilcar Cabral, or an inviolate proclamation of Frantz Fanon or Malcolm X. Nor does it simply reflect the incipient romanticism of the metaphysical poets. Rather, such an option constitutes a prerequisite for liberatory research, that is, research with a practical intent of helping others acquire knowledge and skills to build a more humane and just socialist order.

The goal of critical research is best understood as a means of rethinking teaching, learning, and schooling from the perspective of new languages of social theory. Whilst criticalists borrow a great many theoretical frameworks, conceptual apparatuses, and criteriologies from the fields of sociology, anthropology, philosophy, and literary criticism, for instance, they often give something of importance back to these fields. Much of the value of critical educational research results in applying new frameworks of analysis to educational settings (as in empirical work) or policy issues, or debates surrounding the content and teaching of the curriculum. So in evaluating the work of critical educators it is not always possible to grasp their contributions to education as a series of discrete observations or analyses translated into programmatic suggestions. Any evaluative criteria of their scholarship needs to consider how they have deepened or expanded the range and scope of the very theoretical frameworks they are employing.

My own work has tended to view theory not just as a way of picking through the rag-and-bone shop of rationality, but as an act of critical remembrance. Believing that men and women are not prisoners of inexorable laws of history and that the future is not immanently secured by present historical circumstances, I believe education can lead to 'liberating remembrance' in which the future is clarified through the development of possible horizons of action. This has meant, for me, an understanding of the narratives of struggle of the indigenous peoples of the Southwest, in particular native peoples, and Chicano/as. How can a struggle against capitalism help to unite these groups, along with African-Americans and Whites — in common projects of liberation?

To a certain extent my rejection of radical relativism and my desire to retain the best aspects of the modernist project may be traced to some of Habermas's positions. However, what I find highly problematic about Habermas's work is its incipient universalism and Eurocentrism. His universal model for human rationality which is constructed as a telos for the development of the human species, is essentially a critical theory of advanced capitalism (Santos, 1995). In his work, the West is 'us' and the non-West is constituted as 'other'. When asked if his theories could be of use to democratic socialist forces in advanced countries and/or socialist forces in the Third World, he replied: 'I am tempted to say "no" in both cases. I am aware of the fact that this is a Eurocentric limited view. I would rather pass on the question' (quoted in Santos, 1995, p. 507). I agree with Santos when he remarks:

Habermas's communicative rationality, in spite of its pretense to universality, starts out by excluding about four-fifths of the world population from participation in discourse . . . Habermas's universalism turns out to be an imperial universalism, in full control about the decision about its own limitations, thereby imposing itself in an unlimited way both upon what it includes and what it excludes. (1995, pp. 507–8)

Specific spacio-temporal predicates in Habermas's work severely restricts his discourses of communication. In addition, a certain economy of linguistic practices and power relations as well as an economy of discursive authority limits the scope and force of his arguments. In this context, Latin America becomes, for Habermas, a structured silence, a motivated amnesia that directs attention away from the domination, pacification and homogenization of Latin American countries within past and present geopolitical history.

Whilst I am also trying to rethink democracy from a post-structuralist discussion of universalism versus local knowledge, I am also very wary of the limitations of post-structuralist theory. And whilst my project as a researcher has been specifically motivated by recent attacks on affirmative action and the steady and shameful eroding of race relations in the United States, it has also attempted to challenge ethnicity defined from a separatist and essentialist standpoint.

It should be rather clear by now that I place a different emphasis on structure and agency, policy analysis and praxis, base and superstructure, depending upon which problematic is framing my work. I choose my research projects generally in two ways: in terms of the opportunities that such projects afford me to further an emancipatory theory of agency and identity and in terms of the way my work is able to intersect critically with pressing social issues. What motivates such counter-hegemonic work includes, among other factors, the persistent attack on affirmative action in my own university but also throughout California and the country at large, the growing racism in our schools, the rampant poverty and disease throughout the United States, the growing numbers of the homeless and destitute, the increased segregation of our cities on the basis of race and class, and the attack on public education in general. One of my early decisions was to expand the definition of ethnicity to include an ethical standpoint epistemology centered around the issue of social and economic justice — yet a standpoint theory that I hope does not regress into a radical relativism or a rejection of common struggle. The standpoint epistemologies which I support are those which construe difference not within essentialist or separatist enclaves but which are dialectical and dialogical and which are understood in the context of relations of power and relations of domination and exploitation. We need to situate ourselves from our standpoints (i.e., white, male, black, female) but we need to recognize, too, that commonalities also help define difference. Differences are important but not all differences are significant ones and some are more significant than others.

I have also been drawn both to advances in and criticisms of identity politics largely through my attempt to understand and vigorously challenge my own privilege as a white Euro-Canadian scholar living and teaching in the United States with large populations of students of color. What part can white Anglo males such as myself play in the larger project of liberation? My work in critical literacy has, similarly, been provoked by recent debates, such as the contentious struggle over the university canon. The issue of identity formation is especially challenging for me, especially as an white, Anglo male. I have recently made a decision to speak critically about white culture, to reflect upon my own whiteness, and to make what I call 'ideological whiteness' less powerful in forming the multicultural literature, as well as in daily hegemonic culture. This is achieved, I am convinced, neither by impugning whiteness altogether, nor by uncritically affirming it, but, as George Yudice (1995) notes, by re-articulating whiteness as a form of counter-hegemonic struggle. Yudice notes that the present alternative for our white youth in a culture that does not question its identity structures is participation in white supremacist discourses and practices. I was recently invited to speak on a popular hip-hop radio station in Los Angeles (whose audience is primarily Chicano and African-American) about the concept of whiteness and I was heartened that so many responses from listeners of color affirmed such an attempt to bring the invisibility of whiteness out into the open. My emphasis was — and is — that Whites have a stake in the struggle for liberation and that this mandates that they both recognize their privilege and work against the debilitating social effects of such privilege. In my work I call for an abolition of whiteness, that is, an abolition not of white people but of the social, cultural and material conditions that support, maintain, and regulate white supremacist patriarchal capitalism. It also calls on Whites of good will to commit to democracy, to transcend the liberal myths about diversity, and to work steadfastly with people of color on a global basis in anti-racist, anti-sexist, and anti-homophobic struggles and against neoliberal ideologies and economic practices in order to reclaim dignity and power for the oppressed.

Ideally, I believe that educational scholarship should be part of a developing theory of praxis, a form of social criticism, and a standpoint for political activism and revolutionary struggle. This certainly brushes against the grain of most work carried out within schools of education which seems to be following the ideology of the panoptican, of social control, of the policing of desire, of regulatory practices, of the trend towards the privatization of schools and of placing private profit over the collective needs of the public. Following my commitment to revolutionary praxis, I have, over the years, centered upon certain philosophical questions that I believe should be explored in educational research and acted upon at the level of classrooms and communities of struggle. These include: What is the relationship among ethics, epistemology, and social structure? How can knowledge lead to greater liberation and freedom? Political questions that follow those above include: How can schools function as cultural sites that contribute to equality of educational outcomes for various social groups and to a deepening and expansion of democratic social life? How can educators and educational researchers create the conditions for critical thinking and knowledge production while at the same time serve as agents of social justice? Epistemological questions that follow these sets of questions include: What is the relationship between knowing and acting? How can theories of knowledge be linked to forms of affective engagement in practices of freedom? Pedagogical and policy questions that need to be raised include: How can teaching practices create democratic social relations in classrooms and invite students to link the production of knowledge to a larger practice of liberation outside of school sites? What policies and practices are necessary to create a curriculum that is anti-racist, anti-sexist, anti-homophobic and anti-capitalist? In raising these questions, I acknowledge that my efforts to answer them continue to be but modest attempts at fashioning a praxis of struggle.

Critical Ethnography

My interest in qualitative work grew out of my work as a teacher activist in Toronto's inner-city schools and my effort at developing theory of resistance that took seriously the concept of human agency outside of a theory of rationality. *Schooling as a Ritual Performance: Towards a Political Economy of Educational Symbols and Gestures* is a case study of Italian and Azorean students in a Catholic school located in an inner-city neighborhood in Toronto, Canada, and it utilizes comparative symbology, symbolic interactionism, and ritology (the study of ritual) to uncover elements of the structure of conformity in school settings as well as to explain resistance among students as liminal and antistructural relations.

Schooling as a Ritual Performance follows in the tradition of critical ethnography. When ethnographers attempt to adduce information from reading social texts, too often their interpretations and accounts of social life often appear as authorless. Consequently, critical ethnographers examine their own interpretive accounts by investigating how meaning is produced by a system of signs, by examining the specific meanings produced with particular sign systems, and by analyzing how such sign systems are 'read' differently by different people in different contexts. Critical ethnographers, therefore, begin within the premise that the ethnography's diegesis — the plane of rhetoric supporting the anthropologist's exposition of events — frequently occludes the signs of its own construction. Therefore, in their work, critical ethnographers attempt to read social and cultural texts symptomatically, that is, they attempt to identify where and how ideological masking takes place; and to tease out what a so-called 'natural' or 'authentic' event seeks to hide. From the critical ethnographer's perspective, there exists no natural or authentic events if by that one means that events speak for themselves or exist unsullied or untainted by ideology or interest.

A major idea linked to my concern over issues surrounding the construction of identity is that Marxist accounts of false consciousness and commodity fetishism cannot fully account for why alienated youth participate in popular culture. In this regard I have found Lawrence Grossberg's concept of 'affective investment' useful in drawing attention to the specific ways in which youth consent to forms of popular culture. I refer here to a politics of affect which produces systems of difference which are *asignifying*: for example, economies of mood, structures of feeling or structures of ideological containment (something Raymond Williamson had identified in his works). In other words, I am trying to explore the relationship between the ideological and the affective. How does ideology work outside of rational communication and within the supplementary relations of the popular? In this respect I believe that it is important to develop a theory of pedagogy based on a politics of the body as well as further develop the concept of critical multiculturalism in relation to this. Commodity fetishism has become a public obsession in the psychological sense of the term as capitalism is lived subjectively and as flows of capital are internalized and enfleshed.

Schooling as a Ritual Performance is a systematic attempt to develop an interpretive framework for understanding school culture from the perspective of a critical poststructuralist theory of the symbol. It was one of my first attempts to link symbols used in school contexts to structures of mediation in the wider society, such as the symbolic resources of working-class life. Defining culture as an historically transmitted pattern of meaning embodied in symbols, and defining rituals as embodied and performed symbols and metaphors — forms of enacted meaning — which are constituted in sacred and secular domains, I undertook an ethnographic study of a Catholic school in a working-class urban area of Toronto, Canada. It was my contention that rituals transmitted societal and cultural ideologies and by examining the key symbols and root paradigms of the ritual system of the school, I tried to interpret how ritual performances in pedagogical sites are situated within macro-configurations of unequal power relations. I argued that instruction as a form of disciplinary rites complimented the values reproduced through religious rituals which together constituted a system of enacted meanings that defined 'normal' social relations. Certainly my personal feelings about the institutional role of the Church served as a motor for my critique. I had always felt that the Church played a shameful role in anti-Semitism and sexism and the reproduction of class privilege. I was determined to uncover the marriage between capitalism and faith.

Working from the premise that a body is not defined by its constitutive organization but by its states (an organic plenum, or body without organs, in Deleuze's sense), I was essentially able to identify two 'states' of enacted meaning: the streetcorner state and the student state. Within these states I located rituals which constructed cultures of conformity and rituals and their subsets that functioned to destabilize and resist the root paradigms of cultural consensus.

The myriad of enacted meanings that established and maintained the streetcorner state — in terms of time, space, mood, speech, and bodily rhythms — were mainly premised on the root metaphor of play whereas those of the student state were discovered to be premised on the root metaphor of work. I also analyzed the semiotic 'tension' between these states in the making and remaking of students' identities and the 'sanctification' of work. I analyzed the intertextual transmission of meanings between religious and secular symbols (e.g., the Christian cross and the Canadian flag) and was able to identify gestures of resistance as generally consistent with Victor Turner's concept of the social drama. I was able to identify the root paradigms of instruction as 'becoming a worker' and 'becoming a Catholic'. These paradigms were discovered to be constitutive of a wider ideology of capitalism that works to produce patterned failure among economically disenfranchised minority students, and to maintain a positivist — technocratic approach to educational practice that reinforces a logic of domination and subordination generally, and a logic of capital specifically. I sought to articulate a model of subjectivity that emphasized the more conflictual aspects of agency outside of a dualist framework — a model of subjectivity that attempts to explain the inflection of mind into body and body into mind, and to rethink the relations between the inside and outside of the subject (i.e., the transversal relations between mind and body, subject and object).

Drawing on theories of Michel Foucault, Gilles Deleuze, and Felix Guattari, I set out to undermine the mainstream educational (and modernist) pretension that consciousness can know itself. I explored how bodies are metaphorically inscribed through discursive encounters in classroom and playground sites. Further, I attempted to articulate a theory of the body as inscriptive surface, as a social form, and as a cultural product whose autological and socio-political status needs to be explored. I described as 'enfleshment' the production of ritual knowledge — a process in which the body becomes the ultimate symbol of knowing. In the Coda to the 1993 edition, I further develop the concept of 'enfleshment' in relation to the body/subject: 'By enfleshment I mean the mutually constitutive enfolding of social structure and desire; that is, it is the dialectical relationship between the material organization of inferiority and the cultural modes of materiality we inhabit subjectively.' (1993, p. 274)

Whilst enfleshment is similar to Judith Butler's concepts of performativity and citationality and Foucault's notion of aleatory power (in that it refers to the ways in which discourses produce effects by naming those normative rules in ways that always exceed what is named) I also want to make clear that my use of the term enfleshment differs quite significantly from these ideas. The materiality referred to in the process of enfleshment is not simply the disruptive return of the outside which excludes it; it is not, in other words, simply the materiality of the signifier. Rather, enfleshment is that which sutures the subject into the social division of labor. Materiality does not simply refer to the temporal dimension of the superstructure but is extra-discursive and refers to the materiality of labor. I reject the dismissal of labor that often follows a concern with social relations as mainly or only symbolic organizations or subject positions. Enfleshment is not reversible, it is not simply a form of resignifying the individual or a mode of citationality in the flesh. It is extra-discursive in the sense that it refers to those economic structures that support the production of binary oppositions. It always operates in a dialectical relationship to the mode of production and labor. This perspective fits with Marx's contention that capital acts as the capitalist's surrogate body, that use-value endows objects with corporeal existence, and that the human body extended to society converts the world to its own bodily organ (Eagleton, 1990).

Capitalism has split the human body, according to Marx, into materialism vs. idealism, whereas human freedom represents the full realization of the senses. In arguing that 'gestures and comportment are desire's hieroglyphs', I suggested that 'We can read desire and how it has been ideologically produced by paying attention to students' bodies and how they have been produced both to conform and to resist' (McLaren, 1993, p. 274). Part of the stress in my empirical work on the concept of enfleshment has been influenced by my concern with how individuals and groups are inscribed by myths and narratives, by social dramas, by rituals. In other words, by my concern with how the body is invested outside of signification, subjectification, and totalizable descriptions — in fact, outside of a politics of representation altogether. I have been concerned of late with the ways in which narratives work not just as forms of rationally and systems of intelligibility, but as instruments to structure our feelings, to organize our affective alliances, to shape the feeling body. Why do we live routinized lives of subordination? Why do we continue to be complicitous with dominant regimes of signification, with dominant social practices which alienate and dehumanize most of humanity so that we — the privileged few — can buy our houses in good neighborhoods? Why are revenge and bloodlust such powerful regulating forces in society? The precession of seduction that Baudrillard talks about — does it contradict the possibility of rebuilding the world? Is liberation just one illusion among many? An illusion used to fight perhaps a greater illusion? Why are social relations and signification secured in certain ways and not others? These questions haunt my work and no doubt will continue to influence my future research.

I firmly believe that critical ethnography should utilize an ethics fully grounded in the body primarily because rationality cannot explain why people make the commitments and emotional investments that they do. Current theories of rationality cannot explain fully why people persist in being racists even though they find racism ethically repugnant and rationally irresponsible. Rationality doesn't explain why we invest in behavior that is unreasonable and dehumanizing to others. It can't help us understand how our body thinks. Or how our body works for and/or against the values that we articulate and agitate as logical or spiritual or ethical. In *Schooling As a Ritual Performance* I maintained that rituals as embodied metaphors are able to empower particular articulations of agency in order to win various identities, subjects, knowledges and actors to specific commitments of the capitalist system. The book makes some modest and incomplete efforts to open up analogically the concept of pedagogy to a whole of possible other readings, ultimately to a pedagogy of the body which can be described as haptic, in other words, a pedagogy which seeks to overcome the divisions of materiality and mind. *Schooling As a Ritual Performance* has been to date my most concerted empirical attempt to explore the theme that has occupied me from the beginning of my research on schools: The reconciliation of desire and action, freedom and necessity, understanding and consent. Such a reconciliation is not accessible within a theory of language alone; rather, such a reconciliation (temporary at best) can only be grasped through an investigation of affective economies and the prepredicative structure of experience of the body/subject.

Whilst most pedagogical theories prioritize language in the sense of speech and writing, in *Schooling As a Ritual Performance* I attempted to relocate the primacy of meaning in the feeling body where each configuration of feeling, thought, posture and motion constitutes a symbol (in the sense that informs both Hegel's concept of *Geist* and

Marx's concept of praxis). I am referring to a politics of meaning that is intersubjective — a politics in which the self always embodies the social other.

Working with such an ethnically diverse student body at UCLA has helped me to further resituate my work as a form of cultural criticism and social semiotics, I am beginning to rethink ethnographic research by raising some fundamental questions which I had only begun to address in *Schooling As a Ritual Performance*: On whose authority and on whose behalf do we interpret and evaluate the meanings of others?

Critical Pedagogy and Curriculum Studies

My early writing in the area of critical pedagogy was a response to my six years as an elementary school in Toronto and an attempt to redress the theoretical and political errors that informed my best-selling book, *Cries From the Corridor* (1980), that chronicled those years and which was published in 1980. Realizing that my theory was largely informed by a very white, Anglo liberal view of educational reform that permitted a 'blaming the victim' ideology to tacitly undergird my interpretations of daily life as an inner-city teacher, I attempted to expand on my understanding of ideology and agency. This brought me to a more systematic reading of the work of Albert Memmi, Frantz Fanon, and Paulo Freire. I also looked to Europe in the area of the sociology of knowledge (primarily in London and Birmingham at that time) as this applied to educational issues such as pedagogical practice, curriculum reform and national educational policy initiatives.

In 'Teacher education and the politics of engagement: The case for democratic schooling' Henry Giroux and I (1986) collaboratively developed an alternative model of teacher education that centered around the idea of critical citizenship. In doing so, we argued for the development of a critical language with which to reconstruct the relationship between teacher education programs and the public schools, on the one hand, and public education and society, on the other. We also developed a view of teacher authority and teacher work that attempted to define the political project of schooling as the creation of an emancipatory political agency and ethically based communities. We advocated that teachers should transform their pedagogical role into that of a transformative intellectual — and we attempted to rearticulate the theoretical parameters of this term from the writings of Gramsci (on the organic intellectual) and Foucault (on the specific intellectual). We outlined what we called 'a curriculum for cultural politics' that placed at center stage and in opposition to a content-focused curriculum, the critical study of power, language, culture, and history.

Around the same time, and influenced by post-structuralism and reader reception theory, I took a position contrary to the exponents of cultural transmission in texts, arguing against E.D. Hirsch's notion that meanings can be shared and truth preserved because the objects of understanding have a unitary, fixed, or ideal essence. I argued against Hirsch who claimed that meanings are determinate, possess boundaries and self-identity, and can be directly transferred from the consciousness of one person to that of another. My position was that fidelity of representation is not tantamount to truth and Hirsch's simplistic epistemological frame needed to be challenged since Hirsch only makes sense if we believe the meaning of an utterance is controlled by the intention of a speaker. I argued that an intentionalist grammar of subjectivity needs to be replaced by a stress on the contexts in which utterances are made. Forms of intelligibility are always institutionalized and so are the social practices that accompany them. Consequently, I criticized Hirsch's notion that to share somebody's meaning, we must become subservient to the will or unified with the intentionality of the author of that meaning. In contrast, I argued against the concept of rational volition and the law of identity, and developed a case for the radical discontinuity and fragmentation of the ideal object, purging concepts of their metaphysical foundations, and challenging the idea of the ideal wholeness of meaning which undergirds the epistemology of Mr Hirsch. I do not deny that meanings may be intended and communicated by an author. My central contention is that meanings cannot be essentialized outside of the experiences that readers bring to those meanings, the cultural contexts in which those meanings are generated, and the historical, cultural and economic junctures in which text and reader meet.

In this sense, critical pedagogy, as I am formulating it, attempts to re-engage a social world that operates under the assumption of its collective autonomy and so remains resistant to human intervention. Critical pedagogy, in this sense, remains committed to the practical realization of self-determination and creativity on a collective social scale. When I think of critical pedagogy as a practice of liberation, I frequently think of the figure of Emiliano Zapata who was killed by government forces in the state of Morelos, 75 years ago. Blessed by Nahuatl shamans, Zapata was a spiritual warrior who struggled to protect the sacredness of the land and freedom from oppression. Like Zapata, critical educators need to wage nothing less than a proletarian war in the interests of the sacredness of human life, collective dignity for the wretched of the earth, and the right to live in peace and harmony. Following these imperatives, critical pedagogy can be seen a field of practice rather than a particular structure of inquiry. It is a sensibility, a mode of being, an attitude towards life, a praxis of liberation.

Following from my initiatives to rethink teacher education and to debate the Western canon from the perspectives of critical theory, and because I had been excessively if not obsessively criticized by teacher activists for 'abandoning the people' by writing in an obscurantist, arcane, and inaccessible style, I began to revisit Gramsci's and Freire's writings about praxis. I came to the conclusion that it was politically important to write a book about teaching for prospective teachers that was theoretically grounded but that also incorporated empirical data. The text, *Life in Schools* (1994), centered around empirical accounts of my teaching experiences in Toronto inner-city schools that were previously published in 1980 as *Cries from the Corridor*. The text itself became an opportunity for me to attempt to write a pedagogical text rather than simply a text about pedagogy. In this book I invited readers to be rather ruthlessly critical of my largely liberal humanist teaching experiences in Toronto's Jane-Finch Corridor as depicted in an opening series of diary vignettes. Students were then provided with introductory chapters on critical social theory and invited to re-read the vignettes and re-evaluate my development as a teacher. The philosophy of teaching that emerged from *Life in Schools* centered on the Freirean idea that teaching is a political act of knowing.

Lawrence Grossberg's (1994) articulation of affective pedagogy captures much of the essence of Freire's idea. Grossberg notes that critical pedagogy is about possibility and agency, that it trenchantly refuses to assume that theory and politics can be known in advance, that it should empower students to reconnect their world in new ways and to re-articulate their future in unimagined and unimaginable ways, and that it should assiduously enable students to gain some understanding of their contextually specific involvement in the world. Such a pedagogy deals with formations of the popular and cartographies of taste. It is a pedagogy that is a politicizing instrument in the last instance, since it leaves the field of articulations open. In other words, Grossberg's 'affective' educators try always to leave open their own space of learning as teachers, while constantly questioning the authority of their position as so-called experts as they attempt to invite students to see the global implications of their local learning practices and formation and the local implications of global policies and politics.

Over the years I have come to understand more completely (but no doubt still inadequately) that critical pedagogy needs to be linked to the development of a politics of everyday life in a number of ways. First, it must situate its critical analyses within the realms of local and global cultures, including popular culture and not only as frightening lamentations for the afflications wrought on humanity by post-industrial society, techno-capitalism, hyper-industrialism and the global assemblyline. For instance, it must pay closer theoretical attention to the ways in which everyday discourses and social practices both constitute and reinforce local and global relations of power as well as serve as sites for struggle, resistance, and transformation. It must understand how schools reproduce dominant ideological imperatives through their location within overdetermined material practices such as divisions of labor, state formations, and normative discourses. Thirdly, critical pedagogy must attempt to seize opportunities to make links between new social movements and the networks of power associated with 'school life'. Steps can be taken to achieve this, I believe, by linking the micropolitical (everyday lives of teachers and students) with the macropolitical (larger economic, cultural, social, and institutional structures).

The critical pedagogy that I have tried to develop over the last decade, whilst standing on the philosophical shoulders of others, seeks to analyze the possibilities for the resistance and transformation of social life, both individuated and collective, personal and macropolitical. It engages in such an analysis by making concerted efforts at understanding how wider relations of power are played out in the agential spaces of classroom and community life but also by attempting to investigate how wider structures of mediation at the level of the economy are able to 'take root' in the everyday lives of students and teachers who operate at the level of common sense actions. This means constantly reflecting on the cultural construction of the identities of teachers, students, researchers and also connecting such critical reflection to a wider terrain of political action. This also takes critical pedagogy beyond a discursive politics that sees political activity as merely a text to be deconstructed and interpreted. Instead, it refers to a cultural politics that operationalizes the textuality of political life by linking textuality to materiality. That is, by making connections between the texts that we read (cultural artifacts) and those that read us (the realm of language and discursive structures in general) and the political consequences that these connections bring about in our pedagogies, curricula, and policies.

A critical pedagogy as a form of cultural politics and praxis of transformation is an invitation to students to begin to reconstruct the world and (re)articulate their futures in hitherto unimagined ways, so as to help them to adopt new positions, new political and politicizing engagements, new mobilizations of memories, fantasies, dreams and desires. Critical pedagogy does not attempt to replace such dreams and desires, but to (re)articulate the affective investments students have *already made at the level of popular culture* into a collective vision of a shared political future based on questions that arise from the messy and conflictual terrain of everyday life. Critical pedagogy is premised on solidarity in which a collective 'we' is created out of a multiplicity of group identities. Collective solidarity creates the condition of possibility for our particular identities in terms of race, class and gender affiliations. Because, as consociates we need to take responsibility for each other, our needs, hopes, dreams, and desires can be best brought forward through dialogical forms of pedagogy. And hence I adovcate a revolutionary pedagogy of lived struggle that collides with the limits imposed by the cocktail party activism of school reform efforts and that refuses to submit to relations of exploitation that inform them. Revolutionary pedagogy is committed to a socialist agenda and struggles on behalf of these who continue to endure the most tragic consequences of capitalism.

Critical Multiculturalism

Up to 1993, I had not sufficiently addressed the important theme of multicultural education. After co-authoring an article with Michael Dantley in *The Journal of Negro Education* some years before, I realized that I had largely neglected the concept of multiculturalism as a topic in my own work although writings and research by multicultural educators such as Carl Grant, Christine Sleeter, James Banks, and bell hooks had certainly informed the shape of my work. From my point of view as a criticalist, I began to believe that multicultural education was missing the important work that scholars in critical social theory had advanced on the topic of the politics of difference. I decided, therefore, to focus my energies on bringing critical social theory — specifically resistance post-modernist critique rather than ludic post-modernist critique — to bear on the topic of multiculturalism as a means of bringing something to the debate.

A focus on the post-structuralist articulation of 'difference' rather than the liberal humanist understanding of 'diversity' helped me to develop a critique of neo-liberalism and the politics of diversity which generally 'houses' mainstream approaches to multiculturalism in my book, *Critical Pedagogy and Predatory Culture* (1995a). Yet at the same time I realized that multiculturalism must exceed culture critique in order to resist social relations of capitalist exploitation. Failure to resist capitalist exploitation condemns multiculturalism to consort with its own bourgeoise endorsement of neo-liberalism.

Critical Pedagogy and Predatory Culture is a book I put together when I moved to Los Angeles in 1993. Los Angeles is a city steeped in racism, a fortress of economic barriers behind which identities convulse in rage and terror. In *Critical Pedagogy and Predatory Culture* I argue that acceptance of identity does not refer to simply embracing an essentialist compendium of characteristics of identity, e.g., as Chicanos, Anglos, Asians, or African-Americans. Rather, acceptance of identity is related to failing to notice the very cloth that serves as the backdrop of the discourse of identity, which amounts to an the acceptance of the binary discourses that demarcate the boundaries of identity: e.g., self/other; black/white; masculine/feminine. In other words, identity is not so much identifying with either side of the binary opposition and privileging one side, but identifying with the very concept of binary opposition itself. But can we invent a language that is not informed by such binarisms? If we cannot dethrone the privileging hierarchies of binarisms as they ideologically structure our subjective engagement with the world, we can certainly learn ways to disidentify with such binarisms and attempt to avoid the worst political effects that privileging of any one side of such binarism entails.

I must confess that I am growing dissatisfied with post-structuralist accounts of identity which seem to conclude that all that it will take to build a multicultural society is our recognition of and reinvention as 'hybrid subjectivities'. In other words, all that we need to do is to see ourselves as '*mestiza*'. There is some merit to this idea, to be sure. For instance, we are inevitably 'hybrid' in our identity structures in that most Western subjects have been informed by cultural contact with other cultures and constitute a mixture in this sense. Secondly, hybridity, *créolité*, and *mestizaje* are important in terms of helping us to resist essentialism, to abandon the ventriloquistic illusions of speaking from where one is not and to direct subjects to identify their own local terrains of identity formation (Anzaldúa, 1989; McLaren, 1995a, 1997). The concept of hybrid identities helps us to prevent our standpoints of identity from being conscripted into the universal elsewhere. The concept of hybridity also helps us to understand how the mobile constellation of class, race, gender, and caste and nation come to be asymmetrically articulated in relation to each other. Hybrid identities 'form a changing repertory of cultural modalities' and a movement 'among the diverse performative modes of sharply contrasting cultural and ideological worlds' (Shohat and Stam, 1994, p. 42). But post-colonial hybridity is not unproblematic since it must locate hybridity within the various contexts of historical hegemonies and 'discriminate between the diverse modalities of hybridity: colonial imposition, obligatory assimilation, political cooptation, cultural mimicry, and so forth' (Shohat and Stam, 1994, p. 43). In other words, hybridity is co-optable, power-laden, asymmetrical and can have assimilationist inflections (Shohat and Stam, 1994) and it can also refer to a gradual whitening of identity (Nederveen, 1994).

For me, hybridization brings to mind what Boaventura de Sousa Santos (1995) refers as disorientation of the limits. Santos notes that hybridization 'consists in accosting one of the limits, and seducing the other to join in and be eager to be appropriated or even devoured' (p. 498). It 'orients itself by disorienting the limits, making them confront each other reciprocally while both are outside their particular terrain, and hence vulnerable and easily disfigurable' (p. 498). Santos extends his notion of hybridity through his concepts of frontier subjectivity and baroque subjectivity. Santos notes that by 'displacing the center, frontier subjectivity is in a better position to understand the oppression that the center reproduces and hides by means of hegemonic strategies' (p. 497). Without romanticizing the margin, he notes further that 'To live in the frontier is to live in the margins without living a marginal life' (p. 496), that is, 'experiencing limits without suffering them' (p. 497). Lately, I have been thinking more in terms of what Visweswaran (1994) calls forging the 'coalitional subject' and what William Connolly (1995) calls that 'politics of enactment'. The politics of enactment means developing an ethos of critical responsiveness. This means coming to terms with the relational and contingent aspects of one's identity and responding to the injuries (exclusions, etc.) that occur when universal justice is put into practice. Post-structuralists' theories and their celebration of new decentered modes of subjectivity do not fully account for the ways in which post-modern subjects are conditioned by the collectivized structures of late capitalism and their attendant historically determinate forms of liberalism and neo-liberalism, and how these post-modern subjects are complicit with global capitalist interests and institutions.

I believe that these new 'post-modern subjects' can only avoid restabilizing the interests of the private autonomous agent of capital if they are constructed as revolutionary agents of transformation within the context of a critique of global capitalist relations. We need to remember that identity is decentered, fractured and fragmented rather than multiple. The notion of multiple identities implies some type of mythologized, transcendentalized essence. I prefer to see identity as fluid rather than stable, as differentiated rather than passively complete as in some nativist essence of oceanic wholeness. Identity is surely related to our experiences which can be seen as valid but hardly described as being true (Bondi, 1993). Knowledge of identity never flows directly from experience because experience needs to be interpreted within existing systems of intelligibility. You only learn from experiences that you learn from, in other words: while experience never ensures the truth or authenticity of knowledge, it plays an important role in validating experiences outside of existing regimes of domination and exploitation, so that our location as subjects in anti-hegemonic struggle can be secured (McLaren, 1995a; Bondi, 1993). Let me briefly rehearse what I mean by subjectivity: Human subjectivity is cross-hatched by social relations forged in historical circumstances and linked material struggles. My work on subjectivity is highly influenced by the work of Voloshinov and considers language to be a form of practical consciousness, with consciousness taking 'official' and 'unofficial' formations. In this view, even inner thought is a social process and *all thought* is mediated by relations of class, gender and race (Dawes, 1995). Inner and outer signs organically constitute our inner speech as they are actively registered in our psyche. As a product of social relations, the psyche is also *ideological* in the sense that it is part of a system governed by sets of laws and partakes of a behavioral ideology.

In this sense, self-consciousness is always social and, therefore, so is gender, race, and class consciousness. The sign is consequently an arena of race, class, and gender struggle. Jorge Larrain (1995) has raised some important theoretical points regarding post-structuralist accounts of identity formation that I believe researchers interested in these issues should consider. The idea that post-modern theories are less racist than modernist ones is, for Larrain, troubling. Whilst it is true that many modernist theories which develop from universalistic premises do not accept the other as different, it is also true that post-modern theories often encourage the other to speak for him/herself but consider the other to be living in a totally different, alien world (Larrain, 1995).

Overall, I believe that research in multiculturalism and critical pedagogy must congeal more visibly around the central theme of developing a political economy of historical agency within the context of a polycentric multiculturalism. In this way criticalists can further develop a language that better speaks *to* people, not only *about* them. Tragically, some scholars are more concerned with their reputations as avant-grade theorists than fighting against capitalist exploitation view the reconstruction of theory along with universalist lines as a pernicious totalizing narritive the claims to offer the 'right story' when in fact all stories should remain undecidable: This valorization of 'indeterminacy' and 'excess' only cripples resistance to exploitation at a time when such exploitation has prodigiously intensified.

It is important to always remind our *compañeros y compañeras* who participate in the project (*la lucha*) of liberation from white patriarchal capitalist exploitation, our brothers and sisters in struggle, that they must never cease to resist new forms of consumption and desire which are put before the basic needs of the people. Our example could be that of the *soldadera* of Mexico, the poor working-class women of the Mexican Revolution, who fought alongside the men on the battlelines. Can we not be similarly inspired by the example of Ramona and Subcommandante Marcos of the Zapatistas? To know ourselves as revolutionary agents is more than the act of understanding who we are, it is the act of reinventing ourselves out of our overlapping cultural identifications and social practices so that we can relate them to the materiality of social life and the power relations that structure and sustain them. Do I live in what some might consider an out-dated Marxist imaginary and nostalgia for *el pueblo unido*, for a time before post-modern technoculture's assault on the simple binarisms of oppressor and oppressed, for an era devoid of the multilayered affiliations and dissonances within popular cultures shaped by the multinationalization of the global economy? Perhaps. Yet the challenge remains to continually fight against the bourgeoisification of leftist politics in this era of fashionable apostasy. Leftist educationalists must move radical criticism beyond efforts to unpack the textual un-saids of signifying systems; they must not become paralyzed by what appears to be a social field of unrelated and incommensurable differences. To embrace a postmodern politics bent upon unsettling the certainty of discursive regimes without directly challenging the regime of wage-labor itself is a politics forged in futility and a retreat into the silenced and self-protecting precincts of the bourgeois knowledge industry.

Only fists raised in solidarity with our brothers and sisters in struggle, and a commitment to make critical pedagogy a practical tool for the common good, can bring about the social and educational conditions necessary to rescue those we have lost and betrayed.

It is only after decades of challenging myself through abstractions that I have come to realize the concreteness necessary for the challenge ahead. This is not an attack on theory, but a call for theory to be conjugated with the kind of radical hope that is continually born through political struggle and revolutionary praxis.

Acknowledgment

I want to thank Ramin Farahmandpur for his editorial assistance.

References

ADORNO, T.W. (1967) *Prisms*, Cambridge, MA: The MIT Press.

AGGER, B. (1992) *Cultural Studies As Critical Theory*, London: Falmer Press.

ANZALDÚA, G. (1987) *Border Lands/La Frontera: The New Mestiza*, San Francisco: Spinsters / Aunt Lute.

BENOT, Y. (1970) *Diderot: de l'Athéisme à l'Anti-Colonialisme*, Paris: Maspero.

BOGGS, C. (1995, Dec. 22–8) 'The God reborn: Pondering the revival of Russian communism'. *Los Angeles View*, **10**, 20, p. 8.

BONDI, L. (1993) 'Locating identity politics', in KEITH, M. and PILE, S. (eds) *Place and the Politics of Identity*, London and New York: Routledge, pp. 84–101.

BOURDIEU, P. and EAGLETON, T. (1992) 'Doxa and common life', *New Left Review*, **191**, pp. 111–21.

CONE, J. (1986) *A Black Theology of Liberation*, New York: Maryknoll.

CONOLLY, W. (1995) *The Ethos of Pluralization*, Minneapolis and London: University of Minnesota Press.

DAWES, G. (1995) 'A Marxist critique of post-structuralist notions of the subject', *Transformation*, **1**, pp. 150–88.

DELEUZE, G. and GUATTARI, F. (1977) *Anti-oedipus: Capitalism and Schizophrenia*, HURLEY, R. and SEEM, M. and LANE, H. (Trans.), New York: Viking.

DERRIDA, J. and EWALD, F. (1995) 'A certain "madness" must watch over thinking', *Educational Theory*, **45**, 3, pp. 273–92.

EAGLETON, T. (1990) *The Ideology of the Aesthetic*, London and New York: Routledge.

EBERT, T. (1995–6) 'The knowable good: Post-al ethics, the question of justice and red feminism', *The Alternative Orange*, **5**, 1, pp. 31–9.

EBERT, T. (1996) *Ludic Feminism and After: Postmodernism, Desire and Labor in Late Capitalism*, Ann Arbor: University of Michigan Press.

FRASER, N. (1993) 'Clintonism, welfare, and the antisocial wage: The emergence of a neoliberal political imaginary', *Rethinking Marxism*, **6**, 1, pp. 9–23.

GITLIN, T. (1995) *The Twilight of Common Dreams*, New York: Metropolitan Books.

GIROUX, H. and McLAREN, P. (1986) 'Teacher education and the politics of engagement: The case for democratic schooling', *Harvard Educational Review*, **56**, 3, pp. 213–38.

GROSS, P. and LEVITT, N. (1995) *Higher Superstition: The Academic Left and Its Quarrels with Science*, Baltimore, MD: Johns Hopkins University Press.

GROSSBERG, L. (1992) *We Gotta Get Out of This Place: Popular Conservatism and Postmodern Culture*, New York: Routledge.

GROSSBERG, L. (1994) 'Introduction: Bringin it all back home — Pedagogy and cultural studies', in GIROUX, H. and McLAREN, P. (eds) *Between Borders: Pedagogy and the Politics of Cultural Studies*, London: Routledge, pp. 1–25.

HARRIS, D. (1992) *From Class Struggle to the Politics of Pleasure: The Effects of Gramscianism on Cultural Studies*, London and New York: Routledge.

HAY, C. (1995) 'Narrative as meta-narrative: Post-modern tension and the effacement of the political', *Transformation*, **1**, pp. 243–51.

HENNESSY, R. (1993) *Materialist Feminism and the Politics of Discourse*, New York: Routledge.

HERRNSTEIN, R. and MURRAY, C. (1994) *The Bell Curve: Intelligence and Class Structure in American Life*, New York: Free Press.

HOPPS, W. (1996) *Kienholz: A Retrospective*, New York: Whitney Museum of American Art.

KINCHELOE, J. and McLAREN, P. (1994) 'Rethinking critical theory and qualitative research', in DENZIN, N.K. and LINCOLN, Y.S. (eds) *Handbook of Qualitative Research*, Thousand Oaks, CA: SAGE Publications, pp. 138–57.

LARRAIN, J. (1995) 'Identity, the other and postmodernism', *Transformation*, **1**, pp. 271–89.

LESHER, D. (1996, January 9) 'Wilson makes renewed call for moral values,' *Los Angeles Times*, **1**, 13.

McLAREN, P. (1980) *Cries from the Corridor: The New Suburban Gihettos*, Toronto: Methalen.

McLAREN, P. (1993) *Schooling As a Ritual Performance: Towards a Political Economy of Educational Symbols and Gestures*, London and New York: Routledge.

McLAREN, P. (1994) *Life in schools*, White Plains, NY: Longman.

McLAREN, P. (1995a) *Critical Pedagogy and Predatory Culture*, London and New York: Routledge.

McLAREN, P. (1995b) 'Critical pedagogy in the age of global capitalism: Some challenges for the educational left', *Australian Journal of Education*, **39**, 1, pp. 5–21.

McLaren, P. (1997) *Revolutionary Multiculturalism*, Boulder, Colorado: Westview Press.

NEDERVEEN PIERTESE, J. (1994, January) 'Globalization as hybridisation', *International Sociology*, **8**, 2, pp. 161–84.

SANTOS, B. (1995) *Toward a New Common Sense: Law, Science and Politics in the Paradigmatic Transition*, New York and London: Routledge.

SCOTT, J.C. (1990) *Domination and the Arts of Resistance: Hidden Transcripts*, New Haven and London: Yale University Press.

SEARS, A. and MOOERS, C. (1995) 'The politics of hegemony: Democracy, class, and social movements', *Transformation*, **1**, pp. 216–42.

SHOHAT, E. and STAM, R. (1994) *Unthinking Eurocentrism: Multiculturalism and the Media*, New York and London: Routledge.

SIMON, S. (1996, January 2) 'Job hunt's wild side in Russia', *Los Angeles Times*, **1**, 9.

SIPCHEN, B. (1996, January 31) 'Gun activists yearn for the to electoral trophy', *Los Angeles Times*, **A5**.

TAUSSIG, M. (1993) *Mimesis and Alterity: A Particular History of the Senses*, New York and London: Routledge.

TORRES, R. and GOLDBERG, D.T. (1996) 'After race in Los Angeles', Unpublished proposal.

VALLE, V. and TORRES, R. (1994) 'Latinos in a "Post-industrial" disorder', *Socialist Review*, **23**, 4, pp. 1–28.

VISWESWARAN, K. (1994) *Fictions of Feminist Ethnography* Minneapolis: University of Minnesota Press.

WALLACE, A. (1996, January 8) 'Students back use of race in admission', *Los Angeles Times*, **3**, 13.

YOUNG, R.I.C. (1995) *Colonial Desire: Hybridity in Theory, Culture and Race*, London: Routledge.

YUDICE, G. (1995) 'Neither impugning nor disavowing whiteness does a viable politics make: The limits of identity politics', in NEWFIELD, C. and STRICKLAND, R. (eds) *After Political Correctness: The Humanities and Society*, Boulder, CO: Westview Press, pp. 255–85.

ZAMICHOW, N. (1996, January 23) 'Captains courageous enough not to fight', *Los Angeles Times*, **1**, pp. 9–10.

15   Writing from the Heart

Christine Sleeter

As she entered the graduate seminar, she could hear the students buzzing with excitement. She sat down in the second row, and some of them looked at her curiously. A minute later, the instructor entered briskly and the room quieted.

'We have a guest with us this afternoon, Dr Christine Sleeter. Please welcome her', the instructor said warmly.

Christie stood and walked to the front of the room. Students clapped, some whispering to each other, 'I thought she was another student coming to listen to Dr Sleeter!' 'She doesn't look like I thought she would.' 'I thought she was older, with lots of grey hair.' 'I didn't know she's white!' Christie faced the students and smiled, then asked them, 'Why do you want to write?'

They sat, puzzled. A moment passed, then Christie called on a few students, repeating the question, 'Why do you want to write?'

'Well, you have to, to get tenure. That's what professors do, and I want to be a professor.'

'I want to see if I can get published in *Harvard Educational Review*. If I do that, I know I will have made it.'

'I admire writers like yourself; I want to try it.'

'I want to apply post-modernist principles to constructivist theory in literacy instruction. Not too many people have done that yet, and that is the next wave of cutting-edge theorizing.'

The room was silent again, while the students wondered whether they had given good answers. They sensed that they hadn't. Then one of them raised her hand and asked, 'Professor Sleeter, why do you write? And why do you write so much, and how do you write pieces that catch on? What drives you?'

A smile slowly crept across Christie's face.

That's the key question: What drives you? What is in your heart? What do you care so much about that you simply must say it, in your own way, as clearly and forcefully as you know how? I can tell you my story, but only you can speak to what's in your own heart.

When I was a graduate student, I'm afraid I would have answered the question much as you did. I too was concerned about what it might take to earn tenure. In addition, I had been a good student all my life, and if you put an academic task before me, I worked at it until I mastered it. So in a sense, for a time I viewed academic writing as a technical skill and an academic challenge I would need to master.

At the same time, I was in awe of how much other people seemed to know, and how little I seemed to know by comparison. If the person sitting next to me had just read five books I hadn't read, I assumed I would need to read them also before having anything to say that is 'current'. If the person across from me could talk easily about a theoretical perspective I was still learning how to pronounce, I assumed my own ideas were too unformed and too unsophisticated to voice in public. If I disagreed with an 'authority', it must be that I just didn't understand the issue.

So as I went through graduate school, I assumed the role of a good student and learned as much as I could of the theories, writing techniques, and ideas around me. It wasn't until I had left graduate school, and listened more closely to my own ideas, that I developed my own voice. To illustrate that process, I will tell you about a few pieces of work that I consider my best, and how they came about.

By now the students were fully engaged in Christie's story.

Christie's Story

My writing is intimately connected to my lived experiences, and my inspiration comes from those experiences. As Sue Middleton (1993) explained in discussing her own work, 'The genesis of my research questions . . . lay deep in the tensions and conflicts of my everyday life' (p. 65). I grew up a physician's daughter in a small town in southern Oregon. My ethnic background is mixed European, mostly German. On the surface, it would seem that nothing in my background would prepare me to work passionately in the field of multicultural education. Mainstream as my background was, however, I found myself standing on margins of life in various ways. Most of my experiences with marginalization are not profound, relatively speaking, but they positioned me in a way that I came to view life differently than one might expect.

My father died when I was young, leaving my mother to raise four children. At the time, I was too young to grasp what had happened, and my mother tried hard to minimize the impact of his death on us. As a consequence I grew up with a mother modeling strength and independence. I also grew up sensitive to other people's reactions to differences. In the 1950s, single parent families were very unusual in my hometown, and I was quite aware that my family was somehow different. When people heard that my father was deceased, they often expressed pity; to me, it was a fact of life, and I hated to be pitied. I didn't think of my family as deficient, but was painfully aware of others thinking that.

Another ongoing issue throughout my life has been an attempt to reconcile my sex with my intellectual ability, in a society that penalizes smart women (Kerr, 1985). As a child and young adult, the conflict I perceived between my sex and my intelligence was often a source of pain. The academically capable boys didn't seem to have to choose between peer-group acceptance versus intelligence, but girls did. Academic work came easily for me, and with it, adult praise. Attaining peer group popularity was always much more problematic. I experienced rejection on the part of most of the boys as a hurtful inability to fit in because of personal characteristics I did not know how to change.

My marginal position relative to the 'popular' peer group opened me to seeking friends from other social circles. Largely through my involvement in the school band, I made friends from the 'other side of town'. I then found myself jumping to their defense whenever the middle class kids from my side of town put someone down. Having experienced what it felt like to be looked down on or felt sorry for, I hurt when people I liked were denigrated.

My hometown was about 99 percent white, and people simply didn't talk much about race. Of course the town was racially highly exclusive, but I didn't hear much about people of color except when my mother took us to visit her family in California. My California relatives occasionally made derogatory comments about black people as we passed them on the street. I would try to rise to their defense like I did when working class kids were put down, and would be quickly silenced. I was not comfortable with categorical rejection of an entire class of people and hearing relatives occasionally do just that increased my discomfort.

In college, I spent a summer in Japan, living with a family through the Experiment in International Living. There, I learned what it means to be stared at because one looks different. I learned how it feels to be unable to follow conversations or normal daily routines. But at the same time, my Japanese sister and I learned to communicate on a deeper level than our respective English and Japanese language skills would suggest; I learned to build bridges across wide cultural differences. I also learned to act as a participant observer in a different cultural context — to follow what I saw others doing and to assume that things made sense in their own cultural context, even if I didn't understand the reasoning or the context yet.

These experiences had placed me in margins in various ways, and prepared me to take severe marginalization of other people seriously. My work in multicultural teaching began in 1971, when I moved to Seattle. I had graduated from college without a plan for what to do next and enrolled in an urban education teacher preparation program based in Seattle because it sounded interesting. Much of the central area and south end of Seattle was quite racially diverse, and it was here that I spent most of the next seven years. The program was field-based and we were encouraged to live near the school to which we were assigned. The student body of my high school was about 1/3 Asian, 1/3 white, and 1/5 black, with small numbers of Mexican-American and Native American students.

I immediately fell in love with the students. I quickly got to know their names, and volunteered to spend lunch hour supervising basketball in the gym. From the beginning I oriented myself toward the school from the students' perspectives moreso than from teachers' perspectives. My cooperating teacher used fairly traditional methods of teaching, mainly lecture and textbook reading. My first lesson was to be a formal lecture on feudalism in Europe. I spent much of the night preparing; the next day, trembling, I began. My teacher sensed I had things under control so he left. As I stood at the front of the room, I saw students' eyes glazing over with boredom. So I stopped the lecture and asked them what they would be interested in learning. They suggested various subjects, then converged on 'Women's Liberation', a hot topic in 1971. I had them brainstorm subtopics on the board, then divided them into small groups, each with a subtopic to investigate. Needless to say, my cooperating teacher was very surprised when he returned, although he allowed me to continue.

The students worked enthusiastically for the next two weeks, then either presented oral reports (one group organized a guest speaker) or turned in written reports. Their work was mixed in quality, but they were responsive and inquisitive. In the process, I got to know them fairly well; I also learned that inner-city students would usually respond well if I showed a genuine interest in them and their interests. Over the next few years, as a substitute teacher and then as a classroom teacher, I had plenty of opportunity to get to know many, many inner-city adolescents, who only reaffirmed this lesson and strengthened the basic belief I have in kids. While substituting, I was also giving guitar lessons at a community center. The music I taught came from the Top 40, so the kids loved it. As a substitute teacher in the public schools, I frequently made a deal with kids that if they worked, I'd give them a concert before leaving. This was not simply bribery; my offer usually opened up communication between myself and the students, since they sensed we shared an interest in much the same popular music.

During the years I spent as a teacher in Seattle, I made friends with several African-Americans and lived in racially mixed neighborhoods. Usually when I am around people I listen a lot and take people for who they are. This period of my life transformed much of my view of the world, because much of it was spent with friends who lived on the other side of the color line, and who allowed me to learn how the US works for African-Americans.

For example, I first began to understand institutional racism in the context of housing. I had never spent more than a day looking for a place to live, and I was surprised when an African-American friend anticipated (correctly, it turned out) that it would take him several weeks to find a place. I was incensed that anyone should discriminate against someone based on race; he was used to it and patiently looked until he found a house to rent. At first I did not comprehend that he was facing racial discrimination, but I had to take that interpretation seriously for lack of any other reasonable way of understanding the difficulty he experienced locating decent housing.

I lived in a neighborhood from which black students were bused to desegregated schools, including the high school in which I was hired to teach. I got to know some of them, and gradually began to identify with their perspective. I learned to think of a predominantly white desegregated school as white turf, onto which a small number of black students were admitted. Being on someone else's turf, they were constantly under surveillance and viewed with veiled suspicion, a kind of pressure that I had never experienced. I learned to see where I was living as black turf, in that white friends from college seemed reluctant to visit me there and their white neighborhoods grew increasingly alien for me. Since I had grown up feeling like I didn't exactly fit and feeling very uncomfortable hearing negative judgments made about others, I found myself relatively comfortable in a mixed race and mixed social class environment that seemed more open to differences.

I had been prepared as a social studies teacher, but due to the lack of social studies teaching positions, I became a high school learning disabilities teacher. As a special education teacher, again I found myself standing on the margins looking in. I loved the students and found wonderful strengths and abilities in them. I identified with them, and was frustrated and sometimes angry when they were rejected by peers and other teachers. I got to wondering why I was supposed to spend so much time trying to remediate their weakest learning skills (reading and writing), almost to the exclusion of developing other skills and strengths they had. Sometimes it felt to me and to them as if their strengths didn't count, what counted was what they could not do well. As the first LD teacher in my school, I set up the program and identified the students for it, learning first-hand about the social construction of programs.

So far I have described experiences of marginalization and border-crossing. But at the same time, I always had access to higher levels of education. This access provided me with the tools to name, examine, and eventually write about contradictions and tensions in my own experience. As Sue Middleton (1993) noted,

> My generation's radical sociological and/or feminist perspectives on education had been at least partly theorizations of our experiences of marginality or alienation within it, although — individuals who were to become academically successful — had sufficient 'cultural capital' (Bourdieu, 1971) to enable this marginalization to become the basis of an intellectual critique rather than of educational withdrawal or failure. (pp. 4–5)

I went to graduate school at the University of Wisconsin-Madison. There, I was exposed to a wide range of ideas that shed new light on these experiences: critical theory, multicultural education theory, Marxism, socialist feminism, neo-colonialism.

For the first time, theories named my own senses of things not being right. But at the same time I experienced insecurities that graduate students — particularly those of us who are not white males — often experience: insecurities with new terminologies, new conceptual frameworks and abstract theories springing from the minds of 'authorities', endless new stacks of books to read, and peers who seemed to be more familiar with these ideas than I was. Although I had been good in school all my life, I was good mainly at following the teacher's directions. This is ironic, because in other ways I've always created original products of various sorts, such as paintings, clothing, teaching materials. But I entered academia determined to achieve well by following directions. That meant, as it usually means in school, that one leaves one's personal interests and passions at the door, drawing on them only occasionally.

It was only after completing my PhD and publishing a few pieces that I increasingly reached back into the life I had lived and the experiences I knew, and found my voice. Below, I will discuss a few of my best pieces of work, and where they came from.

Why Is There Learning Disabilities?

According to the dominant paradigm, schools are organized to deliver quality education as equitably as possible. Special education serves children who are disabled; learning disabled students have minimal brain dysfunction. This was the paradigm I was taught until my PhD program. There, I was exposed to alternative paradigms that suggest that schools are organized to reproduce the social class structure, to create consent to white supremacy, to reinforce patriarchal relationships. The alternative paradigms fit and explained much of what I had experienced; once I got past the new vocabulary, I found the new ideas illuminating and exciting.

But what about special education? Were kids in those programs really different, or do special education programs constitute an organizational structure that reproduces inequality? If so, how? In the late 1970s and early 1980s, there was fairly little written on this topic, most of it appearing in British publications (Barton and Tomlinson, 1983; Carrier, 1986; Tomlinson, 1982; 1985) I eagerly read what I could, and attempted to create an alternative analysis of special education in an early paper that was never published. So I let ideas simmer in my head while I plunged into my first job as a professor.

Part of my responsibility in that job was to teach coursework in learning disabilities, which brought me back into direct contact with literature on learning disabilities, which I had been away from for several years. It also stirred feelings, unresolved questions, and frustrations I had as a classroom teacher. I couldn't, for example, simply teach that LD kids have brain dysfunction because my own students had not been tested for this. I couldn't teach about their special learning needs without critiquing the school as a whole for not meeting learning needs of a wide range of children. I couldn't teach remedial teaching strategies without reliving my students' frustration with daily drills on their weakest skills. I couldn't teach how to give specific diagnostic tests without remembering what small slices of information such tests give about complex and interesting kids. And I couldn't pretend there was no connection between learning disabilities as a classification and other race- and class-based ways in which students are divided for instruction.

I wanted to affirm the normalcy of the kids I had taught. To me, affirming their normalcy meant teaching them what they do not know, but it also meant recognizing and building on their strengths, and challenging the contexts that define them as abnormal. It is normal that some people read much better or worse than others, but our education system is constructed such that poor readers are framed as abnormal. Rather than searching for explanations for their abnormality, or treating them as very different from 'normal' kids, I asked: Can't we broaden what counts as normal and structure schools accordingly?

This was really a fundamental question I had been asking most of my life: Can't we broaden what counts as a normal family, or a normal girl, or a normal skin color, or a normal culture? If we saw the best in the people around us, and believed in their strengths and abilities, wouldn't we individually as well as collectively treat each other much differently? How did this complex system of classifying kids come about, and whose interests does it serve?

One day while driving, my mind was juxtaposing the medical model for learning disabilities with my experience as an LD teacher. I knew that the present is historically constructed, so I pondered the historic context during which the first learning disabilities programs were created, wondering what was going on then that would have led to the construction of programs built on a medical rationale that diverged from my own experience 'finding' LD students. Suddenly pieces came together: post-Sputnik school reforms that emphasized increased tracking and higher standards; school desegregation in the 1960s and subsequent white flight; the founding of the Association for Children with Learning Disabilities in 1963; and the limited options available at that time to academically failing children of white professional-class parents. I suddenly had a hypothesis: learning disabilities became a category to protect such children by removing them from other failing students who were presumed to be mentally retarded, 'culturally deprived', or slow learners due largely to poverty homes. While some children probably are neurologically impaired, the category had come to be an acceptable place for children from privileged backgrounds largely because they had to test as 'normal' on an IQ test, and white economically privileged professionals would not regard their reading failure as due to cultural or familial factors (i.e., race or social class).

I practically ran to the library to find out how schools were being discussed in popular literature in the late 1950s and early 1960s, and to find out who was in the various remedial programs in schools. What I found became the substance of two articles that ask, 'Why is there learning disabilities' (Sleeter, 1986; 1987). I knew that what I had to say would not be welcomed by the special education establishment. However, critiques about various dimensions of special education were beginning to grow from within the field itself, and one of its main journals, *Exceptional Children*, at the time was being edited by an 'insider critic' who liked what I had to say. My work even prompted a published critique (Kavale and Forness, 1987), to which I was invited to respond (Sleeter, 1988). People were actually taking my ideas seriously!

I was pleased, of course, that these articles were published. But the main source of my satisfaction was that these articles voiced a perspective about schools and special education that grew from my own experience as a learning disabilities teacher as well as my own life experience. I had framed the world in a way that made sense to me, and used theory, my research and my writing skill to explain what I saw well enough that it made sense to other people. I had learned to use some academic tools to argue that human diversity is normal, even though our social institutions do not support much of the range of who we are as humans.

Multicultural Education As a Form of Resistance to Oppression

As noted earlier, African-American friends sensitized me to the workings of racism and to strategies the black community uses to cope with, and resist, racial oppression. As a teacher in the 1970s, I lacked a good understanding of what challenging racism might mean for classroom instruction, but I was aware that the people around me who were asking the question of what it might mean and who were creating answers were mainly educators of color. I was also aware that when white people involve ourselves in racial issues, we often either try to take over or transform definitions of issues to fit our own perspectives and comfort zones.

When I was contemplating studying multicultural education as part of a PhD program, I almost decided against it because I did not want to be one of the white people who just gets in the way, and am indebted to Carl Grant for his encouragement of my involvement. Before I enrolled in graduate study at the University of Wisconsin-Madison, I consciously pledged to myself that I would try to work with multiracial coalitions, in support of how people of color are framing issues. I also reaffirmed to myself what I had learned in Japan and again in Seattle: That when the sensibilities of people of color seem to be different from those of Whites, it is not because white ideas are more developed. If I try, I can come to understand a good deal of why people of color see things as they do. Even when I do not understand, respect for the integrity and intelligence of other people suggests that I assume other people's viewpoints make sense from the shoes in which they stand.

My PhD program was my first contact with intellectual work of the white left. While initially I was put off by its vocabulary, I found the ideas to be compelling because they explained much of the world as I had experienced it in ways that made sense to me. Neo-Marxism gave me a framework for thinking about social inequality in relationship to the economy and social class structure. Concepts such as hegemony, domination, commodification of culture, and resistance provided conceptual tools for examining the persistance of inequality in the US and globally, and the ways in which people act on their own oppression.

But at the same time, I was puzzled by what appeared to be chasms between the intellectual work of people critiquing social class, race, and gender. Clusters of intellectuals who were mainly white males framed oppression mainly on social class relations, other clusters of white women framed oppression around gender, and still other clusters of intellectuals, mainly of color, framed oppression mainly on race. The latter were the most interested and active in multicultural education. Much of my PhD coursework emphasized social class; mentally I often added 'race and gender', since so many of the concepts seemed useful for examining multiple forms of oppression.

Over time, I became aware that multicultural education was looked on with disdain by some white males who were interested in a class analysis. Often this took the form of simply ignoring it and the people associated with it. Occasionally someone would question my interest in multicultural education, given the weaknesses they saw in it. I can recall instances in which white male leftists have described multicultural education to me as being assimilationist, based on a weak analysis of racism and no analysis of social class oppression, and rooted in the thinking of the dominant white society.

During such encounters, and also while reading leftist critiques of multicultural education, a set of images played over and over in my head. I recalled African-Americans friends in Seattle who talked frequently about how racism constricted their lives, but got up every morning with the purpose of trying to make hostile white schools more accommodating to African-American students. They probably would have spent their energies dismantling white supremacy if they knew how to do that successfully; they didn't, but they did know how to make schools a little more humane. I recalled a Japanese-American educator who had spent part of her childhood in the concentration camps, and as an adult, spent considerable energy organizing a group to develop one of the first multicultural curricula to help elementary children learn to talk about racial and cultural differences. I heard the voice of multicultural education scholars such as Geneva Gay talk about the impact of racism on African-American communities, grounding multicultural education in its ethnic studies roots. And I felt the passion of educators of color who try persistently to get white educators to listen and help.

I also heard white voices from history justifying colonial and racial exclusion policies on the basis of people of color not being educated enough to know how to address their own needs properly. I saw a long stream of white men assuming they knew best how to resolve other people's problems. I saw working class white people historically reaping economic and political advantages by defining themselves as racially superior to non-Whites (Roediger, 1991; Ignatiev, and Garvey, 1996). When members of the white left ignored or dismissed multicultural education, I placed their behavior in that historical context. But it took a long time before I said much because I, as is common among women, felt my own ideas, when questioned authoritatively by men, to be poorly formulated.

Finally I had enough and became angry. I have never regarded multicultural education as a polished and finished product, and most people I have met who work in multicultural education would welcome an exchange of ideas with those who begin with other forms of oppression. But that exchange needs to go in two directions, and when too many male members of the white left saw multicultural education — but not their own work — as needing reconceptualizing, I became angry. I channeled my anger into an article: 'Multicultural education as a form of resistance to oppression' (Sleeter, 1989).

Untempered anger usually does not lead to published articles. In this case, I was initially less concerned about publishing an article than about persuading an audience of the white left to recognize multicultural education as part of a history of work by people of color to challenge racial oppression. In order to persuade, I needed to present clear examples of the problem I was addressing, and frame my argument using concepts both the white left and the field of multicultural education find highly useful. Intellectual work of the white left can connect very productively with multicultural education; there is a great deal of room for dialog and coalescing (Gay, 1995). I wanted to build a bridge, but one that demanded two-way dialog.

So, first I simply wrote my anger down. Then I went back and constructed rational arguments. The article came first from my heart, but I needed to use my head to give it a healthy birth. Once my anger was out and on paper, I could then meticulously employ the skills of scholarly writing (such as doing several drafts) to craft a publishable argument.

White Racism

In any body of work that finds itself under siege, it is difficult to voice problems internal to the work without providing ammunition for external critics. So it has been with multicultural education. In spite of the indignation discussed above, I regarded some of the criticism of the white left, such as the relative silence of multicultural education around issues of white supremacy, as very valid. Increasingly I also encountered criticisms by intellectuals of color, who made some of the same observations.

At the same time, in my own teaching I found myself struggling with the problem of how to help predominantly white classes of teachers and preservice students understand institutional racism, sexism, and poverty. The first few years I taught multicultural education at the university level, my courses focused more on teaching strategies and cultural differences than on racism and other forms of oppression. However, as I continued to teach and became increasingly cognizant of, and frustrated with, the difficulty students had understanding any form of oppression and particularly racism, my teaching focused more and more on those issues. For pedagogical guidance, I found myself reflecting on my own personal learning process, and designing experiential activities to help students see critically for themselves social realities, such as housing segregation, job discrimination, and tracking in schools, that they had learned to view as 'normal'. In so doing, I became fairly comfortable talking about white racism with a fairly wide array of audiences, connecting as best I could the abstract issues with my own life and surroundings, and helping others to engage in similar analysis.

It is difficult to pinpoint exactly when I decided I needed to write about white racism. During the 1980s several developments pushed me in that direction. One development was the growth in the number of educators who wanted to 'do' multicultural education. Too many times I found myself with white or predominantly white groups of teachers who wanted to teach their students about the 'Other', but did not ground multicultural education in unequal power relations. On such occasions I found myself juxtaposing how white teachers tend to frame 'diversity' issues against how educators of color frame the issues. My study of staff development for multicultural education, which culminated in the book Keepers of the American Dream (Sleeter, 1992a), presented such a juxtaposition. Articles based on that study examined how white teachers construct race (Sleeter, 1992b; 1993).

My involvement with women's studies and gender issues also provoked thinking. Although some women's studies programs and organizations do an exemplary job of bridge-building among women, many, by choosing gender as the most important (and sometimes only) basis for analysis, privilege the interests and experiences of white, heterosexual, middle-class women. In various contexts I have participated in all-white women's groups, who occasionally ask the question: Why don't women of color join us? My usual response is something like: Why don't we collaborate with women of color on the work they are doing? The reactions that question provokes are usually either silence, confusion, or an assignment to me to go find out what 'they' are doing. And if 'they' are working on community issues related to racism or poverty, white women often regard these as irrelevant. Some white women become very active allies in anti-racist and anti-poverty work, but many simply regard these as someone else's work to do.

Readers who do not know me personally probably cannot picture the constant struggle in which I engage regarding my own role and work in multicultural education issues. Although I may have a fairly high level of awareness of racism, as a white native-English speaking person I still reap its benefits and often in ways I do not see. Similarly, as someone who has never been poor, I benefit from economic cushions and opportunities I take for granted more often that I critique. The question I had about the role of white people in multicultural education, before leaving Seattle, has never left me.

About four years ago I lunched with Antonia Darder (1991), after having experienced her criticism of white people, myself included, who talk about multicultural education but skim over white racism. She articulated for me what should be obvious from what I've written here, but was still rather muddled in my own mind: that I can't do the work for her that she needs to do with her own Latino/a community, and she can't do the work for me that I should be doing with my own white community. That is, my most useful work as an ally is to help people like myself very directly confront and deal with white supremacy. Shortly thereafter, I looked back over my own writing on multicultural education, and saw that even though I had talked a little bit about racism, I was also skilled at making it sound comfortable and at lumping it in with other things. My teaching was actually more aggressive than my writing was.

When Priscilla Walton, editor of the *Multicultural Education* magazine, invited me to write an article that would challenge the field, I decided to talk with white educators about our own silence about white racism (Sleeter, 1994). In that article I described everyday interactions in which we engage that serve as detours around racism and that help maintain silence about a 'taboo' topic. I intended the article to serve as a beginning for opening up dialog, rather than as a definitive piece on how racism works. Whether it has served that purpose or not, I don't know. I have also written articles describing how I teach about white racism, since my teaching processes are experiential like my own learning processes have been (Sleeter, 1995a; 1995b). (Colleagues who have used the article with white students sometimes contact me in some degree of panic saying, 'Now what do I do? They are so angry I can't get them to listen!').

Finding Your Own Voice

The room was silent for a minute. Finally a young woman who was sitting in the back of the room raised her hand slowly. Christie smiled at her and said, 'Yes?'

The young woman nervously stood up and looked around. She brushed her dark hair off her face and said, 'I never talk in class. I never thought I knew enough to say anything. My brother has cerebral palsy. The rest of you don't know that because it doesn't come up when we talk about the articles we read. I mean, when we are debating post-structuralism, how do you work cerebral palsy into the conversation? But I helped to raise him, and I'm helping him get through college. Luckily he is really smart, because it is very hard. What I've been trying for months to figure out is, what do I write about? All this stuff we study in graduate school is interesting, but my heart is shared with my brother. If I hear you right, what you are saying is — there are connections that only I can make. Is that right?'

Christie smiled broadly. 'That is right. Not only that, but you will give the world your best if you listen to your heart. And maybe your heart will tell you that academic writing is a waste of time.'

'No', the young woman said, 'No, for me that wouldn't be true. How many of us in here know anything about cerebral palsy? Most people only know what they read in a special education book. I do have a lot to say, and what I'm learning here can help me to go deeper in my thinking.'

Another student jumped in. 'But where do you get published? I was an illegal immigrant — I'm legal now. My life is rooted in my experience in Mexico and then coming to the US. I want to write about that — but where do you get published?'

Christie replied,

Let me tell you what I've always done. My best work comes when I first have some-thing to say, which usually happens when I am angered or disturbed by what I see. I listen to my feelings and the voice in my 'gut'. Then I rough out what I want to say, in my own words. Then I browse in different journals. I try to find two or three journals that publish pieces like the one I want to write, and rank order them based on which one I would most like to see accept the piece. My first choice is usually a highly competitive journal; the editor may reject my piece, but sometimes it is accepted. I use that journal as a model for deciding how long to make the article, and how to set it up. If the article gets rejected by that journal, as a friend once told me, the next journal is just a postage stamp away, and I already have that journal identified. One of my favorite pieces, 'Resisting Racial Awareness' (Sleeter, 1992b) took exactly that route, rejected by my first choice but accepted by journal number 2. Incidentally, my first book, *After the School Bell Rings*, with Carl Grant (1986), went to several publishers before it was accepted.

'Why don't you get discouraged when that happens?' a student asked.

It depends on how strongly I feel about what I want to say. If there is a message in what I've written that I feel strongly about, and the message does come through clearly, someone will publish it. If what I have written was a jumble without a clear, strong message or argument, then I put it aside.

   Another strategy I have used has been to write the piece, get it the way I want, then send it to someone for feedback, asking in the process if that person has an idea who might publish it. That was how 'Learning disabilities: The social construction of a special education category' (1986) found a journal. When I wrote it, I couldn't imagine who would publish it! And I have helped authors find publishing outlets when they have sent work to me. Please don't start flooding me with all your work, by the way, I may not be the best resource for what you are doing.

'But how do I find my voice?' asked another student with some frustration. 'I don't know what I have to say that anyone else would find worthwhile.'
   Christie shook her head.

Neither do I. No one but you knows what you have to say. I think the best work is grounded in a strong set of moral values. My work, for example, provokes people and often makes them angry, but I am also told that people are drawn to the moral arguments I try to make. All of you believe in something, in a better world than the one we have at present. That's what is in your heart. Use the ideas you are reading, the theories that help you think and frame ideas, the intellectual tools you are developing — but also listen to your heart. Your heart will ground your writing.

Years later, these students wrote works that inspired the minds and hearts of many, many educators.

References

BARTON, L. and TOMLINSON, S. (1983) *Special Needs and Social Interests*, London: Croom Helm.
BORDIEU, P. (1971) 'Intellectual field and creative project', in YOUNG, M.F.D. (ed.) *Knowledge and Control*, London: Collier Macmillan.
CARRIER, J.G. (1986) *Learning Disability: Social Class and the Construction of Inequality in American Education*, Westport, CT: Greenwood Press.
DARDER, A. (1991) *Culture and Power in the Classroom*, New York: Bergin and Garvey.
GAY, G. (1995) 'Mirror images on common issues: Parallels between multicultural education and critical pedagogy', in SLEETER, C.E. and McLAREN, P. (eds) *Multicultural Education, Critical Pegagogy, and the Politics of Difference*, Albany: SUNY Press, pp. 155–90.
GRANT, C.A. and SLEETER, C.E. (1986) *After the School Bell Rings*, London: Falmer Press.
IGNATIEV, N. and GARVEY, J. (eds) (1996) *Race traitor*, New York: Routledge.

KAVALE, K.A. and FORNESS, S.R. (1987) 'History, politics, and the general education initiative: Sleeter's reinterpreation of learning disabilities as a case study', *Remedial and Special Education*, **8**, 5 pp. 6–12.

KERR, B.A. (1985) *Smart Girls, Gifted Women*, Dayton, OH: Ohio Psychology Press.

MIDDLETON, S. (1993) *Educating Feminists: Life Histories and Pedagogy*, New York: Teachers College Press.

ROEDIGER, D.R. (1991) *The Wages of Whiteness*, New York: Verso.

SLEETER, C.E. (1986) 'Learning disabilities: The social construction of a special education category', *Exceptional Children*, **53**, 1, pp. 46–54.

SLEETER, C.E. (1987) 'Why is there learning disabilities?: A critical history of the birth of the field', in POPKEWITZ, T.S. (ed.) *The Formation of the School Subject Matter: The Struggle for an American Institution*, Barcombe, England: Falmer Press, pp. 210–37.

SLEETER, C.E. (1988) 'The social construction of learning disabilities: A reply to Kavale and Forness', *Remedial and Special Education*, **9**, 3, pp. 53–7.

SLEETER, C.E. (1989) 'Multicultural education as a form of resistance to oppression', *Journal of Education*, **171**, 3, pp. 51–71.

SLEETER, C.E. (1992a) *Keepers of the American Dream*, London: Falmer Press.

SLEETER, C.E. (1992b) 'Resisting racial awareness: How teachers understand the social order from their racial, gender, and social class locations', *Educational Foundations*, **1**, 4.

SLEETER, C.E. (1993) 'How white teachers construct race', in McCARTHY, C. and CRICHLOW, W. (eds) *Race, Identity and Representation in Education*, New York: Routledge.

SLEETER, C.E. (1994) 'White racism', *Multicultural education*, **1**, 4, pp. 5–8.

SLEETER, C.E. (1995a) 'Teaching Whites about racism', in MARTIN, R.J. (ed.) *Practicing What We Teach*, Albany: SUNY Press.

SLEETER, C.E. (1995b) 'Reflection on my use of multicultural and critical pedagogy when students are white,' in SLEETER, C.E. and McLAREN, P. (eds) *Multicultural Education, Critical Pegagogy, and the Politics of Difference*, Albany: SUNY Press, pp. 415–38.

TOMLINSON, S. (1982) *A Sociology of Special Education*, London: Routledge and Kegan Paul.

TOMLINSON, S. (1985) 'The expansion of special education', *Oxford Review of Education*, **11**, pp. 157–65.

16   Research As Praxis: Unlearning Oppression and Research Journeys

Beth Blue Swadener

A more collaborative approach to critical inquiry is needed to empower the researched, build emancipatory theory, and move toward the establishment of data credibility within praxis-oriented, advocacy research. (Lather, 1991, p. 69)

This chapter explores ways in which my interest in social justice and anti-oppression work has taken me through many spaces and enabled me to seek out vehicles for action, voice, and collaboration — in research, teaching, and community work. My passion for social justice issues, full inclusion, and community organizing goes back over 20 years; indeed, some of these ideologies have been with me as long as I can recall. I borrow the title of the chapter from a paper and book (Lather, 1991) which had great influence on me as I was engaging in qualitative research and beginning to re-frame my feminist assumptions. I recall hearing Patti Lather discussing related issues at the Ethnography Forum and sensing that her many challenges to critical ethnography and feminist pedagogy were right 'on time' for my development as a researcher in a field which is not typically known for its contributions to critical or feminist theory, post-modern discourses, or even qualitative inquiry — the field of early childhood education. This is changing, of course (e.g., Jipson and Hauser, 1997; Kessler and Swadener, 1992), and this chapter explores ways in which these and other issues have been at the center of my 'research as praxis' agenda. I have also been influenced by Concha Delgado-Gaitan's framing of 'the ethnography of empowerment' (Delgado-Gaitan, 1993), Liz Ellsworth's interrogation of critical pedagogy (Ellsworth, 1989), and Michelle Fine's continued interrogation of 'ethnographer as ventriloquist' and call to move 'beyond a colonizing discourse of the Other' (Fine, 1994). In this chapter, I draw from personal experiences in community work, teaching social policy and anti-bias, inclusive early education, and from a critical examination of my journey as an educational researcher. I have served in various leadership capacities in volunteer groups focusing on anti-poverty action and child health promotion, advocacy for and with persons with disabilities, child care/early education, and, most recently, worked with street children and their mothers in Nairobi, Kenya. I have done research on anti-bias and inclusive early childhood education, social problem-solving in kindergarten and primary settings, child and family social policy in the United States and in Kenya, and have written on the need to deconstruct the pervasive 'at risk' label and its deficit baggage. I have organized the chapter to examine more closely several of these themes in my research 'as praxis'.

In terms of what guides me in framing research questions and designing and carrying out research related to issues of social justice and multiculturalism, I have divided this chapter into six sections:

1   early memories;
2   race, gender and full inclusion;
3   feminist perspectives and alliance building;
4   toward authentically collaborative research;
5   social policy and equity issues in early childhood; and
6   the 'scholarship of teaching';

each of which reflects an area in which I have conducted research or done critical scholarship. Each section, in turn, frames that topic or issue in at least three contexts: my life experience and major influences on this issue, theoretical frameworks and work which has been particularly influential in this scholarship, and brief examples of some of my work in that area. Boundaries between personal and professional experiences are intentionally blurred, as they are deeply intertwined.

Yearning for Difference: Early Memories

In a workshop with Beverly Tatum focusing on racial identity formation and breaking the cycle of oppression, we began with 'I remember . . .' reflections, as they pertained to learning about difference. I remembered organizing neighborhood clubs, in my early elementary years, which 'did things for others', particularly elderly neighbors and younger children. I also remembered growing up in the 1950s and early 1960s in a white, working class/lower middle class community which had very few families of color and where my first encounters with African-Americans are vaguely associated with an olympic runner from our high school, and trips to Chicago, which was less than 100 miles away. I remember that I was always interested in difference . . . in two neighborhood families who were Jewish, in the few African-American students at our local high school and in the international visitors to our community and home (e.g., from Japan and Pakistan).

I also recall having a friend with cerebral palsy, a girl I knew through my church and through family friends. Three of my parents' close friends had children with disabilities; two of these children were an 'absent presence' — I never saw them. They were institutionalized and both later died. The third, my friend with cerebral palsy, was someone I enjoyed spending time with. We had sleep-overs and visited each others' homes from time to time. She did not attend a local public school, however, was often in 'special settings' and had several surgeries and hospitalizations. (Today she is married and living and working in the community.) Our nextdoor neighbor, a journalist, had polio in his youth and was also in a wheelchair. I recall being impressed that he could drive a car and was quite independent. Another child I remember playing with was hearing impaired and hard to understand at first; she wore a very large hearing aid which looked like a radio.

Thus, I can easily trace some of the more obvious 'roots' of my interest in disability advocacy and full inclusion issues to early exposure in my own community and neighborhood — although not to my school. Unlike so many children who are taught that difference (in this case disability) is bad, scary, and a 'taboo' topic, I recall asking questions and getting answers — often directly from the persons in my life who had a disability or from my parents.

Another, more painful, memory of my childhood and early adolescence was loss. My mother died of cancer when I was in fourth grade. Then, only three years later, my stepmother died. Although younger when my mother died, I was somehow more prepared. My stepmother's death was completely unexpected and came when I was 13 — an emotional age to begin with. Having a father who cooked, cleaned, and cared for me was, I suppose, my first exposure to 'anti-bias parenting' (as I might label it now), as the still strict gender roles of the 1960s needed to be adjusted in our family. My father had support in raising me from a caring community of friends and I did not lack for attention! I believe these experiences have contributed to my focus on the social and emotional well being of children and on the importance of building a caring community in the classroom, and beyond.

Turning to my long-time interest in Africa and affinity with people of color, I recall several years ago finding a picture I had drawn in third or fourth grade of 'what I wanted to do when I grew up'. Interestingly, I had drawn two images: one of me as (white) doctor, working in a rural setting with African children and one of me teaching in an urban school, with the phrase 'teaching in the ghetto' written under the picture. This was in the early 1960s. I was obviously influenced by several icons of the time, as well as the *zeitgeist* of the civil rights era, the growing women's movement, and the war on poverty. Unpacking this drawing provides some of the threads which are deeply embedded in the tapestry of my life, as well as an opportunity to unravel a number of issues, including privilege, power, othering, child-saving, and other less than equitable strands. The missionary zeal with which I initially framed many of my early social projects is now amusing, but also reflects the privileged positions which I held even as a child. I could be a doctor. I could travel. I could 'sacrifice' and I could 'serve' those less fortunate than I. De-colonizing these images and the ideals they represent is a challenge even now.

In high school I had friends from more diverse backgrounds, although still limited by my predominantly white community. I also had a close friend who was gay, although he was not out to many people at that time. (He has since died of AIDS.) In college, one of my house-mates was a lesbian and more of my friends were gay, lesbian, or bisexual. In high school I was the maid of honor in a European-American friend's marriage to a Kenyan and had several African and African-American friends.

As I started taking university courses in the early 1970s, I was drawn to two areas outside my major of child psychology — women's studies and philosophy, particularly socialist theories and Marxism. Although I attended a smaller, regional campus of a state university, I had the opportunity to study philosophy with a former student of Herbert Marcuse, and the matrix for my later embracing of neo-Marxian and social reconstructionist theories in education was being formed. [Much later, when taking courses with Michael Apple, this foundation was re-awakened in powerful and relevant ways to issues in education and curriculum.]

In terms of relationships, it was in the world of work, in group homes for adults with developmental disabilities and mental illness and a residential center for children with multiple disabilities, that I began to connect more with women of color, particularly working class, middle-aged women. These connections to women of color, particularly African-American women, have grown and continue to be very significant today. Creating multicultural alliances to work against racism and other forms of oppression has been a major part of my activism in the past decade, and has clear roots in my coming of age in the early 1970s and participating, in a limited way, in the civil rights and women's rights movements.

Examining Race, Gender, and Full Inclusion in Early Childhood Settings: Changing Paradigms and Perspectives

As a preschool, kindergarten and early intervention teacher, I felt that the early child-hood professions were marginalized (particularly by sexism, as they are highly gender segregated professions with both low salaries and status), yet offered fertile ground for anti-bias pedagogy — where it likely has the greatest impact, in the 'formative' years. Like many feminist early childhood teachers, I tended to focus first on anti-sexist prac-tices or 'gender equity in the nursery school', as some of us called it then. (I suppose, looking back, that I was engaging a sort of 'hierarchy of oppressions', emphasizing sexism and, to a lesser degree, classism and racism. One could also say that I was formulating a materialist feminist framework in many contexts.) Having taught young children from culturally and linguistically diverse backgrounds and supervised student teachers in a number of culturally diverse settings, I became very interested in how children form attitudes about difference and how these attitudes might influence their choices in play and friendship patterns.

As I came to learn more about education that is multicultural and social recon-structionist in the early 1980s (through reading the work of Carl Grant and later studying with him), and became more involved in anti-racist pedagogy, my view of gender issues in early childhood expanded to include the equal importance of addressing issues of race, class, developmental differences, sexual orientation, linguistic diversity and other intersecting aspects of human diversity and complexity. Before I returned to the univer-sity, as a lecturer in Child and Family Studies, I worked for several years developing competency-based staff training modules for group home staff throughout Wisconsin. My first doctoral course in adult education exposed me to a more critical, Friereian perspective and encouraged my critique of many assumptions regarding curriculum development work.

While in the doctoral program at University of Wisconsin-Madison, I also had the opportunity to study with Michael Apple (which rekindled my interest in neo-Marxian theory and introduced me to critical ethnography, Gramsci, and international applica-tions of theory), Mimi Bloch (who helped me find intersections between feminism and early childhood and encouraged my interest in doing early childhood research in West Africa), and with George and Louise Spindler (who introduced me to anthropological studies of education and what it might mean to 'do ethnography'). This exposure to another way of attempting to understand children, child-rearing, peer interactions, and curriculum issues was a turning point or paradigm shift in many ways. Finding methodo-logies which emphasized understanding culture, context, and symbolic interaction was empowering to one who had been steeped in the quantitative, positivist research tradi-tions of developmental psychology and child development.

My dissertation (Swadener, 1986) was an ethnographic study of two mainstreamed, multicultural child care programs which were attempting to implement 'education that is multicultural'. In this study I looked at both formal and informal curriculum as they related to human diversity, and analyzed peer interactions *vis-à-vis* gender, develop-mental differences, race, and language. Some of my most striking findings were related to gender. Gender was used far more than race, language, or ability in 4- and 5-year-old children's friendships and play interactions, reflecting the literature on gender segreg-ated play patterns. Yet, among my more interesting observations was the creative use of language by children who were resisting narrow sex-role ascriptions, including the invention of more inclusive words and the assertiveness of several of the girls to gain access to more of the roles and play props available (e.g., 'Girls *can* be chefs! They're called *cheffahs*!' as asserted by one 4-year-old). Gender equity was actively supported and facilitated by the teachers, several of whom conveyed 'feminist' views in both their teaching praxis and our interviews. Many of these teachers were also quite political, particularly at a center which was involved in organizing a local child care workers union and working for 'worthy wages'.

Other findings which have relevance to contemporary full inclusion issues included different approaches to facilitating mainstreaming in early childhood classrooms. For example, in the center which utilized a team-teaching model in which distinctions between the teacher with early childhood background and the teacher with special education background were minimized, and which also included more children with special needs for the entire day (of a full-day program), children did not view their peers with developmental differences as objects of their help, pity, confusion, or concern. Rather, when interviewing several children about Jimmy, a boy who was delayed in speech and was using sign language, the majority told me that their favorite thing to do with him was, 'learn sign language *from* Jimmy'. Learning from is far more reciprocal than 'doing for', and the teachers and I found this response to be encouraging. Children and parents were also involved in directly discussing children's individual, cultural, and developmental differences. A girl with cerebral palsy and her mother brought in a set of photos on a poster about how her braces were made, and she passed around her 'baby braces', which most children enjoyed manipulating the velcro on her old braces while learning about her growth and development. Although I had sought to document practices of settings which took an even more active, anti-bias stance (education that *is* multicultural), my observations and interviews led to describing both settings as using a 'human relations' approach, emphasizing children's ability to accept each other and form friendships across various racial, ethnic, gender, religious, developmental, linguistic, and, to some degree, class lines. The hardest line for children to cross, overall, was the gender line.

As I further 'unpack' or deconstruct my dissertation research and how my continuing study of the dynamics of oppression has deepened my understanding of complex phenomena such as those addressed in that study, a number of issues become apparent. I have noted a number of limitations of this study, including a 'halo' effect of my high expectations of the participating centers and insistence, at times, that they were actually practicing 'education that is multicultural', when, in fact, they were both closer to a 'human relations' approach to multiculturalism and mainstreaming. I recall having related discussions with both Carl Grant and Christie Sleeter at the time I was writing up my findings. Christie asked me point blank, 'but do you really think those centers are implementing education that is multicultural?' It was a typical case of going in with a title and preconceived notions and needing to be open to what emerged — but within my boundaries and my earnest hope that they *were* taking a more comprehensive approach to anti-bias education than my observations actually supported.

I also neglected to examine class sufficiently in my dissertation, as I was reminded by Michael Apple at my defense. Although there were differences in the average income of the two centers in this case study (i.e., one served primarily graduate student and community children and the other served far more faculty children), both were campus-related programs and not as representative of community-based programs as, for example, a Head Start program and a more typical day care setting might have been. These centers were chosen in part as convenience samples which had been part of a series of workshops on education that is multicultural and were used to learn more about what would happen when centers *tried to enact their interpretations of education* that is multicultural.

I was attempting to apply the construct of education that is multicultural and social reconstructionist to early childhood settings — at about the same time that the anti-bias curriculum was being developed by Derman-Sparks and colleagues (1989).

I also had somewhat blurred boundaries on the two principle roles in which I interacted with these two child care centers, namely, as a researcher (the 'watcher' according to several children) and a student teacher supervisor. An advantage of this dual role was that it enabled me to spend at least one and often two days per week at each center. It also provided further data, in that I often combined notes for the student teacher with notes related to my dissertation. I particularly enjoyed the days in which my role was a bit less ambiguous — the days when I came as participant-observer doing research. During these visits I informally interviewed children and felt more receptive to many types of relevant data — on peer interactions and formal and informal curriculum related to race, culture, exceptionality, gender, and language.

Another issue, which I return to later in the chapter, concerns the degree to which this initial ethnographic study was collaborative with the teachers who were participants in the study. I recall that, although my relationships with teachers in the study were quite good, I vowed to work to make any future ethnographic studies which I might undertake more genuinely collaborative. That is, I did not want to approach another setting or group of teachers, for example, with *a priori* research questions and well developed research design (or title of the study). Indeed, once I had identified another likely site and met a teacher who was open to collaborating on a qualitative study, we negotiated a mutually beneficial design. Specifically, my teacher-collaborator (Dorothy Piekielek Habecker) wanted to have a videotape produced which captured the essence of the consensus decision-making process with children at her Friends School and I was anxious to attempt video ethnography (see Swadener and Piekielek, 1992).

Feminist Perspectives and Alliance Building

Across these varied experiences, I have drawn upon feminist and social justice values which date back to my 'coming of age' in the late 1960s and early 1970s and taking several women's studies courses in college. Among the values which have been most salient in my social policy and child advocacy work have been an ethic of care, the need to engage in authentic collaboration, and a tendency to constantly interrogate the multiple parallel oppressions apparent in much of the discourse, policy-making, and programming for young children and their families. For example, I do not believe in a hierarchy of oppressions (Lorde, 1983), but feel that as a feminist I must constantly be aware of not only sexism, but heterosexism, racism, classism, ageism, ableism, anti-Semitism, and other forms of oppression.

As bell hooks discusses in *Teaching to Transgress* (1994) and other writings, women's studies and much of the earlier work done on feminist pedagogy has been dominated by white, middle class women and often unwelcoming to the voices and perspectives of women of color, whose work was seen more in terms of Black Studies than feminist studies. It disturbs, though doesn't surprise, me that in the mid-1990s, this pattern of exclusion persists in many contexts. I am troubled when women of color who are graduate students express feeling marginalized in courses on 'feminism' and when syllabi in women's studies courses still include few if any contributions of writers of color.

One area in which I have tried to remain active as an academic has been in alliance building work with women colleagues. My work in this area has been greatly influenced by my friendship and many collaborative activities with Mary Smith Arnold (see Arnold and Swadener, 1993) and with Mara Sapon-Shevin (through shared interests in full inclusion, alliance-building, and participation together in symposia on anti-Semitism in higher education at AERA). Mary was among the founders of the Iowa City Women Against Racism Committee and I met her when we both joined the Kent State faculty in 1989. We, in turn, were among the founders of an Institute for Education that is multicultural, a university-community collaborative school change project working with Akron and Cleveland schools.

Our Kent State Institute team included six women, comprised of three African-American and three European-American colleagues from several disciplines and three departments. It became clear to me that even in this bi-racial group of professional colleagues many of our differences and world views were framed as challenges to our collaboration — particularly ideological, theoretical, and at times, personal ones (e.g., disagreements on the degree to which an anti-oppression framework was needed for multicultural education). A number of issues were raised in the wake of our explorations of what it meant to collaborate across several differences and affinity groups (e.g., race, culture, class, religion, academic discipline, etc.). Although we were careful to team up with interracial teams for our major school consultations (i.e., each of the participating schools had two university liaisons), we neglected to balance the grant-writing team racially. When we sought local foundation funding, it became clear that sending two white women likely conveyed the 'wrong' message to potential funders. Looking back, we also involved the school teams in less than fully collaborative ways, with much of the planning being done exclusively by our university team.

There were also disagreements concerning how much time should be spent on 'process' issues, how deep our interpersonal work should go, and how much responsibility each team member should have. We were literally experiencing the tension between Eurocentric and Afrocentric world views, mediated by differing disciplines, theoretical assumptions, personalities, and work styles. We persisted, however, sometimes tape recording our lengthy dialogues and presenting (e.g., at Bergamo) — though never publishing collectively, as I had so hoped we would — our insights and stories. During these years, much of my attention as a researcher was captured by both the multicultural school reform efforts we were part of, as well as the dynamics of our university group. I yearned to be part of a research and school change team which reflected further diversity (e.g., in sexual orientation, linguistic and cultural diversity, and country of origin), and to be involved in a more authentically collaborative project with schools and teachers.

Since 1991, Mary Arnold and I have co-facilitated over 80 'unlearning oppression' workshops for diverse community, school, and university groups. We both believe that this is work which must be lived every day, and our strong ally relationship has enabled us to continue to explore the complexities of building feminist community across many kinds of difference. One of the assumptions of this model is that 'we all stand in the shoes of both targets and perpetrators of oppression'. I have tried to bring this assumption into not both my daily life and into the framing of research questions and my participation in various collaborations. In other words, interrogating unearned privilege allows one to notice arenas in which one has the greatest strength or potential power as an ally. For example, whether on college and university tenure or promotion committees, or other advisory and policy-setting bodies, I have tended to ask 'Who is not at the table?' and 'How might their interests be better represented?' Conversely, knowing that I am not only a perpetrator (often through collusion, typically silence), but also a target of oppression has assisted me in noticing ways in which I have internalized oppression (e.g., taken in myths based on sexism or classism). I have also shared this framework with most of the classes I teach, and Mary and I have visited each other's classes to co-facilitate the unlearning oppression workshop. We have both found that putting our assumptions 'up front' in the classroom context provides critical context for students and a scaffolding upon which to relate many discussions and reframing of issues in our respective fields of counseling and education.

In an attempt to expand the diversity of women involved in alliance-building work locally, we started a group called 'In the Company of My Sisters', which meets bi-weekly to examine how oppression operates in our daily lives and how we can become stronger allies and more effectively interrupt racism, sexism, heterosexism, anti-Semitism, classism, ageism, and other forms of oppression. Our best discussions, in my opinion, have been when more differences were represented in the group — talking across and among race, sexual orientation, religious beliefs, class backgrounds, age and first language. Although this is not part of any formal research agenda, such regular discussions have formed another context in which to interrogate privilege, difference, power relations, and opportunities to form alliances across difference. My 16-year-old daughter has become active in this group, and frequently brings in examples of racism, heterosexism and classism from her high school experiences. She is forming strong alliances with a recently retired union activist and a lesbian mother — relationships which she would likely not have formed outside such a place of 'intentional community'.

In terms of research, several doctoral students in education and counseling professions are part of this women's group and their dissertations clearly reflect 'research as praxis' and unlearning oppression themes. For example, one dissertation is examining the life histories of Head Start teachers who were initially parents in the program and have been with Head Start for 15–26 years, and most of whom are women of color (Jagielo, 1995). Issues of gender, class, and race are interwoven in the women's stories of their lives inside and outside of Head Start. Another dissertation (Haley-Banez, 1996) is examining narratives of lesbian couples in long-term, committed relationships, including women from different race and class backgrounds and couples with their own children. This study examines the strengths and complexities of these long-term relationships and is being actively co-constructed with the participants. It is also transcending the tendency in previous studies to look only at white, privileged women. The group has served as a source of support, guidance, and listening for such research projects. In multicultural feminist alliance building, boundaries between our personal and professional lives are constantly blurred, as other boundaries are bridged.

In another aspect of my 'university life', I have been active in my faculty union (AAUP) and chair of Committee W, which is currently working with the Department of Labor on a gender-based discrimination complaint regarding compensation and promotion of women at Kent State. I have been active in governance, serving on department, college and university advisory bodies and have done 'unlearning oppression' workshops in many colleagues' classes and with colleagues on a few occasions. Thus, research as praxis may also mean using statistical analyses to document gender discrimination in the workplace.

Toward Authentically Collaborative Research in Early Childhood Settings

> Much of qualitative research has reproduced, if contradiction-filled, a colonizing discourse of the 'Other'. (Fine, 1994)

For the past 10 years, my research has emphasized long-term collaborative inquiry with early childhood teachers. While in Pennsylvania, I worked with Dorothy Piekelek in an extended (three year) video ethnography of social justice and conflict management in a Friends (Quaker) primary school, and in Ohio I collaborated with Monica Miller Marsh in a case study of her implementation of anti-bias curriculum and pedagogy in an urban public kindergarten. Both of these qualitative studies involved intensive collaboration within a feminist, action research framework and all presentations and publications have been either co-authored or authored by the teacher-researchers involved (e.g., Marsh, 1992; Swadener and Piekielek, 1992; Swadener and Marsh, 1995).

As Monica Marsh and I have argued recently (Swadener and Marsh, 1998), an irony of much of the research in our field is that groups which are often 'othered' by early childhood researchers include both children and teachers. We are concerned about the 'ventriloquy' which some ethnographers have engaged in, as we are about the often 'colonizing discourse of the Other' (Fine, 1994). I share with Monica and Dorothy the belief that authentically co-constructed research, in which early childhood educators are directly involved in each step of the research process, is one way to move the teacher's and often the children's voices from the margins to the center (hooks, 1984) of qualitative inquiry and discourse.

Monica and I met when she was exploring options for her master's thesis research on multicultural education in early childhood, and I suggested a teacher-researcher collaborative study or action research design, documenting Monica's implementation of the anti-bias curriculum (Derman-Sparks, 1989) in her kindergarten classroom. This led to a two-year collaborative case study, the first year of which culminated in Monica's thesis. Our more recent collaborative work has included co-authoring papers and chapters and participating together in an early childhood project in Kenya. Monica has now completed her doctorate in my former department and we are in frequent communication. She is teaching courses which I teach and we often exchange ideas, recommend readings to each other, and provide mutual support.

Thus, our intertwining interests and collaborative projects continue to flourish, even as we find ourselves in different states — and countries. Our relationship, as colleagues, researchers, and friends is indeed an ally relationship; mutually beneficial, dynamic, and enduring, and provides an example of the possibilities for authentic collaboration in educational research. We have worked to mediate and deconstruct power issues, have sought to be candid with each other, and have also discussed our findings and perspectives with colleagues who contribute life experiences and cultural backgrounds difference from our own (e.g., Swadener, Cahill, Marsh and Arnold, 1995).

I have conducted four qualitative studies in early childhood settings, with data collection ranging from one to three years in length. My research over the past decade has consistently emphasized documentation of culturally sensitive, inclusive, and socially responsible teaching practices and curricula in early childhood settings. I have actively sought to avoid 'teacher bashing' and 'parent bashing', and have also had to be aware of potential 'halo effects' of my positive regard for many of the programs and teachers I have 'studied'. What has changed over the course of these studies has been the way in which I have approached the research and have positioned myself in the work. I have consciously sought to move away from the position of researcher studying 'subjects' who were often 'objectified' or reduced to my descriptions of them and my meaning-making of their activities and interactions, and have moved toward an increasingly collaborative partnership with the participants, particularly the teacher(s). Put another way, I have moved from the 'foreground' of my research, as the primary interpreter and narrator of stories from 'my data', to a position in the background or women into the far more complex and intertextual tapestry of collaborative work, in which the teacher-researcher's voice has replaced mine at the foreground of narration.

Other ethical issues and dilemmas I have faced include questions regarding the degree to which earlier ethnographic work emphasized my voice as a researcher, and to what degree full or authentic collaboration with early childhood educators is possible, in terms of differential incentives for conducting and disseminating research, different priorities for time, energy, and questions for collaboration between teachers and university researchers (Swadener and Marsh, 1996). In one case, the collaborative production of a videotape was more relevant to my teacher-researcher colleague (Dorothy) than making presentations to research-oriented audiences at national conference or publishing in 'scholarly' journals, although we did all these things collaboratively (Swadener and Piekielek, 1992). In this case, the idea of producing a video, and making videotapes of classroom activities available to teachers, was part of our initial 'negotiation' of the collaborative study.

I continue to learn from collaborative experiences, and share a vision with many of my collaborators of far more teacher and student voice in research, the active co-construction and negotiation of meaning and shared writing of interpretive accounts which are multivocal and avoid essentializing descriptions of early childhood settings and contexts. As the life worlds of teachers and university researchers come closer together and form relationships based on intersecting needs and interests, listening, mutual respect, honesty, and openness to change will contribute to research projects which benefit not only teachers and university researchers, but most importantly, children.

Most recently, my collaborative work has been cross-cultural, working directly with Kenyan colleagues in conceptualizing and carrying out a study of changing child-rearing issues and parent and community involvement in early childhood programs. This study utilized interviews with over 460 parents, teachers, grandparents, older siblings of young children, community leaders, and professionals working with families, as well as micro-ethnographic observations in differing child care and community contexts. In each of eight districts of the study I worked with at least two local colleagues and all interviews were conducted by the three of us — with one collaborator asking the questions in the participants' mother tongue and another translating their discussion so that I could be more actively involved.

Following my visits to each district, I transcribed the interviews, typed my field notes and shared both with the local collaborators for checks of accuracy and for their initial interpretations. Local collaborators were also involved in refining and piloting all the interview protocols before we began data collection. At the national level, I continue to work with two collaborating colleagues who also read the transcripts and provided feedback on my initial interpretations of the data. Thus, my collaborative research 'model' has now expanded to include cross-cultural, multilingual, and multiple levels of collaboration.

In my work in Kenya, earlier work in Senegal and The Gambia and recent work in South Africa and Greece, the need to de-colonize assumptions and keep noticing my positions of privilege and power, as well as 'outsider' status has been critical. I have been reminded of Foucault's (1980) discussion of the 'politics of the gaze' and bell hooks' essays on *Race and Representation* (hooks, 1991). I continue to search for examples of cross-cultural researchers who 'write against the grain', (e.g., Tsing, 1993), co-author work with indigenous colleagues, and attempt to enter into authentically collaborative work with insiders of cultures of 'interest'. I have found Faye Harrison's edited volume and writing on 'decolonizing anthropology' (and Richard Feinberg's writing about the ethics of anthropological field work) helpful for my international work, in parallel ways to Michelle Fine's (e.g., Fine, 1992, 1994) influence on my work in the United States. Issues of agency, appropriate representation, and 'othering' continue to be the subject of my thinking, discussion with colleagues, and writing.

In many ways this most recent collaborative research process has felt authentic and the power relations equitable or reciprocal. In other aspects, however, I remain the out-sider, the visiting research, and the privileged 'Mzungu' (white person/foreigner). Other issues, such as the degree to which local collaborators wished to be involved in the data analysis, or how to best include them in writing the final report and disseminating our findings persist.

Social Policy: Equity Issues in Early Childhood Contexts

> More attention must be paid to the linkages between those who suffer and those who care, so that caring becomes a committed advocacy, so that a concrete praxis may emerge. (Polakow, 1993, p. 183)

One of my intents in recent work (Swadener, 1995; Swadener and Jagielo, 1998) is to re-gender discussions of social policy as they apply to issues facing young children and their families in the United States. In recent analyses of social and educational policies affecting children and families (e.g., Arnold and Swadener, 1993; Swadener and Lubeck, 1995; Swadener, 1995), I have sought to deconstruct many of the 'common sense assumptions' (Reed, 1992) about such widely accepted labels and constructs as children and families 'at risk'. This commitment comes, in part, from a feminist ethic which supports listening carefully to (and taking seriously) what members of groups targeted for deficit labels are saying about such pathologizing descriptions and their implicit assumptions about the likelihood of failure. When applied to families, the category of single mothers, particularly low income women of color, has been a frequent target for this deficit framing and has been analyzed by several researchers employing a feminist perspective (e.g., Arnold, 1995; Cook and Fine, 1995; Polakow, 1993; and Weis, 1995). Internationally, some of the 'at risk' rhetoric is being replaced with the phrase 'children in difficult circumstances', which emphasizes the degree to which many contextual and environmental factors contribute to children's problems. My volunteer work during 1994–6 with street children in Nairobi, Kenya reinforced the extremely difficult circum-stances facing growing numbers of single mothers and young children internationally. Yet, my work with a self-help group comprised of mothers with one or more children on the street reinforced my 'at promise' perspective.

As Valerie Polakow and I have discussed (Polakow and Swadener, 1993), it may be privilege which is 'at risk' in America, and without a more thorough interrogation of privilege, the savage distributions in our stratified society and education system will only get worse. This was particularly obvious when deep cuts in social program spend-ing were paired, in several proposed budget bills, with large tax breaks for the highest income Americans. One of the difficult issues of social policy and early childhood, from a feminist and ally perspective, is the distance between the life experience of those setting policies affecting children and families and the life experiences of children and families who are the 'target' of such social intervention, regulation, and, recently, deep budget cuts. Whether watching debates on welfare reform, or analyzing the rhetoric of the 'Contract with America' and many presidential candidates, the degree of othering and judgmental or punitive tone is difficult to mistake for anything other than an instrumental discourse which, ironically, both perpetuates and condemns dependency.

The language of deficiency, whether applied to parenting, academic potential, preparation for success in school, or health-related factors is pervasive in public policy discourses concerning young children and their families. In calling for an 'at promise' view of *all* children and families, my colleagues and I (Swadener and Niles, 1991; Swadener and Lubeck, 1995) have not been attempting to play a semantic substitution game of trading the at-risk label for an 'at promise' one. Rather, we would encourage everyone working with children and families to view all children as 'at promise' and to concentrate valuable energies on building on these strengths, while addressing the many structural and environmental factors which have been argued to place many children 'at risk'. We feel that fields related to early childhood should move beyond the persistent tendency to pathologize the poor (Polakow, 1993) and construct children in poverty and their mothers as an urban (or rural) 'other'. Such othering is inconsistent with a more inclusive feminist perspective, which has an explicit political project of naming exclusions and oppressions and addressing these inequities while advocating for and with families with young children.

Early childhood social policy questions in the United States have not been universal, existential questions (e.g., 'What are the rights of *all* children and families in the United States?') but have been particularized and pragmatic (e.g., 'How can we get low income women to stop having so many children?' or 'How can we get mothers now on public assistance into the labor force?'). Grubb and Lazerson (1982), Polakow (1993), Swadener (1995), and Wrigley (1991) have argued that the US child care and early education 'system' has always been two-tiered, or stratified and caste-like. In the past, day nurseries, which were a form of welfare that existed as little more than custodial care facilities, served poor working mothers, while nursery schools existed for the middle class. This dual market of formal group care is perpetuated as '[p]roposals for child care reform and expansion often assume continued segregation' (Wrigley, 1991, p. 190). If, instead of blaming the victim, the choice is made to look to economic and societal forces that the powerful can control, one is compelled to wonder to whose benefit it is for groups of people in the US to be forced to live in poverty (Swadener, 1995).

The 'Scholarship of Teaching' and Anti-bias Pedagogy

After many years of volunteer work with different anti-poverty and child advocacy groups, I was delighted for the opportunity to teach social policy and help develop a graduate concentration in this area within Early Childhood Education at Kent State. I have also tried to emphasize the personal as political in all my courses, particularly Home–School–Community Relations and Social Studies/Expressive Arts. In my social policy seminar, a major goal has been to cut through the often deeply entrenched belief that individuals cannot make a difference in matters of policy. Through writing letters to the editor and elected officials, learning 'laser talks', a technology borrowed with full credit from the anti-hunger citizens' lobby group RESULTS (Harris, 1994), media workshops, and a combination of existential and instrumental readings (including both CDF reports and books such as *Lives on the Edge*). We spend time discussing ways to 'heal the break between people and government' (Harris, 1994) and participants work on various community-based projects (e.g., volunteering in programs for homeless families, working to get local referenda benefiting children passed, interviewing community activists and opinion shapers, etc.). I do shorter versions of this in workshops for community-based groups, including parents and early childhood professionals, and often include an 'action' (e.g., writing a letter) as part of the workshop. I am currently collaborating with colleagues in two other states to study long-term impacts of welfare 'reform' on families with young children.

In Home–School–Community Relations, participants do a family tree/oral history or legacy interview, a community-based project, popular media analysis, read fiction and autobiographies, and a variety of in-class structured experiences which often have an underlying theme of the 'personal as political'. This theme, in my opinion, is critical to teachers' and future teachers' understanding of some of the complexities of working across an array of differences between home, community and school or child care setting. This course empowers political awareness and advocacy, but in a more gentle, caring way. If my social policy seminar sometimes takes a more 'in your face' view of the plight, yet promise, of children and families, Home–School–Community Relations is far more subtle, as we deconstruct icons, myths, and social/cultural constructions of 'family', 'education', and labels for some children (e.g., 'at risk'). I find that this course has far more reality and 'power' when it is taken concurrently with a six credit course which includes an urban field experience.

That course, which I have team-taught with Mary Louise Holly for the past six years, combines social studies (i.e., anti-bias, culturally inclusive curriculum) and the expressive arts. This course looks more at the social and political lives of children in various contexts — particularly in the early primary years. After participants work together on a curriculum development project, culminating in a workshop which uses hands-on experiences to explore different cultures in ways which (usually) avoid 'tourist curriculum' (Derman-Sparks, 1989); we spend the second half of the semester in an urban, predominately African-American school. Through teaching an integrated, multicultural unit and facilitating an array of arts experiences, participants begin to grapple with day-to-day politics of the school and 'life in classrooms'. They also complete a curriculum critique assignment, which complements a discussion of the hidden curriculum and related policy and praxis issues. Thus, although a 'methods course', this six credit experience can also be described in terms of child advocacy.

Among the challenges of this field-based course is the issue of preparing students for the urban field experience and working to avoid 'tourist curriculum' in the curriculum development projects involved in the course. Student resistance to some of the issues emphasized in this integrated course has also been a factor across the history of the course. The school which has evolved into our principle field experience site is one which operates as an academy (i.e., with school uniforms, emphasis on a strict code of discipline, and active preparation of children to take high stakes proficiency tests). The school serves a diverse population, with approximately 75 per cent of the students children of color and 98 per cent of the children falling below the federal poverty level. Our students generally see the 'promise' in the students they work with, even in the fact of the rhetoric of 'risk' which they frequently here from the school principal and many of the teachers.

Our early childhood majors are also part of a program emphasizing constructivist teaching and learning and are very resistant to the amount of structure and strict disciplinary environment of this urban public school academy. I have struggled to find readings and facilitate discussions which can tease apart the complex issues which this placement raises for our predominantly white, often rural or suburban background students. Students are initially fearful and feel underprepared, but find they have many resources to draw from — most obviously the children's engagement and enthusiasm for their activities. I have drawn from the work of Lisa Delpit, Gloria Ladson-Billings, and recently used *Rethinking Our Classrooms*, a publication of *Rethinking Schools* (a progressive newspaper for and by teachers, published in Milwaukee). By the end of the semester, students are often extremely critical of the school and many of the teachers, but are quite attached to the children and note the difference they feel their anti-bias, hands-on units have made in the children's school lives. It is clear that some now feel they've 'served their time' in an urban school and will try to avoid similar experiences in the future. Others come to me and inquire about changing their student teaching placement to one of the districts where I routinely supervise students teachers (i.e., in Cleveland or Cleveland Heights Public Schools). I currently co-direct a more comprehensive Urban Initiative in Teacher Education involving intense collaboration with Urban teachers, service learning, and a cohort of preservice teachers.

My community-based advocacy activities are beyond the scope of this chapter to discuss, but have included serving on many boards, providing leadership to volunteer organizations, writing guest editorials, and organizing press conferences, candlelight vigils, and public awareness events related to children's issues (e.g., the World Summit for Children in 1990 and Stand for Children in Washington, DC in 1996). I have sought to combine my avocation — advocacy — with my profession, as I have done more policy-related research and writing in recent years. I have observed the power of a few, committed citizens (to paraphrase Margaret Mead) to change policy, and have more frequently experienced the frustration of working in a context in which the 'center' keeps moving further and further to 'the right', and the discourse becomes increasingly one of blaming and pathologizing the poor, while further privileging the wealthy. This is precisely the time when it is dangerous to become too cynical to stay actively involved.

Closing Reflections and Vision of the Future

In conclusion, I am hopeful that some of the previous examples and issues raised will prove helpful for other colleagues who are engaged in multicultural research — in its most inclusive sense. The life of a university researcher and teacher is a privileged one, indeed, although one of hard work and often difficult choices. My choices have been facilitated by supportive family, friends, students, and colleagues. At times my choices have caused my work to be labeled as 'more advocacy than research', or 'too political' (read: 'politically correct'). My dialectical journey as a researcher is intertwined with my experiences as an ally and activist, as well as partner and mother. I feel particularly fortunate to have had opportunities, in different states and national contexts, to connect with research collaborators who share a deep commitment to children and families and who are willing to allow an outsider to enter their classrooms, lives, and cultural contexts. When I teach qualitative methods, I emphasize the importance of moving toward more authentic collaboration in educational research, while discussing the complexities of 'walking the talk' of collaboration.

One of the most difficult aspects of true collaboration can be one's loss of control. For those of us with certain amounts of power and privilege, learning to listen, slow down/be patient when needed, move faster/keep up when needed, or otherwise adjust our personal preferences and habits and cultural assumptions to the patterns, perspectives and wishes of our collaborators and research participants is a challenge, indeed.

Self-interrogation is a good habit to form, both as an ally and as a researcher. I do not advocate a self-obsessed, guilt-ridden form of self-interrogation, but one which asks questions such as, 'How can I be a stronger ally?', 'How are various unearned privileges operating in the dynamics of this research and how can they be minimized?', and 'What is the most culturally inclusive approach this research might take?' Being open to feedback from multiple perspectives, as well as willing to give feedback when asked, and sharing the work [and credit] of writing, re-writing, and disseminating the research all move us closer to a 'research as praxis' which helps unravel multiple oppressions while pursuing a liberatory vision for the future.

References

ARNOLD, M.S. (1995) 'African-American families "at promise"', in SWADENER, B.B. and LUBECK, S. (eds) *Children and Families 'at promise': Deconstructing the Discourse of Risk*, Albany, NY: State University of New York Press.

ARNOLD, M.S. and SWADENER, B.B. (1993) 'Savage inequalities and the discourse of risk: What of the white children who have so much green grass?', *The Review of Education*, **15**, pp. 261–72.

COOK, D.A. and FINE, M. (1995) 'Motherwit: Childrearing lessons from African-American mothers of low income', in SWADENER, B.B. and LUBECK, S. (eds) *Children and Families 'at Promise'*, Albany, NY: State University of New York Press.

DELGADO-GAITAN, C. (1993) 'Researching change and changing the researcher', *Harvard Educational Review*, **63**, 4, pp. 389–411.

DELPIT, L. (1995) *Other People's Children: Cultural Conflict in the Classroom*, New York: The New Press.

DERMAN-SPARKS, L. (1989) *Anti-bias Curriculum: Tools for Empowering Young Children*, Washington, DC: National Association for the Education of Young Children.

DONALDSON, L.E. (1992) *Decolonizing Feminisms: Race, Gender and Empire Building*, Chapel Hill, NC: The University of North Carolina Press.

ELLSWORTU, E. (1989) 'Why doesn't this feel empowering? Working through the repressive myths of critical pedagogy', *Harvard Education Review*, **59**, pp. 297–324.

FINE, M. (1992) *Disruptive Voices: The Possibilities of Feminist Research*, Ann Arbor: University of Michigan Press.

FINE, M. (1994) *Working the Hyphens: Reinventing Self and Other in Qualitative Research*, in DENZIN, N.K. and LINCOLN, Y.S. (eds) *Handbook on Qualitative Research*, Thousand Oaks, CA: Sage Publications, Inc.

FOUCAULT, M. (1980) *Power/knowledge: Selected Interviews and Other Writings, 1972–1977*, GORDON, C. (ed.) New York: Pantheon.

GRUBB, W.N. and LAZERSON, M. (1982) *Broken Promises: How Americans Fail Their Children*, New York: Basic Books.

HARRIS, S. (1994) *Reclaiming Our Democracy: Healing the Break Between People and Government*, Philadelphia: Camino.

HARRISON, F.V. (1991) *Decolonizing Anthropology: Moving Further Toward an Anthropology for Liberation*, Washington, DC: Association of Black Anthropologists.

HALEY-BANEZ, L. (1996) 'Lesbian couples' narratives: A case study', Kent, OH: Unpublished dissertation proposal, Kent State University.

hooks, b. (1984) *Feminist Theory: From Margin to Center*, Boston: South End Press.

hooks, b. (1991) *Race and Representation*, Boston: South End Press.

hooks, b. (1994) *Teaching to Transgress: Education As the Practice of Freedom*, New York: Routledge.

JAGIELO, L.M. (1995) 'Female Head Start teachers' perceptions of the influence of their life experiences upon their professional pedagogy', Kent, OH: Unpublished dissertation proposal, Kent State University.

JIPSON, J. and HAUSER, M. (eds) (1998) *Intersections: Feminisms and Early Childhood*, New York: Peter Lang.

KESSLER, S.A. and SWADENER, B.B. (eds) (1992) *Reconceptualizing the Early Childhood Curriculum: Beginning the Dialogue*, New York: Teachers College Press.

LADSON-BILLINGS, G. (1995) *Dreamkeepers: Successful Teachers of African-American Children*, San Francisco: Jossey-Bass Publishers.

LATHER, P. (1991) *Getting Smart: Feminist Research and Pedagogy with/in the Postmodern*, New York: Routledge.

LEVINE, D., LOWE, R., PETERSON, B. and TENORIA, R. (1995) *Rethinking Schools: An agenda for change*, New York: The New Press.

LORDE A. (1983) 'The master's tools will never dismantle the master's house', in MORAGA, C. and ANZALDUA, G. (eds) *This Bridge Called My Back: Writings of Radical Women of Color*, New York: Kitchen Table Press.

MARSH, M.M. (1992) 'Implementing anti-bias curriculum in the kindergarten', in KESSLER, S. and SWADENER, B.B. (eds) *Reconceptualizing the Early Childhood Curriculum: Beginning the Dialogue*, New York: Teachers College Press.

POLAKOW, V. (1993) *Lives on the Edge: Single Mothers and Their Children in the other America*, Chicago: University of Chicago Press.

POLAKOW, V. and SWADENER, B.B. (1993, September) *Savage Distributions: Privilege at Risk?*, Paper presented at the Third Annual Reconceptualizing Early Childhood Research and Practice Conference, Ann Arbor, Michigan.

SWADENER, E.B. (1986) 'Implementation of education that is multicultural in early childhood settings: A case study of two day care programs', Madison, WI: Unpublished doctoral dissertation.

SWADENER, B.B. (1995) 'Stratification in early childhood social policy and programs in the United States: Historical and contemporary manifestations', *Educational Policy*, **19**, 4, pp. 404–25.

SWADENER, B.B., CAHILL, B., MARSH, M.M. and ARNOLD, M.S. (1995) 'Cultural and gender identity in early childhood: Anti-bias, culturally inclusive pedagogy with young learners', in GRANT, C.A. (ed.) *Educating for Diversity: An Anthology of Multicultural Voices*, Boston: Allyn and Bacon, pp. 381–404.

SWADENER, B.B. and JAGIELO, L.M. (1997) 'Politics at the margins: Feminist perspectives on early childhood social policy and programs', in JIPSON, J. and HAUSER, M. (eds) *Intersections: Feminisms and Early Childhood*, New York: Peter Lang.

SWADENER, B.B. and LUBECK, S. (1995) *Children and Families 'at promise': Deconstructing the Discourse of Risk*, Albany, NY: State University of New York Press.

SWADENER, B.B. and MARSH, M.M. (1995) 'Toward a stronger teacher voice in research: A collaborative study of antibias early education', in HATCH, J.A. (ed.) *Qualitative Studies in Early Childhood Settings*, Westport, CN: Praeger.

SWADENER, B.B. and MARSH, M.M. (1996), 'Reflections on collaborative, and not-so-collaborative, research in early childhood settings', in demarrais, K.B. (ed.) *Reflections on Our Process: Qualitative Research Methods and Ethics*, St Martin's Press.

SWADENER, B.B. and PIEKIELEK, D. (1992) 'Beyond democracy: Consensus decision-making in a friends elementary schools', in KESSLER, S. and SWADENER, B.B. (eds) *Reconceptualizing the Early Childhood Curriculum.*

SWADENER, B.B. and NILES, K. (1991) 'Children and families "at promise": Making home–school–community connections', *Democracy and Education*, **5**, 3, pp. 13–18.

TSING, A.L. (1993) *In the Realm of the Diamond Queen: Marginality in an Out-of-the-Way Place.* Princeton, NJ: Princeton University Press.

WEIS, L. (1995, November) *Intended Use of Ethnographic Data in Policy and Practice: Focusing on White and African-American Low-income Women*, Paper presented at the annual meeting of the American Anthropological Association, Washington, DC.

WRIGLEY, J. (1991) 'Different care for different kids: Social class and child care policy', in WEIS, L., ALTBACH, P.G., KELLY, G.P. and PETRIE, H.G. (eds) *Critical Perspectives on Early Childhood Education*, Albany, NY: State University of New York Press, pp. 189–209.

17　Stumbling Toward Knowledge: Enacting and Embodying Qualitative Research

Becky Ropers-Huilman and Beth Graue

Picture two women walking into a train station, each with her suitcase packed in perfect order. They are engaged in conversation, yet external events unbeknownst to their fellow travelers also flood their thoughts. Their intellectual reading material is tucked purposefully in a side compartment for easy access on this journey, while their under-garments and personal journals are hidden safely away. These women have purchased their tickets months in advance and are taking sure and deliberate strides toward their assigned train. As they walk, though, the train that they were to board begins pulling away from the station. They make a feeble attempt to catch it, but a latch on one suit-case springs open to reveal what was inside. Temporarily dismayed, the women look at each other with questioning eyes for an understanding of how best to clean up that which has sprung open before them and disrupted their order. They realize that neither has a fool-proof answer.

In the Spring of 1995, we became part of an experience in which we both engaged with qualitative research, Beth as a teacher of qualitative research methods and Becky as a qualitative researcher of Beth's teaching. In many ways, we felt that we had a designated train on which we were to travel. We knew what it meant to engage in learning and teaching about research; indeed, we had traveled this route many times before. This time was different, though, and as we began to unpack our experiences, we found pieces of ourselves and our identities scattered on the ground before us and influencing our analysis. What was hidden at the bottom of our traveling bags somehow ended up on the top of the pile. The techniques and strategies that we kept close for easy access were not readily useful.

Throughout this analysis, we propose that qualitative research is learning that comes out of relationships with others. We resist conceptualizing 'subjects' of research as clearly distinguishable from our own beings and interpretations. Meanings that come out of relationships between 'knowers' and 'known' are both flexible and partial as cultures, characteristics, beliefs, attitudes, and perspectives of those involved in know-ing relationships are in dynamic, rather than static, associations. Qualitative research, for us, became much more than data collection strategies or analytic procedures; rather, the ways we judge and interact with qualitative research were integrally related to and implicated by the identities that we brought to our experiences. We do not possess or build cumulative knowledge bases (Geertz, 1995); rather, our knowing is constantly shaped by dynamics of relationships embedded in historical and societal contexts (Lather, 1991).

In this essay, we explore some of the difficult and yet simultaneously useful aspects of enacting qualitative methods. In addition, we consider how teaching and learning in diverse settings both strengthens and problematizes the ways we learn about ourselves

and others. The experience we frame as the centerpiece of our analysis is both representative and unlike any other we have ever had. In what seemed like a simple situation of
one person doing qualitative research on another's teaching, roles shifted, perspectives
blurred, and our knowing took on social dimensions that we have come to realize are
intrinsic parts of qualitative research. These uneasy processes seemed increasingly important to our understandings of qualitative research as we puzzled over a very powerful
series of interactions in Beth's class and our subsequent efforts to understand those
events from methodological, theoretical, and pedagogical perspectives.

This experience reminds us of a fun house, with mirrors that frame images in
surprisingly different ways depending on our vantage points. Oftentimes, we came to
understand classroom events and participants in certain ways, only to be jarred into
different understandings as we looked at the multiple images of possibility that surrounded us. We begin by recounting our perceptions of this experience separately, to
remind both ourselves and the reader that our views of the events were anything but
singular.

Becky's Story

In Spring of 1995, I asked Beth if I could attend a session of her qualitative research
class as part of my dissertation research on feminist teaching. After agreeing on a date,
I had few qualms about attending because, although I was uncertain exactly what to
expect, I was to be an onlooker of her teaching — an observer who would hopefully
sink back into some unnoticeable place where my knowing practice could continue
unencumbered by those who I was researching. While this approach seemed odd and
ironic in some sense, it was one of the primary methodological genres that I had
encountered during my preparation to do research 'on' others. Enactment of qualitative
research, at that time, did not mean that I would have to perform such that others could
view or critique my actions. Nor were the interactions between our experiences and
perceptions a concern.

The class moved along much as did other classes that I had observed until the point
when Beth asked the class to break up into two groups, each one focusing on a specific
assigned text. I chose to stay for the entire time with the group who was discussing
Valerie Polakow's *Lives on the Edge* both because of my personal interest in the topic
and because of the ways that the discussion began to entangle those of us involved. As
group members settled into what I perceived to be a discussion mode, a white man in
the group asked who would like to facilitate. I wondered if his 'leadership' role in this
group was due to his whiteness, his maleness, or some other factor that I was unaware
of. After a pause, and a person or two encouraging him to act as facilitator, he began
with a general question, 'How did everyone feel about the work?'

Even when responding to this seemingly innocuous question, participants in the
discussion quickly seemed to draw lines around their territory, almost as if they were
anticipating a conflict. Polakow's methodological tenets came into question early in the
conversation and it seemed that persons braced themselves for opposition. The two
African-American students and several white students who physically flanked them
seemed intellectually pitted against the four Asian students and several white students.[1]
Questions began to spin for me. Did persons align themselves with positions, persons,
or identities? At what point, if any, did it get to be about identities? Intellectual work is
inherently tied up in struggles of identity, and our identities are never far beyond the

ideas we represent. The outcome of intellectual debates and discussions certainly does affect us personally. Was there a place for a reconciliation and a disruption of these identity questions in my qualitative research? A voice in the back of my mind wondered if my identity was not contributing to my discomfort as well.

Two incidents particularly captured for me the tensions I was witnessing as students tried both to learn how to know through qualitative research and make clear what they were willing to accept as 'quality' knowing. In one situation, an Asian woman made a statement about Polakow's work with which a white woman did not agree. As the white woman challenged her, a white man tried to paraphrase the original point by saying, 'What I think she meant was . . .' The white woman restated her challenge. Another white woman who was literally and figuratively between the two then said, 'Well, I think what she meant was . . .' The challenging white woman interrupted her and said quickly and strongly, 'Let her speak for herself. She has a brain. Otherwise she wouldn't be here.' The white woman who had started her sentence stopped, her face red, and didn't say anything else during the discussion. While it seemed to me that this white woman was trying to empower the Asian speaker to assert a space for her own words and interpretations, this attempt to empower at the same time stifled the speech of another participant. This act of attempted translation reminded me that we all translate our experiences in classrooms into a language that we understand from our own perspectives, whether we are teachers, students, or observers. I thought this was supposed to be a class where students learned about qualitative research, yet something more was being taught and learned through these interactions. I wondered how these interactions and students' diverse interpretations or readings of Polakow's research influenced the development of multicultural research practices.

An additional incident that highlighted tensions for me occurred near the end of the continued heated discussion about Polakow's use of the word 'resilence' to describe the women that she wrote about in her book. An Asian woman was having difficulty pronouncing the word, but understood it well enough to question Polakow's definition and how Polakow was justifying her use of that word. After several interchanges between this Asian woman and an African-American woman, where they disagreed on whether the term resilience was 'appropriately' applied in this case, the African-American woman said, 'Well, maybe this book wasn't written for people whose first language isn't English.' Although the Asian woman had been asserting herself strongly previously, she had no words to respond to that comment excluding her from creating or judging knowing based on this text. She remained silent throughout the rest of the conversation. My role as a researcher conflicted with my roles as a student and caretaker and, hopefully, a multicultural educator. I wanted to remain somewhat distanced from the research, yet I felt morally compelled to intervene. I looked around, hoping that someone else would feel equally compelled. I wondered what other students' roles and responsibilities at this point in the conversation should have been. Were they having the same identity conflicts that I was? Their actions were most certainly being guided by roles other than those inextricably linked to 'student' status. Could any of us have broken out of (or expanded) our roles to disrupt this silencing?

After the class, I left the room quickly, talking only briefly with Beth to set up a future time to discuss the class. My ideas were spinning outside the realms of what I had previously understood to be 'normal' researcher roles. My physical reactions to how students in this class were constructing their relationships with each other were telling me that how I was coming to know was not in a distanced, 'academic' fashion. The questions I was asking inside my head didn't have easy or certain answers — they were not even the questions that I had originally entered the room with. Although it was to have been my main focus, Beth's teaching wasn't in the forefront of my mind as I considered what I had learned from this class. Instead, other areas of interest were asserting their primacy. I was realizing that our actions silence and encourage others in ways that exist far beyond the boundaries of teacher, student, or researcher.

As a graduate student, I have been a participant in more classes than I am able to recall. I have remained silent through many of them. This class stirred thoughts for me and provoked an internal struggle about my place in silence and in silencing others' expressions of their knowing. I wondered how many of my other identity fragments I was willing to give up in order to meet the terms of being a qualitative researcher. Was there any way that I could retain a sanctity about what their synergy produced? Cultural struggles with others and within oneself are inevitable, I believe, in both the celebration of and discrimination against perceived others. Yet in education, as in life, we are all on a journey of knowing. While we regularly part paths with each other to explore other terrain, we walk alongside diverse others in a multicultural world, and that experience affects our processes of and approaches to knowing.

Beth's Story

When Becky asked to visit my class I felt caught in a terrible bind. I had never thought of myself as a feminist teacher but seeing myself as a feminist I was afraid to find out from a researcher that I wasn't. To make matters more uncomfortable, after a fair amount of experience as a qualitative researcher in classrooms, I did not relish the idea of being the object of study. The irony of feeling this discomfort in the context of teaching about qualitative research was not lost on me and I decided to use the opportunity to reflect on the complexity of the roles of researcher and participant in a more organized way. I think that this was the beginning of my interest in how qualitative research is connected to knowledge of self as well as knowledge of others.

I was anticipating intense discussion that week for a number of reasons. Students were reading their first book length qualitative work and I had chosen a couple of methodologically, theoretically, and emotionally challenging works to provoke discussion and to prompt individuals to examine their assumptions about research. The two pieces were Robin Lynn Leavitt's *Power and Emotion in Infant-toddler Day Care* (1994) and Valerie Polakow's *Lives on the Edge* (1993). Each strikes at very emotional-political issues — the quality of day care for young children and the state of the welfare system and its effects on women. In addition, these students seemed fairly polarized into two groups — those who embraced qualitative methods and philosophy and those who were skeptical about its rigor and validity. In previous discussions the skeptics had pushed hard for me to define terms, to distinguish standards in various genres of research and to prove the worth of interpretive work in ways that they could understand. I hoped that we would use the books to help students explore their assumptions about qualitative research, working collaboratively to begin to construct ideas about who they are as researchers.

The class began in much the same way as always, with an opening that focused on general questions and issues. I then asked groups of students to reflect on the qualities of qualitative research. I hoped that this would set us up to reflect on the distinctive characteristics of qualitative research for the focused discussion of the book. We broke into two groups and I moved back and forth between the two as they discussed.

Initially I sat in on the group that was discussing Leavitt's book. While I was physically present with this group, I could feel a tug to my attention by the other group. Perhaps this comes out of experience as a kindergarten teacher — the need to manage multiple activities at all times — but I was attuned to the developing drama of the Polakow discussion.

If we had been living in a cartoon, there would have been sparks flying from those discussing Polakow. The rumble of voices across the room had sharp edges and the body language shouted tension. I quietly moved to sit in on their discussion. I can't map what happened when, or even tell you what I observed. What I have are reactions to interactions that I may have been part of as well as others that were recounted to me later.

At one point, the discussion began to turn to what seemed to be an othering of welfare mothers — characterizing who they were by race and social class. The drift of the conversation was less than positive. For the most part, these portrayals were stereo-typical and contradicted Polakow's point — that women on welfare are a diverse group placed there by the priorities of US society. What was interesting was that the descriptions were constructed as common knowledge images framed from personal experience. The validity of Polakow's case was linked to word match with reader ideology/experience. This played out with two very vocal groups arguing the case explicitly or implicitly. A group of four women — two African-American and two white — articulated the pro-Polakow viewpoint. Five students were forcefully interrogating Polakow's case — one Asian man, two Asian women, a white man, and a white woman, pointing to issues of generalizability and political bias. The remaining students — four white women — did not voice particular sides in the argument but seemed to allow others to ventriloquate their ideas. At one point I thought it might help to have alternative data on the diversity of those on welfare. I went to my office to get statistics published in the *New York Times*.

Things hadn't eased when I got back to the group. While I didn't know what had happened while I was gone, the sparks were now full flames, yet strangely the temperature was as cold as ice. I tried to intellectualize the tension by writing themes that I had heard in discussion — always doing analysis.

Things stopped for me when I heard Chantha, a Taiwanese woman question Polakow's image of resilience as a descriptor of the women studied and as a sampling criterion.[2] She was struggling to make her point in English, wrestling with the interpretive case written in a language that was not her own, a paradigm that was unfamiliar, and a political system to which she was new. Sondra, an African-American woman, offered that perhaps this wasn't a book meant for people whose first language was not English. All conversation stopped. Chantha looked stunned. All I could do was suggest that it was time for a break. This moment has been one that I have replayed in my mind over and over and over again. I'm still at a loss for what I should have done and it's clear that others were affected as well.

This event had reverberations throughout the semester. During the break, students stopped me in the hall to talk about what had happened. After class and all the following week I talked with class members about what had transpired and what we needed to do next. Tonia, who had been ventriloquated earlier on by Matt wanted me to make an announcement in class that we could no longer have that kind of discussion — that we should talk about method not politics. A mid-term evaluation of the course by one student suggested the same. For some, method and politics were not to be considered in the same discussion, for others they were one and the same. The boundaries of method

— defined on a continuum that seemed anchored at two ends with technique and social action — were related to who these students were and how they viewed the world. Somehow I had gotten the relation mixed up. I thought that we would develop a notion of self as researcher as we explored particular genres of research. A self would come out of the process. But each person in that room came to the learning experience with identities that had complex and contradictory implications for their knowing. Their readings of research were framed by notions of self, other, race, ethnicity, gender, independence, science, and research. My understanding of the interactions we had around these ideas were shaped in equally complex ways.

As I reflect on this class I am particularly struck by the role of memory in the construction of meaning of events. My role in this situation was, at the time, as the teacher of a course on qualitative research. Given that role, I have pedagogically related memories of the interactions in the course. But given the nature of the interactions that day, there are fascinating splinters of other perspectives. There are Becky's field notes, which serve as a chronicle and as questions about the meaning of the process from someone who was, in many ways, positioned differently in relation to this experience. We have had numerous discussions about what happened that day so that is another splinter. I also had a number of conversations with students about this incident — in class, in my office, in formal evaluations, and their voices are present in my reconstruction of the event. I no longer have a sense of where ideas come from — what I have at this point is a stew of experience to which I add flavor.

> I slowly came to realize that within the ethnographer, many selves were at play . . .
> Hearing first one, then another, of these different selves, or types of consciousness, helped
> shape what I discovered and how I put my ideas together. (Thorne, 1993, pp. 11–12)

Embodying Qualitative Research

We all engaged with qualitative research in different ways in this experience — students as institutionally placed learners, Beth as the institutionally placed teacher, and Becky as the researcher of Beth's practices in her teaching. All of these roles placed certain expectations on us for our behavior. These expectations, though, were not always clear and, moreover, were not always consonant with other parts of identity roles that were we playing. Further, each of the roles that participants in this class played was deeply informed by relationships among participants and their perspectives on the ensuing interactions. In this section, we discuss how our identities affected our engagement with qualitative research.[3]

As the formal teacher in this interchange of ideas, Beth felt she had a responsibility to teach this group of graduate students to become qualitative researchers. Somehow, they were supposed to adopt an identity as a researcher and add it to the plethora of identity hooks on which they already hung their hats. We realized, though, that Beth's espoused beliefs about qualitative research in some ways contradicted her teaching practices that day. Beth believed that people's cultural orientations and identifications strongly affect their practices — the majority of her training has been related to ethnography, a subfield of qualitative research that characterizes itself by a strong attention to cultural norms and practices. Yet she was hoping for participants to engage with qualitative methods in a provocative way, but one which was primarily intellectual — no mess, no heat, no dirt (where this came from, she'd rather not know). She wanted them to do a situated reading but forgot that they came to class with years of experience that they were living out in front of her eyes. Because identities positioned them to view the world in particular ways, the cultural nature of their interpretations became a hot spot. Researcher identities are formed out of deeply held cultural values about what it means to know, how power operates socially, and status in a world where not all are seen as equal.

Through this experience, Beth also considered how her own identities affected her engagement with qualitative research. As we look back now, we question what Beth's role should have been in this culture clash. In some ways, Beth was attempting to engage students by letting them determine their own rules of engagement. And while that engagement may have been useful in many ways, it made her intervention nebulous. Beth's identity as a teacher may have pulled her to bring the conversation back to a discussion of methodology, yet the standards by which students were measuring both Polakow's and other students' judgments came out of culturally framed conceptions of method. Beth's identity as a white woman urged her to remain silent, letting what she perceived, in one case, to be conflict between two people of color resolve itself without imposition of her agenda. Her identity as a qualitative researcher led her to wonder what sense Becky was making out of this experience, and questioned how Becky was judging her performance as a teacher and as a feminist.

Becky's enactment of qualitative research was also composed within a quagmire of identity. The idea that enacting research is closely related to identities had certainly been an area of exploration for her as she prepared for a dissertation research experience. Readings of post-structural, feminist, and multicultural literature (Flax, 1993; Frye, 1992; Hooks, 1984; McLaren and Lankshear, 1993; Simonson and Walker, 1988) strongly affected her approaches to, and thoughts about, the possibilities for constructions of identities through educational interactions. Nevertheless, when Becky went in to observe Beth, she expected Beth to assume the leading role in this play of classroom interaction because of her teaching identity. Becky assumed that at Beth's request, students would split into their groups, have a 'nice', hopefully somewhat lively conversation, and then would return to their seats and report back to the rest of the class on what they had learned. As a student, Becky knew the routine and had grown, perhaps subconsciously, to expect it.[4] The way the conversation turned was unexpected for Becky as well, though. She did not anticipate the increasing dissonance among students and their eventual arrival at a brick wall which, at the time, no one was willing to climb.

Becky's research focuses largely on issues involved in feminist education. Through her work, she has already seen many examples of practices that would be considered to be outside the norm of university classroom teaching. Yet she was able to reconcile those experiences with a feminist approach to teaching, thereby establishing a new norm of what was characteristic (in her mind) in feminist classrooms. Nevertheless, she still fully expected that students would follow the implicit procedural handbook and would try to work at a reconciling of their views such that they could inform the rest of the class what they had learned. She knew how to research this and was comfortable within those parameters. Because of other identities that strongly inform her life choices and actions, though, she was not comfortable with her role as a researcher in the Polakow discussion. Becky's identities as a researcher and a student allowed her to claim a silence as she was not in charge of or responsible for what she was witnessing. Moreover, according to much of her research training, any interference in the natural course of events may have 'contaminated' the 'validity' of the research findings.[5] As a white woman, Becky realized that her position was privileged in many ways and yet struggled with the simultaneous knowledge that there are certain doors closed to her because of that status. The research conducted in this classroom became much more relational than originally intended, and the focus shifted from one where Becky examined Beth's teaching practice to a consideration of the mixture of identities and qualitative research approaches involved in the relationships among participants.

> I believe a unitary self is unnecessary, impossible, and a dangerous illusion. Only multiple subjects can invent ways to struggle against domination that will not merely recreate it (Flax, 1993, p. 93).

Re-mixing Our Roles

The sections above separated our perceptions of and roles in the enactment of qualitative research into our roles as a teacher and as a researcher. As hinted in the previous section, though, we realize that we have come to inform each other and shape each other's knowing of these experiences, just as we suggest that participants in any stage of qualitative research are affected by the relationships they establish within a context. Identities and relationships are continually fluid, and their presence affects the possibilities for interaction between them and for the knowing of others. Through a discussion that occurred in class the following week, we learned about some of those possibilities.

In the course of an interview about the events in this class, Beth asked Becky if she would come back to the class to share her field notes with the students. For many methodological reasons, they agreed that it may be a beneficial experience. Beth thought it would be important for both Becky and the students to have an experience of being on the other side of the 'field note fence'. For Becky, it could provide a chance to be the object of the scrutiny; and the students could feel the pressure of having their experience narrated by another. It would also allow students to see another field note format. Beth had always shared notes with research participants and it seemed to level the field a bit, equalizing the feeling of power disparity among the researcher and those who were being researched. Always the researcher and teacher, we further thought we could append another dimension to what the notes portrayed, adding more voices to a conversation that was already very rich.

In our conversations at the time, we agreed that our reasons for revisiting the experience were methodological and pedagogical. Yet, in reflections about our decision at a later time, we also realized that we were hoping to foster if not resolution, at least a thoughtful discussion around the conflicts that had occurred the week before. We hoped to open up a space for students to work with each other and with us to craft an environment that would be conducive to learning for the rest of the semester. Perhaps we were also looking for ways to expand the roles we enacted the week before. Our identities beyond those of researcher and teacher were beginning to assert their presence and claim a part of this evolving discourse.

Once in class, Beth passed out Becky's field notes and for several minutes students were silent as they read over Becky's interpretation of their actions and words the previous week. We then asked for any comments or thoughts students may have had about how they were portrayed in this set of field notes. Many of the initial questions were distantly methodological, such as 'Why did you format your notes in this way?' or 'How did you choose what to write or take note of?' The conversation took on a different tone, though, when students started talking more specifically about the *experience* of being an observer in their class and trying to make some sense out of Becky's process of knowing. For example, one student asked Becky if she was nervous coming back to the class to share her field notes. (The answer was quickly and definitively affirmative.) Another asked why she decided to talk about class participants using gender and racial referents. At a turning point in the discussion, Lynn, the student who had urged that others let Tonia 'speak for herself', looked away from both of us and literally faced the class. She asked what they as a class were going to do about the tensions described in the field notes. She appealed to the group that they use this as a positive experience to bring them together, rather than as one that had seemingly great potential to divide.

Lynn's words in this class demonstrated to us a complexity of engagement with/in qualitative research, and reminded us that while we were all positioned in certain ways based on our identities, experiences and relationships to or with each other, we each had a certain degree of agency to expand those constructions. Our positions informed, but did not entirely circumscribe, our knowing. Lynn tried to step out of her role as a 'student' and explore the possibilities that a broader engagement with qualitative research might offer. Through her words, she encouraged others in this relationship to do the same. We realized that none of the positions we took guaranteed certain experiences. Rather, the multiple interactions of classroom texts (persons, readings, events, situations) created experiences which were then viewed differently depending on situated and relational knowing.

Bringing the issues back to class the following week to discuss, we learned that we were coming from many different places and performing many different roles. These roles, or identities, were in dynamic relation to each other both within ourselves and between ourselves and the others in this experience. Peter McLaren and Colin Lankshear's (1993) words seem particularly relevant, 'Culture is best understood as a *terrain of contestation* that serves as a locus of multivalent practical and discursive structures and powers. Knowledge is construed as a form of discursive production' (p. 381). We were experiencing contested roles and expectations; and we were creating both knowledge and culture through those 'terrains of contestation'. We didn't reconcile the contested cultures and knowledge that we saw and enacted through this experience, as if they could be merged into one harmonious classroom culture once and for all. Instead, our perspectives about ourselves and the others in the class were broadened as we shared our perspectives and identities with each other.

We are not solitary what we think; we are full of voices (Young-Bruehl, 1988, p. 17).

Possibilities for Teaching, Learning, and Enacting Qualitative Research

We undertook this analysis with the hope that it would help us to make sense of our practices and ourselves as we interacted with/in the incident described above. Yet this sense-making process has certainly not been a fact-finding inquiry. In a provocative way, our intellectual discomfort with this incident remains and continues to trouble our thoughts. Within the context of teaching, learning and conducting qualitative research, we learned much about the relationships between identities and knowing. While we did not determine, nor were we seeking, correct answers to all the quandaries posed throughout this text, we have constructed several tentative understandings about our future teaching, learning, and researching from our reflections here.

We learned that techniques in research methodology have implications for practice that go far beyond measures of correct application. While some have posed a framework by which methodology, method, and epistemology can be tentatively separated (Harding,

1987), we believe that there are values and practices *linked to identities* that are inherent in each stage, or layer, of research.[6] Through multiple layers and their corresponding lenses, definitions of qualitative research became complicated, with increasingly blurred boundaries. In this incident, we were all playing roles as observers and observed — both objects and subjects of scrutiny. What did this inability to determine 'subject' and 'object' mean for the ways in which we were coming to know each other? Our backgrounds, positions, and assumptions about research informed our classroom involvement and strongly related to the 'knowing' we hoped to have of and with each other.

We learned that identities influenced readings of each other and of all texts that surround us. In this case, Beth hoped that readings of the assigned texts would expand students' conceptualizations of qualitative research and result in students' emergence closer to their researcher 'selves'. Instead, many students initially resisted the Polakow text or other students' interpretations because those expressions clashed with what was already understood to be acceptable or useful from the intersections of their identity or cultural standpoints. In our future learning and teaching contexts, we would like to create space for more 'heated' moments where identities are on the line, so to speak, so that we and others who participate in educational experiences we contribute to can more clearly see how identities and cultures are tied up in everything that we do, think about, know, or understand.

Further, we learned that in teaching and learning situations, engaging with, and problematizing, assumptions and expectations about research and knowing is not easy. We are all deeply invested in the types of knowledge we ascribe to and which form our perspectives and inform our lives. Yet examining how the intersections between identities affect knowledge production is a responsibility to be shared by all who participate in teaching, learning, and research contexts. All of our identities are multi-faceted and unique. Our readings and interpretations of processes of knowing and of knowledge urge us all to examine common-sense understandings or unquestioned assumptions about how our identities are being enacted through our research choices. Simultaneously, they implore us to foster others' embracing of that responsibility as well.

In the classroom context we presented here, we learned that power to shape relationships and, in this case, classroom events was exercised not only by the teacher or the researcher. Rather, all those involved shaped knowing through their access to, and comfort or discomfort with, certain cultures or cultural practices. Simultaneously, the process of knowing shaped both knowledge and those who sought to know. In other research contexts, the situation is similar. Everyone involved in research relationships — as reader, teacher, learner, critic, or presenter — has a power to influence those environments and a responsibility to examine how one is already doing so. Bringing these relationships of power to formal classroom discussion can serve as a useful — albeit complicated — way to analyze how we know and understand ourselves and each other.

Engagement with multicultural research, to us, encompasses research on people of many cultures or positions and research done by people of many cultures or interpreted through multiple lenses. In some sense, all research deals with a wide variety of cultural standpoints and positions. But multicultural research is also a journey of knowing that acknowledges and highlights divergent and multiple themes while considering how cultural practices shape relationships. Teaching and learning about multicultural research, then, through multicultural readings, experiences, participants, or perspectives does not suggest a peaceful and harmonious environment. Rather, intersections of multiple positions can disrupt the knowing and discourses that participants were able and willing to create and engage in both by themselves and with others. With David Damrosch (1995), we believe:

> We need to understand the full extent to which the different phases of our academic life can work in synergy together, recognizing conversely that they undercut one another if we try to hold them too strictly apart. (p. 202)

In supporting multicultural knowing and research, then, we hope to expand and recognize the splinters of our own and students' identities as we seek to create classroom practices that encourage the expression of multiple forms of learning, multiple incorporations of cultures, and multiple 'conclusions' or 'outcomes' from those teaching and learning experiences.

In teaching, learning and enacting qualitative research and knowing in a variety of settings, methods are much more than just techniques and strategies. Standards for measuring the quality of knowing are not simply measures of correct application of certain methods. Rather, our standards for our own and others' knowing are strongly influenced by positioned statuses we bring to that knowing. Our knowing processes exist in synergy with our cultural identities — each enhancing and disrupting the other.

Beth's Story

Revisiting this experience has been disorienting. In many ways, I feel as if I have been forced to reimagine how I come to know. I've always worked from a participant-observer perspective, from the assumption that much of our knowledge of culture comes from direct experience. But this experience was different. I know about this event through others' stories and those stories have been woven into my experience in ways that cannot be separated easily. Does that make a difference? Should it? Theoretically, probably not. Experience does not necessarily form a reality. It heightens attention to how knowing is not singular but highly varied. Knowing is consummately social, shaped by our interactions with people, ideas, problems, and customs.

Becky's Story

For me, this analysis has been both discomforting and invigorating. While the articulation of these dilemmas and concerns with identities paints an overwhelming picture as I wrestle with my understandings of research, the resulting picture also allows me to envision opportunities for identities to swirl around and in between each other. Through the blending and contrast of colors, different pictures are formed and different ways of knowing are available for use. Finding a perfect blend of those identities is perhaps an impossibility, yet cognizance about the ways identities are affecting our ongoing perceptions of the world around us is important. Our knowing of others invariably includes the knowing of ourselves.

Notes

1   Becky's descriptions portrayed a dilemma of knowing others through qualitative research. In this case, she framed students' identities based on her own categories for classifying others.

For example, while she classified some students as 'Asian-American' they may consider themselves Korean or Japanese. In this way, multicultural research is always affected by the views and experiences of those who are constructing interpretations of that research.

2   All students' names are pseudonyms.

3   While we recognize that students' identities certainly had a role in their engagement with qualitative research, we concentrate primarily on our own perspectives as teacher and re-searcher. For ethical and analytical reasons, we concentrate on what we, rather than students, learned about the links between qualitative research and identities, especially as it relates to our knowing processes.

4   While 'niceness' can be seen as a way to foster a comfortable environment for all students' learning, it is also a powerful tool controlling the opportunities for learning that may exist. This class experience did not seem nice when viewed through the cultural lenses with which we are comfortable. Yet we nevertheless believe that through this disruption of 'normal' class-room practices, we opened ourselves to new ways of engaging with, knowing, and learning from others.

5   Despite feminist and post-structural attempts to expand or alter perceptions of qualitative research as being only a 'truth-seeking' activity, many qualitative research texts continue to utilize a language encompassing 'validity' and 'natural environments'. The resulting focus is one that supports the idea that an observer can (and should) seek to report the truth through distanced observations in natural environments.

6   In Sandra Harding's (1987) work on feminist method, she proposed that research can be understood using a three-pronged conceptualization: epistemology, methodology, and method. She suggested that epistemology, or a theory of knowledge, undergirds and influences the entire research process. Methodology refers to 'a theory or analysis of how research does or should proceed' (p. 3). Method, the components of which Harding asserted are not necessarily exclusive to one epistemology or philosophy, encompasses the techniques used for gathering evidence or collecting data.

References

DAMROSCH, D. (1995) *We Scholars: Changing the Culture of the University*, Cambridge: Harvard University.

FLAX, J. (1993) *Disputed Subjects: Essays on Psychoanalysis, Politics, and Philosophy*, New York: Routledge.

FRYE, M. (1992) *Willful Virgin: Essays in Feminism, 1976–1992*, Freedom, CA: Crossing.

GEERTZ, C. (1995) *After the Fact*, Cambridge: Harvard University.

HARDING, S. (1987) 'Introduction: Is there a feminist method?', *Feminism and Methodology*, Bloomington, IN: Indiana University.

HOOKS, B. (1984) *Feminist Theory: From Margin to Center*, Boston: South End.

LATHER, P. (1991) *Getting Smart: Feminist Research and Pedagogy with/in the Postmodern*, New York: Routledge.

LEAVITT, R. (1994) *Power and Emotion in Infant-toddler Day Care*, Albany, NY: SUNY.

MCLAREN, P.L., and LANKSHEAR, C. (1993) 'Critical literacy and the postmodern turn,' in LANKSHEAR, C. and MCLAREN, P.L. (eds) *Critical Literacy: Politics, Practice, and the Postmodern*, Albany, NY: State University of New York, pp. 379–420.

POLAKOW, V. (1993) *Lives on the Edge*, Chicago: University of Chicago.

SIMONSON, R. and WALKER, S. (1988) *The Graywolf Annual Five: Multicultural Literacy*, St Paul, MN: Graywolf.

THORNE, B. (1993) *Gender Play: Girls and Boys at School*, New Brunswick, NJ: Rutgers University.

YOUNG-BRUEHL, E. (1988) 'The education of women as philosophers', in MINNICH, E.K., O'BARR, J.F. and ROSENFELD, R. (eds) *Reconstructing the Academy: Women's Education and Women's Studies*, Chicago: University of Chicago, pp. 9–23.

18 Becoming a Researcher: It's the Trip not the Destination and Studying the Monocultural Preservice Teachers

Mary Lou Fuller

Introduction: Perspectives

Writing this chapter was a daunting experience. To begin with, it meant acknowledging that I was at a point in life where a retrospective examination of my work is appropriate even though I spend my time thinking about today and tomorrow and — until now — I've not given yesterday the reflection it deserves. Finally, there was the question of making observations that others might find either interesting or useful since there is no guarantee that activities which I found pleasing will necessarily be important to others. Thus when Carl Grant invited me to take on this task, I acknowledged how flattered I was to be asked, and began searching for perspectives to make sense of the multicultural education research activities in which I've participated. I discovered two perspectives I would like to share — both interrelated and both productive of insights into the process of multicultural education research as I've experienced it. These perspectives are: The influences of research on the researcher, and the nature and effect of my research. In other words, what did I do and why did I do it.

Influences on the Researcher

I begin with two assertions bearing on life generally and research as a human activity. The process of doing empirical research changes the researcher, and major theories of human behavior describe researchers' lives just as they do others'. It is my hope that by describing my professional (and to a lesser extent) personal life from these viewpoints, others might come to understand better where they are in their personal development as researchers in the area of multicultural education. I make the latter observation based less on anything remarkable in my life and more on the fact that reading another's views often helps one clarify things in one's own mind.

In the first case, I agree with the observation reported by Mitroff and Kilmann (1970) that claims research is an interaction between the object of study and the student. By doing research in multicultural education, for example, I both learn about the process by which people become progressively more multicultural and find that I am changed by what I learn. The study a colleague and I did documenting students progress in shedding their monocultural orientations (Fuller and Ahler, 1991), for example, showed me that this activity was both a developmental process and one needing a specific amount of time to reach maturation.[1] I do not, in short, see the researcher as a dispassionate observer; the researches are changed by what they learn just as surely as nature yields her secrets to the skillful investigator.

I also think that certain descriptions of the human condition are useful in describing how I've approached and made sense of the research I've done. While I'll describe these theories in detail in the following pages, I'd like to simply list them here as a preface. First, developmental theories by Carol Gilligan (1982, 1992), Daniel Levenson (1978, 1996) and particularly Erik Erikson's (1980, 1982) notion of how one's identity matures describes well my movement into the role of a professor responsible for teaching in the area of multicultural education. Second, Donald Schön's *Reflective Practitioner* literature presents an accurate picture of how I examine what I'm learning in light of my past experience; Schön speaks clearly to how I identified regularities in multiculturalism and how I'm changed in the process. And finally, there is the hierarchy of needs Abraham Maslow (Hamachek, 1994) described so well. By using these theories in considering the ways in which I've produced and consumed multicultural research, I can, at least for myself, identify both the motivations for, and the satisfactions deriving from, the work I have done and continue to do.

All of this means that you, as a critical reader, can view these observations on my life as an exercise in understanding how issues such as psychological needs running across the human life span (Maslow) relate to those to specific stages (Erikson) and gender (Gilligan, Levenson) and play out in the kind of thinking (Schön) that allows a person to extract insight from experience. As I've already indicated, I hope that the major value of this chapter will be in allowing others to speculate more skillfully on their own lives as researchers.

Research Traditions

I get weary of arguments about quantitative vs. qualitative research because debates about which methodology is best miss the point. The question should not be which is the right approach, but rather which methodology best addresses the research question. Qualitative methods look for universal truths in observable events, for example, while quantitative techniques estimate how often things occur in nature, and both approaches can support claims of causality. I take this to mean that flexibility is in order, that seeking to understand some phenomenon means using one approach, the other, or both, depending on both the phenomenon under study and the research question being asked. Some examples will clarify what I mean.

Adult Learners on Campus

Three colleagues and I (Slotnick, Pelton, Fuller and Tabor, 1993) studied an existing population of adult learners — especially as they compared to traditional age students. We began with a survey to identify regularities in the lives of both groups of learners. We selected this quantitative methodology because it allowed us to make our estimates while controlling for the important confounding variable of where students were in their educational careers — an issue making it more difficult to identify differences related to age. The results — a series of statements identifying the similarities and differences between the adult and traditional age learners controlling for levels of education — then became the basis for questions used to have learners in both groups describe their own lives. This qualitative approach offered insights into the statistical findings so that we could offer comprehensive and useful descriptions of adult learners. We were subsequently flattered when others recognized the effectiveness of this combination: The National University Continuing Education Association recognized the study with its

1994 Outstanding Research Award. The richness of this study would have been severely decreased if either quantitative or qualitative methodologies hadn't been used.

The Midwest Holmes Group and Monocultural Graduates in Multicultural Environments

The Adult Learners on Campus study contrasted markedly with two others. In the Midwest Holmes Group study, I wanted to estimate the prevalence of selected demographic characteristics and multicultural teaching activities of the 26 member universities of the Midwest Holmes Group, and so quantitative methods were the appropriate choice (Fuller 1992a). They were appropriate because they allowed me to document the numbers of people in each group and use those numbers to compare gender and ethnicity of the faculty to the same characteristics of the student populations across the member universities. This study contrasted with the Monocultural Graduates study where answering the research question meant documenting monocultural graduates' adjustments to teaching in multicultural classrooms. I visited their classrooms, observed them in their school and community environments, and interviewed them as well (Fuller, 1994). Lacking the qualitative data produced by each activity, I'd have been unable to understand how well these new teachers employed multicultural concepts in their teaching — or how thoroughly they missed using that the same concepts to approach and understand diversity.

In other words, multicultural researchers must be open to both qualitative and quantitative methodologies since both traditions can contribute to our understanding of multicultural issues. Pursuing this logic further, I've recently begun adding a medical dimension to my repertoire of research skills. I've begun using epidemiologic concepts and methods. Since epidemiology and multicultural education are seldom used in the same sentence (let alone the same research) it is appropriate for me to turn to the experiences that brought me to this view.

Some Personal Background

My introduction to multiculturalism came from growing up in a small, culturally diverse Arizona community as a member of a family that both respected and prized diversity. Diversity in this community came from the presence of American-Indians (Apache), Mexican-Americans, and African-Americans — populations which were often poorly received by the town's dominant culture. These groups were also significantly less affluent than the 'Anglo' members of the community.

My mother was particularly supportive of the San Carlos Apaches in both attitude and action, and my father's Boy Scout troop was the only one to have African-American and Mexican-American members. I recall that some of our neighbors were less than delighted when scouts of color came to our house so they could ride to meetings with my father.

My parents believed then — and continue to believe — that respect for others is a part of life; you simply do not engage in, or support, behaviors that demean others. My parents, for example, would not enter any restaurant that displayed the sign. 'We reserve the right to refuse service to anyone' since 'anyone' referred to African-Americans, American-Indians, and in some situations, Mexican-Americans.

I learned that respecting others was not a spectator sport to be appreciated from a distance; it was very much a matter of knowing and sincerely appreciating cultures other than one's own. And so it was not surprising that as a teacher I was attracted to environments rich with cultural diversity: I taught in the barrio of Phoenix, on the Navajo Reservation, and in a school where I could look into Mexico from the playground. It also seemed natural that I chose the University of New Mexico for my doctoral program because it offered a multicultural PhD in education.

Considering my background, colleagues and friends were surprised when, nearing the end of my doctoral work, I accepted a faculty appointment at the University of North Dakota where the student body and faculty were primarily white, mainstream, and middle class. This was logical decision to me: Where better to teach multicultural education than to students who have had only the slightest contact with people from backgrounds other than their own? This is especially important since there are many more white, mainstream teachers than teachers of color, and while the proportion of children of color in our public schools is increasing, the proportion of preservice teachers of color is dropping. The public school population is becoming more diverse while the cadre of teachers becomes more homogeneous. Thus it seemed to me then — and I remain convinced now — that the preservice teachers I work with must enter their classrooms armed with knowledge, strategies, and attitudes favorable to diversity if they are to do the best jobs they can for their students.

On Becoming a Researcher: Theorists

The question remaining is one of finding efficient and effective instructional approaches for these preservice teachers. Some of these approaches arose directly from research and some of the outcomes some approaches were documented using research methods. In doing this, however, I'd like to remind the reader that besides being *life* stages the descriptions which follow are also *work* stages. This means that when an adult starts a career, she is developmentally at the beginning of the experience. Thus, for example, when a mature adult enters college as an undergraduate, her experiences are more like those of the traditional age undergraduates (e.g., same anxieties, need to please the instructor, etc.) than those of a graduate student of the same age. Experience in a situation rather than age determines the stage of development (Slotnick et al., 1993). I experienced this when, as an experienced teacher, I began my doctoral studies and felt all the insecurities of my classmates who were many years younger than I.

Erikson and My Motivation toward Research

My current motivations for being a researcher are very different from the reasons for my interest in research in the past, and this has as much to do with where I am in my psychological developmental as it does with my role within the university. As a doctoral student, I learned to recognize both the value of research as a way of understanding the world and the practical importance of producing and publishing research if one is to be on a university faculty. Consistent with Erikson's stage VI, I learned from my professors and my program of study both something about how to conduct research and the role research played in a professors's life.[2] These learnings were both formal (I took research methods courses and did research projects in other courses as well) and informal (I watched professors plan, complete, and publish their efforts, and I noted both how they approached their research and the satisfaction they derived from those activities). I was learning to do and to appreciate research both as a student and as an assistant in the research, and I incorporated the learnings I realized into my emerging professional identity as an aspiring university faculty member.

Consistent with Erikson's stage VII (generativity vs. stagnation),[3] I decided that being a researcher in the area of multicultural education, a teacher, and having a family life (the latter being the most important although often affected by the first two), were the ways in which I wanted to be a generative (i.e., productive) adult.

Levenson

Daniel Levenson's work on the stages of adult life have been both applauded and criticized. The applause was for the contribution to the literature on the developmental stages of adults — the culmination of a 10-year study. The criticism resulted from the fact that he studied only men and was accused of generalizing to all adults — men and women (Levenson, 1978). Levenson recently published the findings of a comparable study done on women (1996) and where he does find differences between the two populations, his categorizations and their characteristics are generally the same. These categories, or *seasons* as Levenson calls them, are identified as: early adulthood; middle adulthood; and late adulthood. Levenson also includes transition periods that overlap each of these major stages.

Briefly, Levenson describes early adulthood as a time of high energy. A period during which individuals are concerned with establishing themselves in family life, love, and occupational advancement. This is a period, '. . . where we are buffeted by our own passions and ambitions from within and demands of . . . society from without' (Levenson, 1996, p. 20). This is a period where budding researchers find themselves trying to identify their own expectations and reconcile them with others' expectations. This period would be comparable to Erikson's stages VI (intimacy vs. isolation) and early stage VII (generativity vs. stagnation).

Early adulthood found me raising three children while working full-time as a primary grades teacher and part-time on masters degrees. I have difficulty now recalling where I found the energy to do all three, but I recall the time that went into making decisions concerning when and how to do what each of these three commitments required. I will describe shortly my views of research at this point in my life.

I've already noted that activity is more important than age when an individual does something more typical of younger people. Thus, my decision to return to graduate school to work on a doctorate forced me to balance my professional needs against the demands placed on me by parenthood. In short, though I was middle-aged, I made some decisions that looked a lot like those I'd made while deciding to work on my masters degrees. The difference now, however, was that instead of having three children at home, I had only one, and she was in high school age.

Levenson sees middle adulthood as a period when those who have met some degree of success become 'senior' members in their various communities. For researchers, this is a time for assuming some responsibility for mentoring and nurturing others (an aspect of Erikson's generativity). Middle adulthood people take a more universal view of their lives and worlds. During this period successful researchers both feel some satisfaction for their achievements and are able to put their research into perspective when viewing both their lives and the arenas within which they work. Indeed the paper you're reading now is an exercise in just such a reflection.

The last stage, late adulthood, is not applicable to the normal working years of most researchers or academicians. Besides, I'm not yet that old.

Feminist Theory and Developmental Stages

I would be remiss not to look at feminist issues since a large number of researchers are women. The feminist literature does not have a common view of developmental stages, and this is not surprising since feminists do not speak with a single voice. Carol Gilligan's work considers stages of development, although primarily in the area of moral development (1982, 1992). Grant notes that in considering developmental stages, 'Gilligan questions the interpretation of male/female difference, not whether there is a difference in the first place' (1993. p. 61). While Grant finds Gilligan's approach problematic (Grant, 1993), Colby and Damon support the use of traditional developmental theories (1987). In addition Levenson, although not a feminist, shows the same general developmental stages for both men and women while acknowledging gender differences (1996).

Erikson points out that the issues that are most important as one enters stage VII (generativity vs. stagnation) are least important at the stage's end, and the converse is true of issues of lesser import early in that stage. None other than Sigmund Freud pointed out that these issues are family and work (work being most important for young men, family being most important for young women), and Karl Jung pointed out that the interests of both genders 'cross' at mid-life. This little vignette exemplifies in my mind the similarities and differences which are at the center of the gender similarities/ gender differences issue. While both men and women consider the same things to be important, the relative value assigned to each is gender dependent.[4]

I've also noticed that the nature of the research institution appears structured more toward the needs of men than women. It is common in the sciences, for example, for a new assistant professor to be 'protected' by his chair for three years during which time he is expected to establish a viable (that is, fundable) research program. In return for this protection, the assistant professor is expected to put in all the hours needed to produce competitive proposals, and this expectation exists regardless of whether she — and not he — is the assistant professor. This expectation exists regardless of family obligations.

Stages As a Researcher

Reflecting on my experiences, I see three different periods in my career as a researcher: An undergraduate fascinated by research, a graduate student and junior faculty member learning to 'do' research, and a more mature faculty member viewing research from a broader perspective. The paragraphs which follow will describe each referring as appropriate to the theorists I've just described.

Fascination with Research

William Perry notes that undergraduates come to campus expecting to learn the truth from experts, and this observation describes me well; as an undergraduate, I put complete faith in research.[5] I had some vague sense that there was 'good' research and 'bad', but no way of the discriminating between the two. Although one of my strengths as a learner has always been that I ask questions, it didn't occur to me to question the research I read. Why should I? I loved research! If an instructor, the text, or outside readings quoted research, I accepted it as truth. Not only did I feel that I had to remember and apply this research, but I also felt responsible for educating others —

Table 18.1 Developmental stages of the researcher: Using 'Adult Stages' to understand the dynamics of growth as a researcher

Model	Beginning	Intermediate	Mature
Maslow	**Safety** (Predictability)	**Love** (Affiliation)	**Self-actualization**
	Making sense of one's environment.	This stage is often misunderstood. Masslow's love hierarchy refers not to love per se but to belonging-affiliation.	A broader view of research and where one fits into the larger picture. A concern for others and a desire to help those less experienced. More altruistic and less self concerned.
	This is the point at which beginning researchers try to understand what is expected of them. Prior to understanding the institutional and discipline's expectations for their research and publications. They need to establish a research agenda. Knowing the expectations makes the research environment safer (more predictable). Even if the researcher has some success (meets expectations), and success is an important part of a predictable environment, she will continue to feel anxious if her professional environment is not predictable.	Establishing one's position in the research community allows one affiliation — actually several affiliations. They belong to a community of researchers who have a common interest, as well as greater acceptance into their college community. (i.e., The assistant professor becomes an associate professor.) Self-esteem When one has an understanding of their environment and it becomes safer (more predictable) and when one is accepted by their peers then their time and energy can turn inward to feelings of self appreciation and confidence. This confidence allows one to take chances, try	
Levinson	**Early Adulthood**	**Early Adulthood, cont.**	**Middle Adulthood**
	Establishing one's self. An era of high energy and trying to identify one's own research expectations and that of the professional community.	A continuation of establishing one's self as a researcher. Finding one's place in the research community.	Becoming a senior member of the research community and nurturing graduate students and junior faculty.
Erikson	**Stage 6 Intimacy vs. Isolation**	**Stage 6 cont.**	**Stage 7 Generativity vs. Stagnation**
	One of the main tasks of this stage is to develop a sense of self (identity). Sorting out who you are. This is also necessary for the beginning researcher. You start to define	As the researcher matures and has had some success with their research and has begun to publish they begin to develop their own style and identity. If they don't	Having completed stage 6 in a positive manner, this is a period one enjoys their successes and feel secure in who they are as individuals. The researcher who feels

Table 18.1 (cont.)

Model	Beginning	Intermediate	Mature
	yourself professionally by establishing a research agenda and developing the necessary skills. See the world from a researcher's perspective	do this, they will most likely feel isolation from the research community of which they would like to be a part and will have a difficult time developing their sense of self as a researcher.	they have made, and continue to make a contribution want to make contributions to the field and to other researchers. They are generous with their time and talent and feel a responsibility toward their research field and the individuals in it. If they have not completed stage 6, they will generally be at a point of little progress — stagnation.

whether they wanted to be educated or not. My opening phrase in more conversations than I care to admit during this period of my life was, 'The research says . . .' And while I was fascinated by research, it didn't occur to me that I could be a researcher.

In retrospect, I believe reading and talking about research at this time addressed a need Abraham Maslow called 'self-esteem' (Hamachek, 1994). By reading and talking about research, I felt confident about myself and the points I was arguing because I had research to support me, and that allowed me to feel good about myself. Was this naive? Of course it was, though I didn't realize that until I gained a graduate student's perspective on research.

From an Eriksonian perspective, I believe I was using the skills and knowledge I felt appropriate for a person who first wanted to become a teacher and then wanted the additional credential of a master's degree. Research, it appeared to me, was important to such people, and so it was going to be important to me. I was, metaphorically, trying on the role I believed I was taking on, and this included holding research in high regard.

Graduate Student and Junior Faculty

I began my graduate work as a classroom teacher working part-time on a master's degree. I took research and research-related classes and did research projects as part of my class assignments. This was a heady experience for me, but most important, it allowed me to take my research into my classroom. It was through my professors' and my evaluation of my classroom research that I came to understand there was a continuum from 'good' to 'bad' research. Also, I learned early that one common source of 'bad' research, for example, was the use of a 'model' (usually a theory or an hypothesis) which was not appropriate to the research question being addressed; I learned the importance of carefully selecting a model appropriate to the research question at hand.

The realization that research — mine in particular — could fall on a continuum from good to bad meant that doing research offered both threats to my safety and opportunities to address those same needs.[6] I could, in fact, address my insecurities as a novice researcher by working with the faculty who supervised me and by the experience I gained through completing, evaluating, and thinking afterwards about what I had done.

This kind of reflection-*in*-action while doing the research, and reflection-*on*-action after my various projects were completed (Schön) provided me with insights into the research enterprise that made me better — though still not good — at what I was doing.

In subsequent master's programs (each time I selected a program appropriate to my needs as an educator), I developed and refined my research skills. I became a more critical reader of the research literature through class projects, for example, and a better producer of research findings through independent studies. It was not until my doctoral work, however, that I came to appreciate the time, energy, and devotion necessary to see a major research project from the inception through to publication.

On reflection, I had three reasons for developing my abilities as a researcher: to answer professional questions arising from my job as an elementary classroom teacher and later as a school psychologist; to satisfy requirements for my various graduate programs; and to refine my skills as a researcher. In all cases, I interpreted my research findings in relation to my practice; research, to me, has always been a practical activity since research findings have always informed my day-to-day teaching. Thus my experiences as a graduate student learning research meant developing my professional identity as an academic including research both as an end in itself (after all, university faculty do research) and a means to an end (research findings contribute to both what is taught and, in the cases such as adult learners on campus, to the way teaching should be done).

After completing my doctorate and becoming an assistant professor, research became part of my professional responsibilities since I was not only expected to do research, I was expected to publish my findings as well. This presented me with a set of almost incapacitating problems. First, where I had always looked to my own professional practice for research questions and used what I learned to address the needs precipitating the studies I did, I wasn't sure what to research. Could I still turn to my own practice as a source of researchable questions? Would anyone else be interested in what I'd learned in response to questions of importance to me? Second, as a student, if my work encountered difficulties I could (and did) turn to others to help solve methodological problems. As an assistant professor, however, I felt insecure about my abilities; I was, after all, supposed to know how to do research of a quality good enough to be published. The third problem also related to publication: Could I write well enough to both describe the work I had done and convince journal referees that I was professionally literate? Although I had published prior to this time, I was concerned by the prospect of my future depending on my ability to be published. Research was no longer as enjoyable an activity as it had been in the past.

I couldn't figure any way out of my problem except to plow ahead: I identified problems of interest to me, sought help (and received sympathetic and useful assistance) from my colleagues, and sent out my manuscripts which were, to my great pleasure, accepted for publication.[7] And, as I began to publish, I began to feel some satisfaction and pride in my scholarly activities. However, while my research now reached a wider audience, I found I was as concerned about what it said about me (I could do respectable research and write in an acceptable manner?) as I was about the answers my research provided to questions of importance in multicultural education. From Maslow's perspective, my insecurities as a novice researcher were being addressed; I could, for example, plan and execute a respectable study. What's more, the fact that my work was read and recognized meant that I was also addressing affiliation needs by becoming a member of the community of multicultural education scholars.[8] Finally, the findings I produced and the fact that addressed issues of importance to me and were well regarded by my colleagues suggested that my self-esteem needs were being satisfied as well.

From an Eriksonian perspective, I was learning the skills and the ethos of being a researcher in multicultural education. Through both my research activities and discussions I enjoyed with others about research, I began learning to look at the world the way a researcher looks at the world; and how to solve problems the way a researcher does. I was living through stage VI (identity vs. isolation).

At the same time, I was doing this as a woman in the still largely male graduate education establishment. As a result, I encountered demands on my life due to my graduate studies that ran counter to the demands I felt due to being a woman and a mother, and I dealt with them as best I could. I accommodated the time I spent on graduate school activities to my daughter's life and, when appropriate and possible, I encouraged my daughter to accommodate her time demands to my needs.

Mature Researcher

About the time I ceased being overwhelmed by the university system and had bought myself some time through my first publications, I again became excited about my research. My success at publishing and the acceptance of my presentations at national meetings meant I was becoming acculturated to academia. And at the same time my concerns about whether I could succeed subsided, the purpose for my research and writing changed; I wanted to become a part of the national conversation on multicultural education, and I could do that through publishing and presenting my research. While formerly the purpose of my research was to answer my questions and develop my skills, I now I wanted to share my findings with a larger and more specialized audience. Where formerly I wanted to validate myself as a researcher, I now wanted to make a contribution to the professional literature. I find that acceptance of my work and the results it has produced has provided me with the opportunity to join, in a small way, in a national discussion that was (and remains) so important to me. I see my research now as a way I have of contributing to improvement of public education, and that pleases me immensely.

At the same time, I've moved through the academic ranks and issues of gaining tenure and promotion are now behind me. The result is that I can take a broader perspective on my research, and doing this allows me to be supportive of the research activities of masters students, doctoral students, and junior faculty. My feeling is that while I evolved from a consumer of research done by others to someone who both consumed research and produced findings for her own consumption, I am now a more sophisticated consumer and a producer. I am now comfortable mentoring others.

I want to turn now to the content of the research I do. Where my early research tended to lack a focus (I wanted to know everything when I first began doing research in my classrooms), I have limited my interests and efforts. I am trying to understand better (i.e., develop a better theory of) what happens to children and so better provide a curriculum and teaching for my preservice teachers and graduate students. Because I have limited the scope of my interests, I can focus my resources more precisely and so learn more about issues of interest to me.

I also find I am becoming an advocate for particular positions, particular views. My research provides insights into both the impact of multicultural issues on the schools and the families they serve and the impact of families (particularly families of color) on the schools, and these insights allow me to argue more cogently for points of view I feel will advance multicultural education and develop among others a better understanding of families. I've also noticed that where I formerly wanted to convince others of the validity of my viewpoint, I now find it is my views of the issues that change. What is important to me is not that I've prevailed or been defeated, but that the research (mine and others) informs my thinking and so allows me to realize insights and to appreciate better the insights of others.

The most important influence of my research has been on my teaching: Research now informs my teaching and my teaching informs my research. Though this sounds like a cliché, research has made my professional life much more integrated, much more coherent. But mostly, the perspectives of research (learning about the world) and teaching (helping others to appreciate those same leanings) allow me more insight into what it is I do and what it is I research than has either activity independently. The whole here is more than the sum of the parts.

Other Influences on My Research: Scholars, Leaders and Mentors

My research has been influenced by a variety of people. While some individuals have been experts in the field of research and their areas of content, others have acted as mentors, and still others have provided me with the opportunity and support to do research. All have played important roles in my professional development.

There are researchers and writers who affect one's view of their professional and personal worlds. I often feel they are professional colleagues although I know them only through their work, and I often carry on wonderful imaginary conversations with these people or ask myself how they would view a given finding in my research. Among these is Jonathan Kozol who I recently had the privilege of meeting. Although I knew I was just one of the multitude that he regularly meets, I was somehow surprised that he did not recognize me; after all, he has been part of my professional life for years.

Early in my professional career Kozol's, *Death at an Early Age* had a tremendous impact on both how I viewed education and my need to know more about poverty and people of diverse backgrounds. It was also at this point in time that I really began to recognize the many faces of research — that research could be the documentation of an experience, a situation, an idea, etc. While each of Kozol's subsequent books have been examples of exemplary qualitative research, Kozol provides the needed demographics to help the reader know who he is talking about and what they look like. But more importantly he gives life to the demographics through an exploration into the lives of those who live in poverty.

I have been very fortunate to have had a variety of mentors who have encouraged and assisted in my growth as a researcher. The first was a former school superintendent (now teaching in higher education) Hank Suverkrupt; the second is a colleague from the medical school at the University of North Dakota, Hank Slotnick; and the third is a multicultural researcher, Carl Grant.

Influence of Public School

Hank Suverkrupt was the superintendent in the Crane School District in Yuma, AZ, during my tenure. He expected educators to be knowledgeable and nurturing, and he also valued professional daring. Teaching for Hank at last placed me in my professional environment, an environment that not only allowed experimentation but encouraged and nurtured it. All teachers were encouraged to read books to widen their professional understandings; in fact the district would pay for them. He often purchased multiple copies of books for each school in the district and the district's teachers would meet as a group to discuss the theories and/or practices proposed in them.

While this might not have been attractive to everyone, it was exhilarating to me. Teachers and administrators got together for the expressed purpose of discussing ideas, and there wasn't a party line — I could agree or disagree without concern for my status within the district. And experimentation followed the consideration of new ideas: Experimentation with ideas, 'What do these ideas mean in relation to what I believe?', and experimentation with practice, 'How do they relate to my current practice?' Hank Suverkrupt understood that if teachers are encouraged to think new thoughts and engage in new practices, the administration could not be punitive about failed experiments. If one can predict the outcome of experimentation, after all, it is not research. One might question whether these classroom explorations were really research because they lacked suitable controls, but they had research questions, methodology on how the data would be collected and analyzed; and later educational implications were drawn.

Perhaps the most important factors in the success of encouraging teachers to continue to grow as thinkers, become more reflective, and apply these skills to the classroom was the fact that the district had a solid philosophy of education against which we could measure the success of our ideas and practices. The Crane School District was a 'child centered' educational environment. What a heady place for someone interested in diversity.

Crane is the only school district I have known where the teachers not only knew the philosophy but, for the most part, measured their practice by it. When we talked about the 'Crane Way' we all knew exactly what the phrase meant. Prior to that time I could voice my philosophy but my philosophy tended to be independent of my actions. Because of the trust and nurturing the district provided, the philosophy became a consistent part of my professional life both as a teacher and as a researcher. A disproportionate number of us continued our interest in research by completing doctorates.

A Fellow Researcher

Mentors seem to appear when you need them and provide you with what you are ready and able to accept. Hank Slotnick became such a mentor as I entered higher education as a tenure-track assistant professor. Slotnick is a biostatistician in the school of Medicine at the University of North Dakota and has a strong background in education. He is respected for his research and publications, particularly in the area of how physicians learn.

Although I entered the world of academia with publications and research presentations to my credit, I entered feeling inadequate and overwhelmed. With the naivete of most new assistant professors, I feared that I might be exposed as an impostor — after all, surely someone would notice I didn't know *everything* about research. Hank Slotnick entered my life at this point with an offer of assistance with and an enthusiasm for research I found contagious. He loved to talk about research (mine, his, anyone's) and so my attitude couldn't help but change and I eventually found myself again enjoying the challenge of research — and not taking myself quite so seriously.

Hank also expanded my research practices by introducing me to a variety of ways of investigating different issues. His minor in anthropology for his first PhD provided an entrée into the world of qualitative research when few educators considered it a legitimate way of studying education, and so he has an appreciation of both qualitative and quantitative techniques and uses both in his research. He encouraged me to try new research methodologies and to relax and have fun with my research, and this is how I discovered a sampling procedure call 'boot strapping' that both addresses messy statistical problems while being fun to use.

He also appreciates my work and genuinely feels that multicultural education is an important area of exploration and an interesting topic for discussion. In addition, he continually encourages me to expand and improve, and there has never been a time that he hasn't been willingly to read and comment on my work. Beyond being a wonderful mentor, he makes excellent spaghetti, and is a terrific husband.

A Leader in Multicultural Research

Carl Grant is one of the most prolific, knowledgeable, and thoughtful people in the field of multicultural education. He is a leader, a scholar, and a friend of all who are dedicated to multicultural education. Before having the privilege of working with him, I was a consumer of his work; his writings helped me consider my work in multicultural research, set a high standard for my performance, and informed me. And as with Kozol, I had imaginary conversations with Carl Grant that allowed me to consider my work from a variety of perspectives.

I met Carl Grant some years ago when we were both involved with diversity issues in the Holme's Group. Meeting someone whose work I held in such high regard and someone whom I saw as a central figure in multicultural education was a little intimidating. I can't help but smile as I remember these feelings since I now know Carl to be the most democratic of people. He is truly interested in his colleagues' and students' work, an interest embodied in the high expectations he has for the quality of the work and his willingness to discuss it. His respect is also evidenced by the fact that he is honest in his critiques.

Carl's generosity is consistent with his other professional characteristics. I have seen Carl Grant repeatedly provide others with opportunities to publish, be involved in organizations, and assume leadership in the multicultural community. As one of the many multicultural researchers who have received just such opportunities and support, I can also report the genuine pleasure he takes in the successes of others.

Mentors are an important part of one's growth as a researcher. While we can learn from the writings and actions of those we don't know personally, those with whom we interact contribute most to the richness of our learning. Though it would be beyond my abilities to list all the contributions that mentors have made to my personal and professional life, the three mentors listed above have exemplified some characteristics that have been particularly important in my growth as a multicultural researcher: They valued multicultural research, they encouraged and supported me, they had important expertise — both in a variety of research strategies and in multicultural research, they had a joy and enthusiasm for their own research and expertise, and they were generous with their time, expertise, and encouragement.

An Introduction to My Research

Some Keys

You now have some idea of how I came to do the research I've worked on and some of the people and ideas that have influenced me. The following pages describe the outcomes of my research and so are best understood from the perspectives that brought me to research in multicultural education.

One of these perspectives is that teaching is an extraordinarily important activity. I find teaching to be one of those activities that benefit everyone: My students learn and grow in the same classrooms in which teaching allows me to better understand both those same students and the content of my teaching — multicultural education.

The other perspective is that my students are progressing through the same stages that I passed through, and are motivated to address the same needs I have. This perspective allows me to better understand both how my students learn and the manners in which they incorporate those learnings into their identities as preservice and practicing teachers. It is critical then, that my teaching addresses my students' needs if it is to succeed. I consider these to include their immediate psychological needs such as security, affiliation, and self-esteem, as well as the developmentally appropriate needs such as allowing students to develop their emerging professional identities. In the latter case, this means providing them with skill and knowledge they can use as practicing teachers. The problem is that the students are unaware of what their needs are, and I cannot turn to them to identify these needs. Instead, I must turn to both my experiences as a teacher and what I have learned from research — both my own and others — to know what skills, knowledge, and attitudes will best serve the students.

Ralph Tyler made popular the idea that goals for teaching have to come from both within and without the students to be taught. Goals coming from within have already been described while those coming from without need to be sketched. I see them as coming from two separable but not independent sources: The identifiable knowledge and skills a teacher needs to create an environment within which children can learn, and learnings expected by the society within which the students will assume positions as adults. In the former case, the skills require that the emerging teacher both understand his students' needs (again, both those coming from within the children and those coming from society more generally) and be able to create effective learning environments. In the latter case, the teacher must have some understanding of both the worlds the child lives in and the worlds the child *can* live in.

Critical Issues

The question, then, becomes one of making the cadre of teachers and preservice teachers more attuned to the needs and expectations of a public school population that is diverse. Two approaches to this problem suggest themselves: More teachers are needed from diverse ethnic, racial, economic, and other backgrounds; and middle class preservice teachers need to be better prepared to work with the diverse children they will encounter in their classrooms. In the first case, people recruited to the teaching profession will already understand some issues facing the children who will be their students; in the second case, preservice teachers will be better prepared to recognize and meet the needs of children from backgrounds different than their own. Though implementing both approaches represents serious challenges ro preservice education programs, every college of education has a responsibility to address them. The reality is that students need teachers who (by dint of coming from similar backgrounds) can be role models for them and teachers who (by representing different parts of the human community) can help them develop the skills they need to succeed in a diverse world. In short, there must never be competition supporting one approach to the detriment of the other.

Mary Lou Fuller

Recruitment and Retention

Universities have established special recruitment offices and created retention programs to help and support students of color. While conferences, books, handbooks, articles, and video tapes address the subject of how to recruit and retain students of color, the number of preservice teachers of color in colleges of education nevertheless continues to decline. And so it's obvious that we must recommit ourselves to their recruitment and retention. Although these programs have not been as successful as originally hoped, they must continue to receive time, funds, and attention with an eye toward making the cadre of public school teachers more like the population of public school children.

Preparing Preservice Teachers for Diversity

While teachers of color play an essential and critical role in our schools, the reality is that these educators comprise only a modest percentage of the faculty. This means children from diverse backgrounds are generally being taught by Euro-American women from middle-class backgrounds. Given this reality, the next question is how do we prepare these preservice teachers to meet the needs of diverse student populations? While this obvious question looms large, only a small amount of time, energy, and financial resources are devoted to exploring potential answers (Fuller, 1992a).

My Research Agenda

This arena — working with monocultural preservice teachers — is where I do the majority of my research. I selected this area because my personal background, professional experiences, teaching situation, and individual interests suggest that my efforts in this area can have a useful impact on education. The question remaining is how I have approached these efforts in the past and how I continue to approach them.

Student Population

I am a professor in the College of Education and Human Development at the University of North Dakota in the Department of Teaching and Learning.[9] We have an undergraduate preservice education program and a graduate program, and our doctoral students represent a disproportionately large segment of the graduate college enrollment. Ours is a very vital, very active program.

It is also a program serving a student body that is more than 90 percent white and middle class. Our students come primarily from rural communities in the upper Midwest where the population is almost exclusively Euro-American. Our university's demographics are somewhat more diverse, but they, too, reflect the communities from which our students come. The largest minority on campus comes from the American-Indian population with African-Americans, Latinos, and foreign students making up the rest.

Perhaps more meaningful, however, is the reality that more than 90 percent of the students taking undergraduate multicultural education classes report not having had any meaningful experiences with people from other cultural and/or racial groups (Fuller and Ahler, 1991). And this is the tip of the iceberg; they similarly lack experience with people from a range of economic backgrounds and family structures. They are truly monocultural in both their knowledge and experience.

This is disheartening because our preservice teachers frequently lack the experience that comes with dealing with people from other cultures. It is a serious problem for the 70 percent of our elementary preservice teachers who leave the geographic area to teach in communities that are culturally, economically, and familially different from those they know and understand (Fuller, 1992b).

Rationale

Our students are similar to preservice teachers elsewhere in that these primarily white, female, middle class preservice teachers, from rural or suburban environments (Fuller, 1994) have had scant exposure to diversity in the schools and communities of their childhood, and in the colleges of education they attend. Though one might expect that the preservice curriculum would attempt to remediate the students' multicultural deficiencies, with few exceptions, this is not true (Fuller, 1992b; Griffith, Frase and Ralph, 1989; Gwaltney, 1990; Fuller, 1992a; Kniker, 1989).

Despite marked demographic changes in classrooms, there is little evidence of change in teacher preparation or teachers' classroom strategies, a situation Sleeter and Grant describe as 'business as usual' (1993, p. 18). When reviewing how teachers teach diverse populations, what they teach, and how these teachers group students, educational changes were not congruent with demographic changes. In other words, while classrooms were designed for the students of an earlier time, for the most part 'business as usual' means schools that don't meet the needs of children of diverse populations.

Clearly, preparing preservice teachers for their future classrooms grows more complex as the school population becomes more diverse. Changing demographics require changing teacher education strategies since 'traditional' approaches no longer fit the realities of a large and growing number of classrooms. Put simply, education faculty must consider the demographics of their graduates' classrooms and they must also inform themselves of their graduates' experiences in these new environments.

I approached the problem of making monocultural students more attuned to issues of diversity through studying three areas: poverty, cultural diversity, and diversity in familial structure. Although the three identified research topics are listed separately, they are intimately related. As Chavez so eloquently states,

> The foundation for a Multicultural Education cannot be unidimensional. Constructs such as culturally and linguistically relevant practices, democratic options, the multiple perspectives that learners bring with them, and liberating practices that acknowledge the diversity in today's classrooms are fundamental. Multiple epistemologies that intensify the need to rethink curriculum as we know it and instruction as it is presently practiced are also crucial to MCE. Liberating otologies that demarginalize learners; interrogate hegemonic structures such as tracking, racism, and sexism; and engender a liberating consciousness to the student populations served make for a Multicultural Education pedagogy that is comprehensive and democratic. (Chavez, 1995, p. 14)

By investigating these issues as they relate to teaching monocultural undergraduates, I hope to contribute to the ongoing conversation concerning multicultural education generally and specifically, monocultural preservice teachers and diversity. I sometimes doubt my own perception of the seriousness of this issue for although I read and hear much support for better preparing preservice teachers for diverse classrooms, I see minimal action on the part of teacher training programs.[10]

In particular, I wondered about both who our public school students are and who are the people who teach them. I wondered about this because if teachers do not understand their students' worlds, they cannot be confident that their educational efforts will be appropriate to either the students' need or their expectations.

The multiculturalism absent on campus is not limited to the areas of ethnicity/culture and race; such limits on multiculturalism ignore major influences on children and the families within which they live. My experiences as both a teacher and a researcher tell me that multiculturalism must necessarily encompass (but not be limited to) income level, gender, special needs, and familial structure. These must be considered because they influence both the ways people interact with one another and the ways individuals see themselves and their places in their worlds. What is more, since African-Americans and Latinos usually attend schools with large concentrations of economically disadvantaged children, monocultural preservice teachers and teachers often have difficulty sorting out the effects of poverty from cultural characteristics. The resulting confusion in their minds colors the ways they approach their students.

Economic Resources

Allow me to clarify what I mean. While it was no surprise that our preservice teachers need knowledge and skills to work with and appreciate other cultures, I was startled by the students' lack of knowledge, understanding, and (sometimes) lack of tolerance in their dealings with low income/poverty and diverse family structures. The disparity between what our preservice teachers and graduates know about poverty and what they need to know is problematic because of the prevalence of poverty. For example, while 25 percent of the children in this country live in poverty (and this number is itself appalling), the figure for families headed by someone less than 30 is 42 percent while a frightening 54 percent of children of female-headed households live below the poverty line (US Census Bureau, 1993). Furthermore, if we added to these totals all those families who live just above the poverty line (people President Clinton calls the 'working poor'), these figures increase dramatically. None of these families are middle class, and consequently the experiences they share with people coming from middle class backgrounds is minimal.

In contrast, 'middle class' is an appropriate descriptor for both practicing and preservice teachers (Webb and Sherman, 1989). These people — like the young teachers and preservice teachers I have worked with — have sensibilities and experiences that are very different from those of their impoverished students. The fact that these sensibilities and experiences color their views of who they are and how they interact with schools means yet a discrepancy teachers must overcome if they are to understand and so work more successfully with public school students.

Several years ago, I took a sabbatical leave to visit with graduates of our elementary education program who were teaching in culturally diverse settings in the Southwest (Fuller, 1994). What I found through observing them in their classrooms, interviewing them, and talking with their supervisors is that, first, they were generally very good teachers. My findings also confirmed that the differences in economic resources available to teachers' families (as opposed to their students) were not understood by our graduates. These differences were less obvious than ethnic/cultural/racial ones and so they had not developed sensitivity to these issues. While these teachers are intelligent, caring people who want the best for children, and the teachers could recognize that a disparity existed between them and their students' economic backgrounds, they failed to realize the disparity created life experiences for them and their students that differed in both quality and quantity. The teachers held stereotypes of low income people that impeded their abilities to work effectively with their low income students. For example, they arrived at their positions expecting 'poor people' to be wane, dirty, and shabbily dressed. Consequently, it took time for them to reconcile the fact that the cute, clean children in their classrooms lived in poverty and were effected by the lack of financial resources. They recognized needs they genuinely wanted to meet but their insufficient understanding of poverty made them inadequate to the task. Because they did not recognize the complexity of poverty, they could appreciate neither its classroom implications nor its broader societal causes.

Lacking this understanding, the participants offered simplistic solutions to poverty and the problems it caused (Fuller, 1992b, 1993b, 1994). They generally agreed that the solution to the dilemmas of poverty was to find better living conditions, to get a job (or a better job), or to go back to school. They did not consider the scarcity and low pay of jobs available to these parents, their lack of skills for higher paying jobs, or their lack of sophistication in dealing with 'the system'. Further, the participants were impatient with their students' parents as evidenced by their if-they-only-worked-harder attitude, an attitude reminiscent of 'blaming the victim' (Ryan, 1971). In addition, a few of the teachers tended to romanticize poverty (e.g., the noble, struggling poor who made the best of the little they had).

Perhaps most problematic was that they tended to see each situation as peculiar to a given family rather than the family being an example of a broader, more complex societal problem. Indeed, only one teacher I spoke with considered the broader societal reasons for the lack of resources for these families.

Ethnicity/Culture/Race

Although our graduates were better informed about ethnic/culture/race than the effects of poverty, they still need to continue developing knowledge and skills in working with children from diverse populations. They must be prepared for the poverty they will encounter in their classrooms.

Approximately 31 percent of public school students are children of color. In fact, children of color make up the majority of school children in some states. Currently, 58 percent of school children in California, for example, are members of under represented groups, and by 2020, these groups are expected to exceed the white mainstream population in the schools (Wise and Gollnick, 1996). These children live in a range of ethnic/cultural/racial, familial, and economic milieus that are frequently different from those in which public school teachers grew up.

The following observation is especially pertinent when considering the striking contrast of the public schools population and that of colleges of education and educators. Despite our talk about multicultural education reform in colleges of education, we still find that,

> The whitest institutions in America, next to churches and corporations, are universities and colleges [and consequently colleges of education]. But unlike churches and corporations, universities claim intellectual leadership, progressive attitudes, and an orientation toward inclusiveness. (Asante, 1996)

The observations I made on my sabbatical leave study confirmed that our graduates recognized that while their students' cultures were different from their own, their cultures were important in the school and community in which these young teachers taught. Further, while the participants were initially uncomfortable with cultures that differed from theirs, they developed an appreciation for some cultural groups. They felt a higher degree of comfort with, and appreciation for, Hispanic families than with low income African-American families.

These teachers were surprised and pleased, for example, at how interested the Hispanic parents were in their children's progress. Although, there initially were some cultural conflicts concerning role expectations, the Hispanic parents were apt to be actively involved in class social activities as opposed to traditional activities such as parent–teacher conferences. The teachers initially misinterpreted this as a lack of interest in their children's progress, and the teachers were initially surprised at the presence of extended family members and siblings at conferences and class parties. However, they subsequently came to prize this cultural behavior (Fuller, 1994).

Since our education program is very humanistic and holistic, it is not surprising that the teachers were pleased with another cultural difference. They liked being seen in more of a parental-type role that encouraged them to be more nurturing than they had anticipated being. They also noted that the children, besides being more affectionate than they had anticipated, were also much cleaner.

These teachers were also particularly appreciative of the manner in which they were treated by the parents. They felt that because they were teachers they had a higher status and were more respected by the Hispanic community than by mainstream parents.

Finally, they were unaware that they came with stereotypes about the Hispanic population. One of the stereotypes that was challenged and abandoned early in their experience was that Hispanics are dirty. Interestingly, the discrepancy between the stereotype and reality created a cognitive dissonance some tried to explain away by using their own experiences. For example, one student told me that Mexican-Americans are simply very much like Norwegians in that both groups prize cleanliness.

Their relationship with African-Americans of limited resources was more difficult for them to relate to and understand. Almost without exception, they had two areas of concern: problems resulting from poverty; and the black English that the children and their parents spoke.

The teachers were not as sensitive to the poverty of this population as they were to the Hispanics with the result that our monocultural graduates felt less comfortable with low income African-Americans. They were also intimidated by black English; they seemed to see their difficulty in understanding their students and their students' parents as a personal failure. Other cultural behaviors accompanying black English included more touching and less personal space than the teachers were comfortable with. Interestingly, both the speech and the cultural behaviors were much more threatening when exhibited by the parents than by the children, the teachers came to prize physical closeness with the children.

In contrast, teachers who taught middle class African-American students reported no discomfort working with their students, and my observations of their teaching confirmed this. They were very interested in their African-American students and tried to make their teaching culturally sensitive. The problems due to poverty were absent and neither the children nor parents used black English — at least not in the school setting. Put simply, these monocultural teachers, in short, were better prepared to work with middle class children than children living in poverty (Fuller, 1993a, 1993b).

Families

The same observations can be made for familial structure. Most of the preservice students and graduates came from intact families and tended to use their experience as the litmus test for families. Structure rather than function was apt to be used to determine the 'quality' of a family.

The participants were not prepared for the great diversity of family structures appearing in their classrooms, and while they generally liked their students' parents, they were suspect of any structure other than the intact home. Not surprisingly, they were most impressed by those families that looked and/or acted most like their families of origin — the family types they understood best.

These young teachers learned that like other varieties of diversity, the range of family types is increasing. Besides intact families (both biological parents and minor children), there are households headed by single-parents, cohabitating couples, and gay parents; and blended families and families headed by grandparents rearing minor children in addition to numerous other structures. In 1970, just under half the families in the US were married couples with children; presently, such families make up only about a third of households nationally. The arrival of reliable, inexpensive birth control means that adults can put off marriage and/or childbirth until they have established themselves, consequently families are smaller and women are older than their mothers were when they had children.

The number of single-parent families has also increased; indeed, it has doubled since 1970 due to both divorce and the number of children born to unmarried mothers (up from 5 percent of all births in 1960 to 27 percent in 1989). In addition, the remarriage rate following divorce has grown, increasing significantly the number of blended families (Ahlburg and De Vita, 1992).

The teachers I interviewed lacked an understanding and appreciation of the range of family styles they encountered in their classrooms and the changes in family structure; indeed the transitory nature of some of the families made them feel uncomfortable. Again there was a cognitive dissonance between the teachers' experiences in their families of origin and their students' experiences. These monocultural teachers had some basic educational skills useful in working with families — parent–teacher conferences, newsletters, etc. — but lacked an understanding of how families function. They needed a sociological background (Fuller, 1992, 1993b, 1994).

These young teachers' perceptions of families are not exceptional; their experiences and perceptions are representative of more experienced teachers.

Research Implications

Research for research's sake is a wonderful intellectual activity, much like a good game of chess; but if the findings aren't in someway useful, the research becomes nothing more than an exercise. Where a good piece of research can be admired and appreciated, it is not a piece art to be valued in and of itself. This is because educators are a pragmatic group who want to know how research findings can be used to help students.

I've already noted that my research has informed my teaching and my teaching has informed my research. The content of all my classes has been affected by my findings, though some classes offer a more obvious fit — graduate 'social foundations', graduate and undergraduate 'multicultural education', 'teaching the Hispanic child', and 'how children learn'. How could a professor effectively teach these classes without looking at economic issues, the family, and culture? They are integral parts of any discussion dealing with public school students.

The question now is how do I use my research findings to better prepare my preservice teachers for the diversity they will encounter? Rather than offer a long list of changes, I will share some changes to my teaching that I find are particularly useful in helping students develop an appreciation of diversity.

Field Experiences

While the community surrounding our university admits of limited diversity, my research helped me recognize the importance of providing preservice experiences with populations that differed from those my students experienced growing up: I am convinced these experiences are essential in helping monocultural students appreciate and feel comfortable with diverse populations. In the absence of school-based field experiences for my students, I looked to our community: Tutoring American-Indian students, working with recent immigrant families, being a big sister (brother)/tutor for a low income, culturally diverse child through the Salvation Army, working with residents at a homeless shelter, tutoring culturally diverse adults for their GEDs, etc. I was surprised and pleased at the number of students who continue the relationships they developed after the semester was over.

I also provide my students with a list of movies (videos) that will provide more exposure to particular groups, and I suggest books that might be helpful. These videos have added an interesting dimension to class discussions since my students occasionally rent a video and get together for popcorn and a multicultural movie.

The students are also given the opportunity to spend a day at a reservation school several hours from campus. This is always a popular trip and the students often write about the stereotypes they had been unaware they held until forced by reality to confront them.

The International Center

We have international students from 34 different countries represented on campus. My undergraduate multicultural education students and I visit the International Center on our campus each semester where some the international students share their cultures. Some students continue to visit the International Center for coffee and conversations with the international students and some close friendships usually develop. Three young women who were planning to backpack around Europe, for example, were invited to spend a week with a friend from the International Center at her home in Germany. It is exciting to see how these experiences help my students become more open toward, and appreciative of, cultural diversity.

College Wide Activities

Based on some of my research, I requested two 'town meetings' for the College of Education and Human Development to examine the issue of poverty. The first meeting was for faculty and graduate teaching assistants, and each participant was given a packet of readings on poverty to read prior to the meeting. All classes were canceled for a morning so the faculty could meet to discuss this information and how it could be integrated into the curriculum. The second 'town meetings' (again all classes canceled for a morning) was for all students and faculty. We invited a sociologist, a school principal from a low income school, and one of our graduates I had observed doing a wonderful job teaching in a poverty environment in Texas. After each speaker's presentation, participants took part in small groups to discussion on how they would use this information in a public school classroom. Poverty became part of classroom discussions.

Conclusion

These few activities are the more obvious results that have emerged from my research. In addition, I have witnessed changes in students' attitudes and behaviors concerning diversity. I hear students whose contributions early in the semester suggested unthinking acceptance of the ultra conservative press and talk radio, later argue with informed and reasoned logic the benefits of multicultural education. As their teacher and as a multicultural researcher I am pleased but something is still missing. I don't often see a real passion for change, or a sense of responsibility for, and interconnectiveness with, the broader issues of multicultural education, or have the idealism that challenges inequalities in all forms or identify and protest injurious political agendas.

Finally, a metaphor for multicultural research can be seen in finding ways to explain an Alexander Calder mobile to students. Certainly, multiculturalism is itself a collection of pieces, each of different shape, color, and texture; and each piece moving in relationship to each other piece. And like a mobile, it is not possible to appreciate multiculturalism from frozen-in-time snapshots; just as the essence of the mobile comes from watching the pieces move in relationship to one another, so the essence of multiculturalism can only be appreciated by seeing each aspect — whether ethnicity, economic status, gender, or family structure — as it relates to each other aspect. Sometimes one part of the mobile obscures another; sometimes the parts appear together in relationships suggesting new and interesting forms.

Being able to appreciate a mobile comes from understanding the sculpture as an art form. Certainly it is possible to appreciate it intuitively, but a studied appreciation is more satisfying, more enlightening. And this — the appreciation of the way the pieces move in relation to one another to create multiculturalism — is what I want for my students. I want them to become connoisseurs, to savor their experiences with multiculturalism in ways causing them both immediate satisfaction and appreciation later as they reflect on things. The problem, then, becomes one of how do I enlighten them, how do I help them to see what is interesting and important about this dynamic system called multiculturalism? This casts me, as a teacher, in the art critic's role: It is not enough for me to see and appreciate multiculturalism on my own, it is important for me to be able to explain it to my students. And so just as a sculpture critic searches for perspectives, for analogies, for ways to help others appreciate the beauty in the mobile, so I see research in multicultural education as my search for ways to increase my vision and so my students' visions. To the degree that my research allows me to be a better critic, it allows my students and me to better understand this art form called multiculturalism.

It is a representation of parts of multicultural education. But it is not a static picture. The pieces of this mobile would be varied in color, shape, size, of course, with each suspended piece bearing particular relationship to the other.

Notes

1 This research conclusion has changed my teaching. I no longer see the abbreviated summer session as the best time to introduce multicultural education to undergraduates. Because they need more time to internalize what they are learning, the summer session comes to an end before the students are comfortable with the concepts and principles they are learning.

2 People in this stage come to understand the world and how they relate to it from the perspective of (in my case) the profession in which they seek membership. In addition to learning the professor's skills, I learned their attitudes and approaches to the world and the problems if presented them. The reason the stage is called 'intimacy vs isolation' is that an important part of the learning concerns how one establishes relationships with others, and these relationships — when successful, allow individuals to function successfully within their worlds.

3 Generativity, it seems to me, is a synonym for *productivity*, and Erikson makes the point that while there are a myriad of ways in which to be productive, each individual has insufficient time and energy to address them all. Thus young men tend to see their careers as more important than their families while young women tend to take the opposite view. Sigmund Freud noted people tend to shift their relative emphases so that by midlife, women are more likely to emphasize career and men have a greater interest in human relationships. The trick for all of us, Erikson points out, is striking a balance for the allocation of our time and energy that allows us to be both generative (productive) and happy.

4 Slotnick and colleagues (1993) described just such differences in the continuing education seeking behaviors of physicians. Young women physicians were disinclined to attend away-from-home activities while young men attended them as much to advance their careers as to learn, while mature women were more likely to attend such sessions than were mature men.

5 Perry's studies go on to show that over the course of their undergraduate careers, students develop more relativistic views so that they can accept and understand how equally credible professors (for example) can hold conflicting interpretations of the same phenomenon. Perry notes that this is often a difficult progression for undergraduates.

6 Abraham Maslow's notion of safety is 'predictability'; if one's immediate future is reasonably predictable, one is secure, and conversely. This means that beginning to do a research project offered opportunities for both success and failure, and, to the degree I felt I had my projects under control, I felt secure.

7 One of the most important insights I had during this time was that a 'revise and resubmit' request from a journal editor was not a rejection; it simply meant that there was more that could be done before the manuscript was ready for publication. I've also found that my work invariable improves through responding to the editors' requests. And so I am as pleased to receive a 'revise and resubmit' as I am to receive an 'accept'; for practical purposes, both summaries of my work have the same meaning.

8 Though I have been publishing for a number of years, I continue to be pleased when I see my work cited in someone else's writings, or when I meet someone at a professional meeting and learn they are familiar with my work.

9 The College of Education and Human Relations was the Center for Teaching and Learning until 1 July 1996.

10 Monocultural students for the purpose of my research can be defined as students who lack meaningful experience with, and knowledge of, other cultures as well as diversities.

References

AHLBURG, D.A. and DE VITA, C.J. (1992) 'New Realities of the American Family', *Population Bulletin*, **47**, 2, Washington DC: Population Reference Bureau.

ASANTE, M. (1996) 'Multiculturalism and the academy', *Academe*, **82**, 3.

CHAVEZ, R.C. (1995) *Multicultural Education in the Everyday: A Renaissance for the Recommitted*, Washington DC: The American Association of Colleges for Teacher Education.

ERIKSON, E.H. (1980) *Identity and the Life Cycle*, New York: W.W. Norton.

ERIKSON, E.H. (1982) *The Life Cycle Completed: A Review*, New York: W.W. Norton.

FULLER, M.L. (1994) 'The monocultural graduate in a multicultural environment: A challenge to teacher education', *Journal of Teacher Education*, **43**, 4.

FULLER, M.L. (1996) 'Multicultural education and classroom management', in GRANT, C.A. and GOMEZ, M.L. (eds) *Making Schools Multicultural: Campus and Classroom*, Englewood Cliffs, NJ: Merrill.

FULLER, M.L. (1992a) 'The monocultural graduate and multicultural students: A demographic clash', *Teaching Education*, **4**, 2.

FULLER, M.L. (1992b) *Monocultural Teachers in Multicultural Environments*, Paper presented at the annual meeting of the American Educational Research Association, Atlanta.

FULLER, M.L. (1993a) *Preservice Attitudes towards Poverty: 'If They Just Tried Harder'*, Jackson Hole, WY: Northern Rocky Mountain Research Association.

FULLER, M.L. (1993b) *Preservice Teachers Attitudes towards Non-traditional Families*, Jackson Hole, WY: Northern Rocky Mountain Research Association.

FULLER, M.L. and AHLER, J.C. (1991) 'Preservice multicultural education: Progressing through developmental stages', *Multicultural teaching*, **9**, 2.

GILLIGAN, C. (1982) *In a Different Voice*, Cambridge: Harvard University Press.

GILLIGAN, G. (1992) *Meeting at the Crossroads*, Cambridge: Harvard University Press.

GRANT, J. (1993) *Fundamental Feminism: Contesting the Core Concepts of Feminist Theory*, Nashville, TN: Routledge.

GRIFFITH, J.E., FRASE, M.J. and RALPH, J.H. (1989) 'American education: The challenge of change', *Population Bulletin*, **44**, 4, p. 16.

GWALTNEY, C. (1990) 'Almanac: Facts about higher education in the nation, the states, and DC', *The Chronicle of Higher Education*, pp. 11–29.

HAMACHEK, D.E. (1994) *Psychology of Teaching, Learning, and Growth*, Boston: Allyn and Bacon, Inc.

KNIKER, C.R. (1989) *Preliminary Results of a Survey of Holmes and Non-Holmes Group Teacher Education Programs*, Chicago: Midwest Holmes Group.

KOZOL, J. (1967) *Death at an Early Age: The Destruction of the Hearts and Minds of Negro Children in the Boston Public Schools*, New York: Penguin Groups.

LEVENSON, D.J. (1978) *The Seasons of a Man's Life*, New York: Ballentine Books.

LEVENSON, D.J. (1996) *The Seasons of a Woman's Life*, New York: Alfred A. Knoph.

MITROFF, I.I. and KILMAN, R.H. (1978) *Methodological Approaches to Social Science: Integrating Divergent Concepts and Theories*, San Francisco: Jossey-Bass.

PERRY, W.G., JR (1970) *Forms of Intellectual and Ethical Development in the College Years: A Scheme*, New York: Holt, Rinehart and Winston.

RYAN, W.B. (1971) *Blaming the Victim*, New York: Vintage Books.

SCHON, D.A. (1990) *Educating the Reflective Practioner*, San Francisco: Jossey-Bass.

SHERMAN, A. (1994) *Wasting America's Future: The Children's Defense Fund Report on the Cost of Child Poverty*, Boston: Beacons Press.

SLEETER, C.E. and GRANT, C.A. (1993) *Making Choices for Multicultural Education* (3rd ed.), New York: Merrill.

SLOTNICK, H.B., PELTON, M.H., TABOR, L. and FULLER, M.L. (1993) *The Adult Learner*, London: Falmer Press.

TYLER, R. (1949) *The Principles of Curriculum and Instruction*, University of Chicago Press.

US CENSUS BUREAU (1993) 'Poverty in the United States', *Current Population Research Series*, Washington DC: US Government Printing Office, pp. 60–185.

WEBB, R.B. and SHERMAN, R.R. (1989) *Schooling and Society* (2nd ed.), New York: Macmillan Publishing Company.

WISE, A.E. and GOLLNICK, D.M. (1996) 'America in demographic denial (National Council for Accreditation of Teacher Education)', *Quality Teaching*, **5**, 2.

19   Circling Toward Research

Reba Neukom Page

As it has turned out, I more or less fell into fieldwork. What I mean with that awkward juxtaposition of tenses is that I never planned to take up educational ethnography. For that matter, I never planned to take up research of any kind, even in 1980 when I began doctoral studies in the School of Education at the University of Wisconsin Madison. Whatever plan I had then entailed, at best, learning something more about schooling, particularly curriculum and, more particularly yet, curriculum for students who experience little success in school and who I had been teaching for about a decade. If I had a long-term view, I expressed it as becoming a teacher of teachers.

Yet I have joined the educational research community. Carl Grant's charge to explain how I have come to do research and to do the kinds of studies of schooling I do has set me musing. In reflecting, I have run up against what seems an ongoing circling of schooling, family, and the times I grew up in. I am somewhat startled to see what could be read as a relatively steady, if slow and circuitous, march right toward field research.

As example of this retrospective constructivism, I begin here by recollecting a project in urban history that I undertook some 30 years ago as an undergraduate at Washington University in St Louis. I can now name the work 'ethnographic', or 'ethnographic-like', with a focus and methods that are quite similar to the interpretive inquiries I conduct today. Recalling it is one way to comment on the intertwining of curricular and cultural differentiation that centers my present research.

*   *   *

In 1964, as a history major at Washington University, I learned I was eligible to take an honors senior seminar. Urban History was to be the topic. I signed on, even though I had no prior coursework in urban history. For one thing, the 'problem of the cities' had re-entered the public agenda. As well, I believe I must have thought a seminar would be 'good' for me: It would make me 'stretch', and it was an academic honor that, for whatever reasons, I should not pass up. I was not concerned particularly about the usefulness of such a course being on my transcript; in the early 1960s, jobs were readily available to college graduates, even students in the humanities. Nor was I thinking about the seminar in terms of graduate school, about which I had little awareness and no plans. In my family, it was enough that I was finishing college.

I remember the professor who would lead the seminar, Samuel B. Warner, Jr, as a young 'Turk', fresh from the halls of Harvard and flush with the success of seeing his dissertation published as the book, *Streetcar Suburbs*. He laid out his version of 'seminar' in the first meeting of the class: We would meet two or three times as a group to talk about how one carries out studies of urban history; after that, each of us would proceed individually, conducting an historical study on a topic of our choosing and writing it up in a final paper that was due the last week of the semester.

During the first meetings, Warner instructed us in what at the time was a new, social science rendition of historical research. In contrast to the 'literary', great-persons and great-ideas history that most of our professors espoused, history as social science promised that contemporary institutions, such as the metropolis, were worth investigation; that the relevant data were in the records of ordinary living, such as tax receipts, hospital manuals, or water treatment plans; and, further, that analyzing data statistically would lead to the discovery of demonstrable social patterns, or structures, which were previously invisible or misconstrued.

We read *Streetcar Suburbs* as an exemplar of the new history. The book documented a kind of if-you-build-it, they-will-come pattern in urbanization. Thus, American cities were not haphazard conglomerations, and the suburbs that began ringing them in the nineteenth century were not simply a spillover response to urban crowding. Rather, suburban expansion correlated with the provision of easy, inexpensive transportation, such as streetcar lines. Streetcars made it feasible for middle-class citizens to emulate the wealthy, with work in the city and a home in the country.

This was heady stuff. The endlessly debatable interpretations and messy details of traditional history would be replaced by succinct, clear-cut statistical relationships, some of them representative even of 'deep' social structures (California freeways replicated the streetcar pattern about a century later, for example). Research would be democratized, too — even undergraduates might contribute! — because data were no longer limited to centuries of texts (and exegeses of texts) about remote events, however interesting. Perhaps most seductive was the promise that scholarship, including history, was directly practical: If people could describe plainly and unequivocally the evolution of important social institutions, they would then know how to plan and manage them better.

Our task as students during those first weeks of lecture included locating a phenomenon in the St Louis metropolitan area whose origins and evolution were worth studying. Influenced by Warner's enthusiasms, I began looking at maps, something I had neglected previously (and a serious lapse for a student of history). I quickly appreciated the complexity, as well as the bird's eye view, that maps of St Louis presented. Patterns replaced my previously inchoate image of the city, as I noticed the bulge of the Mississippi, key transportation arteries, canals and drainage ditches and, especially, the fan-shape of a metropolitan area stretched north–south by the river and west by the frontier. The 'border state' appellation took on new meaning.

I read maps of St Louis with an eye to the local, too, looking for the places I knew and the routes I and my family followed. My eye fell often on the suburb of Webster Groves, about 10 miles from downtown St Louis, where we had lived for five years and where I had spent my last two years of high school.

I had a residue of affectionate curiosity about Webster, left over from those high school years. The move there from Cleveland High School in south St Louis had been nothing short of a liberation. Although the city school had a courtly scholar-administrator (Dr Arthur Svoboda) and an outstanding faculty (Mr Harold Doxsee, my English teacher; a math teacher so excellent I still regret having spent only two years under her tutelage), most students I knew there saw high school as compulsory tedium, girls were not to let on that they were smart, and the thought of continuing schooling if one graduated was simply incredible. By contrast, at Webster High I found peers who admitted to reading books outside of classes and who were eager to talk about them. 96 percent of the 700 seniors in my graduating class went on to post-secondary schooling.[1]

My curiosity about the suburb sharpened when I noticed, in perusing a census map of St Louis County, three, small concentrations of Negro[2] housing floating in the otherwise all-white sea surrounding the city of St Louis.[3] North Webster was one of the three.

The census map disturbed my common sense. I had never thought much about North Webster. I knew its name and that it was the Negro section of Webster Groves, but I was not certain exactly where it was.[4] Nor had I ever thought much about blacks closer to home or noticed how unusual Negro residents were in St Louis County (3 percent of the county population in 1960 versus 30 percent in the city). Common sense told me to look for African-Americans in St Louis;, I took for granted that to volunteer as a reading tutor, I would travel downtown to the Pruitt-Igoe Housing Project. But, that census map set me wondering about 'the history of the Negro community of Webster Groves'.

Dr Warner approved the topic for my seminar project. Within days, I was totally consumed by it. I must have been taking other courses — I am sure a transcript records them — but I confess I cannot recall them (there *was* a second semester of classical history, but the Romans never proved as captivating as the Greeks). By the time the final paper was written, I would have consulted more than 50 books about urban history and black history, as well as scores of novels and stories; pawed over countless maps, deed books, housing reports, and other data sources; and conducted forty interviews with residents of Webster and North Webster.

Part of the project's allure was Dr Warner's social science history. Part was the puzzle, what *were* the origins of North Webster and how *had* the community evolved? Part, too, was the absence of the familiar students' game. I would not be able to look up a topic in the card catalog, read and synthesize references, and write everything up in a 20-page, double-spaced, typed paper. Instead, I would have to live with some uncertainty about exactly where I was going and even what I was looking for. Sometimes, this was anxiety-producing. More often, it was exhilarating. I was young. I don't think I doubted that what I hoped to understand would prove possible.

Thinking back, I recall a more or less *ad hoc* unfolding of the research project, as I let one 'text' lead me to the next, a strategy not unlike that I had learned in traditional history classes. To begin, I headed to familiar territory: the university library. There, I consulted general histories of St Louis, trying to piece together the growth of the St Louis area as a whole, so that I could understand the development of Webster Groves within it, and within Webster, the Negro community of North Webster.

I also haunted the public library in Webster Groves, assuming, rightly as it turned out, that it would have a reasonably good collection of local historical documents and newspaper clippings. I discovered, too, the St Louis Historical Society, where I managed to figure out the cataloging system sufficiently to ask the archivist to bring out volumes of original and facsimile papers and maps dating back to the 1700s. I spent countless hours there, utterly entranced. It seemed (and still seems) a miracle that a young woman with negligible credentials was allowed to handle documents which, by their age alone, struck me as priceless. At various points, too, I became conscious of myself acting like a scholar.

The initial reading spree produced some basic information. For instance, I learned that, beginning in the early 1800s, Webster Groves was principally a rural community of farms, but there were also a few summer estates to which wealthy businessmen in St Louis sent their families so that they could avoid the onslaughts of typhoid and malaria that afflicted the city by the Mississippi. Some decades later, when the businessmen could commute to the city on the Missouri-Pacific Union Railroad, the summer houses became year-round residences. These details explained 'old Webster', or 'the Park', where grand, three- and four-story frame houses with wrap-around porches still stand amid oaks, maples, elms, and hickories.

The same sources told me that North Webster originated with the end of the Civil War, when slaves in Missouri were freed. In Webster, former owners gave former slaves land nearby, 'in the bottoms' along Shady Creek, on which to live. From there, they would also be available to work locally as grounds-keepers, cooks, maids, and in other service jobs.

Comforted by locating some pertinent facts, I puzzled nevertheless about their significance. Were the 'gifts' of land acts of generosity or some kind of enlightened reparation, for example, or were they a cheap and legal means to continue a kind of indentured servitude? Did ownership of land 'in the bottoms' prove economically and socially significant for African-Americans in Webster? Who *were* those black and white people from an earlier century and how *did* they live together?

My questions about what North Webster signified intensified when I came across plat maps — maps which record transfers of property. There, in elegant, now coppery ink script were the tracts into which Webster was gradually subdivided: Mary Gore's Subdivision, Glen Park, Francis Plant's Subdivision, and so forth. Sure enough, too, Warner's hypothesis seemed to hold for Webster Groves: Late nineteenth century streetcar lines *were* followed by an increased division of large estates and farms into middle-class, suburban tracts.

But, as intriguing to me as succinct correlations were the messy details etched on the plat maps: the shapes and names of streets, lot numbers, the names of residents, and the dates of sales and transfers. As I pored over them, some of the names of land-owners in North Webster seemed vaguely familiar. I recalled a Redmond in my graduating class. On a hunch, I picked up a contemporary phone book and, to my astonishment, found listed many of the last names that were inscribed on the nineteenth-century plat maps.

I began driving and walking around Webster and North Webster, maps in hand. The histories I had read re-oriented me, changing what I looked at and how. I now noticed as distinctive and telling Webster's meandering streets, with nothing at right angles. It was all very much like country lanes, even though we were within a short distance of a major metropolis. I marveled at the showboats in 'old Webster', not in terms of aesthetics, architecture, or the money one had to have to buy them, as I had earlier, but instead, in terms of the public health conditions that prompted families a century earlier to leave the city during the summer months; an early transportation system that made the 10-mile trip from St Louis to Webster a journey so onerous that it required a summer house rather than a daily commute; and the conditions of the city for residents who would not have had the means to escape them.

On one walk, I came to the steep ravine in which ran the tracks of the Missouri-Pacific Union Railroad. Informally if quite materially, it marked the border between 'the Park' and an adjoining area at the far edge of which sat North Webster. I had never crossed those tracks in the 5 years I had lived in Webster. I can recall being warned that it was a dangerous passage in a car, with poor visibility of oncoming traffic. More important, I now suspect, was a culture structured symbolically as well as materially, that provided the *absence* of any idea that I might want to travel into North Webster, coupled with some half-realized notion that I was not supposed to travel there.[5]

Armed with a research question, however, I had a reason to venture across the rickety bridge over the tracks. The change in scene was immediate. The homogeneous area of estates in 'the Park' gave way, first, to generous two-story houses occupied by Whites, and then to North Webster, a more heterogeneous neighborhood where moderate-sized, brick and frame houses and lush gardens jostled against deteriorating shacks or overgrown vacant lots. At the same time, North Webster was as 'countrified' as the rest of Webster, replete with wandering streets, large shade trees, and rampant honeysuckle.

My sojourns into North Webster also turned up the information, blazoned on a billboard, that the community was the target of an Urban Renewal Project. I went to the agency's offices in Webster, described my interests, and — again, a marvel — was given free access to shoeboxes full of 4x6 cards describing structures and inhabitants in North Webster. From the cards, I learned, for example, that just minutes from my family's comfortable house were houses without indoor plumbing, electricity, or central heating.

For a time, the boxes from the federal agency reignited the possibility of social science history. However, that possibility gave way because the data were uneven and my knowledge of statistics, meager. As well, I kept returning to a different kind of query, often driven by personal experiences and concerns. I wanted to understand better what North Webster *meant*, sitting there in all-white Webster and all-white St Louis County. Particularly, what did it mean for the people who had lived there a century earlier, and what, for present residents, myself included? What, too, might the two Websters have to say about a racialized 'America'?

The interpretive focus corresponded to shifts in what I was reading, too. Influenced by my walks and the plat maps, I had turned from general social histories of St Louis and the Midwest to black history and literature. Like urban history, these were topics I had not studied in my college courses. I found Booker T. Washington, of course, but also WEB DuBois. Frazier's *Black Bourgeoisie* had just been published and seemed to throw light on features of North Webster.[6] I read Pauli Murray's (1956) *Proud Shoes*, stories by James Baldwin and Ralph Ellison, and Gwendolyn Brooks' (1959) *The Bean Eaters*. I read and, in some cases, re-read, books about the South, too: Faulkner's (1986) trilogy that begins with *The Hamlet;* Warrent's *All the King's Men*; and Lee's *To Kill a Mockingbird*. I began devoting more attention to the burgeoning civil rights movement, particularly its history, by retrieving from *Time* and *Life* articles about federal troops enforcing integration in Little Rock's schools or boycotts in Atlanta.

In time, my interest in the significance of North Webster and its relation to Webster drew me to the idea that I should try to interview community members. In this venture, I was not following methodological conventions that asserted the primacy of 'the native's point of view'. It would be 20 years before I would hear about 'the native', much less the Other, although my history professors taught always about the importance of grasping the *zeitgeist* of an era and about the mistaken and disrespectful anachronisms that result when contemporary values are imposed on earlier eras. Rather, interviewing people in 1964 was a practical expedience. It developed from the dearth of information in the published histories about the suburb of Webster Groves and the Negro section.

At the same time, and however dim my awareness of it, I must have also been working away at comprehending how humans arrange the world into difference and community, just as I do more self-consciously today in the research I undertake. Resonating with Dubois' (1961) words about the value of humane knowledge, I chose them as epigram for the final seminar paper:

> Herein, lies the tragedy of the age: not that men are poor — all men know something of poverty; not that men are wicked — who is good? Not that men are ignorant — what is truth? *Nay, but that men know so little of men* [my emphasis].

I started the interviews with Mr Boulding, a teacher of American history at Webster High whose class I had taken (and the only black teacher on the faculty during the two years I attended). From him, I learned some of the names of community members who it might be important to talk to and who might be amenable to talking to me, and I secured his introductions to several with whom I could begin.

The interviews proved a crucial source of data and perspective. I would not have encountered either, had I limited my inquiry to the history books, plat maps, or the files of the Urban Renewal agency. Nor could I have imagined them or dredged them up from my own world view. Rather, they challenged my world view.

For example, I knew from local sources that there had been a black school in North Webster, the Douglass School. I had not thought much further about it, fitting it instead into a framework with other black schools that had operated separately, unequally, and presumably, badly, for almost a century. However, the local school's existence, both past and present, took on a radically different significance in the interviews when several families pulled out yearbooks to show me pictures of themselves or of their parents or children or prominent leaders in the community. I was dumbfounded: Here were editors of a school newspaper, captains and players on a football team, Prom Queens, a Latin Club, a choir, the Thespian Society, and on and on. I could have been looking at my 1960 yearbook from Webster High, except that here, all of those pictured were African-Americans whereas, in the Webster edition, almost none were.

The interviews held other surprises. For instance, as a young and therefore terribly high-minded liberal, I was stunned to learn that community members in North Webster did not view integration as an unadulterated blessing. They told me — quietly and delicately but firmly and even a bit grimly — that the Douglass School had been a vital center of their community. The worried that their children, even though they were now attending a highly ranked public school, were *losing* educational opportunities. They asked me: Could, and did, their children now participate in and lead clubs or classes at Webster High? Did teachers there credit the children's talents, ambitions, and interests, as teachers had at Douglass? Even though the African-American school had always suffered from inadequate and unequal funds, it was a place where the children belonged.[7] It was also a place of considerable educational excellence, residents told me, with several teachers holding advanced degrees from prestigious universities but teaching at Douglass because jobs for educated Negroes were in short supply in the St Louis area.[8]

Similarly mixed, I learned, were the blessings residents anticipated from the Urban Renewal project. To be sure, houses would be upgraded with indoor plumbing and central heating, and streets would no longer be unpaved or flooded by Shady Creek. But North Webster would also lose houses that had been in families for generations. The rambling, rural-like landscape was threatened and it was not without its charms, as the twisting, inefficient lanes in 'old Webster' attested. Residents worried, too, that reducing the diversity and eccentricity of habitations to standardized, mid-century, 'low-income' modules might lead to an influx of Negroes from the inner city.

These interviews disturbed and complicated my thinking, presenting me points of view I had not anticipated. I was not sure I 'approved' of them either. My version of right thinking was a kind of idealized humanism in which all Americans are brothers and sisters under the skin (or could be, if only certain people — usually 'the South' — could be made to see the light). The testimony from North Webster challenged that view, perhaps most especially its assumption that inclusion and integration were what Whites should be doing 'for' disadvantaged minorities.[9] However incompletely and momentarily, the testimony of North Webster residents gave me a glimpse that the truths I take to be self-evident, aren't.

* * *

I recall a 30-year old seminar project — the final paper marked with an 'A', stuffed into a navy blue folder, and moldering now in a file cabinet — to signal aspects of the interpretive research I practice today. As in 1964, I am easily 'hooked' by the process of conducting research, my energy for it reflecting, at least in part, the years I worked in public schools and other social institutions where the privilege and resources for research might have proved helpful but were rarely available. My methods today are still *ad hoc* so that they vary, depending on the questions I pursue. As in 1964, my reading, too, remains eclectic, probably because, in following one 'text' to others, the satisfaction of connecting the things I happen upon along the way to things I already understand outweighs my anxiety about inefficiency or being too much the generalist.

As important and enduring as the methods I use are the questions that drive them, and me. I continue to be preoccupied with the diverse ways we humans carve up the world and how, using indeterminate symbols, we are nethertheless able to bring meaningful and consequential realms into being. The domain I examine these processes in has shifted somewhat, from a suburban community to school-communities. I give particular attention now to the knowledge that schools teach and distribute, asking about what schools do to knowledge that comes within their purview as they make it school knowledge and, as well, about how and with what effects particular kinds of knowledge come to be enshrined in school curriculum. On both counts, I seek to understand what ordinary school lessons mean, both for the teachers and students who encounter them most directly and for the wider polity, whose resources support public schooling and, which is, presumably, supported by it.

Accordingly, in *Lower-track Classrooms: A Curricular and Cultural Perspective* (1991), I seek to explicate how, in learning lessons about English and history, teachers and students in regular- and lower-track classes also learn about their places in a particular scholastic and social order. More recently, I have been studying high school science (1995). With an eye to the disdain adolescents express for the knowledge that many adults deem the culture's worthiest, I wonder if school science evokes the sociocultural dilemma posed by expertise and experts in a democratic culture. I wonder too how diverse representations of that dilemma may be compounded by gender, age, ethnicity, or other socio-cultural precepts.

While I can thus assert links between present research and a long-past seminar, I am less certain how to account for my unwavering curiosity about symbolic processes. I speculate, therefore, in what follows, when I find traces of the times, family, and graduate studies influencing the ebb and flow of my thinking about how people socially construct representations of self, other, school, and society.[10]

Thus, I am very much a creature of the times in my evolving understanding of the meaning of differentiation, membership, and 'America', even, I find, when I am most non-conforming. For example, my appreciation of differences, which community members in North Webster offered me in 1964, was short-lived. Rather quickly, I reverted to a kind of classic 'do-goodism' (Page, 1994) at which I was quite practiced, even as a girl. My aim in jobs as social worker and teacher, like many of my contemporaries in the war on poverty and subsequent reforms, was not to attend to difference but to eradicate it, almost always in the name of equity, well-being, and 'helping'. Not surprisingly, the results of these efforts were classic, too. As I watched things stay the same, despite all sorts of good intentions to change them (Sarason, 1972), I retreated, baffled. For some time, I turned to a detached relativism, with occasional cynicism: People are different, I learned to say, and they should be able to go their way without my intruding my values on them. This stance is not unlike the individualism that some lament today.

Along with the shifting times, family, too, played into my attentiveness to the diverse and connected 'worlds' people make with words. For instance, a childhood of moving around taught me first-hand the importance of casing a joint before making commitments. It also meant that, having arrived in the seminar at Washington University via Louisiana, Mississippi, Arizona, and Missouri, I was well-equipped with what I can now designate the skills of participant-observation.[11]

The mixed marriage of which I am a product was a significant factor, too, for my alertness to meaning-making and to differences and consensus among people in what things mean. The particular mix in my case involved a southern mother and a Yankee father.

My father went south at the end of the Depression, straight out of medical school, to a first job with Mississippi's Department of Public Health. He had turned to medicine late, after coming close to flunking out of Garfield High in Terre Haute (the first of eight siblings to achieve that 'distinction'), running bootleg liquor up from Kentucky, and riding the rails west to escape Indiana and the family drug store. Practical heroics continued in his parenting. For instance, understanding my disappointment when a storm threatened to dissolve my fifth birthday party and knowing my mother was not about to have 10 screaming children roaming her living room, he rescued the situation by nailing the household rugs over the breezeway so that the party could go on.

He and my mother met in Batesville, Mississippi, where she was a nurse. A taciturn beauty of considerable wit, she was also something of a golddigger (and poor enough to warrant it). One story has it that she was engaged to be married four or five times before she met and accepted my father, and she kept the engagement rings along the way. In time, she was also a victim of chronic illnesses. Yet, even in illness, she emerged occasionally to corral my father's energies. For example, when I announced that, following college graduation and marriage, I was going to work on an organic farm commune, my father only quit asking whether that meant I wanted to take some courses in agricultural management when my mother shushed him with 'George! Just *listen*.'

Without anyone intending it, issues of might and right (and lecturing and listening) were always in the air in my family, as they were in Mississippi, where we lived until I was in the fourth grade. Even the most insignificant acts could be freighted with passion.[12] For example, Civil War was the game of choice in my neighborhood gang in Jackson and preliminary skirmishes were always necessary to determine who would have to be the Yankees. However, whatever my lot, I always risked betraying one parent.

The pilgrimage we made every Christmas to my father's family in Indiana only exacerbated the divided loyalties. There, I was reminded that the North was rich, the South was poor, and the poverty mattered. It signaled a kind of moral failure and, implicitly, a choice between parents.

Schisms were complicated further in 1950, the year I turned 9, when we left the South and my mother's family for the West, where some of my father's siblings had moved in the 1920s. No one in Prescott seemed to know or care much about the Civil War, and our childhood games shifted accordingly. We turned to exploring the out-of-the-way place that Arizona then was. Replete with a spectacular Canyon and spectral

saguaros, turquoise and tostadas, elusive trout and fool's gold, the state's very vocabulary was exotic. Four short years later, we left Arizona. Fittingly enough, it seems now,
we settled in a border state. St Louis also provided my first experiences with the
mysteries and excitement of a city.

Living in diverse regions of the country, within a family oriented around deep,
largely unspoken oppositions, shaped my sensitivity to difference and communion, and
to their forms and consequences. I do not mean that either of my parents or other relatives were neglectful or unloving, Nor were they ideologues. Quite the contrary. Social
ideals or how one should live were rarely topics my family discussed explicitly; no one
was a political activist. My father would never have claimed that 'moral principles'
prompted his venture south or his career in public health. Had I asked him, I think he
would have explained that he needed a job that paid steady and reasonably well, and the
Mississippi Department of Public Health offered one.

Therefore, where others may learn to see social issues, including differentiation, as
clear-cut in the actions they demand, I grew up seeing them as requiring judgment and
choice but always with loyalty and love as complicating factors. For instance, I cared for
my mother, but I never talked with her, or she with me, about her illnesses or how they
separated us. Instead, I assumed I knew what she 'should' do; like my father and me,
she should accept our 'help' and overcome illness by choosing to be strong and healthy.
When she did not so choose, I never thought to wonder about her perspective on the
situation, the way I learned to wonder about the perspectives of people in North Webster.

Similarly complicated in its meaning, if more fleeting, is a two-sentence interchange with an uncle who, along with several of my cousins, met my train in Jackson in
1955 when I was 12 years old. Driving to my grandmother's house, sitting in the middle
of the front seat, I could smell the gasoline on my uncle's clothes from the filling station
he ran. I saw the oil stains on his hands on the steering wheel. He asked me how I liked
'sitting next to n — in school' in St Louis. My cousins waited; someone snickered; 'It
isn't so bad', I ventured.

That interchange sticks with me to this day, emblematic of the layers of signification that even the briefest speech can carry. I recall shame at not naming my uncle's
racism, for example. I also recall anger at the hurtfulness of his 'joke', made at the
expense of a girl too young to defend herself. Later, reading headlines about Little Rock
or watching riots in Detroit or Boston on TV, I imagined my uncle, or any of my
mother's family, or my father's family for that matter, among the screaming Whites.
I worried that I could be them too.

At the same time, my reaction to my uncle was also tentative. After all, he was my
uncle, my family. I knew him well enough to think that he did not mean to be hurtful
and I could remember other times when he was not. I also knew that his own life had
been one of continual poverty, victimization, and striving and, I thought, he might have
some reason to grasp at status when he could.

I think about such fragments of personal history. I am more conscious now of how
they intertwine with public events as well as with the questions and methods that guide
my research into schooling. My reflections on them are influenced by books and university experiences, as well as family and the times.

For instance, Clifford Geertz's (1986) fable of the Drunken Indian and the Kidney
Machine reorients my recollections of mid-century 'America' and my understanding
of difference and community in the 1990s, too. I hear it speak especially to me and
my mother. In the fable, a Navajo is eligible for dialysis but he also refuses to quit the

drinking that has destroyed his body. This disgusts and dismays the Anglo doctors who wish they could refuse him treatment and give it to a more deserving patient. Stuck with each other, both sides proceed self-righteously. The Navajo receives dialysis and continues to drink; the doctors follow procedures and continue to be disgusted; the situation is 'a dribbling out to an ambiguous end' (Geertz, p. 268) until the Indian dies.

As Geertz points out, the tragedy in the story is that neither party knows much of anything about the other and, because of the self-righteousness, neither thinks to learn anything, either. (Echoes of Dubois: The 'tragedy of the age . . . is that men know so little of men.') There is 'helping', moral judgment, mutual accusation, and retreat, but little understanding of the angle at which another person might be coming at the world and, therefore, no understanding either of the slant at which one comes at it, oneself. The essay helps me re-think how I have responded to difference and association — romanticizing it, replacing it with do-good standards, or retreating from it in splendid isolation — and it points me instead toward striving to remain open to comprehending even those with whom we must disagree. In the process, I place myself within the fray rather than apart from it.

I first learned of Geertz's work in 1980, in doctoral studies in the School of Education at the University of Wisconsin, Madison, where gifted teachers introduced me to curriculum and cultural studies. Professors there, particularly Herbert M. Kliebard, Mary Haywood Metz, George and Louise Spindler, and Michael Apple, provided the resources, expectations, and space for conversation that are crucial to beginning to think through issues of differentiation and membership. I am indebted, too, to participants in several midwestern and southwestern high schools who, since the early 1980s, have opened their practices and thoughts to me so that I might learn about them and, at the same time, to learn about my own.

For a long while after leaving high schools to study and, later, to work in the university, I thought (guiltily) that I was using books, teaching, and research in the ivory tower to escape the world. I worried that I was intellectualizing and thereby side-stepping the 'real', 'action-issues' of culturally organized chaos in public institutions and private family. More recently, however, I have clarified that, for me, so-called 'intellectual' pursuits, rather than offering a means to elude demons and divert pressing personal and professional troubles, are a key means by which I gain access to them. Ideas are a more trustworthy means for me than pathos or passion. They open those demons and troubles in a form I can accept, so that I can countenance them — and me.

* * *

When I was in my early 30s, I received as birthday card a poem by Rainer Maria Rilke (1981) from Cynthia Johnson, who was my room mate when we were freshmen at the University of Colorado-Boulder: Struck by my friend's affection and Rilke's images, I kept the card. I re-read it every few years, reviewing the circles I weave as I piece together people and events to make my life.

Spinning meaning about myself and others and considering how and with what I, and others, do the fabricating are what I seem to have a bent for personally. Happily for me, it is what I do professionally too, both in teaching and in research endeavors. I can only speculate, as I have here, about what inspires my inclination for this kind of activity. But I am indebted to Carl Grant, as I am to other teachers, including my parents, people in Webster and North Webster and in contemporary high schools, for presenting questions that prompt me to muse on possibilities.

Notes

1 The CBS documentaries, *16 in Webster Groves* (1965) and *Webster Groves Revisited* (1965), present some of the less enlightened aspects of adolescence in the middle- and upper-middle class suburb.
2 I use the designation, 'Negro', which was current in 1960.
3 Negroes also lived in several unincorporated sections of St Louis County.
4 My ignorance about North Webster was not simply a function of being a relative newcomer. For example, friends who grew up in Webster Groves never played in the park in North Webster or, as teenagers, drove its streets.
5 I and friends sometimes passed *through* North Webster on a small parkway, en route from downtown Webster to other communities.
6 Sara Lawrence-Lightfoot (1994) encountered this text at about the same time and uses it to frame *I've Known Rivers*.
7 Vanessa Siddle-Walker makes this point in her research about segregated black schools in the South.
8 When integration was accomplished in the Webster school system shortly after the Brown decision, many black teachers found themselves unemployed, except for a few like Mr Boulding. Nikki Merchant, a student at Harvard's Graduate School of Education, is interested in the unintended consequences of integration for the careers of black teachers. See, also, Morris and Ambrose (1993) for a photographic history of North Webster.
9 Traces of a populist version of *noblesse oblige* thread through my final seminar paper.
10 30-something years of conversations with my husband, Philip Page, as well as his recent scholarship (1996), are important to my thinking, too.
11 My life continues to unfold as a series of moves across the diverse regions of the US (and a little of the world), including stops along the way at a cash register factory in Berlin, Germany; organic farms (a commune outside Washington, DC; seven acres of Wisconsin's Arlington Prairie); and college and university towns in rural Illinois, Wisconsin, and Maine and urban Boston, Baltimore, and the LA basin.
12 Paterson's (1996) *Sweet Mystery* is a compelling memoir about childhood, North-South marriages, and chronic illnesses.

References

BROOKS, G. (1959) *The Bean Eaters*, New York: Harper and Brothers.
  (1965) *16 in Webster Groves*, New York: CBS News.
  (1965) *Webster Groves Revisited*, New York: CBS News.
DuBOIS, W.E.B. (1961) *The Souls of Black Folk*, Greenwich, CT: Fawcett Publications (Original work published 1903).
FAULKNER, W. (1986) *The Hamlet*, New York: Vintage International (Original work published 1940).
FRAZIER, F. (1962) *Black Bourgeoisie*, New York: Crowell-Collier Publishing Company.
GEERTZ, C. (1986) *The Uses of Diversity. The Tanner Lectures on Human Values*, Salt Lake City, UT: University of Utah Press.
LEE, H. (1960) *To Kill a Mockingbird*, Philadelphia: Lippincott.
LIGHTFOOT, S.L. (1994) *I've Known Rivers*, New York: Penguin Books.
MORRIS, A.C., and AMBROSE, H. (1993) *North Webster: A Photographic History of a Black Community*, Bloomington, IN: University of Indiana Press.
MURRAY, P. (1956) *Proud Shoes*, New York: Harper (Original work published 1910).
NEUKOM, R.J. (1964) 'The Webster Negro community', Unpublished manuscript.
PAGE, P. (1996) *Dangerous Freedom: Fusion and Fragmentation in Toni Morrison's Novels*, Jackson, MS: University of Mississippi Press.

PAGE, R. (1991) *Lower-track Classrooms: A Curricular and Cultural Perspective*, New York: Teachers College Press.

PAGE, R. (1994) 'Do-good ethnography', *Curriculum Inquiry*, **24**, pp. 479–502.

PAGE, R. (1995) 'Who's systematizing the systematizers?: Policy and practice interactions in a case of state-level systemic reform', *Theory into Practice*, **34**, pp. 21–9.

PATERSON, J. (1996) *Sweet Mystery*, New York: Farrar, Strauss and Giroux.

RILKE, R.M. (1981) 'Untitled', in BLY, R. (ed.) *Selected Poems by Ranier Marie Rilke: A Translation from the German and Commentary*, New York: Harper and Row.

SARASON, S. (1972) *The Culture of the School and the Problem of Change* (2nd ed.), Boston: Allyn and Bacon.

SIDDLE-WALKER, V. (1994) *African-American Education, Then and Now: Segregated Schools As a Context for School Reform*, Invited paper presented at the annual meetings of the American Educational Research Association, New Orleans, LA.

WARNER, S.B, JR (1962) *Streetcar Suburbs*, Cambridge, MA: University Press.

WARREN, R.P. (1960) *All the King's Men*, New York: Harcourt Brace (Original work published 1953).

Notes on Contributors

Donna E. Alvermann is University of Georgia Research Professor in Reading Education. Her most recent research explores the potential of feminist pedagogy and poststructural theory for interpreting gendered literacy practices in middle school, high school, and college level classrooms. Having minored in history throughout her undergraduate and graduate programs, she is particularly interested in tracing personal experiences and theoretical underpinnings that guide her present research. In 1997, she received the Oscar S. Causey Award for outstanding contributions to reading research.

Michael W. Apple is John Bascom Professor of Curriculum and Instruction and Educational Policy at the University of Wisconsin-Madison. A former elementary and secondary school teacher and past-president of a teachers union, he has worked with educational systems, governments, universities, and activist and dissident groups throughout the world to democratize educational research, policy, and practice. He has written extensively on the politics of educational reform and on the relationship between culture and power. Among his many books are *Ideology and Curriculum, Education and Power, Teachers and Texts, Official Knowledge*, and most recently *Democratic Schools* and *Cultural Politics and Education*.

Elizabeth Ellsworth is Professor of Curriculum and Instruction and teaches media production and the politics of representation in the Educational Communications Technology Program at the University of Wisconsin-Madison. Her recent work, *Teaching Positions: Difference, Pedagogy, and the Power of Address* asks: 'Who does pedagogy think you are?' and explores the importance of this question to teaching difference.

Mary Lou Fuller This has been a difficult piece to write. For while I take great pleasure in studying, researching and writing about multicultural issues I have rarely thought about myself as a part of my research — though on a cognitive level. I certainly recognize that self and work are inseparable. The nature of this writing task was at once exciting and at the same time uncomfortable. I chose to use this chapter as a vehicle to examine two factors: First, the mechanics of being a researcher and second an examination of some of the research that I've done. It is with trepidation and humility that I've suggested a developmental model for researchers in academia and I would appreciate you, as the reader, sharing your input and personal views on this subject with me.

Dr. Eugene García is Dean of the Graduate School of Education and Professor of Education at the University of California, Berkeley. He has published extensively in the area of language teaching and bilingual development. He served as a Senior Officer and Director of the Office of Bilingual Education and Minority Languages Affairs in the U.S. Department of Education from 1993–1995 and he is conducting research in the areas of effective schooling for linguistically and culturally diverse student populations.

Mary Louise Gomez is an Associate Professor in the Department of Curriculum & Instruction at the University of Wisconsin-Madison where she co-directs a collaborative study aimed at understanding how primary grade teachers think about and practice good literacy teaching to diverse student groups. She teaches graduate courses in methods of narrative inquiry and the teaching of writing to diverse learners. She is co-editor (with Carl Grant) of *Campus and classroom: Making Schooling Multicultural* (Merrill, 1996) and co-editor (with Ken Zeichner and Susan Melnick) of *Currents of Reform in Pre-Service Teacher Education* (Teachers College Press, 1996). Her work has appeared in *Teaching and Teacher Education*, *Language Arts*, *Action in Teacher Education*, and *Teaching Education*.

Carl A. Grant is currently Hoefs-Bascom Professor at the University of Wisconsin-Madison, as well as Professor in the Department of Curriculum and Instruction and Afro-American Studies. He has written widely in the area of multicultural education and has received a number of awards for his distinguished and scholarly contribution to the field.

Mildred J. Hudson earned her Ph.D. from Columbia University, Teachers College in New York City. For seven years, she was a program officer at the DeWitt Wallace-Reader's Digest Fund where she designed and implemented $100 million in education programs. Her work at the foundation included a $50 million national initiative designed to recruit and prepare teachers, particularly teachers of color, for rural and urban public schools. President Clinton's recently proposed $350 million national teacher recruitment and training program attests to the work of Dr. Hudson. She is currently University-Scholar-In-Residence at Morgan State University in Baltimore, MD.

Joyce Elaine King is Associate Vice Chancellor for Academic Affairs and Diversity Programs at the University of New Orleans. She received a B.A. in sociology (with honors) and a Ph.D. in the Social Foundations of Education from Standford University. Her research and scholarship has focused on the sociology of knowledge that functions as ideology and combating dysconscious racism in teacher education and curriculum. A publication that demonstrates her commitment to community-minded research as a tool for education and social change is *Black Mothers to Sons: Juxtaposing African American Literature with Social Practice* (with Carolyn A. Mitchell): NY: Peter Lang (1995).

Peter McLaren is a Marxist social theorist and social activist. He is Professor of Urban Schooling in the Graduate School of Education and Information Studies, University of California, Los Angeles. He is interested in local and global politics in the larger context of anti-capitalist struggle. Professor McLaren serves on the Board of Trustees of the Latino Museum of History, Art downtown Los Angeles.

Sonia Nieto is a product of the New York City public schools. She was born and raised in the Williamsburg section of Brooklyn, a largely Puerto Rican community. There, she began her education as a Spanish-speaking first-grader and still remembers the trauma of learning English. When she was a teenager, her family moved to East Flatbush, the first Puerto Rican family on the block, and she and her sister were among a handful of Puerto Rican students in a student body of 5,600 students at Erasmus Hall High School. When they attended the Brooklyn annex of St. John's University, they were of fewer than a half dozen Puerto Rican students there as well. After graduating from college, she went to Spain to study for her masters in literature and ironically it was there, after meeting her future husband, that she was finally able to appreciate what she had almost abandoned, her Puerto Rican identity. Her experiences have fueled her desire to teach, to share, and to work for social justice for all students. She revels in the riches, the contradictions, the comfort, and the dilemmas of what it means to be a Puerto Rican in the United States. Sonia Nieto is married to Angel, who she met in Spain more than 32 years ago, and they have two daughters and two granddaughters.

Reba Page is Professor of Education at the University of California, Riverside where she teaches about curriculum, interparative research methods, and the social and cultural foundaitrns of education.

Becky Ropers-Huilman is an Assistant Professor in the College of Education and in Women's and Gender Studies at Louisiana State University. Her research and interests primarily focus on critical and poststructural approaches to inquiry, feminist theory and methodology, feminist intersections with higher education institutions, higher education cultures, and teaching and learning in academic environments. Some of her work is published in *Gender and Education, Feminist Teacher, Higher Education: Handbook of Theory and Research, International Journal of Qualitative Studies in Education*, and *The National Women's Studies Association Journal*, as well as in a recent Teachers College Press book entitled *Feminist teaching in theory and practice: Situating power and knowledge in poststructural classrooms*. Her commitment to multiple ways of knowing and understanding feminist practice in educational settings continues to guide her scholarship.

Christine Sleeter is a Professor in the Center for Collaborative Education and Professional Studies at California State University Monterey Bay, where she coordinates the Master of Arts in Education Program. She was formerly Professor of Teacher Education at the University of Wisconsin-Parkside. She has published widely in the area of multicultural education; her articles appear in journals such as *Journal for Research in Mathematics Education, Multicultural Education, Journal of Teacher Education*, and *Theory into Practice*. Her most recent books include *Multicultural Education as Social Activism* (SUNY Press, 1996), *Turning on Learning*, 2nd ed. (with Carl A. Grant, 1997, Merrill), and *Keepers of the American Dream* (Falmer Press, 1992).

Beth Blue Swadener is Professor of Curriculum and Instruction (Early Childhood Education) at Kent State University. She has been active in unlearning oppression work in her teaching, research and community work for many years. Her work has included collaborative studies on anti-bias early education in the U.S., changing child-rearing and the education of street children in Kenya, and, most recently, anti-racism curriculum development in South Africa and Greece. Her books include *Reconceptualizing the Early Childhood Curriculum* (with Shirley Kessler, 1992), *Children and Families 'At Promise': Deconstructuring the Discouse of Risk* (with Sally Lubeck, 1995) and *Does the Village Still Raise the Child: A Colaborative Study of Changing Child-rearing in Kenya* (in press). This book is based on her Fulbright study during 1994–95.

Michael C. Thornton I am what a friend of mine has called a blap; my mother is Japanese American and my father black American. This heritage is reflective of issues I deem important in my research. Most of my efforts revolve around the intersections between communities of color, whether in terms of multiethnic identity, factors influencing interminoirty relations or the role culture plays in influencing these phenomenon.

Index